China's Cultural Diplomacy

This book examines China's contemporary global cultural footprints through its recent development of cultural diplomacy.

The volume presents an alternative analytical framework to examine China's cultural diplomacy, which goes beyond the Western-defined concept of 'soft power' that prevails in the current literature. This new approach constructs a three-dimensional framework on Orientalism, cultural hegemony and nationalism to decipher the multiple contexts, which China inhabits historically, internationally and domestically. The book presents multiple case studies of the Confucius Institute, and compares the global programme located around the world with its Western counterparts, and also with other Chinese government-sponsored endeavours and non-government-initiated programmes. The author aims to solve the puzzle of why China's efforts in cultural diplomacy are perceived differently around the world and helps to outline the distinctive features of China's cultural diplomacy.

This book will be of much interest to students of diplomacy, Chinese politics, foreign policy and International Relations in general.

Xin Liu is a Senior Lecturer and Chinese Course Leader at the University of Central Lancashire, UK.

Routledge New Diplomacy Studies

Series Editors: Corneliu Bjola
University of Oxford
and
Markus Kornprobst
Diplomatic Academy of Vienna

This series publishes theoretically challenging and empirically authoritative studies of the traditions, functions, paradigms and institutions of modern diplomacy. Taking a comparative approach, the New Diplomacy Studies series aims to advance research on international diplomacy, publishing innovative accounts of how 'old' and 'new' diplomats help steer international conduct between anarchy and hegemony, handle demands for international stability vs international justice, facilitate transitions between international orders, and address global governance challenges. Dedicated to the exchange of different scholarly perspectives, the series aims to be a forum for inter-paradigm and inter-disciplinary debates, and an opportunity for dialogue between scholars and practitioners.

Secret Diplomacy
Concepts, contexts and cases
Edited by Corneliu Bjola and Stuart Murray

Diplomatic Cultures and International Politics
Translations, spaces and alternatives
Edited by Jason Dittmer and Fiona McConnell

Sports Diplomacy
Origins, Theory and Practice
Stuart Murray

Countering Online Propaganda and Extremism
The Dark Side of Digital Diplomacy
Edited by Corneliu Bjola and James Pamment

China's Cultural Diplomacy
A Great Leap Outward?
Xin Liu

For more information about this series, please visit: www.routledge.com/ Routledge-New-Diplomacy-Studies/book-series/RNDS

China's Cultural Diplomacy
A Great Leap Outward?

Xin Liu

LONDON AND NEW YORK

First published 2020
by Routledge
2 Park Square, Milton Park, Abingdon, Oxon OX14 4RN

and by Routledge
52 Vanderbilt Avenue, New York, NY 10017

Routledge is an imprint of the Taylor & Francis Group, an informa business

© 2020 Xin Liu

The right of Xin Liu to be identified as author of this work has been asserted by her in accordance with sections 77 and 78 of the Copyright, Designs and Patents Act 1988.

All rights reserved. No part of this book may be reprinted or reproduced or utilised in any form or by any electronic, mechanical, or other means, now known or hereafter invented, including photocopying and recording, or in any information storage or retrieval system, without permission in writing from the publishers.

Trademark notice: Product or corporate names may be trademarks or registered trademarks, and are used only for identification and explanation without intent to infringe.

British Library Cataloguing-in-Publication Data
A catalogue record for this book is available from the British Library

Library of Congress Cataloging-in-Publication Data
A catalog record has been requested for this book

ISBN: 978-0-367-28153-3 (hbk)
ISBN: 978-0-429-32029-3 (ebk)

Typeset in Times New Roman
by Wearset Ltd, Boldon, Tyne and Wear

This book is dedicated to my family.

Contents

List of figures		viii
Acknowledgements		ix
List of abbreviations		xi
	Introduction	1
1	Look beyond and beneath the soft power	18
2	The vehicle and driver of China's cultural diplomacy: the two 'wheels' and two models	50
3	Charting the global cultural terrain of struggle for China's Confucius Institutes	87
4	So similar, so different, so Chinese: analytical comparisons of the Confucius Institute with its Western counterparts	125
5	The last three feet: where citizen diplomacy can dissolve the perception of Chinese sharp power	169
6	Cultural diplomacy with Chinese characteristics	194
	Conclusion	229
	Appendices	242
	Index	255

Figures

1.1	Cultural diplomacy as a mutual process	20
1.2	An alternative three-dimensional theoretical framework	43
2.1	The Nation Brands Hexagon	62
2.2	Brand China Hexagon in 2008	63
5.1	Key words to describe China before the trip	180
5.2	Key words to describe China after the trip	180
5.3	Key words to describe Chinese people before the trip	181
5.4	Key words to describe Chinese people after the trip	181
6.1	Chart of variables	214

Acknowledgements

This is my first book thus I am indebted to so many people for its coming to fruition. Its seed started from my PhD and four journal articles which were published in 2017–2019 based on the PhD thesis. My deepest gratitude and appreciation goes to my PhD supervisors, Dr Petra Bagley and Dr Edward Griffith, my internal examiner, Dr Yu Tao, two external examiners, Dr Michael Barr and Dr Edney Kingsley, and all the anonymous reviewers for the journal articles published on *Journal of Contemporary China*, *Asia Studies Review*, *Cambridge Journal of China Studies* and *Journal of Contemporary Eastern Asia*. Without their support, guidance, insightful feedback and intellectual challenges, this seed could never have sprouted and blossomed.

Meanwhile, I could not be more grateful to my family for their generous and unselfish support throughout my career transition from China to the UK; then from a teacher and translator to a scholar, especially to my husband for having endless stimulating and candid discussions with me that helped develop the ideas, for keeping sending me recommended readings, and for encouraging me to reach high with a free mind to think beyond boundaries. I also want to give a special mention to my daughter, who is the first reader of the completed manuscript and who used her English and computer skills to help me polish the fruit by meticulously proofreading, pointing out the need for clarifications, checking even the smallest details and creating the word clouds. We enjoyed many rounds of delightful discussions over the key words chosen by the respondents in Chapter 5.

Next, I must thank all the interviewees for allowing me to collect primary data and for sharing their insights with me. I am especially indebted to Feixia Yu, Xin Gao, Jinghan Zeng and Meng Zhang, who helped me establish crucial contacts with different organisations that gave this book the breadth of its empirical evidence.

Equally grateful am I to the University of Central Lancashire for its continued support for staff development and for granting me sabbatical leave to concentrate on writing this book. My heartfelt thanks go to Feixia Yu again, who extends all-rounded help to me, from constantly sending me links to the latest news stories to helping me ring fence my time and for covering some of the teaching workload during my sabbatical.

x *Acknowledgements*

I also want to thank Professor Simon Anholt and Dr Wolfram Manzenreiter for giving me permissions to reproduce the National Brands Hexagon and the 2008 China Brand Hexagon respectively, and Mr Jason Bair, Acting Director of International Affairs and Trade at the United States Government Accountability Office, for advising me on the copyright issue and directing me to the other GAO report on the Confucius Institute. I thank Kate at the Copyright unit of Uclan in helping me get a quote to pay for the Country Rating Table produced by Gallup.

I am also extremely grateful to the two anonymous reviewers of my book proposal and sample chapters, the series editors and Andrew Humphrys at Routledge for their inspiring and instrumental feedback and the confidence their positive comments have given me. Last but not least, my sincere gratitude to Bethany Lund Yates, my editorial assistant, for her patience, efficiency and professionalism in guiding me through the production process.

This book has been made possible and better because of each and every one of you.

Thank you all.

Abbreviations

AAUP	American Association of University Professors
ABC	Audit Bureau of Circulations
BBC	British Broadcasting Corporation
BRI	Belt and Road Initiative
BRICS	Brazil, Russia, India, China and South Africa
CAUT	Canadian Association of University Teachers
CC	Confucius Classroom
CCC	China Cultural Centre
CCKF	Chiang Ching-kuo Foundation
CCP	Chinese Communist Party/CPC: Communist Party of China
CI	Confucius Institute
CIUC	Confucius Institute at the University of Chicago
CPAFFC	Chinese People's Association for Friendship with Foreign Countries
CPHRC	Conservative Party Human Rights Commission
CPIFA	The Chinese People's Institute of Foreign Affairs
CPPCC	Chinese People's Political Consultative Conference
DV	dependent variable
EACS	European Association of Chinese Studies
EV	extraneous variable
GAO	Government Accountability Office
GI	Goethe Institute
GPPI	Global Public Policy Institute
HSK	Chinese proficiency test
ICD	Institute of Cultural Diplomacy
IV	independent variable
MERICS	Mercator Institute for China Studies
MOC	Ministry of Culture/MOCT: Ministry of Culture and Tourism (since March 2018)
MOE	Ministry of Education
MOFA	Ministry of Foreign Affairs
MV	mediating variable
NAS	National Association of Scholars

xii *Abbreviations*

NED	National Endowment for Democracy
NPO	non-profit organisation
PGAS	Pew Global Attitude Survey
PPP	Purchasing Power Parish
SCIO	The State Council Information Office
TRA	Taiwan Relations Act
UFWD	United Front Work Department
UKCISA	UK Council for International Students Affairs
USCC	US–China Economic and Security Review Commission
USCCD	US Centre for Citizen Diplomacy

Introduction

> I thought I've seen the whole picture, but no matter how high I stand and how many angles I've changed, I still cannot see it all.
>
> (Xin Liu)

China, the oldest continuous civilisation on earth, has survived 4,000 years' history with a rich cultural heritage, and since 2010 has re-emerged as the second largest economy in the world. However, the perception of Chinese civilisation in the rest of the world has shifted from admiration in the seventeenth and eighteenth centuries, when ancient China was introduced to the West as the model of a secular and humane civilisation by Matteo Ricci (1610),[1] Gottfried Leibniz (1697),[2] Charles de Montesquieu (1748)[3] and Voltaire (1756),[4] to one of growing contempt in the nineteenth century, when China was defeated in the two Opium Wars (1839–1842 and 1856–1860) and the first Sino-Japanese War (1894–1895). Since the time of this negative downturn until today, China's image has been misrepresented in many Western countries. The transformation brought by China's modern development seems to have only changed the colour code, from race to regime: from 'yellow peril' to 'red threat'.

If seen through theoretical lenses, we will be able to see two images of 'otherness' here. First, the dichotomy of East and West as cultural entities was dissected by Said's (1978) critique of Orientalism, in which the Orient was rendered as being the "inferior other" for the Occident to define its own superior identity; in a way, an Orientalist perception of the world is "the West and the Rest" (Hall, 1992: 185), with 'the West' at the centre and 'the Rest' as the inferior. In history, although China had mostly been held as a civilised Confucian utopia until the eighteenth century, it became a rotten Oriental empire towards the end of the Qing Dynasty that had its cultural identity subject to 'otherness'.

Second, this historical legacy was carried on to modern times, when China's authoritarian regime evolved its image from being the 'cultural other' to being the 'ideological other'. Despite the moving of the dynamic hub of the world economy from the developed Western countries led by the USA and Europe to the developing Asian nations led by China and India, the traditional equation of the West with modernity and the Orient with the exotic past remains to be

2 *Introduction*

challenged, and has continued to be a particular obstacle to the Chinese attempt at establishing its political identity. As long as China maintains that the values of its political system are fundamentally different from the leading Western countries, China is still considered as the 'other', if seen through the framework of hegemony and ideology constructed by Gramsci (1971). Moreover, in the discourse of nationalism proposed by Ozirimli (2005), China again falls into the camps of 'us' and 'them'. These polarised 'other' representations uphold each other, and become dual forces of Western domination over China's power of discourse when they come into play with the power and knowledge relations as defined by Foucault (1980). All these, to put it simply, mean that China, as a non-Caucasian, non-Western and non-democratic nation with the largest population and now the second largest economy, "has often been a 'problem' for the world and the world has often been a 'problem' for China" (Scott, 2007: 3). In addition, when American scholars Bellamy and Weinberg (2008) are discussing how to "restore America's image", they quoted the then French President Sarkozy saying:

> it's difficult when the country that is the most powerful, the most successful – that is, of necessity, the leader of our side – is one of the most unpopular countries in the world. It presents overwhelming problems for you and overwhelming problems for your allies.
>
> (cited in Bellamy and Weinberg, 2008: 55)

This image problem is probably even more overwhelming for China. So, the question is: What can China do about it? Among the multipronged efforts made, a state-led cultural diplomacy campaign was launched as part of China's 'Going Global' national strategy.

This book tries to put China's cultural diplomacy endeavours in the context of change that springs from historical, internal and external dimensions, which have all left profound marks on it. While inspired and stimulated by the growing literature in this field, a significant void has been identified in the existing scholarly research that this book attempts to fill. Challenging the adequacy and even appropriateness of using 'soft power' as the mainstream theoretical framework constitutes the point of departure. The book argues for an alternative analytical framework that goes beyond and beneath this Western-defined concept by constructing a three-dimensional model to decipher the multiple contexts China lies in. The analysis touches on Orientalism, Occidentalism, communism, nationalism, cultural hegemony and cultural pluralism, and shows how the development of China's cultural diplomacy is inextricably entangled with all these factors. To a considerable extent, its aim to regain China's great power status that is considered appropriate to its size (in population, geographical and economic terms) and historical heritage is what the China Dream has derived its ultimate motivation from.

The book also attempts to define the unique features of China's cultural diplomacy by putting it in multiple comparative frameworks: both in contrast with its

Introduction 3

Western counterparts and in juxtaposition of different domestic programmes. It should be noted here that the word 'West' has different connotations: although the economic power shift is happening in a geographical domain, and there is also a geographical shift in terms of China studies inside the 'Western world', from Europe-centred study of traditional China (pre-1911) to USA-centred study of modern China (post-1911), 'the West' has often been used as a shorthand narrative for a political and cultural concept. It is "a historical, not a geographical construct" according to Hall, who has remarkably deconstructed the concept as "a tool to think with", "an ideology", "a system of representation" and "a standard or model of comparison" (Hall, 1992: 186). Of course, when East and West are compared, they may appear to be unified and homogeneous, essentially with one view about the other, however, it is fully appreciated that they are used as generalisations for an essentially non-generalisable identity as both the East and West are terms covering enormous historical, cultural and economic distinctions; they are only compared to make a point of the dialectic relationship in a system of global power relations.

To a large extent, Chinese scholars, Chinese state media and even government rhetoric have all helped perpetuate the East–West dichotomy in establishing a binary opposition between China and 'the West'. They used the term, or more recently, the 'Western hostile forces' (*xifang didui shili*), in a way as if it were a monolith entity with a concerted mind: the West wanted this, or the West did that. As Buruma and Margalit pointed out, "anti-Americanism plays a large role in hostile views of the West. Sometimes it even represents the West" (2005: 9). This will be discussed in the book as a manifestation of Chinese Occidentalism, which is revealed as a counter-discourse to Orientalism in modern China where "the image of modern West is used as a cultural and symbolic capital for different ideological agendas" (Chen, 2002: 12).

Another important annotation is needed for Orientalism, which "was the product of a particular moment in the history of European colonialism, and as a result changes and falters with the fate of imperialism" (Dabashi, 2015: 17). Indeed, the whole topography of domination and resistance is changing, the world structure has now shifted from being bipolar during the Cold War era to being unipolar after the collapse of the former USSR, and then to an emerging multi-polar world today. In this process, miraculous economic development has endowed China with a favourable shift of wealth and power. What is at stake today is not so much the "end of history" as once argued by Fukuyama's (1989), but the end of West-centrism. Many of the world's leading powers were negatively affected by the global financial crisis started in 2008, while China continued to achieve rapid growth and overtook the USA as the world's largest economy measured in PPP (Purchasing Power Parity) terms in 2014. The direction of moving to a world that no longer rests upon Western hegemony has generated a sense of crisis for those currently in the dominating positions, which in turn leads to the perception of the rising China as a 'threat'. Since Nixon (1967) believed "Red China [has become] Asia's most immediate threat" in his 1967 article, it has evolved into so many different versions, particularly after it became

4   *Introduction*

topical in the early 1990s: seeing China as a military and economic threat (Roy, 1996; Broomfield, 2003), an ideological threat (Yee and Storey, 2002; Yang and Liu, 2012), a development model threat (Peerenboom, 2007), an environmental threat (Bingman, 2010), a spy threat (Newman, 2011), an energy consumption threat (Richardson, 2014) and an intellectual property rights threat (Roper, 2014). The recently coined term of "sharp power" (Walker and Ludwig, 2017) will be discussed in the book as a latest addition to this whole host of 'threat' vocabulary as a synonym of China's "soft power threat".

In Yee and Storey's book (2002: 0) *The China Threat: Perceptions, Myths and Reality*, the 'China Threat' was named as "one of the most significant debates in international relations since the end of the Cold War". Two actual debates were staged on the Munk Debates, Canada's premier international debate series on major policy issues: one was held in 2011 on "China's Rise – Does the 21st Century Belong to China?",[5] and a more recent one was held in May 2019 on "Is China a Threat to the Liberal International Order?". The winners of the first debate were Henry Kissinger and Fareed Zakaria who argued against "China emerges as totally dominant" as it seems to be "ideologically and operationally ill prepared for it",[6] gaining 22 per cent more audience votes from 40 per cent 'con' pre-debate to 62 per cent 'con' post-debate. The winners of the second debate only won over audiences votes by a small margin of 2 per cent, from 24 per cent 'con' pre-debate to 26 per cent 'con' post-debate, which means that the majority (74 per cent) of the 3,000 audience still believe China *is* a threat to the liberal international order.[7]

The Chinese reaction to these 'threat' discourses is "confused and annoyed, if not outraged", "for the average Chinese feels that the West wants to 'demonise' China, while Chinese leaders interpret the China threat as a threat *to* China" (Yee and Feng, 2002: 33). Lampton has rightly observed that "as China's power has grown, it has wanted to make itself more charming, more effective, to limit counter-reactions" (2008: 27). However, government rebuttals seem to have "failed to reassure regional and global actors" (Goldstein, 2005: 115), even to the extent of being counterproductive as such texts "vigorously reproduce the dangers of the very threat they seek to deny" (Callahan, 2005: 712). Therefore, launching a campaign of cultural diplomacy is believed to be a "strategic communication" that would help China to "get the right message to the right audience through the right medium at the right time" (Anderson and Engstrom, 2009: 36).

In May 2006, *People's Daily* and *China Daily* published an editorial one after the other, titled respectively "China Promotes its Culture Overseas to Dissolve China Threat"[8] and "China Threat Fear Countered by Culture".[9] This shows both an internal and external dimension: internally, China needs to construct a coherent view of its national identity at home that is commensurate with its people's expectation of China's rightful place in the wider world; externally, China wishes to communicate with the world the message of Confucius's belief in 'harmony in diversity', and to re-establish its significance as a major power and culture in today's world, which is marked with economic globalisation, political multi-polarisation and cultural diversification. Guo has summarised this as:

Introduction 5

the international interest in, and recognition of, China's role in the global economy and international politics appear to coincide with a Chinese government's rethink of the image of China as a world power in tune with its reputation as an ancient civilisation.

(Guo, 2004: 30)

In a way, China's cultural diplomacy wishes to challenge the equation of globalisation with Westernisation, while serving the dual aims of countering the China threat argument and advocating cultural pluralism at the same time, corresponding to the aforementioned two images of 'otherness'.

Drawing on empirical materials and perspectives through a number of inter-related frames, this book develops and applies an alternative framework of analysis to examine some of the key programmes of China's cultural diplomacy. Since the Confucius Institute (CI) represents a flagship project, multiple comparative case studies are carried out against its different counterparts: first, between its various host locations overseas across different cultural boundaries with China; then in contrast to other Western global programmes such as the Goethe Institute and the British Council. It is also juxtaposed with other state-sponsored Chinese organisations such as the China Cultural Centre (CCC) affiliated to the Ministry of Culture and Tourism (MOCT), and non-state-organised programmes such as Journey to the East, a student collaboration programme between partner universities in China and the UK. Engaging in multiple comparative case studies represents an attempt at "polyhedron of intelligibility" recommended by Foucault (2003: 249) when there is a multiplicity of force relations to reckon with, as one can only really understand something by looking at it from different directions and using different methods. This way allows a more rounded and more balanced picture of the subject to be developed. Substantial primary and secondary data have been collected and analysed, including 40 interviews carried out over a time-span of six years, and a multitude of source materials in both original Chinese and English, including government documents, academic publications, media reports, as well as internal reports and copies of agreements.

What is in a title?

History is always the preface to the current chapter being written. If we look back at the first two generations of Chinese leaders since the Communist Party came to power in 1949, Mao Zedong and Deng Xiaoping, we can see the former paid more attention to military and ideological power, while the latter placed more emphasis on economic power. Although China has practised cultural diplomacy for many decades, from the famous Ping-Pong Diplomacy in the early 1970s to Panda Diplomacy in the 1980s, it is fair to argue that the practice has been relatively sporadic until it appeared on the agenda of the third-generation leaders as a means to serve a new end. China has mainly been an exporter of manufactured goods and an importer of cultural goods since its opening up in

6 *Introduction*

the late 1970s. Segal's article (1999) argued that China has had such limited cultural outreach not only compared to the 'dominant West' but also in comparison to Japan, that during the first twenty years of opening up, the Chinese government has had to spent more efforts in resisting and controlling the domestic impact of external cultural influences than in attempting to create any specific external influence of its own. It was until quite recently that China is observed to have begun systematically promoting Chinese culture abroad for "pride, influence and revenue" (Lampton, 2008: 140). Though it is a new mission, the way it is handled at the government level is still heavily influenced by the old practice.

'The Great Leap Forward' started by Mao Zedong in 1958 turned out to be such a calamity for the Chinese economy as well as for its traditional culture and values, that it was criticised as the "Great Leap Backward" (Bettelheim, 1978) in modern Chinese history. Six decades have passed since then and China has made great strides in social and economic changes, yet the imprint left by 'The Great Leap Forward', is so indelible and far-reaching that even today the state-run system that features concentrated state power, national investment and mobilisation is still in place: at the word of government command, national level support and resources are allocated in a campaigning style to create a sensational effect, and it is the number that is used as measurement to show the implementer's political achievements – from the Olympic medals to China's GDP growth. The CI as the flagship project of China's new cultural strategy is just another example. In 2006, Hanban Director Xu Lin confirmed in an interview that China aims to establish 1,000 CIs by 2020 (Xinhua, 2006), overtaking the Alliance Française, which was founded in 1883 and is as large as the British Council, Goethe-Institut and Instituto Cervantes combined. This target was announced with pride, as Hanban is confident of achieving it with both policy support and ample financial input from the 'above'. What Paris has managed to realise in 130 years will be achieved by Beijing in less than two decades. It is reminiscent of Mao's slogan of 'overtaking the UK in 15 years' in the 1950s – a slogan brimming with rising nationalism but which triggered the disastrous 'Great Leap Forward'.

However, by March 2013, there were only 400 CIs established worldwide, suggesting the 1,000 target was a bit out of reach; or by using a different calculation, if we include the Confucius Classrooms (CCs) that partners with local secondary schools or primary schools, then the 1,000 target has already been exceeded. Therefore, a new vision was announced to have "a global distribution in 500 major cities all over the world by 2020", according to Xu Lin in another interview with Xinhua (Xinhua, 2013), while specifying a new target of having 500 CIs and 1,000 CCs established worldwide by 2015. The statistics released by the Hanban website by December 2015 indicated there were indeed altogether exactly 500 CIs and 1,000 CCs in total worldwide. This perfectly rounded figure is a bit dubious and possibly artificial, particularly because it was announced back in March 2013. Cultural promotion cannot be planned out numerically like this and made sure the target has to be met. No wonder scholars

Introduction 7

researching China's cultural diplomacy have commented on "the extent to which it attempts to overtly quantify its culture power" as a feature of China's approach to cultural diplomacy (Barr, 2015: 187).

As the term suggests, cultural diplomacy involves both a dimension of 'culture' and 'diplomacy', and this new strategy demonstrates changes in China on both fronts. Although Deng Xiaoping's open-door policy introduced in 1978 was acclaimed as the "Great Leap Outward" (Cheng, 1979), and has propelled China to global prominence in recent decades through its economic might, it was not fully applicable to the diplomatic front during his time when the strategy was "keeping a low profile". A generally more assertive stance on China's foreign policy in the post-Deng era has been observed and articulated by a number of scholars (Unger, 1996; Shambaugh, 2013), and in the Chinese discourse, it is now geared towards "striving for achievements" (Yan, 2014: 154), and Xi Jinping formally presented the latter as the new strategy in his speech at the foreign affairs conference in October 2013. This change of discourse mirrors the shifts in China's self-identity and foreign policies. However, in their new book titled *China's Great Leap Outward: Hard and Soft Dimensions of a Rising Power*, Scobell and Mantas (2014) only explored China's economic and military expansions, while Fallows' overview of China in 2016 was titled "China's Great Leap Backward" as a result of "darkening political climate", commenting that "the country has become repressive in a way that it has not been since the Cultural Revolution" (2016, n.p.).

At the government level, the cultural front was declared to be the third pillar of China's diplomacy after politics and economy in 2004, and Sun Jiazheng, the then Chinese Cultural Minister (1998–2013), pledged to reverse the "huge deficits in the trading of cultural products" (cited in Lai and Lu, 2012: 86). Since the induction of the national strategy of 'Going Global' (*zou chu qu*) in the tenth Five-Year-Plan (2001–2005), the cultural front quickly followed up with *The Implementing Regulations of the Going Global Strategy of Radio, Film and Television* published by the State Administration of Radio, Film and Television in the same year, 2001. A decade later, both the Ministry of Culture and the State Administration of Press and Publication have published their own twelfth Five-Year Plan (2011–2015) on implementing the 'Going Global' strategy (Zhu, 2012), ushering in the age of a 'Great Leap Outward'.

Some milestone events in the last decade or so have marked the fledgling activities of China's cultural diplomacy: from the debut of the 'Year of Chinese Culture' series in France, Italy, Russia and Australia in 2003, to the opening up of the CIs all across the globe since 2004; from launching twenty-four-hour cable news channels (CCTV News, CNC) and newspapers (*China Daily Asia Weekly* and *European Weekly*)[10] overseas in 2010, to staging the Chinese image advertisement in New York Times Square in 2011. The government rhetoric has also shown no ambiguity in its intention to improve China's image abroad: from Jiang Zemin's "Call for Further Propaganda Work to Enhance China's Image Abroad" back in 1999 (cited in Cull, 2009: n.p.), to Li Changchun's appeal to "augment the soft power of Chinese culture and further elevate our national

8   *Introduction*

image"[11] in 2009 (cited in Lam, 2009: n.p.). Wang Chen, who currently heads the Communist Party's overseas propaganda division (*Zhonggong Zhongyang Duiwai Xuanchuan Bangongshi*), added that media and cultural units should enhance their "capacity to broadcast, to positively influence international public opinion and to establish a good image for our nation" (cited in Lam, 2009: n.p.).

After significant investments in various high-profile initiatives and projects, including establishing three national bases for international cultural trade, and the one in Beijing claims to be the 'largest in scale and most comprehensive in scope' in the world, the numbers released by the Chinese government seem to suggest early success: cultural products and services exports grew by 2.8 and 8.7 fold respectively from 2001 to 2010 (Zhu, 2012), and the CIs had expanded to 155 countries all over the world by the end of June 2019.[12] However, despite these impressive figures in input and output, the effects are less satisfactory so far if measured by the major poll results. The Chinese government was disappointed and baffled to find these numbers were not translated into the desired policy result of improving China's national image, which was reflected in a *People's Daily* editorial, asking "How Can We Make the World like Us?" It started with the question of "has China's ascending status brought the nation the admiration and the acceptance of other countries?", the discussion below shows the frustration that when "admiration" is expected, even "acceptance" was not achieved:

> While China continues to exert a more confident image, it is also meeting some resistance from the world, even from its old friends. From the snooty coverage by overseas media outlets to various polls of public perception in foreign countries, these suggest that China is facing a challenge to improve its image.
>
> (People's Daily, 2010)

Although no specifically causal relationship can be established between the decline of favourable values on China's image and the ineffectiveness of China's cultural diplomacy as the causes are complex and open to debate, these poll results at least indicate the challenges faced by it. Such polls include the BBC World Service Country Rating Poll, which saw the negative rating of China increase from 32 per cent when the Poll began in 2005 to 40 per cent in 2009 after the Beijing Olympics, and further up to 42 per cent in 2017.[13] The Gallup World Poll rates of 'very favourable' and 'mostly favourable' views towards China have also decreased from 18 per cent and 46 per cent respectively in 1979 when the poll began, to 8 per cent and 33 per cent respectively in 2019 (see Appendix 1: Gallup, 2019), despite the fact that China has been rated No. 1 since the 2008 Gallup World Poll on the question of "who do you think is the leading economic power in the world today?". Although there are some positive moves in Russia and Africa, these falls could perhaps be seen as a signal to Beijing that having the second largest GDP in the world may not automatically push up its

Introduction 9

national image; instead, the quickly expanding GDP may have raised the volume of the China threat argument and reflected adversely in its image ranking.

There are also two surveys which particularly measure a state's soft power effects. One is the Pew Global Attitude Survey (PGAS), whose systematic and comprehensive data was cited by Joseph S. Nye (2004) to assess America's soft power; the result shows that favourable views of China's image have continued to tumble in the USA and the UK, going down from 50 per cent and 52 per cent in 2009, to 38 per cent and 49 per cent in 2018 respectively (see Appendix 2: Pew Global, 2018,). The other survey is a specific soft power ranking, The Soft Power 30, which was described as the "clearest picture of soft power to date" by Nye (cited in Soft Power 30, 2018: 12). The report provides detailed insights into a country's soft power resources and how they are leveraged by using political values, culture and foreign policy. China was rated at the bottom position of thirty in 2015 but climbed up to twenty-seven in 2018.[14]

These snapshots of opinion polls may provide a revealing picture of China's contemporary international image, but when these figures were cited to explain the mission of China's cultural diplomacy to reshape China's image, they were simply adopted as a benchmark without questioning the background of whom was constructing these polls. They are all organisations based in the USA or the UK: from leading consulting company like Gallup to the research centre at the University of Maryland that produces the BBC poll; from the Pew Research Centre as a non-partisan fact-tank based in Washington DC to Portland Communications, a political consultancy and public relations agency based in London that produces The Soft Power 30 report. Bhabha has argued that, "economic and political domination has a profound hegemonic influence on the information orders of the Western world, its popular media and its specialized institutions and academics" (1994: 19). As listed above, all the major polls were organised by Western institutions, which is a reflection of such "hegemonic influence". This means national image is much more about power and knowledge, and it is this perspective that is lacking in understanding China's image problem. I argue in this book, that this is actually the 'root cause' that must be treated; those poll results are no more than symptoms that cannot be relied on to form any effective diagnosis.

True, as Ramo argues, "in the end, what China thought about itself did not matter so much. What mattered was what the world thought of China" (2007: 12), but two questions must be asked: first, what determining factors are shaping the world's perception of China?; and second, when we talk about the *world's* perception, how much influence does *the Western world's*, in particular the *USA's*, perception of China have in shaping China's international image? With this in mind, Manzenreiter's research offered a more insightful and detailed reading of these statistics in pointing out that since the BBC rating samples include most OECD countries:

> It may come closer to represent the "West" than the Gallup World Poll. Most countries in Europe and North America tend to evaluate China's

10 *Introduction*

influence more negatively than the world average, which is outbalanced by more positive appreciation in Central America, Africa and Asia (with the exception of Japan, down from 22% to 8%).

(Manzenreiter, 2010: 39)

This seems to be consistent with the more negative receptions the CIs have received in Europe and North America than in the rest of the world, since they were rolled out globally in 2004. A series of shockwaves have been sent from these two regions against this 'flagship' of China's cultural diplomacy: first, from the US State Department against visa renewals for CI teachers in May 2012 (Fischer, 2012); and then, to the dozens of CIs closed down between 2013–2019, all of which were located in Europe and North America, from France to Sweden, Germany to the Netherlands, and Canada to the USA. These incidents raised a series of questions that made the author ponder: when the closing down of the CI was interpreted as "heading for a 'soft power' *war* with the West" (Volodzko, 2015: n.p.), and the 2008 Beijing Olympic Games was considered to provide "a platform for an ideological *battle*, between the normative Western forces of a self-defined global consensus and a nation state claiming status as a leader of an alternative to that so-called consensus" (Finlay and Xin, 2010: 895), is cultural diplomacy really a non-menacing platform to showcase China's peaceful rise, or is it actually starting a new battlefield? Why China's similar efforts in promoting its culture were perceived and received differently to other Western countries and encountered unexpected controversies? If cultural diplomacy is a 'prescription' to treat China's image problem, what ingredients in this recipe could potentially generate side effects? And how can we improve the 'prescription' to make sure it not only treats the symptoms but also addresses the root cause?

After exploring answers to the above questions, this book also discusses which measurement will make this cultural 'leap outward' truly 'great', and how not to repeat the mistakes made by Mao's Great Leap Forward when the meaning of 'great' was translated into a blind pursuit of speed and scale rather than, or even at the cost of, effect and impact.

How this book is structured

This comprehensive study of China's cultural diplomacy is divided into six chapters. The first chapter sets out the theoretical premises for this book, arguing the necessity to look through multiple lenses of the historical, international and domestic contexts in which China is endeavouring to reshape its image. It approaches the subject by first discussing the limitations of the mainstream concept of 'soft power' in the current literature: this West-centric concept has not engaged with any historical analysis of the role of Orientalism and hegemony in shaping the current global cultural terrain, or with China's domestic dimension. Its binary view of cultures and values also defies the fundamental vision of cultural diplomacy, which is not a zero-sum game, but a positive sum game of nurturing mutual understanding and respect between cultures. Then, an

Introduction 11

alternative and more sophisticated framework of analysis is proposed to look beyond and beneath the soft power narrative. The political and cultural face of Chinese nationalism is portrayed in detail to shed light on its double-edged role in both motivating and limiting China's cultural diplomacy. The new framework facilitates a broader and deeper understanding and allows one to see a more nuanced picture of China's cultural diplomacy than what is shown through a single lens of soft power.

Following the constructed alternative framework, Chapter 2 focuses on the debates about the vehicle and driver of China's cultural diplomacy. It starts with a theoretical discussion of the competing views internationally and in the Chinese context, and develops an argument that the vehicle of China's cultural diplomacy tries to project soft power on two wheels of culture and political values, to serve the purpose of reshaping China's image away from being the 'cultural other' and 'ideological other' respectively. However, the state-led approach to driving this vehicle is generating some side effects with its sponsorship, censorship and presence in the front seat. Then the chapter analyses the inherent tensions existing in practice both between the two sources of building soft power and between the two means of doing so, attraction and persuasion, with empirical evidence: first, through a comparative case study of the CI with the CCC; then through a comparative case study of the CIs in the USA, UK and South Korea. The finding shows that with the blurred boundary between culture and political values under the soft power framework, China's attempt at reshaping its image as an Eastern cultural contestant is often disrupted by its authoritarian political values, and China's cultural attraction is often reduced by its state-led persuasion.

Chapter 3 then contextualises the operations of the CIs by applying the alternative analytical framework in charting the global 'cultural terrain of struggle' in which China is 'othered' both culturally and ideologically. It develops an argument that the global cultural terrain is an uneven one both in terms of unbalanced powers with hidden barriers for the counter-hegemonic side, and also a hierarchical one affecting the interactions between various players. The complexity of the three-dimensional and conflict-ridden interplays is then epitomised by actual examples of CIs in the field, using both primary and secondary data as evidence to support the theoretical discussions. The process considers the following questions: how was the global cultural terrain constructed in history; what power dynamics underpin the formation and shifting of the terrain conditions; and how has the relationship among different actors been affected by the flow of people and ideas in the inter-cultural connections. Both theoretical reflections and empirical investigations are carried out to reveal the configurations underlying the global 'cultural terrain of struggle', and the challenges faced by the CIs by examining the actual dynamics and intricacies in the field among the multiple players and stakeholders.

Chapter 4 moves from the macro level to the micro level by giving a comprehensive analytical comparison between the CI and its Western counterparts, with a view to answering the question of why the CI with a similar goal is perceived

12   *Introduction*

differently. It reveals a much deeper reading into the differences than what the existing studies have suggested, which has only focused on the CI's government connections and different operating models. The newly developed alternative framework is again employed to show that it is an oversimplification to only focus on the visible difference in *locations*, but does not challenge the Orientalist grounds where hidden difference in power *positions* in this uneven terrain lies at its very core. Apart from the primary data collected by the researcher's first-hand interviews and four copies of CI agreements, secondary data is also drawn on to drive the analysis from the micro level further down to the specific case of the Confucius Institute at the University of Chicago (CIUC), to investigate deeper into this most widely reported closure in the Western media so far.

Chapter 5 starts with discussions of the debatable term of 'sharp power', and then focuses on the role 'citizen diplomacy' can play in dissolving such perception via people-to-people interactions and access to first-hand knowledge and experience. A case study of a student collaboration programme initiated in 2014 between the UK and Chinese partner universities was carried out by combining quantitative and qualitative research methods with questionnaires and interviews. The data shows that autonomy from any political involvement and agenda is the greatest strength of non-government-initiated programmes, and the introduction of 'real China' through interacting with average citizens is very effective in improving participants' perception of China, even if they see all sorts of problems in its quickly evolving society. When Chinese government's political values often become a barrier to the full effects of its state-led cultural diplomacy, citizen exchange should play a bigger role as its most 'unauthoritarian' manner is often far more effective than official efforts.

Chapter 6 moves back to the macro level of the global cultural terrain by combining the cultural boundary theory with nationalism traits to contrast the terrain conditions in the East and West, and to avoid the risk of generalising the prominent features of China's cultural diplomacy. Then, the independent variable affecting the CI's effective operation is identified and contextualised, that is, the CI's ability to localise its product and process to suit different target audiences, along with a number of extraneous variables, including ideology, nationalism, the media environment in the destinations, bilateral relations and different cultural boundaries in between. People-to-people interaction is also an important mediator that contributes to facilitating mutual understanding. A diagram of various variables at play in this process is mapped out to demonstrate the unique challenges China faces in bridging the gaps both between its internal articulations and external communications, and between its own projected image and the world's perceived image of a more powerful China. It then builds on previous chapters to reach the four distinctive features of China's cultural diplomacy, and finishes with discussions of their implications on the practice of China's cultural diplomacy.

The conclusion summarises the research findings and reflects on the messages from the closed down Confucius Institutes. It also shares some final thoughts regarding the recent happenings between China and the USA, and the role cultural diplomacy can play in keeping the looming Cold War at bay. It points to the fact that if a new Cold War is in the making, we can see not only the difference between today's China and yesterday's Soviet Union, but also the division within the Western camp. China's impact on and engagement with the rest of the world, across the East and West, North and South, along with Trump Administration's "America First" foreign policy that has alienated some of its traditional allies, have all prevented the formation of a unified 'camp' against China. However, it also highlights the interconnections between the domestic and international contexts for cultural diplomacy by comparing the different interpretations of the Chinese notion of '*tianxia*', its ancient view of the world, and the government's strategic narrative of 'harmony in diversity'.

I appreciate that a single book like this one cannot cover every aspect of China's multifaceted cultural encounter with the rest of the world, and the issues covered here are by no means dealt with exhaustively, just like the sentence I started with at the beginning: "I thought I've seen the whole picture, but no matter how high I stand and how many angles I've changed, I still cannot see it all." However, I do hope this study sketches out a portrait of China's cultural diplomacy showing its distinctive characteristics. It is a product of a continuous dialogue between myself as both an insider and outsider of Chinese culture, and between the source materials in both Chinese and English. As a native Chinese scholar educated in both China (two BA degrees) and the West (MBA and PhD in the UK), the author tries to use her vantage point to bring in the pluralistic perspectives, and hopefully, stimulate others to explore further the emerging efforts of China to engage with the world.

Notes

1 Nicolas Trigault, S.J. *China in the Sixteenth Century: The Journals of Matthew Ricci: 1583–1610*. English translation by Louis J. Gallagher, S.J. (New York: Random House, 1953); *The True Meaning of the Lord of Heaven* (*Tianzhu Shiyi*), a book written by Matteo Ricci (1985 [1610]), which argues that Confucianism and Christianity are not opposed but are in fact remarkably similar in key respects.

2 The *Novissima Sinica* (*News from China*) was a collection of letters and reports from Leibniz's correspondents, with a Preface written by Leibniz himself, published in 1697 and 1699; Leibniz, "On the Civil Cult of Confucius", 1700/1701, in Gottfried Wilhelm Leibniz, *Writings on China*, translated by Daniel J. Cook and Henry Rosemont, Jr. (Chicago, IL: Open Court, 1994).

3 In the twenty-two books of Montesquieu's *De l'esprit des loix*, published in 1748, references to China appear frequently in the concluding chapters of books or at the end of sequences of arguments to show how the empire serves to illustrate Montesquieu's fundamental principles and to elucidate his method.

4 Voltaire's notable play, *The Orphan of China*, published in 1755, was based on a Chinese play, *The Orphan of Zhao*, which had been translated for European readers by the Jesuit missionaries. In other works, such as his monumental universal history, *Essai sur les mœurs et l'esprit des nations* (*An Essay on Universal History: The Manners and Spirit of Nations*, 1756), Voltaire also showed his admiration for Chinese civilisation.

5 The debate was published in 2011: *Does the 21st Century Belong to China? The Munk Debate on China*, by House of Anansi Press, Toronto.

14 *Introduction*

6 The Rise of China: Be it Resolved, the 21st Century will Belong to China.... Munk Debates, 17 June 2011, available at: www.munkdebates.com/The-Debates/The-Rise-of-China.
7 China: Is China a Threat to the Liberal International Order? Munk Debates, 9 May 2019, available at: www.munkdebates.com/The-Debates/China.
8 See China Promotes Culture Overseas to Dissolve "China Threat". *People's Daily*, 28 May 20106, available at: www.gov.cn/misc/2006–05/28/content_293566.htm.
9 See China Threat Fear Countered by Culture. *China Daily*, 29 May 2006, available at: www.chinadaily.com.cn/china/2006–05/29/content_602226.htm.
10 *China Daily USA* was launched in 2009; and *China Daily African Weekly* was launched in 2012.
11 Li Changchun was the Director of China's Central Commission for Guiding Cultural and Ethical Progress (*Zhongyang jingshen wenming jianshe zhidao weiyuanhui*) from 2002 to 2012, whose main mandate was controlling ideology and propaganda.
12 These are the figures, according to Hanban website: www.hanban.org/confucious institutes/node_10961.htm.
13 BBC World Service Country Rating Poll, 2017, available at: https://globescan.com/images/images/pressreleases/bbc2017_country_ratings/BBC2017_Country_Ratings_Poll.pdf.
14 Soft Power 30 (2018), A Global Ranking for Soft Power, The USC Center on Public Diplomacy, available at: https://softpower30.com/country/china/?country_years=2016, 2017, 2018.

References

Anderson, E. and J.G. Engstrom (2009). China's Use of Perception Management and Strategic Deception. Available at: http://origin.www.uscc.gov/sites/default/files/Research/ApprovedFINALSAICStrategicDeceptionPaperRevisedDraft06Nov2009.pdf.
Barr, M. (2015). Chinese Cultural Diplomacy: Old Wine in New Bottles? In David Kerr (ed.), *China's Many Dreams: Comparative Perspectives on China's Search for National Rejuvenation* (pp. 180–200). New York: Palgrave Macmillan.
Bellamy, C. and A. Weinberg (2008). Educational and Cultural Exchanges to Restore America's Image. *Washington Quarterly*, 31(3): 55–68. Available at: www.tandfonline.com/doi/pdf/10.1162/wash.2008.31.3.55.
Bettelheim, C. (1978). The Great Leap Backward: From China Since Mao. *Monthly Review Press*, 37–130.
Bhabha, H.K. (1994). *The Location of Culture*. London: Routledge.
Bingman, C. (2010). China's Environmental Crisis. *Journal of the Washington Institute of China Studies*, 4(4): 24–34.
Broomfield, E. (2003). Perceptions of Danger: The China Threat Theory. *Journal of Contemporary China*, 12(35): 265–284.
Buruma, I. and A. Margalit. (2005). *Occidentalism: A Short History of Anti-Westernism*. London: Atlantic Books.
Callahan, W. (2005). How to Understand China: The Dangers and Opportunities of Being a Rising Power. *Review of International Studies*, 31(4): 701–714.
Chen, X. (2002). *Occidentalism: A Theory of Counter-Discourse in Post-Mao China*. New York: Rowman & Littlefield.
Cheng, H. (1979). Great Leap Outward? Available at: https://core.ac.uk/download/pdf/6458094.pdf.
China Daily (2006). 'China Threat' Fear Countered by Culture. *China Daily*, 29 May. Available at: www.chinadaily.com.cn/china/2006–05/29/content_602226.htm.

Introduction 15

Cull, N. (2009). Testimony before the US–China Economic and Security Review Commission hearing: China's Propaganda and Influence Operations, its Intelligence Activities that Target the United States and its Resulting Impacts on US National Security. 30 April. Available at: www.uscc.gov/sites/default/files/4.30.09Cull.pdf

Dabashi, H. (2015). *Can Non-Europeans Think?* London: Zed Books.

Fallows, J. (2016). China's Great Leap Backward. *The Atlantic*, December. Available at: www.theatlantic.com/magazine/archive/2016/12/chinas-great-leap-backward/505817/.

Finlay, C. and X. Xin (2010). Public Diplomacy Games: A Comparative Study of American and Japanese Responses to the Interplay of Nationalism, Ideology and Chinese Soft Power Strategies Around the 2008 Beijing Olympics. *Sport in Society*, 13(5): 876–900.

Fischer, K. (2012). State Department Directive Could Disrupt Teaching Activities of Campus-Based Confucius Institutes. *The Chronicle of Higher Education*, 21 May. Available at: http://chronicle.com/article/State-Department-Directive/131934/.

Foucault, M. (1980). *Power/Knowledge.* Brighton: Harvester.

Foucault, M. (2003). Questions of Method. In P. Rabinow and N. Rose (eds), *The Essential Foucault: Selections from Essential Works of Foucault*, 1954–1984 (pp. 246–258). London: The New Press.

Fukuyama, F. (1989). The End of History? *The National Interest* (Summer): 3–18.

Goldstein, A. (2005). *Rising to the Challenge: China's Grand Strategy and International Security.* Stanford, CA: Stanford University Press.

Gramsci, A. (1971). *Selections from the Prison Notebooks of Antonio Gramsci.* Quinton Hoare and Geoffrey N. Smith (eds). New York: International Publications.

Guo, Y. (2004). *Cultural Nationalism in Contemporary China.* London: Routledge.

Hall, S. (1992). The West and the Rest: Discourse and Power. In Bram Gieben and Stuart Hall (eds), *The Formations of Modernity: Understanding Modern Societies: An Introduction, Book 1* (pp. 185–225). Cambridge: Polity Press in association with Blackwell Publishers and The Open University.

Lai, H. and Y. Lu (eds) (2012). *China's Soft Power and International Relations.* Abingdon: Routledge.

Lam, W. (2009). Chinese State Media Goes Global: A Great Leap Outward for Chinese Soft Power? *China Brief*, 9(2): 22 January. Available at: www.jamestown.org/single/?tx_ttnews%5Btt_news%5D=34387&no_cache=1#.VZvXm_lViko.

Lampton, D.M. (2008). *The Three Faces of Chinese Power: Might, Money, and Minds.* London: University of California Press.

Leibniz, G.W. (1994 [1697]). On the Civil Cult of Confucius. In Gottfried Wilhelm Leibniz, *Writings on China*, translated by Daniel J. Cook and Henry Rosemont, Jr. Chicago, IL: Open Court.

Manzenreiter, W. (2010). The Beijing Games in the Western Imagination of China: The Weak Power of Soft Power. *Journal of Sport and Social Issues*, 34(1): 29–48.

Montesquieu, C. de (1748). *De l'esprit des loix.* Geneva: Barrillot et fils.

Newman, A. (2011). China's Growing Spy Threat. *Diplomat*, 19 September. Available at: http://thediplomat.com/2011/09/chinas-growing-spy-threat/.

Nixon, R.M. (1967). Asia After Viet Nam. *Foreign Affairs*, October. Available at: www.foreignaffairs.com/articles/asia/1967–10–01/asia-after-viet-nam.

Nye, J.S. (2004). *Soft Power: The Means to Succeed in World Politics.* New York: Public Affairs.

Ozkirimli, U. (2005). *Contemporary Debates on Nationalism: A Critical Engagement.* New York: Palgrave.

16 Introduction

Peerenboom, R. (2007). *China Modernizes: Threat to the West Or Model for the Rest?* New York: Oxford University Press.

Ramo, J.C. (2007). *Brand China*. London: The Foreign Policy Centre.

Ricci, M. (1985 [1610]). *Matteo Ricci: The True Meaning of the Lord of Heaven (T'ien-chu Shih-i)*. Translated by Douglas Lancashire and Peter Hu Kuo-Chen. Chinese–English edn, edited by Edward J. Malatesta. Saint Louis, MO: Institute of Jesuit Sources.

Richardson, B. (2014). Does China's Quest for Energy Security Threaten the United States? Why Washington Needs to be Concerned about Beijing's Need for Fuel? *Foreign Policy*, 10 December. Available at: http://foreignpolicy.com/2014/12/10/does-chinas-quest-for-energy-security-threaten-the-united-states/.

Roper, C. (2014). *Trade Secret Theft, Industrial Espionage, and the China Threat*. New York: Taylor and Francis Group.

Roy, D. (1996). The "China Threat" Issue: Major Arguments. *Asian Survey*, 36 (8): 758–771.

Said, E. (2003 [1978]). *Orientalism*, reprinted with a new Preface. London: Penguin Books.

Scobell, A. and M. Mantas (eds) (2014). *China's Great Leap Outward: Hard and Soft Dimensions of a Rising Power*. New York: The Academy of Political Science.

Scott, D. (2007). *China Stands Up, the PRC and the International System*. Abingdon: Routledge.

Segal, G. (1999). Does China Matter? In Barry Buzan and Rosemary Foot (eds), *Does China Matter? A Reassessment: Essays in Memory of Gerald Segal*. London: Routledge.

Shambaugh, D. (2013). *China Goes Global: The Partial Power*. New York: Oxford University Press.

Soft Power 30 (2018). The Report. Available at: https://softpower30.com/wp-content/uploads/2018/07/The-Soft-Power-30-Report-2018.pdf.

Trigault, Nicolas S.J. (1953) *China in the Sixteenth Century: The Journals of Matthew Ricci: 1583–1610*. English translation by Louis J. Gallagher, S.J. New York: Random House.

Unger, J. (ed.) (1996). *Chinese Nationalism*. New York: An East Gate Book.

Volodzko, D. (2015). China's Confucius Institutes and the Soft War – With the Closing of Confucius Institutes, China may be Heading for a "Soft Power" War with the West. *Diplomat*, 8 July. Available at: http://thediplomat.com/2015/07/chinas-confucius-institutes-and-the-soft-war/.

Walker, C. and J. Ludwig (2017). From 'Soft Power' to 'Sharp Power', Rising Authoritarian Influence in the Democratic World. National Endowment for Democracy, December. Available at: www.ned.org/wp-content/uploads/2017/12/Sharp-Power-Rising-Authoritarian-Influence-Full-Report.pdf.

Xinhua (2006). Confucius Institute: Promoting Language, Culture and Friendliness. Available at: http://news.xinhuanet.com/english/2006–10/02/content_5521722.htm.

Xinhua (2013). Confucius Institute will Achieve a Global Distribution Network Covering Nearly 500 Major Cities by 2020. *Xinhuanet*, 11 March Available at: www.xinhuanet.com/2013lh/2013–03/11/c_114979560.htm.

Yan, X. (2014). From Keeping a Low Profile to Striving for Achievement. *The Chinese Journal of International Politics*, 7(2): 153–184.

Yang, Y.E. and X. Liu (2012). The 'China Threat' through the Lens of US Print Media: 1992–2006. *Journal of Contemporary China*, 21(76): 695–711.

Yee, H. and Z. Feng (2002). Chinese Perspectives of the China Threat. In H. Yee and I. Storey (eds), *The China Threat: Perceptions, Myths and Reality* (pp. 21–42). London: RoutledgeCurzon.

Yee, H. and I. Storey (eds) (2002). *China Threat: Perceptions, Myths and Reality.* London: RoutledgeCurzon.

Zhu, C. (2012). *Zhongguo Wenhua zouchuqu weihe kunnan chongchong?* [Why is the "Going Global" of Chinese Culture Beset in Difficulties?] *Zhongguo Wenhua Chanye Pinglun* [*Review of Chinese Cultural Industry*], 2: 84–104.

1 Look beyond and beneath the soft power[1]

> East is East, and West is West, and never the twain shall meet,
> Till Earth and Sky stand presently at God's great Judgment seat;
> But there is neither East nor West, Border, nor Breed, nor Birth,
> When two strong men stand face to face, though they come from the ends of the earth!
>
> (Rudyard Kipling, 1889)

One hundred and thirty years after the *Ballad of East and West* was written, we now live in an age of globalisation when the two strongest economies in the world are standing face to face across the Pacific Ocean. Back in September 2012, months before Xi Jinping became the new Chinese leader, the then US Secretary of State Hillary Clinton said that "the Pacific is big enough for all of us",[2] which was widely quoted as a headline in the media. This line has since been continuously repeated, but more by the Chinese side, even as Xi Jinping's 'golden verse' whenever he commented on the Sino-US relations. East and West have not just constantly met each other, they have also interacted with each other across cultural, economic, political and diplomatic realms. Amid China's expanding global presence and growing influence, the China Dream of national rejuvenation staged by Xi Jinping has prompted both the Chinese society and China watchers to rethink China's historical, ideological and cultural heritage.

In China's efforts to carve out a new identity on the global stage, a cultural diplomacy campaign was launched to fulfil this new mission. Academic interest in this area has only recently developed into a substantial body of research. However, its focus has been almost exclusively on how it is functioning as a tool to build China's soft power. The aim of this chapter is neither to measure the soft power generated by China's cultural diplomacy, nor to argue whether or not it has been successful. Instead, its point of departure is to show the limitations of applying the Western-defined narrative of 'soft power' in non-Western contexts, and why an alternative and more sophisticated theoretical framework is needed to look both beyond and beneath the soft power lens to illuminate the complex nature of China's cultural diplomacy.

Unpacking the key concepts

Cultural diplomacy

The hybrid term 'cultural diplomacy' does not have a particularly long history. It first appeared in the 1934 Oxford English Dictionary, as a laudatory reference for English language teaching abroad, but the concept did not gain much currency until the term 'public diplomacy' was coined by Edmund Gullion in 1965 – during the Cold War era. It then appeared across a range of discourses, including academic, journalistic and governmental, to mean the "active, planned use of cultural, educational and informational programming to create a desired result that is directly related to a government's foreign policy objectives" (McClellan, 2004: n.p.). Ham's summary offered a more discerning insight into the contrast with traditional diplomacy, which is "focusing on problems whereas public diplomacy [focuses] on values" (2001: 4).

The above definition explains why cultural diplomacy is often considered to be a core element of public diplomacy, along with "exchange diplomacy and international broadcasting" (Cull, 2008: 33); public diplomacy often assumes the form of cultural diplomacy, which is "the exchange of ideas, information, values, systems, traditions, beliefs, and other aspects of culture, with the intention of *fostering mutual understanding*" (emphasis added) (Cummings, 2009: 1). The definition given in the *Cultural Diplomacy Dictionary* echoes this: "the essential idea is to allow people access to different cultures and perspectives, and in this way, foster mutual understanding and dialogue" (Chakraborty, 2013: n.p.). It is also made clear by the Institute for Cultural Diplomacy that it "is not a promotion of its own culture, but rather of understanding and reconciling, as well as learning from each other" (2011: n.p.).

Its actual practice can be illustrated by the diagram in Figure 1.1 that was adapted from the Double-Swing Model developed by Yoshikawa (1987) for intercultural communication. The diagram shows that cultural diplomacy is inherently relational where both parties of the addresser and addressee play significant roles in this dynamic and cyclical process, and through which both will be changed during the course of cultural diplomacy practice. This model will be elaborated with more evidence-based discussions in the following chapters.

At the heart of this model is an important distinction between "cultural difference" and "cultural diversity" elaborated by Bhabha (1994), who contended that the latter is static and concerns knowledge, while the former stresses the dynamic process and concerns interaction, during which an 'other' culture was involved and where a difference was produced between the 'self' and the 'other'. This further distinguished "cultural pluralism" from the simple fact of "cultural diversity": cultural pluralism addresses the process of mutual recognition, generation and transformation in this interaction with other cultures, particularly between conflicting cultures, and reveals the tensions and exclusions involved in the process when the dominating culture tries to establish and maintain its authority.

20 *Look beyond and beneath the soft power*

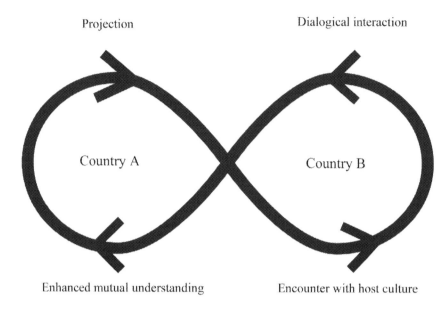

Figure 1.1 Cultural diplomacy as a mutual process.

In Sabbagh's words, it is "a political response to the injustice done to members of formerly oppressed culture" (2005: 100).

China's cultural diplomacy efforts represent such a "political response"; the government wishes to reshape the cross-cultural terrain into a more level playing field as they feel that the Chinese culture was "formerly oppressed". From the above, we can see that cultural difference is the premise for cultural diplomacy, while cultural pluralism underpins its ultimate goal. After clarifying this key concept, we will now look at the mainstream theory of using "soft power" to explain the purpose of China's cultural diplomacy, followed by a critical review that exposes its inadequacy – and even its inappropriateness.

Soft power

Coined by Joseph S. Nye, Jr in 1990, the term "soft power" means "the ability to get what you want through attraction rather than coercion or payment" (Nye, 2004: x). The definition was expanded by adding the word "persuasion" when he explained the new concept of "smart power", a strategy that describes a successful "combination of the hard power of coercion and payment with the soft power of persuasion and attraction" (Nye, 2011: xiii). Again, in another article Nye published in 2012 about soft power in China, he referred to soft power as "the ability to get what one wants by *attraction and persuasion* rather than coercion or payment" (Nye, 2012: n.p.). It is an ideal situation when "attraction" and

Look beyond and beneath the soft power 21

"persuasion" merge seamlessly, but the inherent tension existing between the two, whereby the former draws on intrinsic values while the latter depends on extrinsic aids, was never discussed, although this has huge implications on how to successfully build soft power in practice. Using America's own foreign policy practice towards China as an example, the "persuasion" part has not worked very well. In 1967, Nixon declared in his article in *Foreign Affairs* that: "the world cannot be safe until China changes. Thus our aim, to the extent that we can influence events, should be to induce change. The way to do this is to *persuade* China that it must change" (Nixon, 1967). Since his administration,

> The assumption that deepening commercial, diplomatic, and cultural ties would transform China's internal development and external behaviour has been a bedrock of U.S. strategy. Even those in the U.S. policy circles who were sceptical of China's intentions still shared the underlying belief that U.S. power and hegemony could readily mould China to the United States' liking.
>
> (Campbell and Ratner, 2018: n.p.)

In the Orwellian year of 1984, before President Reagan's first official visit to China, *Time* magazine published a cover story themed "China's New Face: What Reagan Will See". The image used was of a young Chinese man dressed in the traditional 1960s army-style overcoat, holding a bottle of Coca Cola at the Great Wall. The actual story went by the title "China: East Meets Reagan – A Nation with a New Look Prepares to Welcome an Old-Style Anti-Communist", followed by two more reports on China: "China: Capitalism in the Making" and "China: Making Free Enterprise Click".[3] However, over three decades later, from the question posed by *The Economist*: "How the West got China Wrong" in March 2018,[4] to the debates it triggered in *Foreign Affairs* over "Did America Get China Wrong?" in June 2018,[5] then to the answer provided by Harvard scholar William Overholt, "The West is Getting China Wrong" in August 2018,[6] – all showing that China can make changes to embrace what it finds attractive; however, if China is not attracted to following the path voluntarily, then America's plan to induce change by using its "power and hegemony" to "persuade" China hasn't delivered the result. The Chinese government has adhered to the same principle of "Chinese essence and Western utility" (*zhongxue weiti, xixue wei yong*) since the failed Westernisation Movement (1861–1895) in the late Qing Dynasty. Fredman's comments offer a good footnote to its reflection on Sino-US relations: "Since the nineteenth century, the American urge to mould China in its own image has coexisted alongside the Chinese desire to use American technology and know-how to serve China's economic development" (2015: n.p.).

The challenge in using soft power to blend attraction and persuasion is only bigger for an 'authoritarian state' like China than other democracies. According to Li, in China soft power is "primarily utilized to refute the 'China Threat' thesis, facilitate a better understanding of China's domestic social-economic

22   *Look beyond and beneath the soft power*

reality, and *persuade* the outside world to accept and support China's rise" (2009: 31). However, a question worth pondering is: would a state-led *persuasion* campaign increase or decrease the *attraction* of a country's culture, political values and foreign policy – the three sources of soft power defined by Nye? Nye's answer to this question with regard to China was quite blunt, stating that Beijing is "trying its hands at attraction, and failing – miserably" (Nye, 2013: n.p.). Yet, ironically, "soft power" is probably more enthusiastically embraced by the Chinese government than anywhere else, even to the extent of becoming an obsession according to Shambaugh (2013b) and Tao (2015). It has gained considerable currency in both official and scholarly discourse in China, particularly after 2007 when it was adopted into the official lexicon: Chinese president Hu Jintao made it clear at the 17th National Congress that "cultural soft power" has become "an important source of national cohesion and creativity and a factor of growing significance in the competition in overall national strength",[7] and "building cultural soft power" was listed on the agenda in the twelfth Five-Year-Plan (2011–2015). After Xi Jinping took over in 2012, he not only continued to endorse this concept, but also linked it with the new vision of the China Dream, stating in a speech that: "enhancing national cultural soft power is crucial to the realisation of the two 'centennial goals' and the China Dream of national rejuvenation".[8] In 2014, addressing the central foreign affairs meeting, he again emphasised that the government "should increase China's soft power, give a good Chinese narrative, and better communication China's message to the world".[9]

Possibly because of its frequent appearance in the Chinese official rhetoric, despite the academic and foreign policy debates the concept has induced in the USA, there was not much scholarly debate about the concept's relevance to China but instead there have been extensive elaborations on its importance, almost as a timely cure found for China's image problem following its economic and military rise. Therefore, of the myriad literature about China's cultural diplomacy, the great majority has attributed its purpose to "building soft power". To chime with the narrative of cultural renaissance in China, many scholars (Ding, 2008; Li, 2009; Glaser and Murphy, 2009) have pointed to the fact that the theory of "soft power" actually has much deeper roots in China's ancient philosophies. For example, Laozi, the founder of Daoism, used the famous metaphor of water dripping through a rock to say "what is soft is strong"; Mozi, the founder of Mohism and the advocate of the doctrine of non-offense, argued that offensive uses of forces would sow the seeds of long-standing conflicts like theft and murder; and Sunzi, the ancient Chinese strategist, put forward the best strategy as "winning a battle without a fight"; Confucius has said "if those who are distant do not submit, one must cultivate virtue to attract them", and in fact, the core value of Confucianism, which had been China's dominant ideology for more than 2,000 years, advocates that a state should obtain its leadership status by setting a moral example, and win the allegiance of people through virtue, not by force or imposition of one's values on others; Mencius, another great Confucian thinker, was known to elaborate on the value of non-coercion and the necessity for a ruler to cultivate his own virtue to attract others:

Look beyond and beneath the soft power 23

There is a way to gain the whole world. It is to gain the people, and having gained them one gains the whole world. There is a way to gain the people. Gain their hearts, and then you gain them.... When you are correct in your person, the whole world will turn to you.

(cited in Bell, 2006: 25)

Even in the USA, Joseph Nye is only considered the inventor of the term "soft power", but not the originator of the idea. Back in 1961, Etzioni (1961) already noted that power differs according to the means employed to make the subject comply. These means may be physical, material or symbolic, or what Etzioni respectively called coercive, remunerative and normative power. Coercive power relies on inflicting physical or psychological pain or deprivation. Remunerative power is the realm of material inducement; normative power relies on the capacity to motivate through the force of ideas and win compliance through creating group norms which individuals wish to identify with. Then, in another book, first published in 1974, *Power: A Radical View*, Steven Lukes also stated that: "the supreme exercise of power to get another or others to have the desires you want them to have – that is, secure their compliance by controlling their thoughts and desires" (1974: 23).

Nye made use of these ideas and coined the new term of soft power in his 1990 book *Bound to Lead: The Changing Nature of American Power*. This notion of cultural power as an alternative to military and economic might has quickly gained popularity around the world and bred a whole new range of vocabulary qualified by the adjective 'soft', such as 'soft strategy' and 'soft balancing'. It was also warmly embraced by the Chinese government who hopes to use it as the lubricant to transform China's rise from a hard one to a "soft rise" (Wang, 2008: 258). True, if affluence were to lead to influence, the hard power of economic and military strength needs to be combined with cultural and values attraction to make the influence positive.

Nye (2004, 2005, 2012, 2013, 2015) likes to quote changing positions in the opinion polls as an indicator of how successful one's soft power strategy is, which encourages a common view of seeing soft power as a "competition between great powers" to win hearts and minds (Guo, 2004: 20). Although Nye himself claimed that "soft power need *not* be a zero-sum game", the way he pitched China's soft power growth in 2005 as clearly being "at America's expense" actually confirms that it is (2013: n.p.). Nye and Wang's research also found that: "most of these (American) views assume a zero-sum game perspective and cast a more negative rather than positive light on China's soft power growth" (2009: 21). If we remember the purpose of cultural diplomacy as "fostering mutual understanding", we can see why this defies the validity of 'soft power' as being the underpinning theory for cultural diplomacy that clearly does not aim at one side winning over the other, but rather focuses on the notion of a positive sum game of nurturing mutual understanding and mutual respect between cultures. The soft power approach is still a binary one in essence and projects different cultural and value systems as representing identities that are

24 *Look beyond and beneath the soft power*

rivals to each other. The Double Swing illustration (see Figure 1.1) shows that cultural diplomacy transcends the binary opposites of the East and the West in a state of dynamic dialogue, which may lead to a "change of mind" rather than "winning hearts and minds" as its goal is not to eliminate differences, but more as the means to achieve the ends of a better understanding of the differences. The pictorial demonstration shows that the focus is not entirely on one side or the other, but rather a dynamic flow of interactive and dialogical communication between the two sides through cultural encounters.

Another problem with applying the soft power concept is that 'culture' and 'political values' are identified as two separate sources of building soft power, but have a blurred boundary between the two. In addition, the two means of building soft power have further complicated the conceptualisation of China's cultural diplomacy: its focus on showing the '*attraction*' of Chinese 'culture' tends to be interpreted as 'political value' promotion through '*persuasion*'. What is more, since the concept of soft power is affixed vis-à-vis China's rising hard power, which is already causing great concerns internationally, this approach tends to picture China's cultural diplomacy as a softening agent of the China Threat.

Therefore, soft power may be a useful concept in analysing the gap between the soft and hard powers of China and for exploring why China's soft power growth does not synchronise with its increases in hard economic rise as many scholars (Huntington, 1998; Lai and Lu, 2012) have argued for. However, under this lens one will only see that China's drive is stronger in the soft power competition to match its recent rise in hard power, and is thus receiving more funding to support this from the central government. This is too narrow a lens through which to view the purpose of China's cultural diplomacy and to evaluate its effects, as it fails to recognise the unequal power positions associated with culture and ideology. The soft power lens has only put China in the limelight as the projecting side that launches a "charm offensive" (Kurlantzick, 2007), while detaching it from the background of the global cultural terrain: it has not engaged with any historical analysis of the legacies of cultural hegemony, knowledge–power nexus and Orientalism that have shaped national imaginaries and political discourses underpinning the current global cultural terrain. Nor did it address nationalism as the domestic driving force for China to launch cultural diplomacy to communicate its fresh self-perception, which is also connected to and regenerated from its own historical past. The deepseated remnants of the historical contexts, both internationally and domestically, continue to permeate life in China today. As Foucault argued: "We have to know the historical conditions which motivate our conceptualization. We need a historical awareness of our present circumstance" (1983: 209). Without a historical frame of reference, it can only show a lopsided view. Therefore, if the purpose of China's cultural diplomacy is only examined from the perspectives of "building soft power", it has only scratched the surface and seriously underestimated the complexities of intercultural interactions and multicultural relationships.

Strategic narratives

Over time, as some scholars argued, soft power has become a "catch-all term that has lost explanatory power" and the question of how those resources produce effects was not answered (Roselle, Miskimmon and O'Loughlin, 2014), therefore, a new concept of strategic narratives was argued by Antoniades, O'Loughlin and Miskimmon as "tools with which states can project their values and interests in order to extend their influence, manage expectations and change the discursive environment in which they operate" (2010: 3). They are "means for political actors to construct a shared meaning of international politics, and to shape the perceptions, beliefs and behaviors of domestic and international actors" (Miskimmon, O'Loughlin and Roselle, 2012: 1). The relationship of the concept of strategic narratives to the concept of soft power was made clear by Roselle, Miskimmon and O'Loughlin in their article titled "Strategic Narrative: A New Means to Understand Soft Power", which states that "strategic narrative *is* soft power in the 21st century" (2014: 72). From these definitions, it can be understood as a concrete manifestation of the elusive sources used to build soft power named by Nye, that is: culture, political values and foreign policy. When Nye (2014) commented that in today's global information age, victory might sometimes depend on whose story wins, strategic narratives are what constitute the winning stories that showcase the shared consensus. Meanwhile, the concept focuses on the process of power conversion as it "directly addresses the formation, projection and diffusion, and reception of ideas in the international system" (Roselle *et al.*, 2014: 74).

Miskimmon, O'Loughlin and Roselle (2013) have identified three levels of strategic narratives: International System Narratives, National Narratives and Issue Narratives. In the context of China, examples of such narratives at each level may include "harmonious world", "peaceful rise/development" and "the Belt and Road Initiative" (BRI).[10] These more or less correspond to the three narratives of the BRICS countries identify by Noort: "a system narrative of global recovery, an identity narrative of inclusive participation and an issue narrative of infrastructural development" (2017: 121). Although China is a one-party state, every new leadership since Jiang Zemin's time as president (1993–2003) has come up with a newly crafted strategic narrative to mark a new era: from Jiang's "joining the world system" to Hu Jintao's "building a harmonious world", now to Xi's "creating a community of shared future for humankind", clearly show that narratives are "structured to address past, present and future" (Roselle *et al.*, 2014: 75). Some may think such a transcendent narrative of "one world, one dream" is a utopian one that is "enticing, but essentially meaningless" (Parton, 2019: 37). Although it might appear to be divorced from the reality of world politics, China has obviously started to show its ambition to push an alternative vision by using such strategic narratives, which present China as a responsible, stabilising force that seeks pro-active common development and prosperity.

26 *Look beyond and beneath the soft power*

The concept of strategic narratives sheds useful light on the actual practice of cultural diplomacy in the field, particularly "in regards to how influence works in a new media environment" (Parton, 2019: 71); it will be drawn on in the following chapters in discussing how strategic narratives help construct a Chinese identity in building domestic cohesion while making them appealing and persuasive to the target audiences at the same time.

After clarifying the relevant concepts and analysing the inadequacy of the current theoretical framework of soft power, we can now proceed with an overview of the historical, international and domestic contexts specifically for China, where the legacies of Orientalism, cultural hegemony, power–knowledge nexus, communism and nationalism were interwoven into the complex global cultural terrain that China's cultural diplomacy was launched into.

Understanding the historical and international context: China as the cultural other and the ideological other

This section will look at the historical dimension in the international contexts, which is underpinned by Gramsci's concept of "cultural hegemony", Foucault's notion of "power relations" and Said's critique of "Orientalism". What follows is an overview of these key concepts.

A good place to start with is the concept of cultural hegemony, which was first formally put forward by Antonio Gramsci in the 1930s as "intellectual and moral leadership whose principal constituting elements are consent and persuasion" (cited in Fontana, 1993: 140). Gramsci contrasted the functions of "domination" (direct physical coercion) with those of "direction" (consent) in defining hegemony as "a complete fusion of economic, political, intellectual and moral objectives which will be brought about through the intermediary of ideology" (cited in Mouffe, 1979: 181). This process of "manufacturing consent" was further elaborated on by Foucault (1980), who pointed out incisively that discourse was created and perpetuated by those who have the power and means of communication, and power was constituted through accepted forms of knowledge, which was reinforced and redefined constantly through the education system, the media and the flux of political and economic ideologies. Gramsci and Foucault have both highlighted the role played by ideology in producing and maintaining hegemony and power, which is "that part of culture which is actively concerned with the establishment and defense of patterns of belief and value" (Fallers, 1961: 677). These two terms of "establishment" and "defence" capture the essence in this process: it aims at creating something new to cope with the cultural threats posed by the 'other', but it is also a defence of 'our' culture.

Gramsci was visionary enough to take the conventional Marxist theory beyond class struggle to the fight for cultural hegemony as a more significant battle; Foucault's elaboration of power relations revealed how this battle is constant and pervasive in nature, and how power functions in controlling knowledge and vice versa. His research frame suggests analysis to be enmeshed in complex dynamics among truth, knowledge and power (Rowan and Shore, 2009). Based on Gramsci's concept of "cultural hegemony" and Foucault's theory of "knowledge is power", Said developed his critique of Orientalism. Arguing from a different dichotomy of Occident and Orient, which is not about knowledge but about power, Said (1978: 3) dislocated the 'familiar' concept of the Orient to expose how the 'other' helps define the West via contrasting languages, experiences and images in a "Western style for dominating, restructuring, and having authority over the Orient" (Morley and Robins, 1995: 134). In doing so, the West "arrogates to themselves the right to represent all non-Western Others, and thus to provide 'us' with the definitions by which 'we' distinguish ourselves from 'them'" (Morley and Robins, 1995: 134). Said established that power and knowledge were inseparable components of the intellectual binary relationship with which Occidentals claimed "knowledge of the Orient". Just as Dabashi pinpointed, "the critique of Orientalism was a critique of a mode of knowledge production" (2015: 15). It exposed how the relationship between the 'East and West' as potentially cultural contestants was transformed into 'the West and the Rest': the study of the Orient by the Occident is not to achieve a truthful knowledge and perception, but to define the relationship between the two, with Western power standing at its very core. This ideological construction was both persuasive and persistent in Western thought. The idea of the 'other' underpinned the asymmetrical relations between the East and West in which cultural power augmented political power to constitute what Gramsci called "hegemony" (Said, 1978), whose essence is "its ability to diminish diversity by subordinating other cultures to a universal, homogenous culture" (Mulcahy, 2017: 118). In short, Orientalism established the West's cultural hegemony over the East; under Western domination, the East has lost its power or even the right of discourse to the West. This was best summarised by the famous quote of Karl Marx which appears on the preliminary page of *Orientalism*: "they cannot represent themselves; they must be represented" (Said, 1978: viii).

Said further claimed that Western representations of the 'Orient' amounted to a form of cultural imperialism. One meaning of the term is that representations which claim to be objective and universal, are in fact the products of undisclosed relations of power. Huntington elaborated this in one sentence: "What is universalism to the West is imperialism to the rest" (1998: 184). In contrast to Huntington's view that cultural and religious identities will be the primary source of conflicts in the post-Cold War international system, Said has continuously challenged the notion that difference implies hostility, and called for a new way of conceiving the conflicts that have stimulated generations of hostility, war and imperial control. However, in his *Preface* to the 2003 edition of *Orientalism*, Said still lamented the fact that we were imprisoned in "labels and antagonistic debate whose goal is a belligerent collective identity rather than understanding and intellectual exchange" (2003: xviii).

Today, Orientalism is still one of the most powerful analytical concepts as the globalisation of knowledge and Western culture constantly reaffirms the West's

28 *Look beyond and beneath the soft power*

view of itself as the centre of legitimate knowledge. What is probably beyond Said's critique of Orientalism is that this "belligerent collective identity" has produced a mirror image and a whole discourse of Occidentalism, at least in contemporary China, as pointed by Chen (2002) with penetrating insight. She argued that the understanding and knowledge of the 'Western other' is also constructed by a Chinese imagination, prompted by a different motivation and for strikingly different political ends: "not for the purpose of dominating the West, but in order to discipline, and ultimately to dominate, the Chinese self at home" (2002: 3). Chen's book is mainly about how a deliberate misreading of Western cultural texts was adopted to invent a view of the West for internal political purposes by looking at post-Mao literature. I will apply this discerning lens to look at how Chinese Occidentalism is used to support nationalism at home and combat Western cultural hegemony in the domestic context.

For now, let's continue to explore the international context to see how Orientalism is reincarnated in contemporary China. Apart from being the inferior cultural 'other', China also found itself being haunted by another antiquated view as a representation of the 'yellow peril' – a psychological fear that was projected mainly on East Asia. In modern times, the rise of Communist China has reactivated this embedded fear with claims such as the "return of the Yellow Peril" (Williamson, 2015) and the new term "red threat", resonating the continued fear as a recurrent pattern, as Scott notes that: "for the first time, all the core elements of the Yellow Peril paradigm, namely economic strength and military projection based on a large population base were coalescing in reality" (2007: 84). In Tchen and Yeats' words, the fear "becomes part of the politics of a people. It becomes ideology and faith" (2014: 16). The evolution of China's image from being the "yellow peril" to the "red threat" suggests a system of othering. In a way, if we argue for a de-Orientalised cultural China in the modern world, this new vision of 'ideological otherness' re-Orientalises China, that is, the inheritance of being the 'cultural other' has revived itself into being the demonised 'ideological other', making "China, more than any other place" serve "as the 'other' for the modern West's stories about itself" (Pomeranz, 2000: 25). A most recent version of such a mindset in the political rhetoric is the contrast between "noble nations" against "bad actors" in the US Secretary of State Michael Pompeo's speech given at the German Marshall Fund in December 2018:

> *Bad actors* [emphasis added] have exploited our lack of leadership for their own gain. This is the poisoned fruit of American retreat. President Trump is determined to reverse that. China's economic development did not lead to an embrace of democracy and regional stability; it led to more political repression and regional provocations. We welcomed China into the liberal order, but never policed its behaviour. China has routinely exploited loopholes in the World Trade Organization rules, imposed market restrictions, forced technology transfers, and stolen intellectual property. And it knows that world opinion is powerless to stop its Orwellian human rights violations.

Look beyond and beneath the soft power   29

...

In the finest traditions of our great democracy, *we* are rallying the *noble nations* (emphasis added) of the world to build a new liberal order that prevents war and achieves greater prosperity for all.[11]

Compared with the line of 'cultural superiority and inferiority' carved out by Orientalism, more antagonist camps of 'friends or enemies' were created by this ideological otherness. To a certain extent, Gramsci's "cultural hegemony", Foucault's knowledge–power nexus, Said's "cultural imperialism" and Huntington's "clash of civilisations" have all partially explained the coercive use of cultural power in international relations. Foucault also pointed out that: "every relationship between forces is a power relation, with resistance to power as part of the exercise of power" (1982: 793). Culture has always been a weapon of the powerful and cultural resistance is therefore an eternal theme. Cabral (1973) suggested that it may take on new forms (political, economic, armed) in order to fully contest foreign domination, and Wallerstein argued that: "cultural resistance today is very often organized resistance – not spontaneous resistance, but planned resistance" (1991: 100).

Thus, under this theoretical framework, cultural diplomacy can be considered as a new form of planned cultural resistance for emerging powers like China, which has been held as the cultural and ideological 'other' and put under Western hegemonic influence despite the shifts in global economic relations. If viewed from Said, Gramsci and Foucault's perspectives, the purpose of China's cultural diplomacy would be counter-hegemonic, giving it an active defensive edge, completely different from the commonly accepted synonym of launching a "charm offensive" (Kurlantzick, 2007). The mission is not just to wield soft power, but also to shift the power relations underpinning those misperceptions with the 'us' and 'other' ideology embedded in cultural hegemony.

Understanding the historical and domestic context: the double-edged role of Chinese nationalism

After analysing the historical legacies in the international context, we must simultaneously take note of the domestic context, as the inextricable connections between the two dimensions form one of the characteristics of China's cultural diplomacy. Due to this interconnectedness, it is worth noting that the compartmentalisation of the 'domestic' and 'international' context is only meaningful on a theoretical and analytical level, but not in practice. It is also worth noting that both contexts have a historical dimension as well, which forms the bedrock of today's global cultural terrain.

The Chinese government has always been a firm believer in Lenin's famous statement that diplomacy is the extension of domestic affairs. China's domestic political reconfiguration has greatly reconfigured its foreign policy, including the paradigm of its cultural diplomacy; this has special bearing in understanding why cultural diplomacy is now considered a priority on the government agenda.

30　*Look beyond and beneath the soft power*

Building soft power is indeed communicated frequently to domestic audiences as a means of helping to generate national identity, to build national cohesion, to secure popular support and to safeguard regime legitimacy. However, the role played by nationalism is inadequately addressed in the current literature. Although the subject of Chinese nationalism per se is not under-researched, it is mostly focused in the spheres of national sovereignty, security and international relations; Chinese nationalism's double-edged role in both driving and limiting China's cultural diplomacy is yet to be explored.

Nationalism as the new ideology

In the last four decades, China has been through unprecedented transformation both in terms of scale and speed – culturally, economically, socially and politically. While massive developments are shaping up a new China, the old ideology underpinning the regime legitimacy is being shaken. As argued by Hroch (1985), nationalism becomes a substitute for factors of integration in a disintegrating society. Many scholars have argued that in today's China, nationalism is considered to be one of the two pillars that the national coherence and regime legitimacy rest on alongside rapid economic growth. Before we delve into further discussions, we need to clarify the meaning of the term employed here.

Of the myriad and competing definitions of nationalism, I found the one offered by Guibernau most applicable to China. In his view, "nationalism is a sentiment that has to do with attachment to a homeland, a common language, ideals, values and traditions, and also with the identification of a group with symbols which define it as 'different' from others" (Guibernau, 1996: 43). The strength of nationalism derives above all from its ability to create a sense of identity. As Robinson put it, it "describes the creation of an ideology that serves to celebrate and emphasise the nation as the preeminent collective identity of a people" (2014: 9). Hall (1991) has famously pointed out that self-identity is always a structured representation which has to go through the eye of the needle of the 'other': "Only when there is an other can you know who you are ... and there is no identity that is without the dialogic relationship to the other" (Hall, 1996: 344). This coincides with Ozkirimli's (2005) view that the discourse of nationalism divides the world into 'us' and 'them', and shows a tendency to perceive the world in terms of 'friends' and 'enemies'.

Since nationalism is both a "style of politics" and a "form of culture" (Smith, 1991: 91), these dual attributes of nationalism are sometimes referred to as "cultural nationalism" and "political nationalism" (Yoshino, 1992: 1). He and Guo's (2000) discussion of cultural nationalism sees the Chinese nation and Chinese people as being rooted in Confucian tradition and philosophy, and emphasises the ideological function of traditional Chinese culture in maintaining political order. This shows a particular blending feature between the cultural and political attributes in the Chinese context. Another two categories of Chinese nationalism defined by them are "state nationalism" and "popular nationalism", with the former referring to any doctrine, ideology or discourse in which the Chinese

Look beyond and beneath the soft power 31

party-state strives to identify itself as the nation, while the latter comes from below and represents unsystematic, popular national sentiments. These two categories can be associated with the two fundamental attributes of nationalism argued by Guibernau (1996): its political character as an ideology, and its capacity to be a provider of identity for individuals conscious of forming a group based upon a common culture, past, project for the future and attachment to a concrete territory. The combination of these two attributes creates an ideology that emphasises the nation as the pre-eminent collective identity of a people that comprises an "inter-stitching of state-inculcated patriotic political appeals, Han ethnic identification, and cultural pride; a confusion of aspirations for national greatness alongside growing sub-national assertions of regional identity; open-minded optimism and anti-foreign resentment" (Unger, 1996: xvii). To understand this complexity, we must explore the historical context by tracing the driving forces of social changes in China – a country that has always prided itself on being a historically powerful nation with a distinguished civilisation.

China's name itself, 'the Middle Kingdom', suggests its ancient belief of being the centre of '*tianxia*', under the heavens, which is more than a geographical term. Surrounded by much smaller neighbouring countries throughout history, the tributary system developed after the Han Dynasty gave the Middle Kingdom a strong sense of cultural superiority that the world revolves around China. Therefore, the series of defeats by foreign gunboats in the late Qing Dynasty – the two Opium Wars (1839–1842 and 1856–1860) and the first Sino-Japanese War (1894–1895) that were later taught at school as the "century of humiliations" – have ripped apart China's cultural superiority and triggered generations of efforts to reform the country and regain the glory: from Dr Sun Yat-sen's revolution to establish a republican and reinstate the Han ruling by overthrowing the Manchurian Qing Dynasty, to Mao Zedong's consolidation of a communist regime by winning the Anti-Japanese War (1937–1945) and rising against American imperialism; from Deng Xiaoping's re-adaptation of the common aspiration to economically develop China and negotiate for Hong Kong and Macao to be returned to China; to Hu Jintao's initiative to put soft power and cultural diplomacy on the top of the government agenda for the first time and roll out Confucius Institutes to help implement the strategy; leading eventually to the current government led by Xi Jinping, whose ambition is best summarised in the new vision of "realizing the dream of the great rejuvenation of the Chinese nation". This China dream is not to build something brand new, but to build a future based on the memory of 4,000 years of history. Therefore, only after a historical review can we fully understand Townsend's comments:

> The waters of nationalism steadily engulf all that stand in their path – imperial, republican, and Communist institutions, elite and popular classes, coastal and interior regions, reformist and conservative factions, Chinese at home and abroad. Other movements and ideologies wax and wane, but nationalism permeates them all.
>
> (Townsend, 1992: 97)

32 *Look beyond and beneath the soft power*

The cultural faces of Chinese nationalism

Nationalism exists in all counties and societies, but the cultural attributes differ from nation to nation, and it is the cultural imprint upon Chinese nationalism that is not adequately understood by the West. First of all, China's strong collectivist culture glues the state nationalism and popular nationalism together in that the state goal of strengthening the Chinese nation is shared by virtually all the Chinese people, thus state nationalism functions like a strategic means to gain popular legitimacy. This perception is common in academic treatments of Chinese nationalism (Unger, 1996; Zheng, 1999, Mitter, 2004; Saich, 2004), and we can easily see the national vision of the Chinese dream is more of a collective ambition than an individual aspiration compared with the 'American dream'. It seems to support the generalisation made by Guibernau (1996) that nationalism can be utilised by authoritarian regimes that place the interest of their nation above everything and always seeks to unify people's mind.

Second, the word '*guojia*' in Chinese could mean nation, state and country at the same time and they are all associated with '*jia*', which means family. The most famous of Confucius' teaching is to "cultivate the moral self, then regulate the family, then govern the state rightly, which eventually will lead the world to peace" (*xiushen, qijia, zhiguo, ping tianxia*). This historical legacy indicated that in a way, the Chinese state is run like a family and its leader is like a father figure. Mao Zedong and Deng Xiaoping were both known as "Grandpa Mao" and "Grandpa Deng" for school children during their ruling times and the nickname of "Uncle Xi" for Xi Jinping was even used in the state media. A most widely quoted line in his inaugural speech in 2012 was "to meet Chinese people's desire for a happy life is our mission".[12] This explains why economic development and nationalism are the two pillars that the CPC's[13] regime legitimacy rests on: although it is not voted into power, at least its domestic legitimacy can be maintained by improving people's livelihood and welfare, just like a father bringing more and better food to the table. This family sentiment touches on the other two distinctive attributes of Chinese culture: people's emotional attachment to their country and the importance of hierarchy. Just as the father is the authoritative figure to be obeyed at home, government decisions are to be implemented rather than challenged at work.

Third, patriotism, which literally means 'love the country' in Chinese (*aiguo*), is the 'right' form of nationalism in China. As Zhao explained, "the sentiments of the Chinese people are not described as nationalistic but patriotic. In the vocabulary of the Chinese communists, 'nationalism' carries a derogatory connotation and is used to refer to parochial and reactionary attachments to nationalities" (2004: 79). He further explained that, after 1989, the Party has effectively "equated patriotism with support for the government and its policies" (Zhao, 2000: 20). In a *People's Daily* editorial on China's National Day in 1996, it asserted that: "patriotism requires us to love the socialist system and road chosen by all nationalities in China under the leadership of the Community Party" (cited in Zhao, 2004: 76). Since Mao Zedong defined the party as being "great, glorious and correct", these three adjectives have become the definitive descriptions used in all the slogans. Today, at the entrance to Zhongnanhai, China's 'White House', two large slogans still remind people of this on the side walls: "Long Live the Great Communist Party of China" and "Long Live the Invincible Mao Zedong Thought". By identifying the party with the nation, Zhao argues, the regime makes "criticism of the party an unpatriotic act" (2004: 76). This may also explain why the Chinese are "more nationalistic in their reactions to foreign criticism and condemnations of China" (Jia, 2005: 15), even if such criticisms are actually targeted against the Communist Party. Just as Chinese people would react very strongly if any disrespectable remarks were made against their 'parents', what they are defending is not necessarily the 'acts', but the person that they feel morally obliged to defend.

When "love for Chinese cultural traditions" was also included as "an essential component of patriotism, in additional to love for the CCP and love of socialism" (Guo, 2017: 150), Hubbert (2019: 25) commented that Chinese officials have been "forthright about efforts to instrumentalise culture as a form of patriotic ritual". This is reflected in the intensity of the emotional investment of individuals, who are like sparks easily enflamed in a country like China where its ancient and continuous civilisation gives unity to the Chinese nation and the deepest cultural attachment to its people. To a considerable extent, China's ancient historical grandeur and the deep scar inflicted during its modern history by Western humiliation are ingrained in China's national psyche. The combination of these cultural attributes means that China tends to care tremendously about preserving and gaining face on the international stage. For example, when China hosts major international events, production from polluting factories and work at construction sites would be suspended to create "Olympic Blue" or the "APEC blue" sky. Even people's mobility would be restricted to help make the city appear more presentable with lighter traffic. Gries called this "face nationalism", defined as "a commitment to a collective vision of the 'national face' and its proper international status as presented to other nations" (1999: 67). The original Chinese word for face, '*mianzi*', has been adopted in English to distinguish this strong Chinese cultural feature from the familiar concept of 'face', but what is not fully understood is that it only matters when there is an 'outsider' involved: you don't 'lose face' in front of your own family members and loved ones, but it becomes a big deal if you are offended or criticised by 'others' in public.

For example, in Foreign Ministry's press conferences, rhetoric such as "deeply hurting Chinese people's feelings" and "we solemnly demand a formal apology" are often used to comment on incidents that violate China's core national interests. A most well-known example is the China–US aircraft collision incident which took place over the South China Sea in April 2001, when China lost one pilot and an aircraft. The Chinese side insisted on receiving a full apology from the US side, when their first statement only expressed "regrets". Beijing was still not satisfied when Washington used the word "sorry", until ten days later, after a series of intense negotiations, a "very sorry" was used by the

34 *Look beyond and beneath the soft power*

American Ambassador in his letter to the Chinese Foreign Minister, which was reported widely in headlines by domestic media as the "letter of apology".[14] This military collision incident reflects a cultural level of 'collision' as well in the importance of face-saving. As Gries explained: "treating China as an equal, the Chinese people will feel that China has gained face in international society" (1999: 71). Guo also pointed out that the government's "continued emphasis on mutual respect in international relations is motivated by the desire to avoid criticism and that tackling criticism is a top priority in foreign policy" (2017: 154). This "priority" can only by understood by understanding the cultural traits of Chinese nationalism.

The political face of Chinese nationalism: Occidentalism in contemporary China

Chang has made a forceful depiction of "contemporary Chinese patriotic nationalism" as a "volatile mix of potentially troublesome attributes that social scientists have identified to have a high propensity toward aggression" (2001: 182). These attributes include:

> an ethnic-racial conception of nationhood; a reactive nationalism that nurses memories of China's historical humiliation at the hands of the imperialist powers; a collective sense of victimhood and insecurity; xenophobic narcissism; a preoccupation with power; cultural-moral relativism; an illiberal worldview; an irredentist resolve to reclaim lost territories; and political authoritarianism.
>
> (Chang, 2001: 182)

Out of the mix are some elements that contribute to the forming of the political face of Chinese nationalism: Occidentalism. If the Occidentalist picture of the West has been coloured by religious sources in the Muslim world, in China, it is done through:

> playing up a history of painful Chinese weakness in the face of Western imperialism, territorial division, unequal treaties, invasion, anti-Chinese racism, and social chaos, because eliminating the "century of shame and humiliation" is at the heart of a principal claim to CCP legitimacy.
>
> (Zhao, 2004: 84)

Callahan (2006: 187) called it an "enduring narrative of modern Chinese history and identity", and Chang (2001) named it "wounded nationalism" with "great hypersensitivity", while Mufson (1996: n.p.) regarded the rise of Chinese nationalism as "a potent force in a country that is striving to shake off its image as the sick man of Asia and regain ancient glory". This Chinese representation of the Western forces who invaded, exploited and carved up China and forced a series of subjugations on a once-proud civilisation is its "deepest and most recurring

Look beyond and beneath the soft power 35

images of the Other" (Said, 1978: 1). Remembering China's national humiliation afflicted by the 'used-to-be barbarians' has been used as a way to depict the West as an enemy in order to mobilise internal support for the state. As Chen stated, "such Occidentalism may be considered as a counter-discourse, a counter-memory, and a counter-Other to Said's Orientalism" (2002: 6).

As explained earlier, this discourse was created and perpetuated by those who have the power and means of communication, and then reinforced constantly through the education system and the media, both of which are under the state control in China. Back in the 1980s, there were two media campaigns staged nationally against Western-inspired liberal ideas: the first was against "spiritual pollution" that "run counter to the country's social system" (Iyer, 1983) declared by the Party's Propaganda Chief in 1983; the second wave was "anti-Bourgeois liberalisation" in 1986, when a CPC Plenum defined "bourgeois liberalisation" as "negating the socialist system in favour of capitalism" (Abrams, 1986). This shows that Occidentalism in modern China is not a perfect mirror of Orientalism: its bigotry in projecting the 'other' may be just as reductive, but the reflection is more of a Chinese version of "Westoxification" – a term coined by Ahmad Fardid, a professor of philosophy at the University of Tehran, and later popularised by another Iranian intellectual Jalal al-e Ahmad, to describe "the twin dangers of cultural imperialism and political domination" due to "intoxication or infatuation that impairs rational judgment and confers an inability to see the dangers presented by the toxic substance, that is, the West".[15] In China, it is used to imply a Western intention to "peacefully evolve" China, a theory of conspiracy that China believes the West maintains a strategy to infiltrate and subvert socialist countries by spreading Western political ideas and lifestyles, inciting discontent and encouraging groups to challenge the Party leadership. As Shambaugh observed in the early 1990s,

> peaceful evolution is the main threat to China's stability today. The ideological struggle will be the most important factor in future Sino-American relations. The U.S. will again become the major threat to China, but not a military one. The Taiwan problem will remain important, but the ideological struggle – particularly peaceful evolution – will be primary.
>
> (Shambaugh, 1991: 275)

Although the term "peaceful evolution" was dimmed in official discourse after 2000, "hostile Western forces" became the new reference in Hu Jintao's time (2012):

> *The hostile forces* in the international community are hastening their steps to *westernize and separate/disintegrate* ('fenlie' is the original Chinese word used) our country. The ideology and culture fronts have been their key areas of infiltration. We must deeply understand the seriousness and complexity of ideological struggles, and take powerful measures to cope with them.
>
> (cited in Sahlins, 2015: 7)

36 *Look beyond and beneath the soft power*

Hu specifically warned Xi over this threat in 2012 (Wu, 2012), when Xi Jinping took over. According to Guo, at the heart of Xi's China Dream discourse is:

> a two-pronged strategy, namely political de-Westernisation and cultural re-Sinicisation. The former is an ideological defence that is designed to counter the influence of "universal values" detrimental to the CCP's grip on power and to maintain the political identity of the Party and the state.
>
> (Guo, 2017: 151)

A US State Department inspector general's appraisal of the embassy in Beijing in 2017 described how the Chinese government called American public affairs diplomats "hostile foreign forces" (Perlez and Ding, 2018). An actual example is the Umbrella Movement (pro-democracy protest) which happened in Hong Kong in 2014. According to Van Oudenaren (2015), state-run media alleged that a high-level official at the National Endowment for Democracy (NED) "had met key people from 'Occupy Central'" months before the Umbrella Movement got underway. The *People's Daily*[16] and *Global Times*[17] both claimed that the West was the "pushing hands behind the scene" by using "universal values" such as democracy to alter the internal societal, cultural and normative composition of socialist states with the objective of precipitating regime change and undermining unity. Just like Said (1978: 55) described how the Orientalist "seeks to intensify its own sense of itself by dramatising the distance and difference" between 'us and them', such discourses also seek to polarise the two systems as being implacable foes and give people a sense of what they are fighting against and fighting for. As Chen (2002: 2) has incisively pointed out, "the Chinese Orient has produced a new discourse, marked by a particular combination of the Western construction of China with the Chinese construction of the West", it "serves an ideological function quite different from that of Orientalism", which is for Western world domination; "Chinese Occidentalism is primarily a discourse that has been evoked by various and competing groups within Chinese society for domestic Chinese politics" (Chen, 2002: 3). In other words, the 'othered self' uses the discourse of being the 'ideological other' as evidence of anti-China bias for its own political agenda.

It has also been reinforced by a government-sponsored Patriotic Education Campaign, through textbooks, museum exhibitions and monuments. For example, the Chinese participation in the Korean War in 1950 is always taught in schools as "the War to Resist US Aggression and Aid Korea", where Chinese troops fought against the "American devils" ('*guizi*', a general derogatory term used for all foreign forces that have invaded China throughout history, but more commonly used to refer to the 'Japanese devil' and 'American devil' in modern history). Over time, it has become a taken for granted way of constructing and interpreting history. It is even used in the teaching materials on the Confucius Institute Online platform, with the video materials stating that the "US manipulated the UN Security Council to pass a resolution to organise a UN command consisting mainly of US troops to enlarge the aggression against Korea"; the

Look beyond and beneath the soft power   37

material stating that the USA had "tried to seize the whole peninsula" was later deleted, after being criticised as "Anti-US propaganda" (Robertson, 2012: n.p.). However, in 2015, the state media's online portal people.cn is still commemorating the war's 65th anniversary, and an event themed "let history tell future" was reported with an aim to "let the younger generation better understand patriotism, heroism and internationalism, so that they can carry forward the invincible spirit of 'the War to Resist US Aggression and Aid Korea'".[18] Outside state media, identity and public memory are also fused in popular culture where nationalism is not imposed by the state so much as it resonated with people's feelings. For example, there is a genre of patriotic films and television series of fighting against the 'foreign devils', and the Beijing Opera show, one of the 'red classics' based on a plot of the Korean War was re-aired in 2015; its poster with the slogan of "Beat the American ambitious wolf"[19] went viral again in 2019, following the China–USA trade war.

In the early 1990s, Shambaugh (1991) has attributed Chinese perceptions of the USA to recurring cycles of amity and enmity. Today, China's complex love–hate relationship with the West is reflected in a paradox of rejection and mimesis: the emerging middle class and new rich are allowed to embrace Western technology, pursue a Western lifestyle, send their children to America to study at private schools and universities, and flaunt the latest gadgets and luxuries, but are not however, allowed to embrace the freedom and democratic norms. For example, you can queue to get a newly released model of an Apple smart phone on the same day as the USA but you cannot use Google or Facebook – another example of the government's stance of 'Chinese essence and Western utility' (*zhong ti xi yong*). While the ancient Great Wall is now used to attract foreign tourists rather than defending against foreign invaders, the Great Firewall of China – controlling domestic Internet use – has been erected to protect its 'essence' from being attacked.

The above shows how a deeper understanding of the historical and domestic influences on Chinese nationalism can help one make sense of China's behaviour, explicate how the Chinese view the world around them, how they tell their history, and what China wants the most – and fears the most.

The changing face of Chinese nationalism

Compared with the deep-seated and long-standing cultural attributes, perhaps another dimension just as significant for understanding contemporary China is its quickly evolving nature: its goal is constantly evolving in dynamic relationship with the rest of the world, driven by the implicit changes in the Chinese nationalism domestically. Wang (2005: 41) has come up with a three-P incentive structure to explain China's policy goals: Preservation, Prosperity and Power/Prestige. The first two Ps represent the domestic priority of maintaining regime legitimacy and economic growth, while Power/Prestige needs to be gained from external interactions. As Wang (2005: 40) further observed, "in a more open, richer, and confident China, the popular aspirations for power may inevitably

38 *Look beyond and beneath the soft power*

push Beijing to demand more influence and presence", and the government must respond to such aspirations to gain popular legitimacy and international legitimacy.

Nationalism is not monolithic as argued by Whiting and Chen (cited in Lampton, 2008: 147), who identified three types of nationalism: the first type is "affirmative nationalism", which "fosters patriotism and targets attitude" and centres exclusively on 'us'. Here we see an essentially constructive patriotism directed towards inward change and constructive international participation. This reflects the completion of the first stage of building a national identity. The second type, "aggressive nationalism", "arouses anger and mobilised behaviour". According to Whiting, "this is the form of national feeling that most concerns China's neighbours as it is focused on 'them'" (cited in Lampton, 2008: 147). Callahan (2006) argued that since 1989, national humiliation discourse has aimed to maintain and contain the Chinese nation by focusing on the external other. Finally, "assertive nationalism" has the potential to become either affirmative or aggressive nationalism because it "adds 'them' as a negative out-group referent to the 'us' of affirmative nationalism" (Lampton, 2008: 148).

Once mainly internal in orientation, Chinese nationalism today shows an implicit dynamic shifting from being "affirmative" to swinging between "aggressive" and "assertive", where the "intellectual level of nationalism" has a particular influence. Zhao argued that between the two levels of the state and popular nationalism, that is, a top-down effort to promote and make use of patriotism, and a bottom-up populist sentiment against foreign pressures, there is a "sandwiched intellectual level", where the "Chinese cultural nationalism developed and called for a *fanshi zhuanyi* (paradigm shift) to redefine intellectual discourse in terms of Chineseness" (2004: 67). This has profound implications for China's foreign policy making and its cultural diplomacy.

As explained by Ozkirimli (2005), since nationalism requires the constant defence of one's own culture as being either equal or superior to other national cultures, it ultimately turns the language of national identity into a language of morality, and renders it the very horizon of a political discourse that reflects a profound conviction that a counter-hegemonic stance is needed. If we apply the lens of Orientalism and cultural hegemony in looking at Chinese nationalism, we can see how the deeply and widely embedded pride in Chinese culture was turned into a strong desire to rise against Western domination, and the political character gives the government a sense of mission that goes beyond the cultural scope. The drive to regain glory and dignity, the deeply held and long-standing aspirations for restoring China's position as a great power in the world is behind the China Dream of "great rejuvenation of the Chinese nation" proposed by Xi Jinping. He and Guo have concluded that: "the core goal of Chinese nationalism is not only to promote and protect the national interests of China, but also to restore its 'greatness', or to reassert China's role in international politics" (2000: 2). In this sense, cultural diplomacy in China naturally converges state nationalism with popular nationalism, which is passionate about achieving an international status commensurate with Chinese people's conception of their

Look beyond and beneath the soft power 39

country's rightful place in the world. As Zhao explains, "nationalism as a shared value between the Chinese state and Chinese populace has played an increasingly important role in shaping the trajectory of China's rise" (2013: 553). However, Nye explicitly mentioned the "undercurrent nationalism as a potential roadblock" when commenting on the increase of China's soft power in 2005, and concluded that "as long as China fans the flames of nationalism and holds tight the reins of party control, its soft power will always remain limited" (2005: n.p.). Then in 2015, he simply claimed that Chinese nationalism was "the No. 1 factor limiting China's soft power". Why is that?

Because the dual characteristics of nationalism could often render culturally sustained boundaries and identities into the subject of political conflicts, and the nationalistic discourse involves a strong sense of morality that can be volatile in nature. On the one hand, nationalism can strengthen the regime's legitimacy and unify the nation by joining people together, across the disintegrating fractions of the right and the left, as well as polarised social classes of the rich and the poor; but on the other hand, uncontrolled nationalism can also pressurise the government into adopting a more aggressive stance to avoid being seen as weak in the face of external challenges. During the Cold War era, nationalist emotions were used to carry out an ideological war against the enemy camp, while in today's stronger China, popular nationalism has infiltrated deeper down and taken root outside the state itself. For example, the top grossing film in the box office in 2012 had a strong nationalist theme: *Wolf Warrior*, and its sequel *Wolf Warrior 2* set a new box office record of Chinese-speaking films in 2017. Zhao also observed that:

> Seeking status, acceptance and respect on the world stage, popular nationalists routinely charged the communist state as neither confident enough or competent enough in safeguarding China's vital national interests and too chummy with Japan and soft in dealing with the United States.
>
> (Zhao, 2013: 540)

Both Chinese and Western scholars (Xiao, 1996; Zhao, 2000; Shambaugh, 1996) have pinpointed the reactive nature of Chinese nationalism. Shambaugh called it "defensive nationalism", which is "assertive in form, but reactive in essence" (1996: 205), while Xiao argued that, "the intensity of the reaction is in proportion to the intensity of negative stimulus from abroad" (1996: 62). The incidents such as the anti-US protests against NATO's bombing of the Chinese Embassy in Belgrade in 1999, anti-Japanese protests that erupted across China following the Diaoyu Island dispute in 2012, popular reactions to China's territorial disputes with its Asian neighbours in 2015, and the boycott of South Korea as a holiday destination and its supermarket in China in response to its decision to deploy the THADD missile defence system in 2017, were all such reactions not mobilised by the government. They have, however, raised particular concerns that China's growing presence in the world economy and the political stage has begun to "feed Chinese pride, and potentially invites thoughts of Great Power

40 *Look beyond and beneath the soft power*

muscle flexing ... making it of special importance today whether Chinese nationalism remains relatively benign or becomes jingoistically assertive" (Unger, 1996: xii). This "whether or not" discussion soon evolved into being a given which was argued by other scholars such as White, who simply stated that "no wonder Chinese patriotism often shades into nationalism and even jingoism – just as patriotism in other countries often does" (2013: 47). Shambaugh (2013a: 58) also commented on a more assertive Chinese nationalism emerging out of the current domestic discourse on China's global identities, while Zhao elaborated on the delicate change in such domestic voices among the state media in "a dangerously stunted version of a free press, in which a Chinese commentator may more safely criticise government policy from a hawkish, nationalist direction than from a moderate, internationalist one" (2013: 544). This means that however moderate or pragmatic the government seeks to be in its diplomacy, there are powerful domestic forces and voices that call for a more muscular foreign policy; and it appears that the more prominent China's rise on the world stage becomes, the more salient the double-edged nature of Chinese nationalism appears. Thus, while it is filling the vacuum of ideology domestically, it is also fuelling the China threat argument internationally at the same time. If China's non-Western ideology is the breeding ground for the China threat perception, its rising nationalism at home is like an undercurrent that supplies water to sustain its life.

The above shows the strategic tight rope walking which is required between the international and domestic contexts. It is critical to have a more nuanced understanding of the two sides: on the domestic side, the government goals have always been affixed to staying in power as the absolutely dominant party; however, on the international side, the quest is on a changing scale with its prominence on the world stage. At the turn of the century, what China wanted to achieve was more respect and understanding, not to challenge the dominant powers, but at best to "balance" them (Rozman, 1999), or even just to have "the approval and support" from the existing powers (Wang, 1999). In 2005, scholars like Deng may have convincingly argued that Beijing saw a recognised "international status" in some ways "better than power" (2005). By 2007, Zhao appealed that China "should not only listen, but talk back" (2007), or fight for more power of discourse. Then, 2008 marked a turning point according to Callahan, when the combination of the Beijing Olympics and the start of the global financial crisis made Chinese elites suggest: "say Yes to calls for Beijing to lead the globe" (2012: 34). By 2012, the "grand shift of power from the West to the East" has become "common sense" and Beijing shifted from "being a rule-taker to rule-maker" (Callahan, 2012: 33). It seems today's China has started to gain 'more lines to say' as one of the leading roles on the world stage, and gain the confidence to say 'now listen to me'. In 2016, Xi added "cultural confidence" to the "three confidences" that the CCP wishes to boost – confidences in the development path, guiding theories and political system.[20] As argued by Guo, unlike Deng, Jiang, and Hu before him, "Xi does not beat around the bush with his opposition to 'universal values', American-style democracy, and Western political

Look beyond and beneath the soft power 41

system or modes of development" (2017: 152). Then at the 19th Party Congress in 2017, "Xi Jinping left no doubt that he regards China's illiberal concepts of political and economic order as superior to so-called Western models, and that he seeks to export 'Chinese wisdoms' to the world as a 'contribution to mankind' " (Benner, *et al.*, 2018: 7).

Inspired by Wang's (2005) three-P incentive structure for China's policy goals, I argue there is also an emergent trajectory along three-Ps in the evolving goals of China's cultural diplomacy: from changing *Perception*, to improving *Position*, then to enhancing *Power.* This evolvement also resonates with Chinese culture – an image of a 'new rich' person who buys into the 'great power club' is low in status, and it does not match with China's self-identification as being a sophistic-ated civilisation that can contribute Chinese wisdom to solving global issues. It may not be a planned-out journey at the start, as China does not choose to or aim at becoming the "center of gravity of world affairs" (Kissinger 2005), but it has certainly become a central theme of contemporary world politics when the "tipping point" came, as Kynge describes, "quite suddenly, or so it seemed, China became an issue of daily international importance" (2005: 6). Chinese scholars such as Xiang explained this outcome as "no one, not even the Chinese themselves, can prevent China's influence from spreading into politics, values and ideology" (2006, cited in Scott, 2008: 17). This defines a turning point in the journey of China's cultural diplomacy, starting from *responding to* the international misper-ception of China's own image to *repositioning* itself and now to *reshaping* a global picture involving all with an alternative discourse. As Scott has put it,

> one's place in the world is an objective and subjective thing, what one's position is and what one hopes its position should be and will be. One's place in the world looks back to what it has been, as well as forward to what it might or could be.
>
> (Scott, 2007: 7)

In both directions, looking back and looking forward, China sees nationalism.

Despite the rich literature regarding nationalism in China, very few have linked it to China's undertaking of cultural diplomacy. I argue that at least in China's case, we have to fully acknowledge the interplay between the two: on the one hand, nationalism, as one of the major sources of identity formation gives the driving force for China to launch cultural diplomacy: the desire to elevate China's cultural position and counter-cultural hegemony informs the party-state's decision making, while the popular nationalism gives the state moral support and even a sense of urgency to pursue cultural diplomacy. On the other hand, nationalism is also limiting its effects as has been argued by Nye and is evidenced by my primary research, which will be fleshed out in the following chapters. Meanwhile, cultural diplomacy can also play a dual role in balancing the 'double-edged' nature of Chinese nationalism: when an observable change in its external dimension is showing an increasingly zero-sum approach in China's foreign policy, cultural diplomacy can help rein it in with its positive-sum approach; and when its internal

42 *Look beyond and beneath the soft power*

dimension was criticised to "represent a backward-looking ideology, keeping an eye on the past and obsessed with China's historical and cultural superiority" (Lei, 2005: 495), cultural diplomacy could turn China from inward-looking to outward-looking by engaging with other cultures.

Therefore, viewing China's cultural diplomacy through only one lens of soft power falls short due to its inability to recognise the complexities and intricacies of this endeavour; it misses the critical ways in which cultural diplomacy actually works, and will only lead to a misinterpretation or mischaracterisation of it. The best cultural diplomacy strategy must seek a balance between internal and external forces from its domestic and international contexts, and both have historical legacies deeply ingrained, thus pointing to a three-dimensional framework of analysis needed.

An alternative analytical framework

Cultural diplomacy is an endeavour spanning over different nations, territories, races, development stages, social and political systems and cultural traditions. In many cases, it also spans over different civilisations in Huntington's terms (1998). Due to these variations and the constantly evolving power relationships, it is a very complex subject. Understanding a subject of such a complex nature requires a complex approach. So far, there are many commentary types of analysis of current events which use concepts developed in the West to test the Chinese case. I have argued that the soft power concept is incompatible with the very purpose of cultural diplomacy and lacks a historical perspective in locating the 'root cause' of the unique challenges faced by China, which is a complication co-produced by vestiges of Orientalism, Western cultural hegemony and the power–knowledge nexus. It is also an inappropriate framework as it applied the same lens to look at China as other Western countries and failed to recognise the unequal power positions associated with culture and ideology, as it neglected the crucial processes through which hegemony has been produced and maintained, underpinning the current global cultural terrain. It also fails to address the domestic context where nationalism is a driving force for China to launch cultural diplomacy that converges state nationalism with popular nationalism. Therefore, this lens is not able to provide a holistic view of China's cultural diplomacy; positioning China's cultural diplomacy as a projection of soft power is highly charged and at the same time is oversimplified.

Following the explanatory arguments laid out above, an alternative analytical framework constructed on historical, international and domestic dimensions, and drawing on the tripartite theories of Orientalism, cultural hegemony and nationalism is developed (see Figure 1.2). It offers a more comprehensive perspective to investigate the prominent features of China's cultural diplomacy and allows us to see a much more sophisticated discourse. At the core of this complex is power, as every relationship between forces is a power relation (Foucault, 1982), thus all the arrows in Figure 1.2 represent a power relationship, which connect each interface of this new analytical framework.

Look beyond and beneath the soft power 43

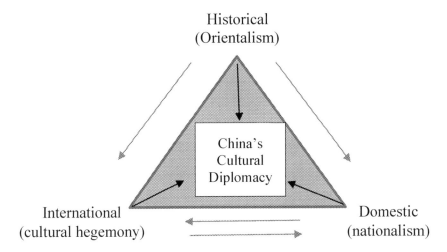

Figure 1.2 An alternative three-dimensional theoretical framework.

While inspired and stimulated by the growing literature about China's cultural diplomacy, this alternative framework of analysis challenges the existing ones and argues for the necessity to look through multiple lenses of the historical, international and domestic contexts to examine China's endeavours to reshape its image. It has re-conceptualised China's cultural position in the world from the pre-modern period to contemporary times, and developed new lines of academic inquiry. It has found that both culture and ideology helped to draw the line between the two sides of hegemony and counter-hegemony in the global cultural terrain of struggle. It also demonstrates how "the domestic–international nexus compels the Chinese leaders to be highly attentive to their country's vulnerabilities in both fronts" (Deng, 2009: 73), as how domestic issues are handled or reported may impede its cultural diplomacy abroad. Therefore, the framework reveals a three-dimensional picture of an uneven terrain that is both imbalanced and hierarchical at each interface. Only by capturing the intricacies between the intertwined, multiple contexts can we begin to acquire a deeper and more precise understanding of China's cultural diplomacy. The following chapters will draw on empirical data to reveal the fine line that must be navigated between the interfaces to strike a delicate balance.

Notes

1 This chapter is derived, in part, from an article published in *Cambridge Journal of China Studies* on 1 December 2017, available online: www.repository.cam.ac.uk/handle/1810/274412.
2 See Clinton says Pacific Big Enough for US, China, *South China Morning Post*, 1 September 2012, available at: www.scmp.com/news/asia/article/1027607/clinton-says-pacific-big-enough-us-china?edition=international; Hillary Clinton: Pacific "Big

44 *Look beyond and beneath the soft power*

Enough for all of Us", the *Telegraph*, 15 November 2012, available at: www.telegraph.co.uk/news/worldnews/australiaandthepacific/9679778/Hillary-Clinton-Pacific-big-enough-for-all-of-us.html; and Steven Lee Myers, Clinton Begins Asia Trip, Trying to Ease Tension With China, *New York Times*, 1 September 2012, available at: www.nytimes.com/2012/09/02/world/asia/clinton-tries-to-ease-tension-with-china-on-asia-trip.html.

3 China's New Face: What Reagan Will See, *Time*, 30 April 1984; China: Making Free Enterprise Click, *Time*, 30 April 1984; for the *Time* magazine cover, published in *Time*, 123(18) 30 April 1984, see http://content.time.com/time/magazine/0,9263,7601840430,00.html.

4 *The Economist*, How the West got China Wrong, 1 March 2018, available at: www.economist.com/leaders/2018/03/01/how-the-west-got-china-wrong.

5 Wang Jisi *et al.*, Did America Get China Wrong?: The Engagement Debate, *Foreign Affairs*, 14 June 2018, available at: www.foreignaffairs.com/articles/china/2018-06-14/did-america-get-china-wrong.

6 William H. Overholt, The West is Getting China Wrong, *East Asia Forum*, 11 August 2018, available at: www.eastasiaforum.org/2018/08/11/the-west-is-getting-china-wrong/.

7 Hu Jintao's report at 17th Party Congress, *Xinhua*, 24 October 2007, available at: http://news.xinhuanet.com/english/2007–10/24/content_6938749_6.htm.

8 See *Tigao guojia ruan shili* [Improving National Cultural Soft Power], speech given by Xi Jinping, 30 December 2013, available at: http://cpc.people.com.cn/xuexi/n/2015/0720/c397563–27331770.html.

9 Xi Eyes More Enabling International Environment for China's Peaceful Development. Addresses the central foreign affairs meeting held on 28–29 November 2014, available at: http://english.cri.cn/12394/2014/11/30/189s854461_1.htm.

10 The Belt and Road Initiative (BRI), changed from the original English translation of "One Belt One Road Strategy" after careful deliberations because "strategy" has more connotations for serving one's own national interests while "initiative" is offered as an open solution to solving a problem of common concern.

11 The full speech, Remarks by Secretary Pompeo at the German Marshall Fund, in Brussels, 4 December 2018, is available at US Embassy in Ukraine: https://ua.us embassy.gov/remarks-by-secretary-pompeo-at-the-german-marshall-fund/.

12 The full transcript of Xi Jinping's Speech at the Unveiling of the New Chinese Leadership, at the 18th Party Conference, 15 November 2012, is available at: www.scmp.com/news/18th-party-congress/article/1083153/transcript-xi-jinpings-speech-unveiling-new-chinese.

13 CPC is the official acronym for the Communist Party of China, but CCP is also very commonly used for the Chinese Communist Party, especially by Western scholars, it is kept as it is in some citations in this book.

14 Tan Jiaxuan, Tang Jiaxuan Reveals the Behind-The-Scenes Incident of the Sino-US Plane Collision: The US Apology Letter is Six Times, 6 December 2010, available at People.com: http://history.people.com.cn/GB/198305/198865/13408190.html.

15 See Westoxification, *Oxford Islamic Studies*, available at: www.oxfordislamicstudies.com/article/opr/t125/e2501.

16 Qingbo Zhang, Stop the Violence and Quell the Chaos, Cutting Off the Black Hands Behind the Curtains, *people.cn*, 19 August, 2019, available at: http://opinion.people.com.cn/BIG5/n1/2019/0810/c1003-31287267.html.

17 Lan Ye, Hong Kong Society Asked to have the Black Hands Revealed Behind the Curtains, 10 April 2019, available at: http://china.huanqiu.com/gangao/2019-04/14694601.html?agt=15422.

18 The report Commemorating the 65th Anniversary of the Chinese People's Volunteers Fighting against the US and Aid Korea [*Jinian Zhongguo Renmin Zhiyuanjun Kangmei Yuanchao ruchao zuozhan 65 zhounian*], *People.cn*, 27 October 2015, is available at: http://military.people.com.cn/n/2015/1027/c1011-27746142.html.

19 The poster can be viewed at: http://5sing.kugou.com/fc/14631430.html.
20 See Li Kun, Cultural Confidence Becomes New Buzz Words, *CCTV.com English*, 21 July 2016, available at: http://english.cctv.com/2016/07/21/ARTI8yXZ2iF1htJyq BskYBXs160721.shtml.

References

Abrams, J. (1986). Communist Party Issues Guidelines for Social Values. 28 September. Available at: www.apnews.com/b4537305d9622699ee3e977352ec66bd.

Antoniades, A., B. O'Loughlin and A. Miskimmon (2010). *Great Power Politics and Strategic Narratives, CGPE Working Paper 7*. Brighton: Centre for Global Political Economy.

Bell, D. (2006). *Beyond Liberal Democracy: Political Thinking for an East Asian Context*. Princeton, NJ: Princeton University Press.

Benner, T., J. Gaspers, M. Ohlberg, L. Poggetti and K. Shi-Kupfer (2018). Authoritarian Advance: Responding to China's Growing Political Influence in Europe. Global Public Policy Institute and Mercator Institute for China Studies. Available at: www.merics. org/sites/default/files/2018-02/GPPi_MERICS_Authoritarian_Advance_2018_1.pdf.

Bhabha, H. (1994). *The Location of Culture*. London: Routledge.

Cabral, A. (1973). *Return to the Source: Selected Speeches of Amilcar Cabral*. New York: Monthly Review Press.

Callahan, W. (2006). History, Identity, and Security: Producing and Consuming Nationalism in China. *Critical Asian Studies*, 38(2): 179–208.

Callahan, W. (2012). Sino-Speak: Chinese Exceptionalism and the Politics of History. *The Journal of Asian Studies*, 71(1): 33–55.

Campbell, K. and E. Ratner (2018). The China Reckoning, How Beijing Defied American Expectations. *Foreign Affairs*, March/April. Available at: www.foreignaffairs.com/articles/china/2018–02–13/china-reckoning.

Chakraborty, K. (ed.) (2013). *Cultural Diplomacy Dictionary of the Academy for Cultural Diplomacy*. Berlin: Center for Cultural Diplomacy Studies Publications. Available at: www.cd-n.org/content/pdf/Cultural_Diplomacy_Dictionary.pdf.

Chang, M.H. (2001). *Return of the Dragon: China's Wounded Nationalism*. Boulder, CO: Westview Press.

Chen, X. (2002). *Occidentalism, a Theory of Counter-Discourse in Post-Mao China*. New York: Rowman & Littlefield.

Cull, N. (2008). Public Diplomacy: Taxonomies and Histories. *Annals of the American Academy of Political and Social Science*, 616(1): 31–54.

Cummings, M.C. (2009). *Cultural Diplomacy and the United States Government: A Survey*. Washington, DC: Centre for Arts and Culture.

Dabashi, H. (2015). *Can Non-Europeans Think?* London: Zed Books.

Deng, Y. (2005). Better Than Power: International Status in Chinese Foreign Policy. In Yong Deng and Fei-ling Wang (eds), *China Rising: Power and Motivation in Chinese Foreign Policy*. New York: Rowman & Littlefield.

Deng, Y. (2009). The New Hard Realities: "Soft Power" and China in Transition. In M. Li (ed.), *Soft Power: China's Emerging Strategy in International Politics*. (pp. 63–79). Lanham, MD: Lexington.

Ding, S. (2008). *The Dragon's Hidden Wings: How China Rises with Its Soft Power*. Plymouth: Lexington Books.

Etzioni, A. (1961). *A Comparative Analysis of Complex Organizations: On Power, Involvement, and Their Correlate*. New York: Free Press of Glencoe.

46 *Look beyond and beneath the soft power*

Fallers, L. (1961). Ideology and Culture in Uganda Nationalism. *American Anthropologist*, 3(4): 677–678.

Fontana, B. (1993). *Hegemony and Power: On the Relation Between Gramsci and Machiavelli*. Minneapolis, MN: University of Minnesota Press.

Foucault, M. (1980). *Power/Knowledge*. Brighton: Harvester.

Foucault, M. (1982). Subject and Power. *Critical Inquiry*, 8(4) (Summer): 777–795.

Foucault, M. (1983). Afterword: The Subject and Power. In H. Dreyfus and P. Rabinow (eds), *Michel Foucault: Beyond Structuralism and Hermeneutics*, 2nd edn pp. 208–226). Chicago, IL: Chicago University Press.

Fredman, Z. (2015). Fredman on Wheeler, The Role of American NGOs in China's Modernization: Invited Influence. *The H-Diplo* (June). Available at: https://networks.h-net.org/node/28443/reviews/73557/fredman-wheeler-role-American-ngos-chinas-modernization-invited.

Glaser, B. and M. Murphy (2009). Soft Power with Chinese Characteristics. In *Chinese Soft Power and Its Implications for the United States* (pp. 10–26). Washington, DC: Centre for Strategic and International Studies. Available at: https://csis-prod.s3.amazonaws.com/s3fs-public/legacy_files/files/media/csis/pubs/090403_mcgiffert_chinesesoftpower_web.pdf.

Gries, P. (1999). A 'China Threat'? Power and Passion in Chinese 'Face Nationalism'. *World Affairs*, 162(2): 63–75.

Guibernau, M. (1996). *Nationalisms: The Nation-State and Nationalism in the 20th Century*. Cambridge: Polity Press.

Guo, Y. (2004). *Cultural Nationalism in Contemporary China*. London: Routledge.

Guo, Y. (2017). The Impact of Chinese National Identity on Sino-US Relations. *Joint U.S. Korea Academic Studies*, (August): 146–158.

Hall, S. (1991). The Local and the Global: Globalization and Ethnicity. In Anthony King (ed.), *Culture, Globalization and the World-System*. London: Macmillan.

Hall, S, (1996). Ethnicity: Identity and Difference. In G. Ely and R.G. Suny (eds), *Becoming National*. Oxford: Oxford University Press.

Ham P.V. (2001). The Rise of the Brand State. The Postmodern Politics of Image and Reputation. *Foreign Affairs*, September–October, 80(5): 2–6.

He, B. and Y. Guo (2000). *Nationalism, National Identity and Democratization in China*. Aldershot: Ashgate Publishing.

Hroch, M. (1985). *Social Preconditions of National Revival in Europe*. Cambridge: Cambridge University Press.

Hubbert, J. (2019). *China in the World: An Anthropology of Confucius Institutes, Soft Power and Globalization*. Honolulu, HI: University of Hawaii Press.

Huntington, S. (1998). *The Clash of Civilisations and the Remaking of World Order*. London: Touchstone.

Institute for Culture Diplomacy (2011). *Cultural Diplomacy Outlook Report 2011*. Available at: www.cd-n.org/index.php?en_cd-outlook-2011_content. n.p.

Iyer, P. (1983). China: Battling "Spiritual Pollution". *Time*. Available at: http://content.time.com/time/magazine/article/0,9171,926379,00.html.

Jia, Q. (2005). Disrespect and Distrust: The External Origins of Contemporary Chinese Nationalism. *Journal of Contemporary China*, 14(2): 11–21.

Kissinger, H. (2005). China: Containment Won't Work. *Washington Post*, 13 June. Available at: www.globalpolicy.org/component/content/article/152/25775.html.

Kurlantzick, J. (2007). *Charm Offensive: How China's Soft Power is Transforming the World*. Cambridge, MA: Yale University Press.

Look beyond and beneath the soft power 47

Kynge, J. (2005). *China Shakes the World*. London: Weidenfeld & Nicolson.

Lai, H. and Y. Lu (eds) (2012). *China's Soft Power and International Relations*. Abingdon: Routledge.

Lampton, D.M. (2008). *The Three Faces of Chinese Power: Might, Money, and Minds*. London: University of California Press.

Lei, G. (2005). Realpolitik Nationalism: International Sources of Chinese Nationalism. *Modern China*, 31(4) (October): 487–514.

Li, M. (2009). Soft Power: Nurture not Nature. In Mingjiang Li (ed.), *Soft Power: China's Emerging Strategy in International Politics* (pp. 1–18). Lanham, MD: Lexington.

Lukes, S. (1974). *Power: A Radical View*. London: Macmillan.

McClellan, M. (2004). Public Diplomacy in the Context of Traditional Diplomacy. Vienna Diplomatic Academy. Available at: www.publicdiplomacy.org/45.htm.

Miskimmon, A., B. O'Loughlin and L. Roselle (2012). *Forging the World: Strategic Narratives and International Relations. Working Paper*. London: Centre for European Politics/New Political Communications Unit.

Miskimmon, A., B. O'Loughlin and L. Roselle (2013). *Strategic Narratives: Communication Power and the New World Order*. New York: Routledge.

Mitter, R. (2004). *A Bitter Revolution: China's Struggle with the Modern World*. New York: Oxford University Press.

Morley, D. and K. Robins (1995). *Spaces of Identity, Global Media, Electronic Landscapes and Cultural Boundaries*. London: Routledge.

Mouffe, C. (1979). *Gramsci and Marxist Theory*. London: Routledge & Kegan Paul.

Mufson, S. (1996). China's New Nationalism: Mix of Mao and Confucius. *Washington Post*, 19 March. Available at: www.washingtonpost.com/archive/politics/1996/03/19/maoism-confucianism-blur-into-nationalism/1bd76add-66c6-450b-8a80-465d952edd34/?noredirect=on&utm_term=.13988c520cb7.

Mulcahy, K.V. (2017). *Public Culture, Cultural Identity, Cultural Policy: Comparative Perspectives*. New York: Palgrave Macmillan.

Nixon, R.M. (1967). Asia After Viet Nam. *Foreign Affairs*, October. Available at: www.foreignaffairs.com/articles/asia/1967-10-01/asia-after-viet-nam.

Noort, C. (2017). Study of Strategic Narratives: The Cases of BRICS. *Political and Governance*, 5(3): 121–129.

Nye, J.S. (1990). *Bound to Lead: The Changing Nature of American Power*. New York: S.I. Basic Books.

Nye, J.S. (2004). *Soft Power: The Means to Succeed in World Politics*. New York: Public Affairs.

Nye, J.S. (2005). The Rise of China's Soft Power. *Wall Street Journal Asia*, 29 December. Available at: http://belfercenter.hks.harvard.edu/publication/1499/rise_of_chinas_soft_power.html.

Nye, J.S. (2011). China's Soft Power. Carnegie Council for Ethics in International Affairs. Available at: www.youtube.com/watch?v=RmW1gZPqFDs.

Nye, J.S. (2012). China's Soft Power Deficit. *Wall Street Journal*, 8 May. Available at: www.wsj.com/articles/SB10001424052702304451104577389923098678842.

Nye, J.S. (2013). What China and Russia Don't Get About Soft Power: Beijing and Moscow are Trying their Hands at Attraction, and Failing - Miserably. *Foreign Policy*, 29 April. Available at: http://foreignpolicy.com/2013/04/29/what-china-and-russia-dont-get-about-soft-power/.

48 *Look beyond and beneath the soft power*

Nye, J.S. (2014). The Information Revolution and Soft Power. *Current History*, 113(759): 19 -22. Available at: https://dash.harvard.edu/bitstream/handle/1/11738398/nye-information-revolution.pdf?sequence=1.

Nye, J.S. (2015). The Limits of Chinese Soft Power. *Project Syndicate*, 10 July. Available at: www.project-syndicate.org/commentary/china-civil-society-nationalism-soft-power-by-joseph-s-nye-2015-07.

Nye, J.S and J. Wang (2009). Hard Decisions on Soft Power: Opportunities and Difficulties for Chinese Soft Power. *Harvard International Review*, (Summer): 18–22.

Ozkirimli, U. (2005). *Contemporary Debates on Nationalism: A Critical Engagement*. New York: Palgrave.

Parton, C. (2019). China–UK Relations Where to Draw the Border Between Influence and Interference? RUSI Occasional Paper. February, *Royal United Services Institute for Defence and Security Studies*. Available at: https://rusi.org/sites/default/files/20190220_chinese_interference_parton_web.pdf.

Perlez, J. and L. Ding (2018). China Thwarts U.S. Effort to Promote American Culture on Campuses, *New York Times*, 30 December. Available at: www.nytimes.com/2018/12/30/world/asia/china-American-centers-culture.html; a Chinese version is available at: https://cn.nytimes.com/china/20190103/china-American-centers-culture/.

Pomeranz, K. (2000). *The Great Divergence: China, Europe, and the Making of the Modern World Economy*. Princeton, NJ: Princeton University Press.

Robertson, M. (2012). Chinese History According to the Confucius Institute. *The Epoch Times*, 12 June. Available at: www.theepochtimes.com/chinese-history-according-to-the-confucius-institute_1484249.html.

Robinson, M.E. (2014). *Cultural Nationalism in Colonial Korea, 1920–1925*. Seattle, WA: University of Washington Press.

Roselle, L., A. Miskimmon and B. O'Loughlin (2014). Strategic Narrative: A New Means to Understand Soft Power. *Media War & Conflict*, 7(1): 70–84.

Rowan, M. and S. Shore (2009). Foucault's Toolkit: Resources for "Thinking" Work in Times of Continual Change. *Australian Journal of Adult Learning*, 49(1) (April): 57–74.

Rozman, G. (1999). China's Quest for Great Power Identity. *Orbis*, 43(3): 383–404.

Sabbagh, D. (2005). Nationalism and Multiculturalism. In Alain Deieckhoff and Christophe Jaffrelot (eds), *Revisiting Nationalism: Theories and Processes* (pp. 100–121). London: C. Hurst & Co.

Sahlins, M. (2015). *Confucius Institute: Academic Malware*. Chicago, IL: Prickly Paradigm Press.

Saich, T. (2004). *Governance and Politics of China*. London: Palgrave Macmillan.

Said, E. (1978). *Orientalism*. London: Penguin Books.

Said, E. (2003). *Orientalism*, reprinted with a new Preface. London: Penguin Books.

Scott, D. (2007). *China Stands Up, the PRC and the International System*. Abingdon: Routledge.

Scott, D. (2008). *The Chinese Century? The Challenge to Global Order*. New York: Palgrave Macmillan.

Shambaugh, D. (1991). *Beautiful Imperialist: China Perceives America, 1972–1990*. Princeton, NJ: Princeton University Press.

Shambaugh, D. (1996). Containment or Engagement of China. *International Security*, 21(12) (Fall): 180–209.

Shambaugh, D. (2013a). *China Goes Global: The Partial Power*. New York: Oxford University Press.

Shambaugh, D. (2013b). China Is "Obsessed" with Soft Power. *Asia Society*. Available at: http://asiasociety.org/video/david-shambaugh-china-obsessed-soft-power.

Smith, A. (1991). *National Identity*. London: Penguin Books.

Tao, X. (2015). China's Soft Power Obsession: China Needs to Rethink its Quest for Soft Power. *Diplomat*, 14 April. Available at: http://thediplomat.com/2015/04/chinas-soft-power-obsession/.

Tchen, J.K. and D. Yeats (2014). *Yellow Perils! An Archive of Anti-Asian Fear*. New York: Verso.

Townsend, J. (1992). Chinese Nationalism. *Australian Journal of Chinese Affairs*, 27 (January): 97–130.

Unger, J. (1996). *Chinese Nationalism*. New York: An East Gate Book.

Van Oudenaren, J.S. (2015). Beijing's Peaceful Evolution Paranoia: The Chinese Communist Party's Obsession with the Threat of a Color Revolution is Revealing. *Diplomat*, 1 September. Available at: https://thediplomat.com/2015/09/beijings-peaceful-evolution-paranoia/.

Wallerstein, I. (1991). The National and the Universal: Can There be Such a Thing as World Culture?" In Anthony King (ed.), *Culture, Globalization and the World-System*. London: Macmillan.

Wang, F. (2005). Beijing's Incentive Structure: The Pursuit of Presentation, Prosperity and Power. In Y. Deng and F. Wang (eds), *China Rising: Power and Motivation in Chinese Foreign Policy*. New York: Rowman & Littlefield.

Wang, J. (1999). Managing Conflict: Chinese Perspectives on Multilateral Diplomacy and Collective Security. In Yong Deng and Fei-ling Wang (eds), *China Rising: Power and Motivation in Chinese Foreign Policy*. New York: Rowman & Littlefield.

Wang, Y. (2008). Public Diplomacy and the Rise of Chinese Soft Power. *The ANNALS of the American Academy of Political and Social Science*, 616(1): 257–273.

White, H. (2013). *The China Choice, Why We Should Share Power*. Oxford: Oxford University Press.

Williamson, K.D. (2015). Return of the Yellow Peril. *National Review*, 22 April. Available at: www.nationalreview.com/2015/04/return-yellow-peril-kevin-d-williamson/.

Wu, Z. (2012). Hu Warns Successors over "Peaceful Evolution". *Asia Times Online*. 11 January. Available at: www.atimes.com/atimes/China/NA11Ad02.html.

Xiao, G. (1996). *Zhongguo minzu zhuyi de lishi yu qianjing* [The History and Prospect of Chinese Nationalism], *Zhanlue yu Guanli* [*Strategy and Management*], 2: 58–62.

Yoshikawa, M.J. (1987). *The Double-Swing Model of Intercultural Communication between the East and the West*. In D. Lawrence Kincaid (ed.), *Communication Theory: Eastern and Western Perspectives*. San Diego, CA: Academic Press.

Yoshino, K. (1992). *Cultural Nationalism in Contemporary Japan: A Sociological Enquiry*. London: Routledge.

Zhao, Q. (2007). Better Public Diplomacy to Present a Truer Picture of China. *People. cn*, 30 March. Available at: http://en.people.cn/200703/30/eng20070330_362496.html.

Zhao, S. (2000). Chinese Nationalism and Its International Orientations. *Political Science Quarterly*, 115(1): 1–33.

Zhao, S. (2004). Chinese Nationalism and Pragmatic Foreign Policy Behavior. In Suisheng Zhao (ed.), *Chinese Foreign Policy: Pragmatism and Strategic Behavior*. New York: An East Gate Book.

Zhao, S. (2013). Foreign Policy Implications of Chinese Nationalism Revisited: The Strident Turn. *Journal of Contemporary China*, 22(82): 1–33.

Zheng, Y. (1999). *Discovering Chinese Nationalism in China: Modernization, Identity, and International Relations*. Cambridge: Cambridge University Press.

2 The vehicle and driver of China's cultural diplomacy

The two 'wheels' and two models[1]

> In establishing virtue in life and in writing, one should not care if the foundation is based in the East or West.
>
> (Anthem for Tsinghua University, 1924)

Following on from Chapter 1 which focuses on a theoretical discussion of understanding the purpose of China's cultural diplomacy (the 'why'), this chapter will trace the contours of the prevailing research on cultural diplomacy and China's undertakings in the sense of 'what' (vehicle) and 'who' (agent).

The end of the Cold War started new debates about the remaking of the world order; it marked the change from a world of geopolitics and power to a post-modernist world of images and influence. Many scholars (Huntington, 1998; Ding, 2008) contended that cultural factors had now emerged as the *force majeure* in international relations, and culture has become a global paradigm for explaining differences – as a means for locating 'the other'. But what is culture?

A most elusive term, culture's definitions abound and range from the very complex to the very simple. Geertz, with reference to the American anthropologist Clyde Kluckhohn's *Mirror for Man* (1949), noted sarcastically that:

> in some twenty-seven pages of his chapter on the concept, Kluckhohn managed to define culture in turn as ... [what follows is 11 different definitions]; ... and turning, perhaps in desperation, to similes, as a map, as a sieve, and as a matrix.
>
> (Geertz, 1973: 4–5)

According to *The UNESCO Universal Declaration on Cultural Diversity* adopted by the 31st session of the General Conference of UNESCO in November 2001, culture is a "set of distinctive spiritual, material, intellectual and emotional features of society or a social group and that it encompasses, in addition to art and literature, lifestyles, ways of living together, value systems, traditions and beliefs" (UNESCO, 2001).

As explained in Chapter 1, cultural diplomacy in China is mostly understood, both in the academic community and in the government sphere, as an endeavour to build and project soft power, which draws on three sources according to Joseph S. Nye, Jr: "culture, political values and foreign policy" (2004: 11). Since cultural diplomacy represents aspects that fall outside the remit of traditional foreign policy, its function in China is mainly implemented on two 'wheels' of the vehicle: one wheel of 'culture' serves the purpose of reshaping China's image away from being the 'cultural other', and the other wheel of 'political values' aims to change the perception of China as the 'ideological other'. The question of how to coordinate these two wheels has generated much discussion.

The vehicle of cultural diplomacy: a theoretical discussion of the two wheels

There are currently two positions in China contending against each other regarding the vehicle of China's cultural diplomacy. One asserts that 'culture' should indisputably be the core of cultural diplomacy, and China is rich in its cultural heritage. One of the leading scholars is Hu Wentao (2008); he divides cultural resources into three sets: political culture, spiritual culture and popular culture. Hu believes that as the current political culture in China is vastly different to the Western one, which still dominates the international community, it would be more of an uphill struggle on this front; therefore, a wise choice is to focus China's cultural diplomacy on the other two aspects: spiritual and popular culture. After all, Chinese Gongfu and pandas arrived in the USA long before McDonald's and Hollywood came to China. This position can be considered as the 'cultural wheel' of the vehicle, aiming to serve the purpose of reshaping China's image away from being the 'cultural other'.

However, a dilemma is revealed, as Young (2008) has highlighted two interrelated issues that concern China's spiritual and popular cultures: first, whether and how far to break with the past; second, how much to borrow from overseas. Both issues involve nationalism, underlying the dialectical tension between a political nationalism that emphasises a revolutionary break with the past, and a cultural nationalism that constantly refers to China's past. When China presents itself as a modern power on the international stage today, this dilemma is reflected in the conflict-ridden official version of Chinese national culture that the government is attempting to promote: it embodies inherently contradictory elements such as Confucianism, Maoism, socialism, capitalism, modernism and globalism. Although it is fair to argue that all cultures are fragmentary in their own ways, perhaps no other culture faces the challenge to the extent of such complexity as China because of the history it carries, and the two 'otherness' factors it holds at the same time. There are simply too many dimensions and links to establish perfect coherence.

The second issue regarding foreign influence demonstrates a particular challenge for China's popular culture. Many scholars have argued that contemporary popular culture is actually a soft belly for Mainland China. In a 2008 survey on soft power in Asia conducted by the Chicago Council on Global Affairs (Whitney and Shambaugh, 2009), China's historical and cultural links were the

52 *Vehicle and driver of cultural diplomacy*

strongest and would presumably have the greatest impact. However, China's cultural soft power was only rated as "middling" and continued to trail behind – not only behind the USA, but also behind that of Japan and South Korea. Both Japan and South Korea have traditional cultures which are closely related to China's, but both also have their own distinct popular cultures represented abroad by such phenomena as manga and anime in Japan, and television dramas and pop music in South Korea. Unfortunately, China has no such readily accessible point of convergence between its popular culture and the rest of the world (Ren, 2010). This may help to explain why China's current focus is on promoting the traditional aspects of Chinese culture, because they represent 'Chineseness', whereas its contemporary popular culture is etched with all sorts of foreign influence that does not fit in with the 'socialist culture' defined by the 2011 Plenary Session of the CPC Central Committee. In other words, both the spiritual and popular cultural dimensions also face the contradiction of having the imperative to be promoted as a world culture and the requirement of a more specific political nationalism, with the two often in tension. Young's conclusion (2008: 15) that "China is somehow trapped in itself" depicts the dilemma faced by the cultural position.

Many scholars including Deng have argued that "the country has largely refrained from projecting soft power on the political front, presumably because it is an area of China's comparative disadvantage" (2009: 72). When China's ranking slipped down across a number of international polls, both Nye (2011) and d'Hooghe (2011) commented on the enormous gap between China's political values and the Western prevailing norms as being one of the intrinsic reasons for this slip, yet the contending position emphasising the wheel of 'political values' has actually been gaining more ground in recent years. It was championed by Professor Yan Xuetong from the Tsinghua University. He argues that "the central point of soft power is not cultural strength, but political strength" (Yan, 2007: 5), believing that China should not cede its political ground, but rather should directly contest Western political domination. Although Yan believes that good governance and China's political norms of non-Western origin should be the main source of "attraction and persuasion" of Chinese soft power, in his later work (Yan, 2011), ancient Chinese thoughts were emphasised as the foundation that sustains the modern Chinese power. This position has taken a clear counter-hegemonic stance against the domination of Western values, thus representing the other wheel serving the purpose of countering China's image as the 'ideological other'.

Another prominent scholar for this position is Zhang Zhizhou (2012), a senior researcher at the Centre for Public Diplomacy Studies, who also demarcates culture into three sets: tangible culture, spiritual culture and ideational culture or values. He further argues that although the three sets comprise the richness of a nation's cultural image, only values are directly relevant to the nation's soft power. No matter how magnificent a country's material and spiritual culture may appear, its contribution to building soft power would be limited in the absence of value identification. Zhang's (2012: 193) conclusion

Vehicle and driver of cultural diplomacy 53

that "in a way, cultural diplomacy is value diplomacy" was confirmed in the *Annual Report of China's Public Diplomacy* 2011–2012, which defined the goal of China's public diplomacy as to "improve China's international image, safeguard national interest and the independence of values" (Public Diplomacy Research Centre, 2012). As a policy suggestion put forward in this *Report*, Zhang further explained that given the two preconditions for values to be accepted by others – they either accord to the public expectations of their existing values, or the value is in the position to lead or persuade the target country's public – in China's case, the way forward is to aim at more power of discourse to redefine the international significance of Chinese values, whereas the current focus is on China's tangible heritage and spiritual culture, thus less satisfactory in generating soft power.

We can see that both groups tend to blame each other as the cause behind the less than satisfactory effects of China's cultural diplomacy so far; and a more intriguing observation is that they both claim to be the mainstream view endorsed by the government, based on the same reference to Hu Jintao's 2007 speech at the 17th National Congress.[2] The 'culture' advocates quote Hu on "enhancing the country's cultural soft power" by "creating a thriving cultural market and enhancing the industry's international competitiveness", while the 'political value' advocates quote him calling for "building up the system of socialist core values and making socialist ideology more attractive and cohesive". Although Glaser and Murphy's research (2009: 16) argued that the "core role of culture was clinched" when the term soft power was included in Hu's report, thus the cultural wheel "had had the greatest impact on policymaking" (2009: 13), Yan and Zhang's political value stance was adopted by the Centre for Public Diplomacy Studies, established in 2010 as a direct response to Hu's speech.

It is notable that the growing influence of the political value position synchronises with the evolving goals of China's cultural diplomacy discussed in Chapter 1. In 1999, Wang commented that: "Beijing has a peculiar but persistent mentality of being politically under siege ..." She further commented that: "the growth of China's capabilities has ironically enhanced Beijing's political insecurity, as the West is now compelled to increase its scrutiny and criticism of the CCP's political system in the rising Chinese power" (Wang, 1999: 40). After two decades, however, the latter statement still seems to be true, but a more confident China is slowly playing an advocate role, with a stance gradually shifting to feeling stronger in countering the criticism with the Chinese alternatives. Who will win this tug-of-war between the two positions as representing the mainstream view very much depends on the next layer of debate regarding political values, which will be unfolded in the following section.

Political values: universalism versus relativism

It is not hard to see that ideology is the backdrop to many debates in the foreground or centre stage, revealing a key question lurking at the crux of the

54 Vehicle and driver of cultural diplomacy

two-wheel debate: are the 'political values' specified in Nye's concept of soft power universal, or, like the first element of culture, does their appeal actually come from distinctiveness? If universalism is used to define political values, it means China faces insurmountable constraints in carrying out its cultural diplomacy, as this notion of a unitary and homogeneous model marginalises the distinctive Chinese way: its authoritarian political culture is constantly under assault by the Western model of democracy. As long as China maintains that the values of its political system are fundamentally different from those of the modern Western world, its soft power would be considered lame; and thus the impact produced by cultural diplomacy would be very limited. So in terms of universal 'political values', which is supposed to be the strongest cornerstone of building soft power, China seems to have the soft belly in place.

Therefore, the Chinese answers are inclined to base their arguments on relativism, frequently stressing the relative nature of culture and ideology, to the extent of some scholars arguing for "Chinese exceptionalism" (Zhang, 2011). This could be considered as a way of China 'othering' itself in relation to the West, whereas their Western counterparts tend to believe that political values attract due to universal attributes that can transcend one's own country and appeal to others, culminating in Fukuyama's claim for the "end of history" (1989). When this claim proves to be premature and China's economic success prompted Western scholars to coin the notion of "Beijing Consensus" as a challenge to "Washington Consensus" (Ramo, 2004), the Chinese government has not been keen on promoting the new consensus, partly because this may aggregate the China threat perception, and partly because China does not believe in universalism, nor does it have the tradition of a "missionary culture" as explained by Nye:

> We come from a tradition of missionaries who believe in our values and want to sell them to the rest of the world, the Chinese tradition has been attractive to some of the neighbours in East Asia but it has not been a missionary culture. They haven't been selling ideas.
>
> (Nye, 2005: n.p.)

The Economist cover story (2010) "The Beijing Consensus is to Keep Quiet" says that: "In the West people worry that developing countries want to copy 'the China model'. Such talk makes people in China uncomfortable". When addressing the Summit of the CPC in Dialogue with World Political Parties in December 2017, Xi Jinping said that "we will not 'import' a foreign model, nor will we 'export' a China model, nor ask others to 'copy' Chinese methods".[3] It is fair to argue that this difference actually lies at the very core of the perception gap: China and the USA want very different things. Kissinger showed his expert understanding in his masterpiece *On China*:

> Like the United States, China thought of itself as playing a special role. But it never espoused the American notion of universalism to spread its values

Vehicle and driver of cultural diplomacy 55

around the world.... In the Chinese version of exceptionalism, China did not export its ideas but let others come to seek them.

(Kissinger, 2011: 17)

The USA has a global mission to promote their consensus as the orthodox, while China's desire is not to replace one consensus with another, nor to export or persuade others to adopt their model, but it seeks to replace the unipolar domination with a multipolar world order so that it is not judged on its political system. Zhao has articulated well that: "China is a reformist/revisionist power, dissatisfied not with the current order but its position in the order" (2016: 14). In other words, its central appeal is more us-centred "to increase China's voice and weight in the existing institutions" (Zhao, 2016: 14). Fredman has compared the two countries' quests as "the missionary impulse is as deeply ingrained in America's DNA as the search for wealth and power is in China's" (2015: n.p.), except that for China, when wealth is achieved through economic development, its new goal is not to seek power to dominate the world, but to gain more power of discourse to refute some of the universal values that are imposed by the West. Yan Shuhan (2018), a professor from the CPC Party School, has written fiercely that:

We are resolutely opposed to 'universal values'. This is because 'universal values' spoken by Western countries, especially the United States, are really only their values which are promoted as values that are universally applicable to all countries in the world. They also require that all countries implement them. If some countries say No to this, they attack and vilify these countries, and some even use this as an excuse to intervene in these countries.

(Yan, 2018)

If we look at the actual definition of cultural diplomacy, we will see relativism is more applicable to its purpose of "fostering mutual understanding". In this sense, the Chinese concept of "harmony in diversity" explains better the purpose of cultural diplomacy, which is not about building universalism but about embracing cultural differences. I argue that the Chinese philosophical concept of Yin and Yang can be applied here to transcend the binary divisions of 'us' versus 'other', and even the dualistic conceptualisation of dichotomies: to think of Eastern and Western culture as Yin and Yang that inspire each other, contain a drop of each other, complement each other and depend on each other to form a whole. Their relationship is a symbiotic one, and the most important essence in this concept is that its centre is where the Yin and Yang meet. This idea, which aims at nurturing compatibility and harmony, is considered to be one of the major reasons why Chinese civilisation stands as the oldest continuous civilisation on earth today, owing to its ability to embrace and incorporate different cultural and belief systems throughout its long history: from the introduction of Buddhism to China during the Han Dynasty, to Christianity and Islam during the Tang Dynasty, Chinese civilisation survived and thrived through all these cultural encounters.

56 *Vehicle and driver of cultural diplomacy*

Even in terms of modern-day ideology, Deng Xiaoping has reformed Mao's communist China into 'socialism with Chinese characteristics' by incorporating some capitalist ideas with his pragmatic belief that "never mind if it's a black cat or a white cat, it is a good cat as long as it catches the mice". This shows a genuine open-mindedness, just like the Tsinghua anthem goes, when we adopt virtues, we need not ask if it comes from the East or West. Meanwhile, the Five Principles of foreign policy formulated in 1954 were firmly adhered to, namely, mutual respect for sovereignty and territorial integrity, mutual non-aggression, non-interference, equality and mutual benefit, peaceful coexistence. These five principles and the 1955 addition of "seeking common ground while reserving differences" (*qiu tong cun yi*) are still the cornerstones of China's foreign policy today. All these show that relativism and mutual respect are the established beliefs shared by the Chinese understanding of culture, political values and foreign policy.

However, the notion of soft power is built on universal appeal, the different perceptions of universalism versus relativism may explain why China's efforts at creating a global dialogue between the Eastern and Western cultures tends to be read by the West as an attempt to export Communism, a label for the 'ideological other', and thus is constantly met with suspicions and resistance. The above discussions reveal that within the construct of soft power, the two sources of attraction are not working in harmony in the case of China, who has abundant cultural heritage and traditions to offer on the 'cultural wheel', but non-universal and non-Western values to offer on the 'political values wheel'. This may reflect the "odd paradox" argued by Shambaugh (2013): on the one hand, China is extraordinarily proud and confident in its historical identity, but on the other hand, it shows extreme insecurity. These dual aspects give Chinese cultural diplomacy both a defensive and offensive edge. If the two wheels of the vehicle are not heading in the same direction, it may end up not going very far. This makes the driver's role, or the agent of cultural diplomacy, particularly important and precarious, which will be the focus of the discussions in the next section.

Agent of cultural diplomacy – diverging and changing views

As a specific subset of public diplomacy, does the cultural dimension require any special consideration about who should be the leading agent for cultural diplomacy: state or non-state actors? If hard power can be built through government funding, will state involvement function productively or counterproductively when it comes to soft power? The next section will examine the diverging views about the appropriate agents of cultural diplomacy both internationally and domestically.

The international debates on agents of cultural diplomacy

Mainly springing from its varying definitions, the international debates on the agents of cultural diplomacy are reflected in the three positions summarised by

Gienow-Hecht (2010: 9). The first sees cultural diplomacy as first and foremost "an instrument of state policy", lacking in the participation of private individuals. In the Special Issue of the *International Journal of Cultural Policy* titled "Cultural Diplomacy: Beyond the National Interest?", cultural diplomacy is contrasted to cultural relations in that the former is "essentially interest-driven government practice" while the latter is "ideals-driven and practiced largely by non-state actors" (Ang, Isar and Mar, 2015: 365). Because of this, some cultural institutes have changed their rhetoric and now keep a distance from "cultural diplomacy", repositioning themselves as actors that pursue "international cultural relations" according to Fouseki and Kizlari (2018). Similarly, Arndt argues that cultural diplomacy can only be said to "take place when formal diplomats, serving national government, try to shape and channel this natural flow (of culture) to advance national interests" (2006: xviii); this echoes the clear articulations made by Hartig (2018) and by McDowell, who states that "for it to be diplomacy, it has to entail a role for the state" (2008: 8). It is obvious that this position dwells on the 'diplomacy' side of the concept.

The contrary position looks at cultural diplomacy as a way to act outside of politics, but actually shares the belief that "non-state agents enjoy greater authority compared to state entities working in the same field" (Chartrand and McCaughey, 1989). Their understanding of the concept of cultural diplomacy has a clear focus on the 'culture' side: it does not address cultural diplomacy as a synonym of public diplomacy, but as a subset that has its own distinctive features. As argued by Ogoura (2006), scholarship and culture should be independent of political power and, in fact, are often a means of resisting authority. In Carter's words, "being suspicious of governments is almost second nature, especially when culture is the other item in the equation" (2015: 478). Further, Leonard, Stead and Conrad made it clear that if a government wants its voice to be heard or to influence people's perceptions, it should work "through organisations and networks that are separate from, independent of, and even culturally suspicious towards government itself" (2002: 55).

A third group of scholars define cultural diplomacy as a hybrid term in concept that requires matching hybrid actions in practice: apart from the state, it also needs participation from and coordination between government and non-governmental institutions. This was endorsed by the definition given in the Cultural Diplomacy Dictionary: "Cultural diplomacy is practiced by a range of actors including national governments, public and private sector institutions, and civil society" (Chakraborty, 2013: 30).

If these diverging views are mostly over definitions, in practice, Seiichi (2008: 191) has proposed the government role as a "network hub": it should focus on low-visibility efforts to create a fertile environment where actors are connected to one another horizontally; ideas and culture are freely created by the private sector, as government involvement is liable to be seen as a meddlesome intrusion by the authorities into matters of personal taste and beliefs, raising suspicions, reducing cultural attractiveness and causing a reflexive backlash. This is exactly in line with the recommendations made by the British Council report,

58 *Vehicle and driver of cultural diplomacy*

that the government role is to "create the conditions for cultural exchange to flourish: by allowing freedom of expression and enabling artists and tourists to travel and visit ... Support cultural exchange through independent, autonomous agencies – because direct government involvement invites suspicion and ultimately, hostility" (Holden, 2013: 34).

Chartrand and McCaughey's research (1989: 3) offers an illuminating model to spell out different government roles in support of fine arts with a model country for each type: Facilitator (USA), Patron (UK), Architect (France) and Engineer (Russia). As explained by Mulcahy, "depending on their political cultures, governments vary in the ways that their cultural policies are conceptualised and implemented" (2017: viii). For example, there is no Ministry of Culture in the USA; the tradition has been one of separation of church and state, free market competition and private philanthropy, and "the basis of the American approach to culture eschewed any collective state intervention" (Mulcahy, 2017: 3). Based upon these traditions, the USA has adopted the Facilitator role; while in the UK, the concept of cultural diplomacy even appears to bear negative connotations as a result of its use during the Cold War (Saunders, 1999; Gienow-Hecht, 2000), that is, "due to its connotations as with colonialism, imperialism and propaganda, and the unethical and immoral practices associated with such activity" (Nisbett, 2012: 558). Chartrand and McCaughey (1989: XXX) argued that: "the susceptibility of public culture to ideological coloration, and the politically sensitive nature of cultural programs has been the case for arguments that cultural policy should be formulated and implemented 'at arm's length'", leaving the government role more as a 'hidden hand'. The autonomous British Council is such an example in keeping distance from the state. In comparison, France as a 'cultural state' claiming "its language, literature, philosophy, and fine arts are universal accomplishments worthy of preservation and emulation" (Mulcahy, 2017: viii), has a "long tradition of administrative centralisation" as "cultural diplomacy has been an integral part of its foreign policy for over a hundred years" (Mulcahy, 2017: 33). The state funds the fine arts through the Ministry of Culture, but the artistic enterprises maintain autonomy in artistic decision-making. This contrasts to the Soviet Union, where the Czarist autocracy combined with communist ideology has resulted in adoption of the Engineer role, defined as one who "owns all the means of artistic production. The Engineer supports only art that meets political standards of excellence" (Chartrand and McCaughey, 1989: 5).

This can shed useful light on looking at different state roles in cultural diplomacy. An important point made by Chartrand and McCaughey (1989) is that although these roles are mutually exclusive in theory, in practice most countries have, to varying degrees, adopted all four modes of public support. The next section will now present the diverging views in China, and how the different government roles are reflected in different activities and initiatives in practice.

The domestic debates on agents of cultural diplomacy

Needless to say, all views have their fair share of followers, and even have their corresponding institutions in China, but probably it comes as no surprise that the government-led and multi-agent views are better represented in China. Both domestic and foreign scholars researching China's cultural diplomacy, such as Hartig (2012a), Barr (2015) and Zhou and Luk (2016) have observed the government-centred approach as its main feature. Li clearly defines cultural diplomacy as "the diplomatic activities through cultural means to serve a political or strategic end undertaken by a sovereign state" (2005: 24). His clear stress on the role played by government is based on his fundamental understanding that cultural diplomacy is, after all, diplomacy, which is of course carried out by the government. Other scholars, such as Bian (2009), even argue that because of this, it is only natural for cultural diplomacy to take on a strong political colour in its implementation.

In 2013, the Communist Party's 18th Central Committee declared that public diplomacy should be led by the government; in practice, it is implemented by a complex network of state actors including the Ministry of Culture (renamed to be the Ministry of Culture and Tourism since March 2018), the Ministry of Education and the Communist Party's Publicity Department (Zhang *et al.*, 2015). The State Council Information Office (SCIO) was set up in 1991, but in 1998, the SCIO was merged with the International Communication Office of the CPC Central Committee, becoming 'one institution with two titles', a distinctive Chinese feature of serving both the party and the government at the same time. This 'dual track' is the norm for domestic practice, but the overlap with the party organ often seriously plagues programmes of cultural diplomacy. There is also a lack of coordination among the key agents as pointed out by Zhao (2005): they are parallel organisations of the same ministerial levels; despite some overlapping functions, they all go their own way, which has resulted in a waste of resources and sometimes competition against each other, giving a false picture of bountiful activities in full swing, but with little actual effect or impact.

As the British Council has reported, the appetite to invest in cultural diplomacy is especially high in newly emerging nations such as China, whose government is deploying heightened cultural diplomacy activities to raise its international profile and standing, as is befitting its rising global economic power (Holden, 2013: 26). All the milestone events that marked the fledgling of China's cultural diplomacy so far have been clearly state led and government sponsored. However, Nye has specifically named China as "making the mistake of thinking that government is the main instrument of soft power" (2013: n.p.). Guttenplan commented (2012: n.p.) that the Chinese government wants to change the perception of China by "combating negative propaganda with positive propaganda", for example, "countering hostile foreign propaganda" was listed as one of the main objectives of SCIO (Shambaugh, 2007), but this actually revealed the crux of the problem as there is no such thing as "positive propaganda"; it will only meet with a negative reception if it is identified as "propaganda", let alone when

60　*Vehicle and driver of cultural diplomacy*

it is self-claimed. The classic example was when Li Changchun was quoted in *The Economist* stating that the Confucius Institute was "an important part of China's overseas propaganda set-up" (*The Economist*, 2009) – a statement that has been frequently seized upon by critics and used as evidence to associate the CI with politicised missions. According to *A Chronology and Glossary of Propaganda in the United States*, propaganda is "*a form of purposeful persuasion* that attempts to influence the emotions, attitudes, opinions, and actions of specified target audiences for ideological, political or commercial purposes through the controlled transmission of one-sided messages via mass and direct media channels" (Nelson, 1996: 115). Therefore, "what propagandists do is to utilize their own interpretation of the truth in order to sell an ideological point of view to their own citizens and to the world at large" (Welch, 2014: 4), and the most important thing is that:

> Propaganda is most effective when it is less noticeable. In a totalitarian regime – indeed any "controlled" society – propaganda is more obvious and visible and largely tolerated for the fear of the consequences. In a so-called "open" society propaganda is much more problematic when it is hidden and integrated into the political culture.
>
> (Welch, 2014: 17)

This telling statement has sharply pointed to two issues of propaganda, being implicit and explicit. Propaganda also exists in so-called "open societies" – its muted undertone is integrated into the political culture and it becomes an invisible power. In a way, it means that anything 'they' produce is deemed to be propaganda, what 'we' do is called lobbying or persuasion.

Explicit propaganda has always been integral to the post-1949 Chinese state with a dedicated Propaganda Department of the CPC Central Committee taking firm control of all forms of media to further its ideological objectives. Then an Overseas Propaganda Department under the CPC Central Committee was established in 1990. It was only after 2009 that the English translation was changed to the Publicity Department, and the old term of "external propaganda" was gradually replaced by "public diplomacy". However, some scholars, such as Edney (2012) and Sun (2015), note that the term "external propaganda" is still in use in Chinese policy writings, and the propaganda system still shapes the way the Chinese party-state approaches soft power. Whenever Liu Yunshan's speeches were being quoted, he was always referred to as the Propaganda Minister (2002–2012). As Nye has pointed out, "information that appears to be propaganda may turn out to be counterproductive if it undermines a country's reputation for credibility" (2008: 100). Kuhn (2012: n.p.) has used the expression of "instant killer for credibility" to refer to explicit propaganda, as when the information communicated is 100 per cent good and positive, the credibility rate with American audiences is zero. When decisions are driven by a domestic agenda and made on the 'tracks' of domestic standards, they sometimes cannot reach the international domain. A common phrase in use in China since its opening up is to "connect to the international railway", meaning to adapt to the international standard, but in order to do so, it needs re-engineering and not just repackaging. Otherwise, it is not hard to understand why the authoritarian nature of the Chinese Party-state, and the blurred boundary between state involvement and the social cultural realm would generate caution among foreign academics who fear that the strings of propaganda are attached. What is more, government-led approaches also tend to demonstrate progress by reporting the number of activities that have been carried out rather than measuring the actual effects of opinions that have been influenced. As pointed out by Lukes, "power is at its most effective when least observable" (1974: 23). Cultural diplomacy must remain subtle; any attempt to make it a government campaign will reduce its impact.

Recognising this, there is also a representation of the mixed-agent view in China. Hu has clearly stated that:

> Cultural diplomacy is diplomacy carried out by government or non-governmental organisations to serve the end of promoting mutual under-standing and mutual trust between nations and peoples, constructing and elevating a country's international prestige and soft power, through the means of educational and cultural exchanges, exchanges of people, arts and performances, and trade of cultural products, etc.
>
> (Hu, 2008: 32)

He also points out that it is imperative to curb the government's role, while more non-state actors should be drawn in, especially because most Western countries have an innate and deeply rooted aversion to any government-manipulated culture. This will only aggravate the deep-running misunderstandings and mis-conceptions already existing between China and the Western countries. Hu's view has received increasing support in recent years: an important endorsement came from Zhao and Zhang (2010), who made it clear that public diplomacy can be performed by any state departments, by society or even by individuals. This was confirmed in the *Annual Report of China's Public Diplomacy 2011–2012*, which represents a different stance to the mainstream view at least in academic circles (Public Diplomacy Research Centre, 2012). Zhao Qizheng, editor-in-chief of the *Public Diplomacy Quarterly*, outlines different actors' roles in which: "the government is the leading party. Non-governmental organizations, social organizations and social elites constitute the backbone forces, and the general public is the foundation" (2012: Preface).

Following Hu Jintao's speech on building cultural soft power in 2007, a number of new task forces have been assembled in China: an independent, non-governmental think-tank, Charhar Institute, was founded in 2009 with public diplomacy as one of its top priorities. In 2010, a Public Diplomacy Office was established in the Chinese Foreign Ministry and in 2011, the Centre for Public Diplomacy Studies – the first one of its kind – opened at the Beijing Foreign Studies University. In 2012, the China Public Diplomacy Association was

62   Vehicle and driver of cultural diplomacy

established in Beijing as a national non-profit social organisation, to strengthen the soft power of China by mobilising, coordinating and organising social resources and the public for the promotion of China's public diplomacy in an inclusive and pioneering manner.[4] These numerous institutions represent a joint effort of state, academia and social organisations, which appears to indicate an emerging pattern of multi-agency in implementing public diplomacy in China.

I believe the multi-agent view not only accords with the international trend, but more importantly, it fits better with China's distinctive features at two levels. First is China's unbalanced image. According to the national brand hexagon developed by Anholt to measure global perceptions of countries (see Figure 2.1), which visualises and construes the contribution of each of the six scores to a nation's overall ranking, Brand China in 2008 was pictured as the Figure 2.2. It is clear to see that "culture and heritage" and "governance" are at the two ends of China's ranking, rated at the 9th and 48th out of the 50 countries respectively, accounting for the divergence in perception between China as a polity and China as a civilisation.

What is more, as Ramo has argued,

China's greatest strategic threat today is its national image.... Its problem is more complex than whether or not its national image is "good" or "bad", but hinges on a more difficult puzzle: China's image of herself and other nations' views of her are out of alignment.

(Ramo, 2007: 12)

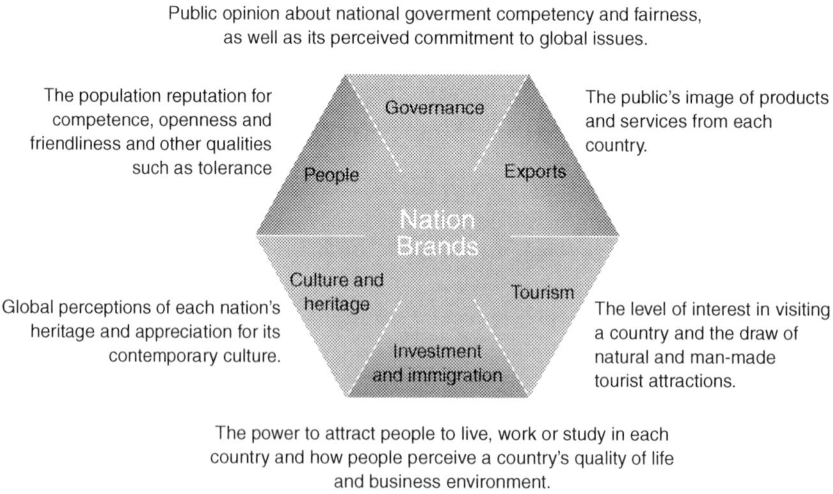

Public opinion about national goverment competency and fairness, as well as its perceived commitment to global issues.

The population reputation for competence, openness and friendliness and other qualities such as tolerance

The public's image of products and services from each country.

Governance

People   Exports

Nation Brands

Culture and heritage   Tourism

Global perceptions of each nation's heritage and appreciation for its contemporary culture.

Investment and immigration

The level of interest in visiting a country and the draw of natural and man-made tourist attractions.

The power to attract people to live, work or study in each country and how people perceive a country's quality of life and business environment.

Figure 2.1 The Nation Brands Hexagon.

Source: Nation Brands Index.

Vehicle and driver of cultural diplomacy 63

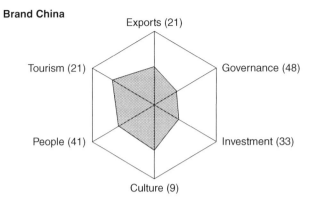

Figure 2.2 Brand China Hexagon in 2008.

Source: W. Manzenreiter, The Beijing Games in the Western Imagination of China: The Weak Power of Soft Power. *Journal of Sport and Social Issues*, 34(1) (2010), 37.

This is linked to the second level of China's distinctive feature. As Goodman (2004) points out, it has been the norm for Chinese government to equate the Chinese state with the government and even specific political parties. When a national culture is promoted through state organs led by the ruling party, it becomes government behaviour, and if the target country holds negative perception towards the Chinese government, then government-led cultural diplomacy would have a very limited role to play, if not counterproductive, particularly if the recipient country has a completely different model for state involvement. Government rhetoric such as "make sure that all cultural battlegrounds, cultural products, and cultural activities reflect and conform to the socialist core values and requirement" (Sahlins, 2015: 6) reveal the contradiction existing between the cultural goals of the Chinese government and its political system's ability to deliver those goals: the CPC wants to see China acknowledged as a cultural superpower; yet at the same time, the CPC's role in the determination of cultural production works against this goal. Therefore, it is fair to argue that cultural power per se is not necessarily a soft power, it is the soft use of it by the right agent that can work the transition. It seems that the dose of government defining, planning, funding and leading the cultural diplomacy is causing the side effect of reducing China's cultural appeal. This assumption will be explored by empirical evidence provided in the following chapters.

There is also a representation of the public-as-agent position in China, the leading organisation is the Chinese People's Association for Friendship with Foreign Countries (CPAFFC), which claims to be "a non-governmental diplomacy organisation" that is committed to people-to-people diplomacy (*renmin waijiao*) or non-governmental diplomacy (*minjian waijiao*).[5] One of its main functions can be described as "elite capture" (Parton, 2019) by engaging in exchange activities with retired politicians and officials, dignitaries and scholars,

64 *Vehicle and driver of cultural diplomacy*

or "old friends of Chinese people", so their interactants are more targeted and selected, not based on the grass-roots level. According to Xin and Wang's research, ironically enough, this non-governmental organisation has shown a "strong government colour" due to "its source of funding, staffing and channels of organising activities, which are all closely government-related" (2015: 14). Its Statutes also specify an aim at gaining "extensive international support for its socialist cause with Chinese characteristics",[6] therefore, it probably can be better understood as a supportive arm to the mixed-agent position. The actual practice of China's non-government-initiated citizen diplomacy will be looked at separately in Chapter 5.

In sum, there are changing dynamics in China from the mainstream view of seeing cultural diplomacy as a government-led endeavour to wider acceptance of the multi-agent view. China is also learning from its successes and lessons in the actual implementation of cultural diplomacy on various fronts. For example, the success of the CIs that have rolled out at an incredible speed to 155 countries by June 2019 has been accompanied by very mixed receptions, and much criticism is about its top-down operation model as state-led enterprises, thus triggering many controversies about their being used as propaganda tools. In contrast, the most eminent agents of American cultural diplomacy come not from the government but civil society: everything from Hollywood to Harvard. Compared with the Facilitator's role played by the American government, the Chinese government roles can mostly be found in the other three models, though not a perfect match with Chartrand and McCaughey's descriptions. Its role in media production is more like an Engineer, which will be discussed in Chapter 3. In the section below, I will compare the Architect model showcased by two government-sponsored initiatives: one is the CI under the auspices of the Ministry of Education, and one is the China Cultural Centre (CCC) affiliated to the Ministry of Culture and Tourism.

At arm's length versus the overseas arm: comparison of the CI and the CCC

In my interview with Mr Anders, Director of the Goethe-Institut in Beijing, he made an interesting remark that the CI is indeed "not comparable" to the Goethe-Institut, not because of its government connection, but because the Goethe-Institut's official counterpart is actually the CCC in Berlin. CCCs were set up as government-sponsored cultural centres since the 1980s through Agreement on Mutual Establishment of Cultural Centres between China and XXX (name of the host country), the ones set up in Berlin and Madrid have made it quite clear on their official websites that they are the counterparts of the Goethe-Institut and Instituto Cervantes respectively. Their aim is to "enhance cultural exchanges and relations between countries, improve mutual understanding and friendship",[7] which perfectly echoes the definition of cultural diplomacy.

By the end of 2017, a total of thirty-five centres have been established all over the world and a target of fifty is set for the year 2020.[8] They follow the same model and are all based in prime locations in the host country and fulfil similar functions, including holding cultural activities, teaching and training, and providing information services. However, in my interview, most CI Directors either disagree that they are parallel organisations to the CIs, or have never even heard of them. Although they are both government-sponsored, the CI Chinese Directors and teachers are sent by the home universities, in other words, they are from the partner academic institutions, while the CCC Directors and staff are expatriated by the Ministry of Culture and Tourism or Cultural Bureau at the local (provincial) level, which means they are from government institutions. To highlight this important difference at the operational level, I have described the CI as "under the auspices" of Ministry of Education, and the CCC as "affiliated to" Ministry of Culture and Tourism, to put it differently, the former is *at arm's length*, while the latter *is the overseas arm* of the Ministry.

Though earlier in establishment, CCCs are much slower in global expansion with much lower visibility, thus causing very few disputes. There is currently little research about the CCC: one recently published was Zhang and Guo's (2018) chapter on the effectiveness of CCCs in China's public diplomacy, comparing it with the CI. Not convinced by some of their research findings, this section aims to extend the discussions regarding the vehicle and driver of China's cultural diplomacy to explore the different features between the two organisations, and seeks to provide different answers to the same questions raised by Zhang and Guo:

1   Since the CCC attracts less criticisms, does that mean the CCC is more effective than the CI in promoting Chinese language and culture and if so, why? (2018: 186)
2   The activities of CCCs are not very different from those of the CIs. Why should one (the CI) be greeted with suspicion, receive a great deal of criticism and face significant resistance, while the other (the CCC) receives little criticism? (2018: 189)

Their answer to the first question is clearly Yes, as confirmed in that "the chapter concludes that CCCs have so far been more successful", and the prime reason they gave to question two is that "Because it (the CI) works with partners in the education sector, it has given rise to concerns of politically motivated academic interference" (Zhang and Guo, 2018: 189).

Before arguing for a different answer, how to define "success" and how to measure "effects" need to be clarified first. Although the authors made the point that "the effectiveness of public diplomacy is measured by minds changed rather than cash spent" (Zhang and Guo, 2018: 195), instead of giving evidence of how the CCC has managed to do a better job of changing people's mind than the CI, they did give evidence to the point made later that their "level of activities is not constant":

Both the Chinese and German versions of the website of the CCC in Berlin show intensive activities in 2015. But after the activities held in July 2015,

66 *Vehicle and driver of cultural diplomacy*

nothing has been posted on the bulletin board when it was checked in November 2016, suggesting that there had not been much going on since then. A check on the website of the CCC in Benin, Africa, also yielded little activity from July 2015 to November 2016.

(Zhang and Guo, 2018: 192)

Therefore, it seems that an implicit equation has been established between "less criticism" and "more successful", and those reasons given to explain why the CCCs are "more effective" can at best explain why it has attracted less criticism: their gradualist and much less intrusive approach, their choice of host countries, and less visible role played by the government. I don't think the last reason is an accurate representation; it has more to do with the visibility of the CCC than the role played by the government. If it is put under the same level of scrutiny as the CI was, the government role is only more explicit. Other reasons listed by them also applies to the CI approach, such as collaboration with local civil societies and organisations, thus does not distinguish the CCC from the CI. It is not my intention here to draw a conclusion of which organisation is more successful or more effective due to lack of comparable data regarding their impacts, what I want to discuss below is to apply the lenses of the vehicle and driver of cultural diplomacy to compare the two organisations.

As discussed earlier, as the two sources of building soft power, culture and political values can be considered the two wheels of the vehicle. Unlike the CI which sees itself as 'the cultural wheel' but tends to be seen as also straddling over 'the political value wheel', the CCC distinguished itself better as the former – both from its affiliation to the Ministry of Culture and Tourism, the name of the organisation itself, and its model of reciprocal agreement, all help it define its role more narrowly and clearly. This links to the actual activities carried out at the two organisations. They may seem very similar as argued by Zhang and Guo (2018) and indeed have some overlaps as confirmed by BGD1, but a closer look will show that all the CI activities that actually attracted controversy or criticisms are not carried out by the CCC – research for example, which is the flashpoint leading to a number of CI closing downs and censorship controversies, only apply to the remit of the CI and will be look at in more details in Chapter 4.

If the above concerns the 'what' is delivered between these two organisations, let's now look at the 'how' – relying on both attraction *AND* persuasion or mainly on attraction. It is a fair argument that cultural products are mainly relying on its natural attractiveness, while value promotion may involve more persuasion, which may apply more to the part of the job carried out by the CI – both intentionally or unintentionally. This relates to the different target audiences. For the CCC activities, the general public are attracted to attend, they make their own decisions of whether to participate or not, while for the CI, the Chinese curriculum may have already been delivered by a teacher from the host institution before, or by locally hired staff from China, or even by someone from Taiwan, now replaced by someone sent from mainland China (because they are 'free') who may implicitly try to persuade the students to see the stance of

Vehicle and driver of cultural diplomacy   67

Chinese government. Of course, there are many cases where only the existence of a CI enables the provision of a language programme that was not viable before, but either way, delivering to a classroom embedded in a host university is why the CI's approach is considered more intrusive.

Then we can look at the 'where'. So far, there are no CCCs in North America and the UK, which happens to be the area with the largest number and most concentrated distribution of the Confucius Institutes. According to statistics released by the Hanban in June 2019, the USA alone is home to the biggest number of CIs (88 CIs) in the world, (reduced from 110 by the end of 2017), while the UK has the most concentrated coverage (29 CIs) in Europe. If "how many minds were changed" is one of the measurements for the effectiveness, then the winning side would definitely be the CI as the CCC has no presence in these areas at all where the Cold War mindset is more prevalent according to Chinese government, and the majority of the CI controversies all sprung up in these areas: this can be best demonstrated by looking at the dozens of reported CI closing downs between 2013 and 2019: twenty-two out of the thirty-three were all located in North America – two in Canada and twenty in the USA. Again, the non-presence of CCC in these areas is one of the most important reasons why they did not attract much criticisms, but I consider the controversies and heated debates the CIs have stirred as evidence that it _is_ "changing people's mind", to the extent that it triggers the alarm of some who are scared to see such changes. This was shared by DPEC in the interview, who suggested that the criticisms which the CI received could be viewed "the other way round as a sign for its 'success', it means the CIs are producing effects". Even with these closures, there are still a total of 284 CIs in full operation in Europe and North America, compared with 13 CCCs in Europe and none in North America. Therefore, it is not tenable to list "choice of host countries" as one of the reasons accounting for the CCC's 'success', it can only be used to explain its record of little criticism received and indicate the different challenges they are facing: visibility for the CCC versus credibility for the CI, which will be further discussed in the following chapters.

Now let's turn our comparisons to the agent, or driver of the vehicle. As stated earlier, both the CIs and CCCs are sponsored by the government and both are quite open about this connection as well. However, the puzzle is, CCCs do not have any official local partners in the host country and are staffed by people from Chinese government, while CIs are mainly operated as a partnership with a host institution, then how come the CCC is questioned much less for its government connection? Zhang and Guo put the blame on the very fact that the CI "works with partners in the education sector" (Zhang and Guo, 2018: 189), while at the same time, CCC's collaboration with "both government and non-government organisations in both China and the host countries" (Zhang and Guo, 2018: 195) was stated as a contrasting feature accounting for its success, so the question is: aren't universities in China and the host countries part of such organisations? Plus that CIs also work closely with the local communities and civil societies in reaching out and engaging with the general public, for example,

68 *Vehicle and driver of cultural diplomacy*

the Chinese New Year performance is also staged by non-official organisations in China, and the lion dance was often performed by local Gongfu Society in venues provided by the local City Council. I find such reasoning very unconvincing, almost to the contrary, I argue that the CI's model of partnering with local universities lies at the very core of its effects, however, as the Chinese saying goes, "a tell tree catches the wind", the CIs are more liable to attacks because they are hundreds times more in presence.

Now that the different operating models of the two organisations are mentioned, they do constitute the key dimension of the contrast. One key difference is that the CI was designed as a platform for international collaboration, while the CCC is affiliated to a Chinese ministry, thus functioning as its overseas arm. Unlike the triangular model of the CI between Hanban and home/host institutions, the CCC follows a strict rule of reciprocity in signing Agreement on Mutual Establishment of Cultural Centres between China and XXX (name of the host country). On the one hand, this model reassures people of its intension and standard, thus leading to less controversy; on the other hand however, it is also the reason for its slow growth and challenge in realising reciprocity in the real sense. As Zhang and Guo mentioned in their article, "lack of reciprocity" (2018: 193) is actually listed as the second challenge, and the Benin Centre was used as an example in that "while Beninese people were becoming more familiar with Chinese culture, it would take a long time for China to know 'Africa' (not Beninese) culture because he believed China was not investing enough in this direction". What is harder to change than the lack of investment from government is perhaps the lack of interest from the general public as revealed by the interviewee: "A Chinese who knew Beninese culture is abnormal because the Chinese are too proud of their own culture" (Zhang and Guo, 2018: 194). This point will be elaborated in Chapter 3 when a cultural terrain of struggle is mapped out for the CI: the global cultural terrain is not an level playing field with some cultures taking up the hegemonic position, reciprocity is not easily achievable when no equal position between cultures is established. This is a hidden barrier for the CCC's model, as cultural attractiveness is not a result of persuasion, if it is not viable to set up a Culture Centre of a certain country in China, then the reciprocity agreement means that no official CCCs can be set up in those countries. This may explain why there is only one CCC established in East European countries so far (Bulgaria). Even for countries that agree to set up a CCC, usually there is only one at the capital or major city, while the CI model is based on institutional partnerships between universities, it allows a huge growing space. Cultural centres can of course be established by other means, such as a number of similarly named Chinese Culture Centres were set up in the USA by overseas Chinese diaspora in New York, San Francisco and other cities, but no counterpart of the CCC is established in the USA or the UK sponsored by the Ministry of Culture and Tourism, while the CI's model has allowed it to achieve the widest spread in these two countries.

When the CCC's expansion clearly picked up speed after 2014, it was explained as partly a response to "its competition with the CI" (*China Daily*,

Vehicle and driver of cultural diplomacy 69

2012, cited in Zhang and Guo, 2018: 187). It is simply as unadvisable for the CI to adopt the CCC's model as for the CCC to catch up with the CI's speed. It is fair to say both models have its merits and challenges, the point is not for them to compete with each other, but to build on the strength of each other while reflecting upon how to manage their own challenges and magnify the impacts of their activities.

To summarise, the similarities between the CIs and CCCs include their government sponsorship and their function as a window for cultural diplomacy by offering similar cultural activities including language teaching, lectures, events, exhibitions, performances and holiday celebrations, etc. An interesting observation is that while the CCC is actually the Ministry of Culture and Tourism's overseas arm, the government role in the driver's seat is not causing as much controversy as the CI, which is operating at arm's length from the Ministry of Education in the host country, but the government role in the front seat is questioned more. It should put itself in the backseat and let the two partner institutions sit in the front. CIs and CCCs differ from each other in their models of operation, which can explain largely both the very different expansion scope and the share of criticisms received. However, I challenge the implicit equation established between "less criticism" and "more successful" or "more effective" by other researchers such as Zhang and Guo (2018).

Another big difference is that the CCC's activities are mostly confined to bringing Chinese cultural products and activities to the host countries for the people there to taste 'a slice' of the complexity of Chinese civilisation, while the CI offers abundant opportunities to enable more students and staff from their host institutions to visit China or spend one or two years studying there to gain first-hand knowledge about contemporary China, develop deeper and more comprehensive understanding of the real China, and benefit from the opportunities a more developed and prosperous China can bring them. This would arguably work better in winning or changing people's mind, in a way, one's heart can be persuaded by one's eyes, as after all, seeing is believing. First-hand knowledge and experience will always produce bigger impact on people's perception than second-hand information. What the CCC can consider doing in this direction is to take advantage of the merge of the Tourism Bureau into the Ministry of Culture in 2018, and its partnership with a corresponding cultural bureau at local government level in China, for example, the CCCs in Belgium, Greece, Australia and Sri Lanka are co-founded by Shanghai, Beijing, Guangdong and Tianjin cultural bureaus respectively, more activities can be staged to promote their home provinces/cities as tourist destinations to attract more people from the host country to visit China.

As Shambaugh has articulated, soft power is "largely about the capacity of a society to attract others, rather than a government to persuade others" (2013: 209). The comparison between the CI and CCC has raised questions to be answered: will a state-led *persuasion* campaign, especially for an authoritarian state like China, increase or decrease the *attractiveness* of a country's culture and political values? Will the two sources of soft power – culture and political

70   *Vehicle and driver of cultural diplomacy*

values – enhance or complicate each other's attractiveness? The next section will try to answer these questions by looking at how the driver's identity and driving practice affect people's reception and perception of the vehicle. The case study is carried out by comparing challenges faced by Confucius Institutes in the USA and UK with those in South Korea by providing multiple sources of evidence including academic publications, media reports and interviews made during site visits to the Confucius Institutes in South Korea and the United Kingdom in 2014 and 2019.

A comparative case study: CIs in the USA, UK and South Korea

As "China's most globally visible, ubiquitous, and controversial soft power project" (Hubbert, 2019: 2), the CI has already been referred to a few times in the discussions so far, and will be examined again in the following chapters to gain more in-depth knowledge and understanding. Since the first CI's establishment in 2004, thirty-five CIs have ceased to operate so far (till May 2019),[9] along with one cancellation[10] and seventeen rejections.[11] The first two closed in 2010 were not extensively reported: one was the CI at Osaka Sangyo University in Japan, which was closed in March 2010 due to spy concerns (Lumsden, 2015). When the *People's Daily* reported the written apology on behalf of the university, it included the original remarks made by Toshiyuki, former secretary for university affairs: "Although the Confucius Institute is not an invasion by the Chinese government, it can be seen as a 'soft landing' for China's expansionism" and "we should recognise Hanban as a cultural spy department and should not cooperate with it".[12] The other one was closed by the local Security Bureau in Yakutsk of Russia on accusations that it was "promoting the penetration of the Chinese ideology and economic expansion to the territory of Russia" (cited in Tîrnoveanu, 2016: n.p.). The second CI closure in Russia happened in 2015 to Blagoveshchensk State National Normal University for "violating Russian laws by being registered as a foreign cultural centre" and "South China Morning Post reports that prosecutors say the Confucius Institutes are organizations of foreign agents".[13] It was not captured by much media attention either, but the other thirty-two CI closures from 2013–2019 received much more media attentions and triggered a lot more debates: apart from the Lyon Confucius Institute that was closed by Hanban in 2013 (Hughes, 2014), the other decisions to terminate their renewable CI agreements were all made by the host institutions, including two in Canada, one in Denmark, one in the Netherlands, two in Germany, two in France, three in Sweden, and twenty in the USA. The full list can be found in Appendix 3. There was also one university in Canada, the University of Waterloo, who decided to "withdraw" from the four-party partnership in the CI in June 2015 following a campus consultation, leaving the CI remain open hosted only by its affiliated Renison University College (Montgomery, 2014).

As the above section shows, the CI defined itself as a language institute functioning as an organisation in overseas educational establishments, domestically,

Vehicle and driver of cultural diplomacy   71

they are under the auspices of the Ministry of Education, thus only partially playing the role of the 'cultural wheel', as that is the CCC's remit as an affiliation to the Ministry of Culture. However, most of the CI controversies are caused by its perceived role in soft power projection based on cultural and political value promotion. It has attracted hyper media attention for both its remarkable growth and the debates it has triggered, resulting in a number of investigations into them by various types of organisations: reports produced by the American Association of University Professors (AAUP) in June 2014, *On Partnerships with Foreign Governments: The Case of Confucius Institutes* (the full text can be found in Appendix 4); the US National Association of Scholars (NAS) in April 2017, *OUTSOURCED TO CHINA Confucius Institutes and Soft Power in American Higher Education*;[14] the UK Conservative Party Human Rights Commission in February 2019, *China's Confucius Institutes: An inquiry by the Conservative Party Human Rights Commission*;[15] and the US Government Accountability Office (GAO) on 27 and 28 February 2019: *CHINA: Agreements Establishing Confucius Institutes at U.S. Universities Are Similar, but Institute Operations Vary*,[16] and *CHINA Observations on Confucius Institutes in the United States and U.S. Universities in China.*[17] However, there are still limited conceptually based academic research about the CI, and this gap has allowed the ill-matched interpretations to become the main frame to understand the CIs. This section will focus on using the relevant data collected for cross-case synthesis in answering the two specific questions raised above for this Chapter.

Data and method

The CI was selected to be the comparative case study based on three major considerations. First, it represents the most watched effort of China's cultural diplomacy and a highly controversial one. Since the first CI was opened in November 2004 in Seoul, South Korea, the latest statistics indicate that by June 2019, there were 532 Confucius Institutes opened in 155 countries and regions around the world (Hanban website). Both its impressive speed of expansion and global coverage of the CIs, and the extension of the starting contract period from three years to five years with Hanban-guaranteed funding can be seen as evidence for its early success. However, in the short time-frame of its rapid expansion, the CI has also received its share of criticisms along with approbations, which can be found in a growing body of literature, both in influential media outlets and prestigious academic publications. It was also cited as an example when the new term 'sharp power' was coined in 2017, as it was part of China's "Going Global" strategy of "establishing a brand new image of China and building China into an international cultural centre" through the means of "infiltrating into mainstream international community" as described by the then Chinese Cultural Minister Sun Jiazheng (Yang, 2014). Therefore, it makes a very illustrative case to show both the opportunities and challenges faced by China's cultural diplomacy.

The second reason is that the CI is indeed a complex entity located in a milieu of contexts: the case study is undertaken in the historical, cultural, political, and

72 *Vehicle and driver of cultural diplomacy*

international relation contexts, as contextualisation is a necessary step for comparative analysis and for appropriate generalisation of results. It enables the researcher to explore issues such as the relationship between domestic and international contexts, multiple power relationships among the stakeholders, and the communication process involving both domestic and overseas audiences, which makes the CI an ideal subject for the case study method in its capacity to explore complex processes as they unfold in organisations.

The third reason is that despite the growing interest in the CI reflected in recent studies and media reports, most of the case studies that have been done by academics so far have only focused on CIs in one country, such as the USA (Stambach, 2014), Germany (Hartig, 2012b), Australia (Gil, 2017; Hartig, 2012c) and South Africa (Hartig, 2014). The only comparative analysis was done between CIs in Germany and Australia in Hartig's book (2016) *Chinese Public Diplomacy, the Rise of the Confucius Institutes*, which claimed to be "the first comprehensive analysis of CIs". As the author himself recognises (Hartig, 2016: 9), there are many similarities between the two chosen countries, not to mention the fact that they are both "Western countries", and that the concept of public diplomacy was used as "the theoretical framework for analysing CIs". This study has selected CIs from four different continents and cultural spheres spanning from East to West, and applied the newly developed alternative framework of analysis to examine it, making this comparison a valuable complement to previous studies.

Careful thoughts have been put into making a representative selection of the CIs and the case study was carried out in three phases. Five CIs from four different continents were selected in the first phase by taking cultural spheres in Huntington's terms into consideration: South Korea in the Confucian cultural sphere of East Asia; UK and France in the Western civilisation of Europe; Mexico in Latin America, and Morocco in the Muslim world of Africa. Nine people were interviewed during the summer of 2013, with seven of them from the Chinese home universities, and two from the host universities. Though the coverage offers a good geographical spectrum, no access to the same spectrum of data sources from each continent was available. Given the special nature of the CI as a partnership between home and host institutions, it would be ideal to interview both directors sent by the home institutions and those appointed by the host institutions; similarly, it would gather more balanced views if teachers both seconded from China and locally hired are interviewed.

Therefore, in the second phase, four CIs were selected for field visits in 2014: two in South Korea, including the very first CI in the world, Seoul Confucius Institute, which was approaching its first ten-year anniversary when the interview took place in the summer of 2014, and a second sample deliberately chosen for its location in a smaller city in South Korea, and the fact of being awarded the '2010 Confucius Institute of the Year'; and two in the UK, one represents a featured CI with both home and host institutions being among the most prestigious universities in their respective countries, and one allows me to carry out some non-participant observations and three repeated interviews to compare

Vehicle and driver of cultural diplomacy 73

notes with the first phase. These selections were made with an intension to keep the contrasting angle between a generally East and West cultural perspective, while allowing both intra-country and cross-region comparisons to enhance validity of the research findings. On top of this, secondary data were collected for CIs based in the USA, which hosts the biggest number in the world and saw twenty setbacks so far. To facilitate the comparison of the CI with its Western counterparts, Goethe-Institut is selected as there was already a cooperation treaty signed in 2010 between Hanban and Goethe-Institut in Beijing, based on continuous exchange of new developments in pedagogical methods and teaching techniques. They hold regular meetings, and since the Goethe-Institut plays the role of a consultancy to Hanban, its founding director in Beijing, Mr Kahn-Ackermann, became an advisor to Hanban after he retired in 2011. This layer of comparison offers particularly important insights to answer the question of 'why' China's similar efforts in launching the CI are perceived and received differently and encounter unexpected controversies by comparing 'what' is the vehicle, 'who' is the agent, and 'how' it is implemented in the field. Its succeeding director, Mr Anders, was interviewed in his Beijing office in summer 2015.

Following the domino effect of the CI closing downs from 2018–2019 in the USA and Europe, more than the total number of all the closing downs in the first fourteen years since 2004, a third round of interviews were carried out in spring 2019 in four more CIs, two based in Belgium and two based in the UK, and one senior diplomat in charge of education and cultural affairs in a diplomatic mission; Meanwhile, three British teachers and three groups of students were interviewed as well, with a view to adding another level of comparison between the CI with other non-government-organised programmes such as Journey to the East, a student collaboration programme between partner universities in China and the UK. Appendix 5 lists all the codes, dates, venues and corresponding roles of all the interviewees. A short questionnaire was distributed to the thirty participating students as well, and the collected data is presented in Chapter 5.

In sum, the overall data profile of this research composes multiple sources of documents and reports, including agreements with Hanban, Annual Reports of the CIs interviewed; *CI Annual Development Reports* and the *Confucius Institutes Magazine* published by Hanban; substantial literature review from both English and Chinese sources; observations carried out over a period of eleven years from 2008 to 2019 at one of the CIs; and primary data were collected from a total of forty interviews carried out in a time-span of six years from 2013–2019, with people of five different roles sharing their insights and experiences at twelve different CIs.

Cross-case primary data was then drawn on to lend validity to the research findings. The methods employed include text analysis, observation, questionnaires and semi-structured interviews, covering the three subtypes of data triangulation proposed by Denzin (1978: 295) in terms of time, space and person. Because data collected by each method reveals different aspects of empirical reality, by drawing on multiple sources of evidence, data triangulation can

74 *Vehicle and driver of cultural diplomacy*

provide more information and better insights towards a more comprehensive answer while corroborating the findings and helping reduce the likelihood of misinterpretations.

Both the aim of China's cultural diplomacy to improve its global cultural position and the means through global coverage of projects such as the CI give this endeavour a global nature. However, the world is not one monolith. By drawing on the triangulated data collected, the section below will examine how the driver's identity and driving practice affect people's reception and perception of the vehicle in different destinations, namely, the USA, UK and South Korea in this comparative case study.

Tensions between the 'wheels' and the 'driver'

According to its mission statement, the CI aims to "develop and facilitate the teaching of the Chinese language overseas and promote educational and cultural exchange and cooperation between China and other international communities" (Constitution and by-laws of the CIs, Hanban website). Its intentional focus on promoting Chinese language and culture defines its own role as the 'cultural wheel' of the vehicle. Actually, even 'culture' is considered an auxiliary function of the CI, which is primarily a language-teaching institute. This was emphasised by a number of interviewees such as DPEC and BGD1, who actually opposed the idea of regarding the CI as a vehicle of China's cultural diplomacy, rather, "it is just a language institute that offers some cultural activities, but calling it cultural diplomacy is an overstatement – we come from an university in China and work at an university here, what we do is nothing diplomatic" (BGD1). UKD5 also mentioned that during the CI Annual Conferences, they only discuss how to improve teaching standard and quality as a language service provider, just like the Goethe-Institut and Alliance Française in China, there is no political value related items on the agenda. Therefore, it is only natural for the CI to evade such discussions in its teaching and cultural exchange activities. This can be observed at the CI classrooms as described by Hubbert in her empirical research:

> Inside the classroom, the CI teachers reinforced an idea of a China defined by its cultural glories and modernization feats, not its political practices. Whenever politically laden topics emerged from classroom discussions, I observed that the teachers quickly refocused students on language acquisition and cultural activities.
>
> (Hubbert, 2014: 330)

Hanban's explanation is that political discussion is not the CI's remit, and CI teachers do not necessarily have the expertise or knowledge to handle such discussions. A genuine difficulty faced by Hanban and will be elaborated in Chapter 4 is its lack of quality teachers, even just as language tutors. Due to its rapid expansion, many CIs have to rely on volunteers or postgraduate students to work

Vehicle and driver of cultural diplomacy   75

as language teachers. They are not expected, nor in the capacity, to deliver any content discussions in this regard. Just as the Deputy Director of the CI at the Erlangen-Nurnberg in Germany said, the CIs "may not be the correct venue for debates on Tibet and other sensitive issues; such topics are better left to Sinology departments" (cited in Sahlins, 2013: n.p.). This view was echoed by my interviewee UKSC5: "after all, I am not a teacher of politics, I cannot offer an expert answer, and I would not want my language class to evolve into a politics class". Nor does Hanban want this – all the CI secondees interviewed said that during the pre-departure training organised by Hanban, they were instructed to either respond with government rhetoric, or try to divert the topic when politically sensitive discussions arise in the classroom. According to UKSC5:

> The advice Hanban gave us in pre-departure training is to take the Chinese government stand to speak for China, tell students Chinese official views.... They also advised us not to engage in extended debates with students, if students stick to their views, we can only present our views in a mild manner and avoid head-to-head confrontations.

UKSC2 explained her approach like this: "I would not say the students are wrong, but I think it is necessary to let them know the Chinese views. Then it is up to them to decide if they support this view or not". This accords with UKLH3's explanations: "our main purpose is to offer a platform where different views can be put forward, not to argue who is influenced by who". This approach of "just letting them know" is how counter-discourse gains access to the knowledge centre from the Chinese perspective, but it is also identified and resisted as "ideological infiltration" from the hegemonic side, thus keeping the two sides wrestling in this terrain of struggle.

According to Hartig's (2018) empirical research based on fifty internal work reports from CIs in Asia, Africa, Europe, America and Oceania, the percentage of all CI activities that dealt with state and politics in one way or the other only accounts for 11.8 per cent, 7.5 per cent 3.1 per cent, 1.8 per cent and 1.2 per cent respectively in the continents they are located in. However, even the language-focused approach cannot be immune from criticisms for the CI "only teaching simplified characters, which are used on Mainland China but not in Taiwan, Hong Kong or Singapore, estranging language learners from Chinese texts produced anywhere but the Mainland" (Epstein, 2018: n.p.). Such politically charged reproach give the impression that it is the CI's intentional choice to do so, but it is not the CI who banned teaching traditional characters, rather, it is simply due to a lack of demand or a viable market and available expertise at the same time: even the majority of well-educated population born in mainland China after the 1950s were only taught simplified characters at school, which literally means that there is very little expertise available in the current workforce to teach traditional characters, plus the fact that simplified characters are already symbols of one of the most difficult languages to master in the world. I am sure no CI would object to the host university to offer such courses if there is indeed

76 *Vehicle and driver of cultural diplomacy*

such a demand and they can find suitable teachers. Actually, in one of the universities I interviewed, there is also a Taiwan Institute based in the same School and runs its own programmes. Students learning Chinese there can also choose to apply for Taiwan scholarship to complete the year abroad.

A much more serious and unanticipated consequence of this language-only approach is its paradoxical effect. As Hartig (2015) argues, the approach is complicated by the fact that it is precisely those sensitive topics that are probably most familiar to the CI target audiences, as they regularly appear in the media. Evasion is recognised as censorship and hampers the credibility of CIs. What is even worse, as Hubbert's (2014) research concludes, is that because China is routinely imagined as politically repressive, the purposefully apolitical nature of its pedagogical materials and classroom practices sometimes works counterproductively, as this "political absence" is interpreted as "authoritarian presence", thus "reinforcing perceptions of a repressive Chinese government apparatus". All of her interviewees recognised that Hanban's "attempts to depoliticise the classroom had this paradoxical effect" (Hubbert, 2014: 339) in that "its invocation of culture" "augments, rather than diminishes perception of threat and distrust" (Hubbert, 2019: 18).

This paradoxical effect was also shown by Lueck, Pipps and Lin's research finding that despite the Confucius Institute's self-proclaimed role of focusing only on Chinese language and culture, the narrative of the CI reports in the *New York Times* defined it as "a tool that was being used by the Chinese government to favourably influence American perceptions of China's domestic policies and international actions. Contributions of the Confucius Institute to Americans' knowledge of China's language and culture went largely unreported" (Lueck, Pipps and Lin, 2014: 344). I argue this is another paradoxical effect: the Confucius Institute was not credited for what it meant to provide, but discredited for what it did not mean to provide, and the negative perception based on what *did not* happen could wipe out the positive effects of what *did* happen.

Many domestic scholars do not seem to see any problem for the CIs to "function as agents of the state by relaying knowledge and information regarding China's language, cultural traditions, way of life and foreign policies, in order to foster international recognition of China as a civilised and harmonious society" (Pan, 2013: 29), but in Western scholars' eyes, this made CIs be "understood fundamentally and rightly as politically motivated institutions. And because the programmes are from China, and that carries with it broadly articulated assumptions about political value and practices, the expectations are especially politically laden" (Hubbert, 2019: 104). For example, Professor Hughes from the London School of Economics that hosts a CI referred to it as "an institution that has the mission of promoting the values and interests of the CCP to have a long-term base on campus" (Hughes, 2014: 57). This shows, in disregard of the cultural wheel function identified by the CI itself, it was understood as an influence project aiming to promote China's political agendas abroad via targeting overseas universities.

Vehicle and driver of cultural diplomacy 77

This is exacerbated when the CI's voluntary compliance with its role as the 'cultural wheel' is interpreted as censorship on the one hand, and its being given a double mission in government rhetoric on the other hand: in a plenary session in October 2011, the CPC Central Committee has published a key resolution on promoting the development of "socialist culture" in which the CIs were described (along with the Xinhua News Agency and China Central Television) as part of the drive to "create new methods of propaganda to strengthen our international right to speak, respond to foreign concerns, improve international society's understanding of our basic national conditions, to display our country's image of civilisation, openness and progress" (Hughes, 2014: 55), and in a speech given by Li Changchun at the CI Headquarters, he was even quoted saying "*using the excuse* of teaching Chinese language, everything looks reasonable and logical" (cited in Sahlins, 2018: n.p.), though I doubted the accuracy of this English translation.[18]

The above discussions seem to support Hu's (2008) view and the author's argument earlier regarding the counter-productivity of the government-led approach, because even though culture and political values are defined by Nye as two separate sources of soft power, it is not possible to draw clear lines between the two in reality, particularly because the two 'otherness' of China (culturally and ideologically) have developed into a complex whole over time, and the government role as the driver or agent only aggravates the entangledness. While the CI only wants to focus on its language and cultural function, the government rhetoric always assigns more significance to it, which makes the separation of the two wheels a one-sided wishful thinking. For example, Hu Yongqing, a deputy of the NPC was quoted to say "promoting the use of Chinese among overseas people has gone beyond purely cultural issues" (cited in Kurlantzick, 2007: 67), and Wang Gengnian, Director of China Radio International, was quoted in a 2011 speech that "we should quietly plant the seeds of our ideology in foreign countries, we must make good use of our traditional culture to package our socialist ideology" (Sahlins, 2015: 8). As Paschalidis has argued, politicisation of culture during the Cold War era has "turned culture from a vehicle for ideology into a synonym of ideology" (2009: 282).

A more recent example is when the UK decided to also host an investigation into the role and influence of the Confucius Institutes in April 2018 following the NAS investigation carried out in the USA. Professor Hughes believes that this is because the CI is "being politicised": "some of this is driven by China's trade practices and some of it is driven by increasing concerns over how Xi Jinping is behaving, clamping down on domestic dissent and using China's economic resources to expand its geopolitical influence" (cited in Bothwell, 2018: 6). If we link this to the national brand hexagon cited earlier, we can see a nation's image hinges on the overall, while culture is only one section within a larger repository of images that constitute the world's perceptions of China. Unless 'governance' and 'export' practice also improves, the cultural dimension alone has a limited role to play in transforming China's national image, nor can it stay immune from the impacts of other dimensions. Besides, a number of

78   *Vehicle and driver of cultural diplomacy*

'flash points' in China's relationship with many Western countries, such as the Falun Gong and Dalai Lama issue, do straddle over the 'two wheels' of both culture and political values. As commented on by Nye (2004: 89), China's influence through global dissemination of cultural programmes was yet to be realized, primarily because the country's "domestic policies and values set limits on the development of its resources".

If the above suggests that the two wheels seem to complicate each other in some Western countries as the two sources of culture and political values create the operating contexts for each other in practice; on the other side of the globe, political values do not seem to be a barrier to the CI's mission of culture promotion. In July 2014, I visited two CIs in South Korea and interviewed a total of four directors and four Chinese teachers working there. All the Chinese teachers interviewed answered the question of "how do you handle sensitive questions?" in a very relaxed manner: "Korean students are generally very reserved and quiet", commented one interviewee, which was echoed by another interviewee working at a different CI: "Korean students are very polite, they genuinely care about the feelings of the teacher, if they think the question would upset a Chinese person, or make the teacher uncomfortable, they would not ask". A third interviewee described a typical scenario in class:

> Generally, Korean students do not like to talk about politics, when sensitive topics arise, they would say, 'let's not discuss politics' and change topics to something that interests them, mostly about where to go for travelling and eating, topics that would not hurt people's feelings. So politics is off the table.

Rather than intentionally avoiding discussions of politics, cultural traits are an important reason for this, according to Jin:

> Owing to the far-reaching historical influence of Confucian thought in South Korea, and the homogeneous nature of Confucian culture in Korean society, the fact that the CI was identified as a tool of enhancing Chinese soft power did not lead to more criticisms or opposition to it; instead, the reactions are more focused on the revelations this may have for South Korea.
>
> (Jin, 2013: 239)

These primary data seem to suggest that Confucius Institutes in South Korea do not face the same challenges posed by the tensions or complications between the 'two wheels' as in the USA and UK, due to different relations they have with China at multiple levels, culturally, economically, historically and geographically. If we continue to use the metaphor of 'vehicle', the difference between the CI's practice in different target countries can probably be likened to driving in left-driving and right-driving countries: in South Korea, it is like driving on the same side of the road as home, things go smoothly due to similar driving habits; however, in the USA and UK, the CIs need to be more careful in adapting

Vehicle and driver of cultural diplomacy 79

to the left-driving practice, otherwise, they may run into unexpected problems and be 'honked at' without realising what went wrong.

Meanwhile, the answers to whether China's state-led approach increases or decreases its cultural attraction seem to be more consistent across the globe. When asked: "How does the CI differ from its Western counterparts", "government presence" was blurted out as an answer without hesitation by one South Korean Director:

> Cervantes/Goethe Institutes are non-governmental while the CI is governmental, and often takes on a political colour. The CI should be a nongovernmental organization for cultural transmission, but it serves a national strategy and the Chinese government has spent a lot of money on it every year, so they have their stand and want to show this through their visits.

Another South Korean Director commented on such visits:

> When state leaders visit other countries, they would normally attend unveiling ceremonies for CIs, it is good this time Xi Jinping *did not* visit a CI in South Korea, but the Halla CI in Jeju was unveiled by Li Changchun, giving it a strong political colour. The CI's image among the media and general public is very government-related, we were often questioned why we are serving the Chinese government.

While such questioning is causing discomfort in South Korean, it can lead to closure of some CIs in the USA. These cases will be elaborated in Chapter 4. The empirical evidences collected from the three countries show a contrasted operating context of the CIs. The cross-case synthesis seems to support the answer that the government-centred approach makes the cultural programme look like a state-led persuasion campaign, and reduces cultural attractiveness due to government presence in the foreground and the blurred boundary between state involvement and the cultural realm. While the attraction of language and culture can be retained and separated from political values in some destinations, it may be disrupted by the latter in others. There are tensions existing in practice both between the two sources of building soft power, and the two means of attraction and persuasion as evidenced by the comparative case studies. The different receptions and perceptions of CIs' activities in the USA, UK and South Korea suggest that the global vision of China's cultural diplomacy can only be achieved through localising its practice by adapting to local conditions.

The comparisons between the CI and CCC and among CIs in the USA, UK and South Korea show different challenges: the CCC is more like a wheelbarrow, functioning on one cultural wheel with very limited delivery, so no one seems to worry about who is pushing it, while the CI is perceived to be driving fast on two wheels, the driver's identity and some driving practice is causing concerns. A remedy can be found by evolving from a government-centred approach to a network-based one with multiple agents to engage the local

80 *Vehicle and driver of cultural diplomacy*

community and create more collaborations. China needs to reflect its current practice of funding a mass production of vehicles like the CIs. When a domestically made vehicle, running on a state-controlled engine, drives on the road of a host country situated within different geopolitical, ideological, cultural and historical contexts, the most important thing is to make sure the driver adapts to the local driving practice, and of course, a good knowledge and understanding of the local road conditions is critical to avoid accidents. The next chapter will attempt to do this by charting out the global cultural terrain of struggle for the CI.

Notes

1 This chapter is derived, in part, from an article published in *Journal of Contemporary Eastern Asia*, summer 2018, available online: https://static1.squarespace.com/static/59823f57197aea3038e12bc7/t/5b5e963e8a922d8f9e58ac8f/1532925504463/17_8_Liu.pdf.

2 Hu Jintao's Report at 17th Party Congress, *Xinhua*, 24 October 2017, available at: http://news.xinhuanet.com/english/2007–10/24/content_6938749_6.htm.

3 *Xi Jinping: bu "shuru" waiguo maoshi, ye bu yaoqiu bieguo "fuzhi" zhongguo zuofa* [Xi Jinpung: China will not "Import" Foreign Models, Nor Ask Others to "Copy" Chinese Methods]. *Guancha.cn*, 1 December 2017, available at: www.guancha.cn/politics/2017_12_01_437446.shtml.

4 Z. Li, Message from President. China Public Diplomacy Association, 14 April 2014, available at: www.chinapda.org.cn/eng/xhgk/hzzc/.

5 See Statutes of the Chinese People's Association for Friendship with Foreign Countries, adopted by the Tenth National Council Meeting in May 2012, on the website of the Chinese People's Association for Friendship with Foreign Countries (CPAFFC): http://en.cpaffc.org.cn/introduction/rule.html.

6 Ibid.

7 See China Cultural Center website, at: http://en.cccweb.org/.

8 State Council Information Office, *Haiwai Zhongguo Wenhua Zhongxin: buju chucheng, runwu wusheng* [Layout of Global Distributions of Chinese Cultural Centre], 2018, available at: www.scio.gov.cn/31773/35507/35514/35522/Document/1623215/1623215.htm.

9 This figure is based on my own research, the *Report of the Conservative Party Human Rights Commission* (p. 16) released in February 2019, available at: www.conservativehumanrights.com. The report listed the twenty-five closures in total, not including the first two incidents that were rarely reported, and the latest closure at Leiden University, which was announced after the report was produced, and Redden (2019), Three More Universities Close Confucius Institutes, *Inside High ED*, 1 May 2019, available at: www.insidehighered.com/quicktakes/2019/05/01/3-more-universities-close-confucius-institutes.

10 Toronto District School Board in Canada.

11 These include: the University of Manitoba, the University of British Columbia, the University of Melbourne, the University of Copenhagen, Aarhus University, Southern Denmark University, The University of Oslo, the University of Pennsylvania, the University of California, Berkeley, Cornell University, Harvard University, University of California, San Diego, the University of Wisconsin, Tokyo University, Kyoto University (Sahlins, 2015). Montgomery (2014) also mentioned that both Concordia and McGill Universities in Quebec said they had been approached by the Chinese government to start a Confucius Institute programme, but did not sign up for it. The figure provided by the Report of the Conservative Party Human Rights Commission (p. 16) released in February 2019 was sixteen rejections.

Vehicle and driver of cultural diplomacy   81

12 Japanese University Apologizes for Calling Confucius Institute Spy Agency, *People's Daily* online, 12 June 2010, available at: http://en.people.cn/90001/90782/7023278. html.
13 Russia to Close Another Confucius Institute, *The New Lens*, 3 August 2015, available at: https://international.thenewslens.com/article/21748.
14 National Association of Scholars, Outsourced to China, Confucius Institutes and Soft Power in American Higher Education, A Report by the National Association of Scholars, 2017, available at: www.nas.org/images/documents/NAS_confuciusInstitutes.pdf.
15 Conservative Party Human Rights Commission Report, *China's Confucius Institutes: An Inquiry by the Conservative Party Human Rights Commission*, 2019, available at: www.conservativehumanrights.com.
16 GAO, China: Agreements Establishing Confucius Institutes at U.S. Universities Are Similar, but Institute Operations Vary. Publicly Released: 27 February 2019, available at: www.gao.gov/assets/700/696859.pdf.
17 GAO, China: Observations on Confucius Institutes in the United States and U.S. Universities in China, Testimony Before the Permanent Subcommittee on Investigations, Committee on Homeland Security and Governmental Affairs, U.S. Senate. Publicly Released: 28 February 2019, available at: www.gao.gov/assets/700/697156.pdf.
18 I tried to locate the original Chinese speech. A few website sources says: "*shiyong zhege jiekou lai jiao zhongwen, yiqie kanqilai dou hen heli he hehu luoji*", which reads like a word-for-word back translation of Sahlin's citation and there was no original source given, available at: https://botanwang.com/articles/201804/%E2%80%9 C%E5%AD%94%E5%AD%90%E5%AD%A6%E9%99%A2%E2%80%9D%E6%97 %A0%E5%AD%94%E5%AD%90.html. From Hanban's own online portal, I found the Chinese speech he gave while visiting the Confucius Institute Headquarters in 2012: "*yong yuyan qieru, shenli chengchang*", which can be translated as: "using language as a breakthrough point is very natural and reasonable" or "language teaching is a natural point of entry", available at: http://chinese.cn/college/newsexpress/article/2012-11/28/content_473552.htm.

References

Ang, I., Y.R. Isar and P. Mar, (2015). Cultural Diplomacy: Beyond the National Interest? *International Journal of Cultural Policy*, 21(4): 365–381.
Arndt, R. (2006). *The First Resort of Kings: American Cultural Diplomacy in the Twentieth Century*. Washington, DC: Potomac Books.
Barr, M. (2015). Chinese Cultural Diplomacy: Old Wine in New Bottles? In David Kerr (ed.), *China's Many Dreams: Comparative Perspectives on China's Search for National Rejuvenation* (pp. 180–200). New York: Palgrave Macmillan.
Bian, Y. (2009). *Wenhua waijiao zai guoji waijiao zhanluezhong de shuangchong xiaoying ji qishi* [The Dual Effects of Cultural Diplomacy in International Diplomatic Strategy and the Implication]. *Lilun Qianyan* [Theory Frontier], 13: 30–31.
Bothwell, E. (2018). Confucius Institutes Face International Official Inquiries. *Times Higher Education*, 12–18 April, No. 2352: 6–7.
Carter, D. (2015). Living with Instrumentalism: The Academic Commitment to Cultural Diplomacy. *International Journal of Cultural Policy*, 21(4): 478–493.
Chakraborty, K. (ed.) (2013). *Cultural Diplomacy Dictionary of the Academy for Cultural Diplomacy*. Berlin: Centre for Cultural Diplomacy Studies Publications. Available at: www.culturaldiplomacy.org/academy/content/articles/ICD_Academy_Flyer.pdf.
Chartrand, H.H. and C. McCaughey (1989). The Arm's Length Principle and the Arts: an International Perspective – Past, Present and Future. In M.C. Cummings Jr. and Mark

82 *Vehicle and driver of cultural diplomacy*

Davidson Schuster (eds), *Who's to Pay For the Arts?: The International Search For Models of Arts Support.* New York: American Council for the Arts. MA: Lexington Books.

Deng, Y. (2009). The New Hard Realities: 'Soft Power' and China in Transition. In M. Li (ed.), *Soft Power: China's Emerging Strategy in International Politics* (pp. 63–79). Lanham, MD: Lexington.

Denzin, N. (1978). *The Research Act.* New York: McGraw-Hill.

Ding, S. (2008). *The Dragon's Hidden Wings: How China Rises with Its Soft Power.* Plymouth: Lexington Books.

The Economist (2009). A Message from Confucius: New Ways of Projecting Soft Power. 24 October. Available at: www.economist.com/node/14678507.

The Economist (2010). The Beijing Consensus is to Keep Quiet. 6 May. Available at: www.economist.com/asia/2010/05/06/the-beijing-consensus-is-to-keep-quiet.

Edney, K. (2012). Soft Power and the Chinese Propaganda System. *Journal of Contemporary China*, 21(78): 899–914.

Epstein, E. (2018). How China Infiltrated U.S. Classrooms, *Politico Magazine*, 16 January. Available at: www.politico.com/magazine/story/2018/01/16/how-china-infiltrated-us-classrooms-216327.

Fouseki, K. and D. Kizlari (2018). Cultural Diplomacy: Arm's Length Strategies under the Microscope. *EconomistsTalkArt*, 14 February. Available at: https://economiststalkart.org/2018/02/14/cultural-diplomacy-arms-length-strategies-under-the-microscope/.

Fredman, Z. (2015). Fredman on Wheeler, "The Role of American NGOs in China's Modernization: Invited Influence". *The H-Diplo*, June. Available at: https://networks.h-net.org/node/28443/reviews/73557/fredman-wheeler-role-American-ngos-chinas-modernization-invited.

Fukuyama, F. (1989). The End of History? *The National Interest*, (Summer): 3–18.

Geertz, C. (1973). *The Interpretation of Cultures: Selected Essays.* New York: Basic Books.

Gienow-Hecht, J.C.E. (2010). What Are We Searching For? Culture, Diplomacy, Agents, and the State. In Jessica C.E. Gienow-Hecht and Mark C. Donfried (eds), *Searching for a Cultural Diplomacy.* New York: Berghahn Books.

Gil, J. (2017). Dragon in the Room: Who's Afraid of Confucius Institutes? *Asia Times*, 21 December. Available at: www.atimes.com/dragon-room-whos-afraid-confucius-institutes/.

Glaser, B. and M. Murphy (2009). Soft Power with Chinese Characteristics. In *Chinese Soft Power and Its Implications for the United States* (pp. 10–26). Washington, DC: Centre for Strategic and International Studies. Available at: https://csis-prod.s3.amazonaws.com/s3fs-public/legacy_files/files/media/csis/pubs/090403_mcgiffert_chinesesoftpower_web.pdf.

Goodman, D.S.G. (2004). China in East Asian and World Culture. In Barry Buzan and Rosemary Foot (eds), *Does China Matter? A Reassessment: Essays in Memory of Gerald Segal.* London: Routledge.

Guttenplan, D. (2012). Critics Worry About Influence of Chinese Institutes on U.S. Campuses. *New York Times*, 4 March. Available at: www.nytimes.com/2012/03/05/us/critics-worry-about-influence-of-chinese-institutes-on-us-campuses.html.

Hartig, F. (2012a). Soft Power in China: Public Diplomacy through Communication. *Chinese Journal of Communication*, 5(4): 477–480.

Hartig, F. (2012b). Confucius Institute and the Rise of China. *Journal of Chinese Political Science*, 17(1): 53–76.

Hartig, F. (2012c). Cultural Diplomacy with Chinese Characteristics: The Case of Confucius Institutes in Australia. *Communication, Politics & Culture*, 42(Part 2): 256–276.

Hartig, F. (2014). The Globalization of Chinese Soft Power: Confucius Institutes in South Africa. In *Confucius Institutes and the Globalization of China's Soft Power*. With contributions by R.S. Zaharna, Jennifer Hubbert and Falk Hartig (pp. 47–63). Los Angeles, CA: Figueroa Press. Available at: www.uscpublicdiplomacy.org/sites/uscpublic diplomacy.org/files/useruploads/u25044/Confucius%20Institutes%20v2%20(1).pdf

Hartig, F. (2015). Communicating China to the World: Confucius Institutes and China's Strategic Narratives. *Politics*, 35(3–4): 345–358.

Hartig, F. (2016). *Chinese Public Diplomacy: The Rise of the Confucius Institutes*. London: Routledge.

Hartig, F. (2018). China's Global Image Management: Paper Cutting and the Omission of Politics. *Asian Studies Review*, 42(4): 701–720.

d'Hooghe, I. (2011). The Expansion of China's Public Diplomacy System. In J. Wang (ed.), *Soft Power in China: Public Diplomacy through Communication* (pp. 19–35). New York: Palgrave Macmillan.

Holden, J. (2013). *Influence And Attraction: Culture and the Race for Soft Power in the 21st Century*. London: British Council.

Hu, W. (2008). *Meiguo Wenhua Waijiao Jiqi zai Zhongguo de Yunyong [American Cultural Diplomacy and its Practice Related to China]*. Beijing: Shijie Zhishi Publishing House [World Affairs Press].

Hubbert, J. (2014). Ambiguous States: Confucius Institutes and Chinese Soft Power in the U.S. Classroom. *Political and Legal Anthropology Review*, 37(2): 329–349.

Hubbert, J. (2019). *China in the World: An Anthropology of Confucius Institutes, Soft Power and Globalization*. Honolulu, HI: University of Hawaii Press.

Hughes, C.R. (2014). Confucius Institutes and the University: Distinguishing the Political Mission from the Cultural. *Issues & Studies*, 50(4) (December): 45–83.

Huntington, S.P. (1998). *The Clash of Civilizations and the Remaking of World Order*. London: Touchstone.

Institutes in Australia. *Communication, Politics & Culture*, 42(2): 256–276. Available at: http://mams.rmit.edu.au/bd8e4ha8e4t8z.pdf.

Jin, X. (2013). *Hanguo meiti guanyu Kongzi Xueyuan de baodao yu pinglun* [Media Reports and Commentaries Concerning the Confucius Institutes in South Korea]. In L. Zhang (ed.), *Zhongguo Wenhua Yu Waijiao [Chinese Culture and Diplomacy]*. Beijing: Intellectual Property Publishing House.

Kissinger, H. (2011). *On China*. New York: Penguin Group

Kuhn, L. (2012). China Still Has Much to do in Promoting Cultural Influence. *Xinhuanet*, 26 October. Available at: www.xinhuanet.com/english/indepth/2012–10/26/c_13193 2296.htm.

Kurlantzick, J. (2007). *Charm Offensive: How China's Soft Power is Transforming the World*. Cambridge, MA: Yale University Press.

Leonard, M., C. Stead and S. Conrad (2002). *Public Diplomacy*. London: The Foreign Policy Centre.

Li, Z. (2005). *Wenhua Waijiao, Yizhong Chuanbo Xue de Jiedu [Cultural Diplomacy, An Interpretative Mode of Communication]*. Beijing: Beijing University Press.

Lueck, T., V.S. Pipps and Y. Lin (2014). China's Soft Power: A New York Times Introduction of the Confucius Institute. *Howard Journal of Communications*, 25(3): 324–349.

Lukes, S. (1974). *Power: A Radical View*. London: Macmillan.

Lumsden, A. (2015). Big Dragon on Campus: China's Soft Power-Play in Academia. Council on Hemispheric Affairs. Available at: www.coha.org/big-dragon-on-campus-chinas-soft-power-play-in-academia/.

84 Vehicle and driver of cultural diplomacy

McDowell, M. (2008). Public Diplomacy at the Crossroads: Definitions and Challenges in an Open Source Era. *The Fletcher Forum of World Affairs*, 32(3): 7–16.

Montgomery, M. (2014). University Teachers call for an End to Confucius Institutes. *Radio Canada International*, 9 September. Available at: www.rcinet.ca/en/2014/09/09/university-teachers-call-for-an-end-to-confucius-institutes/.

Mulcahy, K.V. (2017). *Public Culture, Cultural Identity, Cultural Policy: Comparative Perspectives*. New York: Palgrave Macmillan.

Nelson, R.A. (1996). *A Chronology and Glossary of Propaganda in the United States*. Westport, CT: Greenwood Press.

Nisbett, M. (2012). New Perspectives on Instrumentalism: An Empirical Study of Cultural Diplomacy. *International Journal of Cultural Policy*, 19(5): 557–575.

Nye, J.S. (2004). *Soft Power: The Means to Succeed in World Politics*. New York: Public Affairs.

Nye, J.S. (2005). The Rise of China's Soft Power. *Wall Street Journal Asia.* Available at: http://belfercenter.hks.harvard.edu/publication/1499/rise_of_chinas_soft_power.html.

Nye, J.S. (2008). Forward. In Y. Armonk, Watanabe and D.L. McConnell (eds), *Soft Power Superpowers: Cultural and National Assets of Japan and the United States* (pp. ix–xiv). New York: M.E. Sharpe.

Nye, J.S. (2011). China's Soft Power (speech given to Carnegie Council for Ethics in International Affairs in 2011). Available at: www.youtube.com/watch?v=RmW1gZPqFDs.

Nye, J.S. (2013). What China and Russia Don't Get About Soft Power, Beijing and Moscow are Trying their Hands at Attraction, and Failing – Miserably. *Foreign Policy*, 29 April. Available at http://foreignpolicy.com/2013/04/29/what-china-and-russia-dont-get-about-soft-power/.

Ogoura, K. (2006). The Limits of Soft Power. *Japan Echo*, 33(5): 60–65.

Pan, S.Y. (2013). Confucius Institute Project: China's Cultural Diplomacy and Soft Power Projection. *Asian Education and Development Studies*, 2(1): 22–33.

Parton, C. (2019). China–UK Relations Where to Draw the Border Between Influence and Interference? RUSI Occasional Paper. February, *Royal United Services Institute for Defence and Security Studies.* Available at: https://rusi.org/sites/default/files/20190220_chinese_interference_parton_web.pdf.

Paschalidis, G. (2009). Exporting National Culture: Histories of Cultural Institutes Abroad. *International Journal of Cultural Policy*, 15(3): 275–289.

Public Diplomacy Research Centre (2012). *Annual Report of China's Public Diplomacy 2011/2012.* Beijing Foreign Studies University, Beijing: Current Affairs Press.

Ramo, J.C. (2004). The Beijing Consensus. The Foreign Policy Centre. Available at: www.xuanju.org/uploadfile/200909/20090918021638239.pdf.

Ramo, J.C. (2007). *Brand China*. London: The Foreign Policy Centre.

Ren, Z. (2010). Confucius Institutes: China's Soft Power? *Rising Powers Initiative*, June. Available at: www.risingpowersinitiative.org/wp-content/uploads/policycommentary_jun2010_confuciusinstitute.pdf.

Sahlins, M. (2013). China U. *The Nation.* Available at: www.thenation.com/article/china-u/.

Sahlins, M. (2015). *Confucius Institute: Academic Malware*. Chicago, IL: Prickly Paradigm Press.

Sahlins, M. (2018). Confucius Institutes: Academic Malware and Cold Warfare. *Inside Higher ED*, 26 July. Available at: www.insidehighered.com/views/2018/07/26/confucius-institutes-function-propaganda-arms-chinese-government-opinion

Saunders, F.S. (1999). *Who Paid the Piper? The CIA and Cultural Cold War.* London: Granta Books.

Seiichi, K. (2008). Wielding Soft Power. In Yasushi Watanabe and David McConnell (eds), *Soft Power Superpowers: Cultural and National Assets of Japan and the United States* (pp. 191–206). New York: M.E. Sharpe.

Shambaugh, D. (2007). China's Propaganda System: Institutions, Processes and Efficacy. *The China Journal*, 57: 25–58.

Shambaugh, D. (2013). *China Goes Global: The Partial Power*. New York: Oxford University Press.

Stambach, A. (2014). *Confucius and Crisis in American Universities, Culture, Capital, and Diplomacy in U.S. Public Higher Education*. New York: Routledge.

Sun, W. (2015). Slow Boat from China: Public Discourses behind the "Going Global" Media Policy. *International Journal of Cultural Policy*, 21(4): 400–418.

Tirnoveanu, D. (2016). Russia, China and the Far East Question. *Diplomat*, 20 January. Available at: http://thediplomat.com/2016/01/russia-china-and-the-far-east-question/.

UNESCO (2001). Universal Declaration on Cultural Diversity. Available at: http://portal.unesco.org/en/ev.php-URL_ID=13179&URL_DO=DO_TOPIC&URL_SECTION=201.html.

Wang, F. (1999). Self-Image and Strategic Intentions. In Y. Deng and F. Wang (eds), *In the Eyes of the Dragon: China Views the World*. Oxford: Rowman & Littlefield.

Welch, D. (ed.) (2014). *Propaganda, Power and Persuasion, from WWI to Wikileaks*. London: IB Tauris.

Whitney, C.B. and D. Shambaugh (2009). Soft Power in Asia: Results of a 2008 Multinational Survey of Public Opinion. Available at: www.brookings.edu/wp-content/uploads/2012/04/0617_east_asia_report.pdf.

Xin, C. and W. Yang (2015). *Zhongguo feizhengfu zuzhi kaizhan gonggong waijiao de chengxiao, zu'ai yu lujing yanjiu -yi Zhongguo renmin duiwai youhao xiehui duimei gonggong waijiao weili* [A Research on Effects and Obstacles of China's NGO in Implementing Public Diplomacy: A Case Study of CPAFFC's Activities with the USA]. *Forward Position*, 7: 10–16. Available at: www.hprc.org.cn/gsyj/wjs/mjdw/201606/P020160628382370046716.pdf.

Yan, S. (2018). *Gaige kaifang de chenggong wei jiejue renlei wenti gongxian le Zhongguo zhihui Zhongguo fang'an* [The Success of Reform and Opening Up Provides Chinese Wisdom and Solutions for Problems of the Whole Mankind]. *Wenhua Ruanshili* [*Cultural Soft Power*], 4: 18–25. Available at: www.qstheory.cn/llqikan/2019-04/15/c_1124368931.htm.

Yan, X. (2007). *Ruanshili yu Zhongguo de Jueqi: Beijing daxue yu shijie yanjiu zhongxin Yanjiu Baogao* [Soft Power and the Rise of China, Research Report Produced by the Centre for Chinese and Global Affairs – Peking University]. 5: 1–18. Available at: http://wenku.baidu.com/view/727d65d33186bceb19e8bbbb.html.

Yan, X. (2011). *Ancient Chinese Thought, Modern Chinese Power*. Princeton, NJ: Princeton University Press.

Yang, L. (2014). *Xinshiqi Zhongguo wenhua "zouchuqu" zhanlue de yiyi* [The Significance of the "Going Global" Strategy of Chinese Culture in the New Era]. *Renmin Luntan* [*People's Tribune*], 11 August. Available at: http://chapter.people.com.cn/rmlt/html/2014–08/11/content_1475959.htm.

Young, N. (2008). Culture as Ideology. *China Rights Forum*, 3: 15–21.

Zhang, F. (2011). The Rise of Chinese Exceptionalism in International Relations. *European Journal of International Relations*, 27 October. Available at: http://journals.sagepub.com/doi/abs/10.1177/1354066111421038.

86 *Vehicle and driver of cultural diplomacy*

Zhang L. *et al.* (2015). China's Cultural Diplomacy: Strategy, Policy and Implementation. Available at: http://carnegietsinghua.org/2015/04/17/china-s-cultural-diplomacy-strategy-policy-and-implementation.

Zhang, X. and Z. Guo (2018). The Effectiveness of Chinese Cultural Centres in China's Public Diplomacy. In Daya Kishan Thussu, Hugo deBurgh and Anbin Shi (eds), *China's Media Go Global.* London: Routledge.

Zhang, Z. (2012). How Cultural Diplomacy Wields Soft Power. *International Communications*, 10: 36–38.

Zhao, K. (2005). *Ying waijiao, ruan zhuolu, shilun Zhongguo waijiao xin siwei de xingcheng yu yingxiang* [Hard Diplomacy, Soft Landing: The Forming and Influence of New Thoughts of Chinese Diplomacy]. *Guoji Guancha [International Observation]*, 5: 26–29.

Zhao, Q. (2012). *How China Communicates: Public Diplomacy in a Global Age.* Beijing: Foreign Languages Press.

Zhao, S. (2016). China as a Rising Power Versus the US-Led World Order. *Rising Powers Quarterly*, 1(1): 13–21.

Zhao, X. and J. Zhang (2010). *Dui dangqian jieduan Zhongguo gonggong waijiao de zai renshi* [Reconsideration of China's Public Diplomacy at the Current Stage]. *Xiandai Chuanbo* [Morden Communications], 6: 56–81.

Zhou, Y. and S. Luk (2016). Establishing Confucius Institutes: A Tool for Promoting China's Soft Power? *Journal of Contemporary China*, 25(100): 628–642.

3 Charting the global cultural terrain of struggle for China's Confucius Institutes

> This is a contested terrain between Eurocentric cultural hegemony and Sino-centric counter hegemony. Perhaps the first step towards achieving the ultimate goal of cultural diplomacy is to view the global cultural terrain in a de-centred way.
>
> (Xin Liu)

The term of "contested ideological terrain" was defined in Messner's (1988: 198) research as a theoretical framework that looks at cultural practice that reinforces both the existing power dynamics and the agency of human groups and individuals. If as argued by Tomaselli, "culture now provided a vehicle for the explanation of the active and deliberate production of counter-meanings by groups of people responding to structurally imposed political, economic and social conditions" (1987: 12), thus becomes "something produced in and struggled over in communicative practices" (Howarth, 2011: 2) and "a web of interacting levels of meaning through which a particular social order is communicated, reproduced, experienced, and explored" (Williams, 1982: 13), then planned inter-cultural interactions can be argued to be attempts at reconfiguring the global cultural terrain.

As Foucault (1980) pointed out, discourse joins power and knowledge, and its power follows from the general public's casual acceptance of the 'knowledge' that the culturally privileged produce to reinforce its own power-knowledge equation. In his eyes, there are three types of struggles: against forms of domination, against forms of exploitation, and against forms of subjectivity (Foucault, 1982: 793). Gramsci (1971) also argued that although hegemony is formed through "consent", it is constantly readjusted and renegotiated, as there will always be a counter-hegemonic struggle. Where there is hegemony, there is resistance, and this is a two-way process: while the counter-hegemonic side will be engaged in "a war of position", another Gramscian term referring to the cultural struggle of much longer duration and complexity to gain positions of influence that can develop counter-hegemony, the hegemonic side will resist any emerging new forces that could challenge its position. In the case of the Confucius Institute (CI), its rapid expansion was

88 *The global cultural terrain of struggle*

quickly identified by the hegemonic side as a potential threat to its hegemonic position in the global cultural terrain.

This chapter will employ these conceptual frameworks as well as the double-swing model and the alternative analytical framework developed in Chapter 1 to chart the shifting global cultural terrain by looking at the cultural interactions taking place on a global scale between structured organisations (such as academic institutions, the media, and the government) and the individuals who are involved in such interactions (such as the academics and the general public as the target audiences). It will investigate the simultaneous multi-level interactions going on in the field, and use the rich data collected as 'bricks' to construct a three-dimensional view of the global "cultural terrain of struggle" where the CI is launched into: as an endeavour to counter Western cultural domination and subjectivity of the modern-day reincarnation of Orientalism. It will contextualise the operation of the CIs by showing a holistic view of the terrain and focusing on the intercultural interplays among various forces between the two sides: the projecting side and the receiving side in terms of cultural diplomacy practice; and the hegemonic side and counter-hegemonic side in terms of the current terrain conditions, with a view to revealing the actual configurations underlying the 'power struggles'. To this end, three steps will be taken, which corresponds to the three sections of the chapter:

1   Framing the broader context for the CI's position in the global cultural terrain of struggle;
2   Presenting various actors holding different positions in this terrain;
3   Epitomising the complexity of the multiple interactions among various players with some actual examples in the field.

Step one: framing the broader context for the CI's position in the global cultural terrain of struggle

Like the natural terrain, the cultural terrain is also historically determined. We have witnessed the shaping and changing positions of different civilisations in the long course of history. As the oldest continuous civilisation on earth today, China has survived four millennia's vicissitudes, from being a most sophisticated and admired culture in the world until the seventeenth century, to the decline in the eighteenth century, which eventually gave way to the "century of humiliations" from the mid-nineteenth to the mid-twentieth century when China was defeated by Western gunboats, its culture was also degraded into being the inferior 'other'. Perhaps a much less recognised reversal is when this *inferior* position was twisted by Orientalism into being *opposite* to the Occidental: it means Chinese culture was considered inferior *not* because China was defeated, but because it represents all the qualities of a mortal danger to the rest of the world. The growing revulsion Chinese culture received culminated in the "yellow peril" stigma, which revealed the hidden logic shrouded in Orientalism and its legacy lingering today: being different implies being everything the

The global cultural terrain of struggle 89

Occidental is not, while the Occidental represents all the universal values, thus grants legitimacy for one side and breeds hostility against the other side. I do not think this legacy is going away anytime soon and argue that they are only becoming *hidden* as this 'conversion' has become a form of 'knowledge' that is consolidated through power of discourse. This power is invisible when it forms hegemony, which means domination by one culture as the universally valid ideology that justifies the social, political, and economic status quo as natural, perpetual and beneficial for everyone (Gramsci, 1971). When it is accepted as the *normal* state, it means oppression of the 'other' groups becomes hidden, to the point that if cultural diversity is not lost, equality is, thus the general public do not see any injustice in this terrain where the 'other' cultures are despised.

During the Cold War era, China was again deemed to be in the opposite camp, that of Communism, although a 'communist China' is more of an 'ideological mask' that the West has put over China's face as representing the other end of binary opposition to freedom and democracy. As Said put it, "nothing is easier for people to deal with something that is different than to portray it as dangerous and threatening and to reduce it ultimately to a few clichés" (1993: 238). Communism is such a cliché for a changing China constantly exploring its development road of "socialism with Chinese characteristics". I argue this is a 'mask' painted with Western subjectivity and arbitrarily imposed on China, covering the actual face of a real China that they failed, or rather, refused to see. Instead, they used the hegemonic position in discourse to turn the 'mask' into 'knowledge' that became accepted as the true face of China over time; and when one stays under the 'mask' for a long time, it becomes part of one's identity. In a sense, if a general Western 'culture hegemony' was formed in the post-colonial world, a more specific 'ideology hegemony' was also formed in the post-Cold War era. The end of the Cold War with the collapse of the former Soviet Union seemed to have consolidated the Western belief of universalism, as alleged by Fukuyama:

> What we may be witnessing is not just the end of the Cold War, or the passing of a particular period of post-war history, but the end of history as such: that is, the end point of mankind's ideological evolution and the universalisation of Western liberal democracy as the final form of human government.
>
> (Fukuyama, 1989: 4)

However, the history has not come to an end as predicted by Fukuyama. In direct response to his argument, Huntington came up with the notion that "the clash of civilisations" would be the new framework in understanding "the remaking of world order", claiming that culture would replace ideology to become the new defining factor in global politics, which has "evolved into multipolar and multicultural for the first time in human history" (1998: 2). It is important to note though, there is a critical difference between the existence of a multicultural world and the appeal for cultural pluralism: "multicultural" just means more than

90 *The global cultural terrain of struggle*

one, a synonym to cultural diversity, it does not mean any equal positions among the 'multi' players, actually, it is far from being an equal distribution of power and influence among these multi-cultures coexisting in this terrain. Mere diversity without real encounter and dialogue does nothing to remove our ignorance of one another, and "leaves in place the stereotype, the half-truth, and even fears that underlie old patterns of division", while cultural pluralism is an achievement through the "active seeking of understanding across lines of difference" (Eck, 2006: n.p.). It is not just an end to universalism, but a beginning to shift intercultural relations from superior–inferior to a more level playing field where all cultures are seen as different, but equal.

Although promoting cultural pluralism and constructing a harmonious world is claimed to be the goal of China's cultural diplomacy, so far, it has been a little more than a grand rhetoric in a terrain that is still dominated by the unrivalled Western culture. China has now secured at least the nominal status of a great economic power in the world, which has given it unprecedented confidence to interact 'equally' with other nations on the table of business negotiations, but it is "as yet not fully accepted as a legitimate member of the US-Centred great power club, defined by shared in-group collective identity" and was assigned to an "outlier status" that "Chinese analysts tend to blame Western discrimination, ideological hostilities and fear of rising Chinese power" (Deng, 2005: 54–55). As a result, "the Chinese are eagerly seeking stature, acceptance, honour, and respect everywhere on the world stage" (Wang, 2005: 39). However, as Zhang Yijun observed, the vice-chairman of the Foreign Affairs Committee of the Chinese People's Political Consultative Conference,

> China's troubles stem from the fact that it feels it has already made an enormous effort to participate in the international system and abide by international rules, but it is still subject to discrimination and attacks because its political system and cultural background are different.
>
> (Zhang Yijun 2000, Cited in Deng, 2005: 55)

This was further explained by Deng (2005) as a consequence of being cast outside the like-minded great-power group, which will determine how image is formed, as out-group would be subject to various forms of negative stereotyping. Foucault (1980) has explained this "power cycle", in which discourse is created and perpetuated by those who have the power, and the discourse created by them will constantly reaffirm their position as the centre of power. In other words, the hegemonic discourse functions like 'trenches': it keeps the hegemon in the powerful position, and keeps the others off at the periphery or in inferior positions.

As a subset of public diplomacy that intends to "influence citizens of other countries" (Melissen, 2005), cultural diplomacy naturally involves interactions between two sides as the double swing model illustrated in Chapter 1: one side tries to influence the general public of the other side, but because it is meant to "achieve the desired geopolitical aims of the sponsor" (Osgood and Etheridge,

The global cultural terrain of struggle   91

2010), the receiving side may suspect and even resist this kind of influence, or redefine the influence with their own interpretations, especially when the sponsor is an authoritarian government, and the cultures and values on both sides are not held as compatible equals. While this 'inequality' may be the very reason for the projecting side to be engaged in cultural diplomacy, the receiving side may want to counter that influence to maintain its own position. Thus, we can well imagine the practice field of cultural diplomacy is actually a contested "terrain of struggle" – Gramsci had highlighted the constant nature of the fight for cultural hegemony in the 1930s: for the hegemonic side, the need to keep fighting to maintain its hegemonic position is made ever more pressing by the shifting new terrain, in which the counter-hegemonic side is fighting for cultural pluralism.

The historical context that has shaped the terrain today is essential to understanding the current interactions among all forces in the terrain who are already influenced, to a different extent, by the pre-existing 'isms' in their perceptions: be it Orientalism, universalism or communism. The rhetoric may change when there is a changing wind in the discourse, but not the perpetuated binary mindset: when it is not politically correct to dismiss the ideal of cultural pluralism or cling to any racist allegations in the globalised modern world today, people can still be openly vocal about anti-Communism. For example, when the Stop Higher Education Espionage and Theft Act was billed and triggered debates in the USA in 2018, while some criticised it as an "irresponsible" attempt to "categorize an entire country of people en masse as spies", some openly claimed that "Opposing Communist Chinese Spies Isn't Racist" (Peterson, 2018: n.p.).

Meanwhile, there is also a dimension of domestic audiences that needs to be examined in this context frame: the role played by nationalism. As argued by Joseph Levenson (1968), the key transition to modernity in China was the move from culturalism to nationalism, which has been rejuvenated as the new ideology for contemporary China. As discussed in Chapter 1, it clearly provides a strong driving force for China to implement cultural diplomacy, but its double-edged nature also entails cultural resistance according to Guibernau (1996), which works both ways between the projecting side and the receiving side, adding another source of tension to this terrain of struggle.

The above has briefly contoured the historical, international and domestic contexts for the current global cultural terrain that the CIs have been launched into. Unlike the natural terrain, the cultural terrain is much more dynamic and ever-shifting, driven by all sides' endeavours of cultural diplomacy, therefore, it can be reshaped in a matter of decades, due to the dynamic relationships among all forces at play. The next section will take a closer look at such forces in the terrain: who they are, which positions they take, and how the changing positions affect their interactions.

92 *The global cultural terrain of struggle*

Step two: presenting various actors holding different positions in this terrain

This part will present the ecology for the CI by looking at all the stakeholders at play, including:

- The Chinese government and Hanban;
- The CI, a joint force of host and home institutions locked in a triangular relationship;
- China-related scholars;
- The media (both in China and the host country);
- The general public in host countries as the target audiences.

The Chinese government and Hanban

The CIs are managed and funded by the Office of Chinese Language Council International, known as Hanban in Chinese abbreviation. Directly affiliated to the Ministry of Education, Hanban was established in 1987, but a new plaque of 'Confucius Institute Headquarters' was hung in April 2007 in direct response to Hu Jintao's speech on enhancing China's cultural soft power to show its new remit of administration and supervision of the CIs. Although the new office building in Beijing only identifies itself as the Confucius Institute Headquarters, and Hanban is only kept in parentheses after the CI Headquarters as the official title of the organisation, it is still the most widely used name in English.

Hanban is registered as a non-profit organisation (NPO) with corporate status, but it is the Chinese government that covers all of the expenses for the CI headquarters and its work of expanding CI activities overseas, as they are considered to serve the national strategy of building cultural soft power. According to its official website, Hanban actually comprises of representatives from twelve state ministries and commissions.[1] On top of all these, its first chairperson of the Council, Madame Liu Yandong, was also the Minister (2002–2007) of the CCP's United Front Work Department (UFWD). When she retired in 2018, the new Chairperson of the Council, Madame Sun Chunlan, was also the UFWP Minister from 2014–2017. This was often used to indicate CI's connection to UFWP's remit, which involves "both domestic efforts to quell dissent within China through clamping down on political ideals and social philosophies that might threaten CCP control and international efforts to improve China's public image" (Hubbert, 2019: 12), although the connection is more in the background of individual leaders than the institution itself. However, it is true that Hanban's top management are all high-ranking government officials: the Chairperson of the Council is also China's Vice-Premier; and the first Hanban Director, Madame Xu Lin who retired in December 2016, was also a Counsellor of the State Council (with the rank of vice-minister). Therefore, regardless of its de jure status, it would be no overstatement to describe it as a quasi-governmental organisation under effective government control and strongly reflects government views. The following

The global cultural terrain of struggle 93

speech given by Xu Lin clearly shows Hanban is in the vertical hierarchical structure of the Chinese government:

> Every year since 2004, Li Changchun gave numerous important instructions to the CI and visited CIs in 15 countries when traveling abroad. He has established a favourable image as a Chinese leader in the international society. The series of important instructions by Li Changchun on the CI are theoretical treasures of the CI undertaking. We studied them in the past, and we must continue to study them now and in the future.
>
> (cited in Sahlins, 2015: 7)

This often incurs speculations of CIs as having a hidden agenda beyond their stated objectives, or posing "a threat to academic freedom and shared governance because of the way they involve the Chinese government in colleges' affairs" (Schmidt, 2010: 648). In the operation of the CI, Hanban provides funding and controls the budget, it convenes the annual assembly, examines the CI reports, and organises training for both Chinese directors and tutors from the home institutions before their departure, and also pays for directors from the host institutions to fly to China for the annual conference and training programmes. From each of these remits, Hanban can exercise authoritative control: they decide on whether to approve the budget or not; who needs to be trained on what and by whom; and censor news releases on their official website. About the latter, UKD2 gave an example in my interview, it is about one report submitted to Hanban about a guest lecture which in content was favourable to China, but since the topic itself contained a derogatory term, even if it was disputed in the lecture, the whole entry was deleted, as Hanban has zero tolerance for discord – every word showing on the official website must be 100 per cent positive. If an event staged cannot be included in the work report, it naturally nurtured self-censorship and similar topics would be avoided in the future. It also seems understandable why UKD2 says the No. 1 "rule of thumb" is to "do less, err less".

On its tenth anniversary, the CI received congratulatory letters from both President Xi Jinping and Premier Li Keqiang,[2] showing the highest level of national endorsement. Li mentioned the hope that the CI would carry forward the Confucian philosophy of "harmony without uniformity", reaffirming the aim of China's cultural diplomacy in advocating cultural pluralism. At least, this represents the grand vision held by the highest level of the Chinese government, with abundant financial support channelled down to the next level, where the CI is considered a key project to implement this national strategy, whose day-to-day activities are delivered in the host country by a joint force of host and home institutions.

The CI, a joint force of host and home institutions locked in a triangular relationship

A typical CI is born out of a triangular partnership: Hanban, a home institute from China and a host institution overseas. A typical CI's team is composed of a

94　*The global cultural terrain of struggle*

(foreign) Director appointed by the host institution, an office administrator (or two) paid by the host institution, a Chinese Co-Director, and a number of tutors sent by the Chinese home institution and paid by Hanban. What is worth emphasising is that there is no three-party agreement but two separate ones: the first agreement is only signed between Hanban and the host institution to establish a CI on its premise, which is "funded and arranged in part by Hanban" (GAO, 2019: 6). And then the host and home institutions will sign an executive agreement to detail activities and operations of the CI, which does not include Hanban as a signatory. Another important mechanism is that each CI has a Board of Advisors whose members usually comprise of the president and professors of both home and the host institutions as decision makers and advisors. The Director from the host institution also takes the leadership role in approving CI plans, whereas the Chinese Co-Director is mainly responsible for implementing the plan, communicating with Hanban, and managing the Chinese secondees. There is thus a structurally conflicting hierarchy embedded in this three-party partnership: Hanban is above the home university, while the host university holds decision power through the Board over "significant issues, such as teaching, research or operations of the institute" (GAO, 2019: 17).

In essence, the CI functions like a joint venture, serving a common goal but also different interests vested by the two partner institutions. As UKD1 commented,

> it is fair to say Yes, both partner institutions have common understanding of the CI's goal in the main, as it was actually written into the (executive) agreement and it will add to the reputation of both universities, however in reality, each side has its own agendas and expectations.

For the Chinese home institutions, the CI is often used as a flag or poster for internationalisation and an opportunity to travel abroad. For prestigious universities, the decision is partly driven by the need to "support work of the Ministry of Education" (UKD4), as their privileged position means they "have closer relationship with the Ministry and comes with it more responsibilities" (BGD1), many such top-rated Chinese universities have more than ten CIs set up overseas. One MRD stated quite candidly that "the choice of having a CI in Morocco is to respond to the university's grand strategy of internationalisation in different continents, and Morocco is chosen as our presence in Africa". UKD4 gave a very revealing answer about the three-point mandates he was given by the home university president before he left for the post: "Number one, do not get into any trouble (political misstep or diplomatic faux pas); Number two, nurture a good relationship with the partner institution; Number three, try to do a good job for Hanban". This comes as the last point. This is an honest reflection of the priorities from the perspectives of the home institution. A common theme in the Chinese Directors' pre-departure training is the teaching of Zhou Enlai, China's first Premier and Foreign Minister, "there is no small matter in foreign affairs" (*waishi wu xiaoshi*). With such admonishments, it is understandable why some Chinese Directors tend to be overcautious and lack initiatives in their roles.

The global cultural terrain of struggle 95

For the overseas host institutions, a common expectation is to use the CI as a platform to leverage more benefits beyond the Chinese programme and better position themselves in gaining more from China's economic rise. It is interesting to note that all the interviewees have mentioned China as a subject they want to interact and connect with, not just their partner universities, and not just about learning the language. As a matter of fact, in BGD2's words, "they (the host institutions) have no obligations to promote Chinese language and culture, what they want through the CI is to understand the rising China, and learn how to cope with a rising China". The CI was used in a way as a proof of connections with China and a commitment to developing long-term relations. In this sense, having a CI on campus is a bonus point. This is particularly the case for CIs established in a relatively small city. The FRD in such a situation mentioned the value of the CI in the eyes of the local city council as a platform to build and expand relationships with China, the rising economic power. But sometimes, staging cultural promotional activities in small cities can be a challenge, especially in Western countries. As complained by UKLH2:

I feel Chinese culture is considered as a weak culture here, it is not really a level field we can play in. Because you are trying to promote and sell your things, which would naturally put yourself in an inferior position.

An example given was that of a Chinese New Year performance, which is paid for by Hanban but not always staged by a very high-calibre professional art troupes, so the CI has to first deal with the unenthusiastic theatre, then face the challenge of filling all the seats, even with complimentary tickets. UKD1 from the same CI also added:

the popularity of our programme or event in the local area is no match for a Hollywood blockbuster, or a European exhibition in China. At least in China, people are willing to pay for such performances, while here, we need to give complimentary tickets to schools to fill the theatre.

An interesting observation is the recurring theme among the answers given by Chinese directors and secondees to the question of the CI's mission, most of them have addressed it from the state perspective first: "to build a bridge for spreading Chinese culture" (UKD2), "to open the information channel to foreigners who do not have enough understanding of China, and reduce the bias from the media" (UKD3); "to play a role as people-to-people diplomacy" (UKSC2). As explained earlier, the majority of Chinese home universities are all directly under the auspices of Ministry of Education, which is also Hanban's immediate superior in the hierarchy. The CI is a mission entrusted by the Ministry of Education to Hanban to be accomplished through these home institutions, but the state-run system may be very alien to and incompatible with the host institutions: the relationships between universities and governments are starkly different in China and most Western countries, where university autonomy is

96 *The global cultural terrain of struggle*

strongly upheld. It would be hard to imagine a British university talking about "serving the national interests" in institutional partnerships. In this sense, the "interests are different in scale and character" as argued by Sahlins (2013: n.p.): as an instrument of the Chinese government, Hanban wants to spread the influence of the Chinese state worldwide; by contrast, host institutions are concerned only with their parochial welfare as academic institutions. For example, according to UKD6, such welfare includes more international students and research funding from China. DPEC also used this to explain why there are not yet any CIs closing down in the UK, where high education is a 'pillar industry' and China is their number one source country of international students. However, when there are other channels or platforms to achieve the same benefits, the host institution may decide not to renew the agreement. To put it simply, to have or not to have a CI, and to keep or not to keep the CI, are all entirely up to the host institution.

Therefore, between the two levels of government and academic institutions, we can see a contrast between long-term strategies against relatively short-term moves, or a gap between the overall mission of Hanban and specific objectives of the CIs, as the mission is set by the Chinese government, while the objectives are set by the host universities who are self-interested entities. Sometimes, there are mismatches between the macro and micro levels, leaving the CI caught in the middle. For example, UKLH1 complained about the two partner institutions not

> sharing the same understanding about the CI's roles, as the host institution hopes that the CI should contribute to income generation and put a lot of pressure on us, which has nothing to do with the original intention of setting up a CI – they are funded by Chinese government to teach Chinese here.

Other times, this structurally conflicting hierarchy among the three parties could even lead to the closing down of the institute. The Pennsylvania State University, which shut down its Confucius Institute in 2014, can be used as an example here. According to a written statement posted by its Dean on the university website, "over the past five years, we worked collegially with our partners at the Dalian University of Technology. However, several of our goals are not consistent with those of the Hanban" (Redden, 2014); it was "Hanban's regular rejection of their research plans, including those on the environment, science and politics, saying they were beyond the scope of CI's mission" that led to the termination of the partnership. (Jacobs and Yu, 2014: n.p.). It is clear to see they are putting the blame on Hanban while stressing their good relationship with the home institution.

Other complications could be caused by the Chinese embassy/consulate in the host country as explained by MOD and UKD1. The staff working at the Education Section of the embassy or consulate are seconded from the Ministry of Education, where Hanban reports to, and their remit includes supporting, monitoring and supervising overseas Chinese organisations. On the one hand, the CI needs the support from the embassies, including some resources provided by them; they are always invited to important CI events, and the annual report submitted to Hanban is also copied to them. On the other hand, this extra party could further complicate the CI's mission from originally prescribed in the agreements. For example, when there are some politically sensitive activities on campus, the embassy may ask the CI to try to block them, which is beyond the CI's remit. When there is no CI in situ, the embassy has to do it by themselves, such as in 2013, the Chinese embassy in Sydney sanctioned the Australian Centre on China in the World at the Australian National University by alleging its China Story Yearbook "lack of balance" and blocked internet access to the report from mainland China. The Chinese diplomats visited the centre and lodged complaints with the Australian government. The centre's director, Professor Geremie Barme, wrote back in a letter to the Chinese embassy: "I for one do not see how such a crude interdiction benefits mutual understanding [and] respect".[3]

The interactions between the CI and its home institution are relatively trouble-free according to all interviewees, as all home institutions have a special CI Office designated to communication with Hanban and with the host institutions abroad. However, according to SKD1, "once the directors/teachers are expatriated, the home institution pay little attention to what's going on out there, they just pay 'ear service' to the annual report once the CI is set up", echoing the earlier statement that having a CI set up and running is considered as 'mission accomplished' by some home institutions, so "as long as you don't bother them, they won't bother you much. But if you need support from them, usually they are very supportive" (UKD4). The Hanban's role in the CI's daily operation is consistently confirmed by my interviews: all the UKDs and SKDs interviewed denied government interference in their day-to-day operations, and none reported Hanban ever said No to their activities. It is just that the budget may not be fully approved according to UKD1:

> More or less, it's half-half: half of the activity budgets will be approved. But usually we would still carry them out even if we did not get Hanban's funding, we just make the scale smaller, in other words, for things listed on our plan, we'll make sure they happen, but the scale depends on if we can get Hanban's funding to make it big or not.

UKD2 also commented that:

> I think the CI is trying to play down its government involvement, CI has become part of the school at the host institution, subordinate to the Board whose members are from both partner universities; Hanban does not play a part in CI's day-to-day management, and the finance is managed by the host institution, we do not have our own 'little coffers' (hidden reserve).

If we can use the metaphor of intercultural marriage for the CI's partnership between a Chinese home institution and an overseas host institution, we can see it experiences common problems faced by such relationships: cultural differences in

98 *The global cultural terrain of struggle*

handling daily affairs, trivial or major, could potentially lead to conflicts. In a traditional Chinese family hierarchy, the mother-in-law is a very powerful figure to whom the young married couple should show reverence if not obedience, Hanban's role is like a rich 'mother-in-law' who provides for the new couple generously to build a new life. The intercultural marriage only further complicates the relationship, as the 'Chinese wife' looks up to her mother and expects the 'foreign husband' to also listen to his 'mother-in-law', which is not always compatible with his native culture, plus the fact that their matrimonial home is overseas while the rich 'mother-in-law' can only speak Chinese. Even if the 'foreign husband' is learning the Chinese language, he may find it hard to communicate with her in the Chinese way, or find her way an interference in their life in his own country. The positive side is that the 'mother-in-law' does not live with them and tries to give them autonomy to make their daily decisions. This is a most important but often overlooked point: the CI model only follows the same framework of a three-party partnership, which functions like a similar house for different families to live in – each married couple would certainly have their own ways of living and stories to tell. The actual CIs are as different to each other as individual universities and households are different to one another. Therefore, although by the same name, CIs come in many forms: a less prestigious university with a smaller budget would see the CI as a good trade-off for serving its own students' needs while recruiting more students from China; while more elite institutions feel they can make a deal, as Hanban wants to borrow their prestige to improve the CIs' credibility. In their day-to-day operations, some are more language focused, some are more cultural activity focused while others may be more research-focused.

To summarise, as a player stationed in 'the receiver's side', the CI is a joint force based in a host institution with staff provided by its home institution and funding provided by its headquarters in Beijing. As one entity, the CI is at the forefront of the counter-hegemonic side from China's perspective, though physically, it can be based in a host country that is well resided in cultural hegemony, thus in a head-to-head position against the hegemonic side. We can see there are common grounds for both partners, but also different angles to consider their own individual interests: the common ground is to provide Chinese language programme and introduce Chinese culture; the angle from the home institution is more for the international face of the university, and gaining work credits for the Ministry of Education, while for the host institution, it may serve as a leverage to better position themselves in gaining more from China's economic rise. The common agreement framework is spelt into different specific objectives by the different players situated in different positions, resulting in different challenges for different CIs as showcased in the contrasting case studies in Chapter 2.

China-related scholars

Foucault has explained the function of the education system, the media, and the flux of ideologies in forming power of discourse. Therefore, a change of China's cultural image may only happen when a new counter-discourse begins to gain

The global cultural terrain of struggle 99

access to the centre of legitimate knowledge, that is, host universities in the case of the CI. As academics standing at this very centre of knowledge, China-related scholars are more sensitive to this new discourse, and their perceptions and receptions of the CI's presence on overseas university campuses are rather divided. Some view the CI's existence as a welcomed addition to institutional collaboration while others sounded alarm at this as "ideological infiltration", using government speeches loaded with propaganda and "socialist ideology" as evidence to show China's intention through expanding CIs overseas. The most sensational alarmist talk was from American socialist Steven W. Mosher (2012), who dubbed CI a "Trojan horse", seeing this external 'other' now becoming part of a living community of 'us'. Such remarks were refuted by other American scholars, such as Paul Smith, a professor at Harverford College, who worried that the frustration of the USA's own ability to fund academic projects eroded by the economic downturn could "fuel unproductive resentments against China" (cited in Redden, 2012: n.p.). Strong counterarguments were also offered by other China scholars, such as Nakagawa (2011) who has concluded after speaking to a range of people (including China scholars, journalists and CI directors) that "I've seen little to support the notion of Confucius Institutes as ominous propaganda". This is supported by Robert Saunders, an assistant professor of history and politics at the State University of New York: "the Chinese government has reaped so much benefit from the CI, that doing anything that might jeopardize their image and their acceptance by foreign government and institutions is just not worth it" (Ding and Saunders, 2006).

As a matter of fact, many posts of CI Directors and members of the Board are taken by pro-China scholars, such as Tim Wright, professor of Chinese Studies and executive board member of the CI at Sheffield University. He was quoted to say:

> The Chinese government is well aware of the danger of the CI being perceived in this way. We are given more or less a free rein to do what we want. Someone who wished to undermine China might not be welcomed at the institute, but then the British Council didn't exactly put on talks about the IRA.
>
> (cited in Shepherd, 2007: n.p.)

The most heated debate amongst academics was started after Professor Sahlins published the article "*China U*" in 2013, which received a rebuttal from Professor McCord of George Washington University. Both scholars work on campuses with CIs, but McCord believes CIs are "hardly a threat to academic freedom" and we should "let a hundred flowers bloom", while Sahlins believes CIs are "academic malware" (China File, 2014), quoting many government speeches as evidence. The 'Debate Over Confucius Institutes' was intensified after the American Association of University Professors (AAUP) submitted a report in 2014, calling on *all* American universities to rethink their relationship with the CIs. The debates were published in two parts on China File in July

100 *The global cultural terrain of struggle*

2014, focusing on "the costs and benefits of having a CI on a university campus, the economic forces at play, and the role of China in university life more broadly" (China File, 2014). These debates involved twenty-four scholars, but only a handful of them had first-hand experience with the CI. One important observation was that most of the counter-arguments came from people who had either done research, or worked with/for the CI first-hand, while those accusing the CI of being a propaganda tool were those who either shut the doors to the CI, or judged it based on speculations or media reports. McCord (2014: n.p.) has pointed out that the greatest problem with the "anti-CI literature is that it often leaps from suspicions and concerns to a conclusion of fact". This was echoed by the GAO report which interviewed officials from a sample of ten case study schools, including those that have closed their CIs or declined to set up CIs: "Several of these school officials told us that they believed such criticism were not backed by evidence or based on specific incidents, but instead were rooted in a lack of understanding about CIs" (2019: 28).

A resurgent debate was started in 2017, after a report titled *Outsourced to China, Confucius Institutes and Soft Power in American Higher Education* was released by the National Association of Scholars (NAC). Based on case studies of twelve Confucius Institutes in the USA, the report found four areas of concern, namely intellectual freedom, transparency, entanglement, and soft power, and again "recommend that *all* universities close their Confucius Institutes" (Peterson, 2017). Though this report mainly repeated similar concerns raised in the 2014 debates; an article published in *The Chronicle of Higher Education* 2018 anticipated that "the growing economic and geopolitical rivalry between the US and China, a rising global power, is likely to be another source of the renewed scrutiny of Confucius Institutes in recent years" (Bauman, 2018). This has unfortunately come true when the UK Conservative Party Human Rights Commission (CPHRC, 2019) also carried out an investigation into CIs and released a report in February 2019, *China's Confucius Institutes: An inquiry by the Conservative Party Human Rights Commission*, reaching a similar conclusion and recommending *all* British universities to take similar measures to the NAC report.

Back in the 2014 debate, Professor Heilmann at the University of Trier in Germany, also the founding director of a China think-tank in Berlin, Mercator Institute for China Studies (MERICS), had made a point that overall, the CI issue looked far less ideologically charged from a European perspective, and that "the overtones of great power rivalry with China (or cold war allusions) that appear to drive parts of the U.S. debate about CIs, are mostly missing in Europe and Germany",[4] suggesting a regional difference as an important feature of the global terrain. Even Xu Lin has commended on a CI conference in Edinburgh that: "the US government hurt our feelings, but Confucius Institutes across Europe have done a great job, especially with cultural promotion, which is not surprising given Europe's rich history and culture".[5] This was also supported by my interview with UKD5 who commented on the "open-mindedness" and a "generally welcoming environment in the UK". However, in February 2018, a

The global cultural terrain of struggle 101

report was published by MERICS and another German think-tank Global Public Policy Institute (GPPI) under the title of *Authoritarian Advance: Responding to China's Growing Political Influence in Europe*, claiming that from the perspective of liberal democracies, *all* areas of interaction with China are potentially problematic and deserve scrutiny. After all, China's political model is based on an authoritarian regime intent on strengthening a deeply illiberal surveillance state at home while also exporting – or at least trying to popularise – its political and economic development model abroad. Thus, today, *all* areas of Europe's interaction with China have strong political undertones.[6] Following the report, more CIs were closed down in Europe, including France, Sweden, Germany, Denmark and the Netherlands, seeming to indicate that such a regional gap is narrowing in the Western world (a full list can be found in Appendix 3).

Therefore, the China-related scholars are only classed as one group because of their positions at the very centre of knowledge; however, there are divergent views concerning the CI's ideological overtone across the globe, and even if they are physically standing at the same host institution of the CI, their viewpoints could be miles apart, or even stand at opposite ends of the spectrum, which sets the conflict-ridden context in which the CIs are operating. Chicago University, which closed its CI in 2014, could be a handy example to show the divide. Hanban Director Xu Lin told the BBC reporter during the 2014 interview that:

> Chicago University visited us many times, they are strongly interested in establishing a Confucius Institute, so they chose us, it is not Hanban who pushed them.... the concerns are only from very few people, but the sound is very strong.
>
> (cited in Sudworth, 2014)

Their case will be looked at in detail in Chapter 4.

On the other side of the terrain, Chinese academics tend to follow closely the official line as:

> in most cases, the Party appoints university presidents, who in turning appoints department heads. In addition, at every level of the academic establishment, there is a parallel Party structure, with cadres playing a leading role in the development of their work units.
>
> (Chan, 1999: 57)

The Hoover Institute's report also pointed that: "because of the pervasiveness of the party-state, many nominally independent actors – including Chinese civil society, academia, corporations, and even religious institutions – are also ultimately beholden to the government and are frequently pressured into service to advance state interests" (2018: 3). Because of this, although Chinese scholars involved in those controversial CIs can speak, but the "political subjectivity" means they are considered as speaking in one voice as the government. Actually, Guo pointed that:

102 *The global cultural terrain of struggle*

The voices of officialdom and academia have become harder to distinguish than at any other time since 1978. This is coupled with tighter political control over expressions, which has induced greater conformity among intellectuals to the Party line, encouraging larger numbers to support and repeat the line in the mass media and academic journals.

(Guo, 2017: 155)

Therefore, counter-discourse is considered stronger if it comes from inside the 'Western world'. For example, Eric Einspruch, who chairs Portland State University's Confucius Institute, clarified that the CI simply offers "non-credit Chinese courses, cultural programs of interest to the community, and faculty-initiated scholarly activity" (cited in Epstein, 2018: n.p.). Although the main trust of Epstein's article (2018) is to provide evidence for his title "*How China Infiltrated U.S. Classrooms*", he did include many counter-narratives based on his "recent interviews at several US universities with Confucius Institutes, none expressed regret or indeed much concern". Nancy Gutierrez, at the University of North Carolina at Charlotte, responded directly to the accusation of CI's interference at academic freedom: "We made the decision to host a [Confucius Institute] because we believe that this partnership will allow us to expand understanding of Chinese culture very broadly – for community members and for our students", she says, and "a faculty advisory committee will provide the intellectual guidance … ensuring that we are guided by principles of academic freedom" (Epstein, 2018: n.p.). Other examples include Western Kentucky University (WKU), where the Confucius Institute is expanding; its Director Terrill Martin defended its partnership candidly:

I don't believe the Confucius Institute program is controversial at all. I just believe that people don't understand, don't ask the right questions and make a lot of unfounded assumptions about the program, based on the failures of a few.

(Epstein, 2018: n.p.)

However, based on a different reason –

the University could not secure a waiver from the Department of Defense that would allow WKU to operate both the CI and the Chinese Flagship Program. Defense spending legislation passed in 2018 prohibits institutions from hosting Confucius Institutes if they receive DOD funding for Chinese language programs.[7]

WKU has notified its partners that "the University has ended its agreement with the Confucius Institute Headquarters to operate the CI at WKU" in April 2019.[8]

The above represents the few interviews that speak for the CI in the CI-related literature. As commented by my own interviewee UKLH1, "people who disagree have the loudest voice, people who benefit from the CI are not as outspoken". Or

The global cultural terrain of struggle   103

rather, their voices are not heard. Mr Anders, the Goethe-Institut Director in Beijing, made an interesting comment during the interview:

> Most of the media reports I *read* about the CI are negative, about the Communist influence, but I've also *heard* the contrary, people who are involved in the business saying 'No, we're free to do what we want. What are you writing there? Ask me! I can tell you it is not true'.

Yet, their voices are only heard among a small circle, while those scholars who dwelled on the Orientalist discourse have their stances amplified by the mainstream media, reinforcing their discourse. This brings us to the role of media, another influential player in this terrain that could magnify the scholars' debates and works hand-in-hand with the education system in reinforcing and redefining the accepted forms of knowledge and 'truth'.

The media (both from China and the host country)

As one of the most effective tools for reinforcing power and hegemony, media is a very powerful player in shaping people's minds through the languages it uses, the stories it tells, and the images it conjures up.

No matter how objective one media outlet claims to be, each serves its own purposes and interests. Western media are a tool to consolidate Western culture's hegemonic position with West-centric knowledge, while the Chinese media try to counter this biased media environment. Actually, 'issue rebuttals to distorted overseas reports about China was listed among the main aims of China's public diplomacy, along with "form a desirable image of the state", "improve the international environment surrounding China"; and "influence the policy decisions of foreign countries" (Zhao, 2015). To achieve these goals, an internationalisation campaign of Chinese state media was also sponsored by the government: Xinhua news agency, CCTV and *China Daily* all received vast sums of money to 'go out' and explain China's point of view to the world. For example, according to Parton's report (2019: 3), "the *Telegraph* accepting £750,000 a year to include a supplement from the CCP's *China Daily*". Barr provided a statistical comparison in terms of government funding:

> China has committed US$6.5 billion for the overseas expansion of its main media organisations. A little comparison may help put this into perspective: the USA currently spends about US$750 million annually on international broadcasting, whilst UK funding for BBC World Service runs at less than US$400 million per annum.
>
> (Barr, 2011: 45)

But what really sets Chinese media apart from its Western counterparts is not that they are government-sponsored, but that they are state-run, thus the state plays more of an Engineer's role against the 'arm's length principle' that applies in most

104   *The global cultural terrain of struggle*

Western countries, which is "the basis of a general system of 'checks and balances' deemed necessary in a pluralistic democracy to avoid undue concentration of power and conflict of interest" (Chartrand and McCaughey, 1989: 7). In the UK, with its unwritten constitution, freedom of the press is made explicit through the arm's length status of the British Broadcasting Corporation (BBC), while in China, media is subject to the leadership of a number of competent ministries, including the CPC Publicity Department, the Ministry of Culture, the General Administration of Press and Publication, and the State Administration of Radio, Film and TV. They hold the power of appointment of key staff, resource allocation and final approval of content. Chartrand and McCaughey (1989) have proposed a five-point methodological framework to study the arm's length relationship in cultural diplomacy, namely, funding, agenda setting, evaluation, hierarchy and appointment power, all of which are institutionally embedded in the Chinese system, hence their effect is continuous and the impact more profound. Therefore, it is not an overstatement that the Chinese media are the conduits of government's voice, actually, the Chinese word 'throat and tongue' (*houshe*) is used to refer to its role as the mouthpiece. Domestic rhetoric is also rather explicit and open about media control. For example, the following remarks were made by Li Changchun in a speech to the All-China Journalists Association in 2011:

> The journalist front must have a high sense of political responsibility and historical mission, deeply studying, propagating and implementing the spirit of the Sixth Plenum of the 17th Central Committee in order to promote the great advancement and flourishing of socialist culture.
>
> (cited in Hughes, 2014: 61)

After Xi Jinping came to power, an even tighter control of state media can be observed. First from his tour of the top three state-run media outlets in February 2016, when a sign of 'the central television's family name is the Party' was displayed to welcome him, and acknowledge that all media must "love the Party and serve the Party" (Wong, 2016); then in a speech given to the All-China Journalists Association in November 2016, he urged the country's journalists to follow "the correct political direction", conform to the CPC Central Committee, adhere to the Marxist view of journalism, stick to the standpoint of the Party and the people, and uphold socialism with Chinese characteristics (Xinhua, 2016).[9]

In the Soft Power 30 report, UK was rated No. 1 in 2015 and BBC was named among the pillars of British soft power: "Over 1700 foreign correspondents are based in the UK, and with a dynamic media market of its own, London is the global media capital" (The Soft Power 30 website). In contrast, the lack of "political and press freedoms" was listed under the weakness of Chinese soft power, and the 2017 report of the Foreign Correspondents' Club of China reveals that around half of surveyed journalists reported interference, harassment or violence; problems with visa renewal were up 150 per cent from 2016, and 6 per cent (up from 2 per cent in 2016) had been threatened with cancellation or non-renewal of visas

The global cultural terrain of struggle   105

(cited in Parton, 2019: 20). Such explicit control of the domestic media environment contributes to China's ranking at 177 out of 180 in the 2019 World Press Freedom Index produced by the Reporters Without Borders.[10]

This type of vertical media structure does not travel well outside China, especially to destinations with a more horizontal structure of information exchange. The English translation may take partial blame as well: the Chinese word '*xuanchuan*' is a neutral one meaning 'publicity', but it has been routinely translated as 'propaganda' during the Cold War era and was largely kept in use till today. Awkward English translations offered by many of the Chinese government websites and news outlets often lend themselves as evidence to be used against China. For example, in attending a national conference on propaganda and ideology, Liu Yunshan was quoted as saying journalists "must vigorously sing the praises of the achievements of the CCP, socialism, the reform policy, and [the glories of] the great motherland" (cited in Lam, 2009: n.p.).

This open rhetoric nurtures an almost knee-jerk reaction that anything produced by the Chinese government is deemed to be propaganda that must be resisted, and the Confucius Institute was often associated with "propaganda" in many media headlines all over the world. For example, the Indian Ministry of External Affairs has openly opposed the establishment of Confucius Institutes in universities, arguing that they were nothing more than a Chinese design to widen influence by "using culture as a propaganda tool".[11] The Swiss press also carried such headlines as "Propaganda Tool of the People's Republic" and "Chinese Culture Centres Spark Propaganda Fears" when reporting the opening of the Geneva CI in 2012.

Another example of awkward translation is Zhao Qizheng's (2007) article on the English website of *People's Daily* titled "Better Public Diplomacy to Present a Truer Picture of China". There is no such thing as a 'truer' picture, and in the article, Zhao said:

> We can't expect foreign media to portray China justly, or close the opinion gap they have created. China must present an accurate picture of itself to the world. The expansion of reform and opening up is necessary for the nation's peaceful development. In this regard, China should not only listen, but *talk back*. As the 2008 Beijing Olympic Games and 2010 Shanghai Expo approach, we must *ensure these occasions are grand gatherings that present an accurate image of China* and increase its influence.
>
> (Zhao, 2007)

A reading of his remarks indicates that "foreign media's" portrayal of China is unjust, and only China can present an accurate picture of itself, which can be done through grand gatherings of mega events such as the Olympics and the World Expo. As the deputy director of the Foreign Affairs Committee of the Chinese People's Political Consultative Conference (CPPCC) National Committee, Zhao's words will be widely quoted. What he meant is probably "to engage in a dialogue" (instead of "talking back") so that a more comprehensive picture could be shown and a "fairer" understanding could be established. But

106 *The global cultural terrain of struggle*

the indication that rejecting international criticism and hosting grand events can present an accurate picture of a mega country like China is a bit over simplistic and problematic.

True, one of the goals of China's cultural diplomacy is to fight against the subjectivity of Western media by unveiling the "true" face of China to the rest of the world, or to give the world an 'accurate' understanding of China. But the question is: can this be done by a medium that is also biased? As argued by Hartig, "CIs do not present the 'real' China to the world, but rather a 'correct version' of it, which limits their ability to project China's strategic narratives effectively" (2015: 252). This "correct" version, as described by Perry Link, is an "overly rosy portrait of Chinese society", "not only smaller than the whole but crucially different in nature" (China File, 2014). This means when the Chinese government aims at unveiling the 'true face' of China, it is actually using cultural diplomacy as plastic surgery to show a 'beautified face' of China without realising there is any problem in doing so.

Meanwhile, the love for "grandness" is often reflected in the laudatory style of Chinese reports, not only for mega events, but also for government 'leaders', which can have a fatal effect on the CI partnership as shown by the closure of Chicago University Confucius Institute: the only official reason given by the university for suspending negotiations with Hanban concerning the CI agreement is that one Chinese newspaper, the *Jiefang Daily*, disclosed in an admiring and flattering tone that: "the University panicked at Xu Lin's firm stance after receiving her personal letter and phone call, and immediately agreed to keep the CI open" (Wang, 2014: n.p.). This actually pushed the result in the exact opposite direction: the ongoing negotiations were immediately aborted and decisions were made by the university to terminate the agreement. This is obviously a result that Hanban regrets, probably more so in knowing the trigger – they would never imagine such a local media report written in Chinese and meant entirely for domestic readers, would fall under the scrutiny of the American media. This suggests an urgent need for domestic media to develop an awareness of the 'sans frontiers' nature of its audience today in the globalised and digitised world.

As for Western media influence, UKD3 commented that: "information in the West about China is often filtered and selected by journalists who know little about China or have a biased view of the country". Both overt and covert biases can be observed in the international media reports regarding the CI. For example, in Guttenplan's *New York Times* article (2012) titled "Critics Worry About Influence of Chinese Institutes on U.S. Campuses", Mosher's "Trojan horse" accusation and other criticisms were elaborately reported, but they do not point out to readers that the criticisms all come from people who do not work with the CI, and only use their secondary information or so-called 'knowledge' to judge it, nor do they show the profile of Mosher as an advocate for human rights in China, using ideological differences as a sweeping allegation to ignore the CI's focus on language teaching that does not necessarily has any political aims. The only counter-argument in the article came from Mr Byrne as a CI Director from London School of Economics, who denied that

The global cultural terrain of struggle   107

there had been any pressure from his Chinese partners to steer clear of any areas. "Our focus is on the language of business and culture. We're not here to engage with difficult issues". No views from China were ever represented in this article, even when there are people-in-the-know available with important first-hand experience of the CI; they are not fully engaged with. When the media decides what to write, what not to write, how much to write, who to interview and what questions to be answered, these decisions are loaded with the power of discourse.

Abundant evidence of this kind of selective reporting can be found in second-ary data: the only two universities that hosted a CI and cancelled the Dalai Lama's visit were repeatedly reported and used as evidence of the CI's infringe-ment on academic freedom in both the 2017 NAC report and the 2019 CPHRC report: the University of North Carolina (in 2009) and the University of Sydney (in 2013) (reported by BBC, *Bloomberg*, the *Sydney Morning Herald*, etc). In contrast, a number of other universities hosting a CI have all invited Dalai Lama to visit and give a speech; these include the University of Stanford (October 2010), the University of Miami (October 2010), the California State University in Long Beach (May 2011), the University of Maryland (May 2013) and LSE (June 2014), just to name a few. Actually, Emory University has hosted the Dalai Lama a few times for a series of public and campus events, as he holds the title of Presidential Distinguished Professor there. The CIs in these universities were not involved in these activities, nor did they intervene or try to block such visits. Yet, these facts were never mentioned by the media as counter-evidence to show that the CIs did not infringe on academic freedom there.

Similarly, there were reports about the University of Calgary being delisted as a recommended institution for Chinese students heading abroad after it awarded the Dalai Lama an honorary degree in February 2010 (reported by the *Globe and Mail*, CBC News). However, no Western media ever bothered to point out that a number of other universities that also awarded honorary degrees to the Dalai Lama, such as UCLA, the University of Michigan, Emory Univer-sity, Rutgers University and the University of Aberdeen, all had a CI opened on their campus after the award. Their application to and recognition by the Minis-try of Education was not affected by this incident at all. Actually, there are even a number of universities, including the University of Maryland, Miami Univer-sity and the University of Minnesota, which awarded the Dalai Lama an honorary doctorate *after* a CI had been set up on their campuses. In my own interviews, UKD5 also mentioned that at an event celebrating cultural diversity, the CI banner appeared in the same room as a Dalai Lama portrait presented by another religious group.

Moreover, the terminations of CI agreements in 2015 with Chicago Univer-sity, Penn State University and the University of Stockholm have been played up all over the press as sensational news (reported by Reuters, *The Economist*, *The Times Higher Education*, *New York Times*, *Wall Street Journal*, *Forbes*, *South China Morning Post*, to name a few), yet the new opening of the 101st Confu-cius Institute in the USA following these incidents in February 2015 at the

108 *The global cultural terrain of struggle*

University of California Santa Barbara did not appear in any major news outlet. There is no doubt that if it were another 'closing down', it would not have fallen off their radar.

All the above incidents can serve as direct evidence of selective media reports, which is a form of 'covert bias', based on which sweeping accusations were made concerning the CI's infringement of academic freedom. It shows that media reports can often be an attempt to exploit pre-established assumptions. It plays a clear "agenda-setting role" by deliberate coverage of events with the goal of influencing, and sometimes with the effects of swaying public opinion.

Of course, it is only fair to mention that there are also different views and voices in the Western media. For example, the *Guardian* carried a report titled "Not a Propaganda Tool" in 2007 (Shepherd, 2007); and in 2011, another article in *The Economist* (2011) stated that China "has been careful not to encourage these language centres to act as overt purveyors of the party's political viewpoints, and little suggests they are doing so". There were also voices from the Chinese media outlets in English offering counter-arguments, such as the *China Daily USA*, which carried an article in 2015 in response to the "chorus of concern" following those CI closures, stating that: "Confucius Institutes are building bridges rather than Great Walls to share knowledge about the history, culture and language of a rising world power which has been in the shadows" (Watkins, 2015). The article also finished with a quote from Confucius: "Real knowledge is to know the extent of one's ignorance". Another example is the answer given in the *Global Times* (2012) article to "Why is Washington so Scared of Confucius?": "The issue shows the US cultural confidence is not as strong as we thought. Only culturally weak countries have such sensitivity".[12] Interestingly, a very similarly titled article "Why is the US so Scared of the CI?" was published in the Chinese portal of the *Financial Times* in 2019, but provided very different answers: lack of academic freedom, transparency and reciprocal treatment.[13]

Another head-to-head example is when the *Global Times* (2019) directly responded to the *New York Times* report (Perlez and Ding, 2018) regarding the American Culture Centres in China. The *New York Times* article, "China Thwarts U.S. Effort to Promote American Culture on Campuses", stated that "today, the American centres have closed after the Chinese authorities denied American officials entry to them and state security agents interrogated an American academic working on a Chinese campus", citing President Xi's "campaign against liberal democracy" and "the rise of nationalist sentiment" as the reasons (Perlez and Ding, 2018). Although it also mentioned that "funding American culture in China became particularly unpopular in Washington as the Trump administration worked to distance the countries and anger built over Beijing's propaganda in America", and "in all, the State Department spent $5.1 million on 29 centres, though about ten of them never opened". In response, the *Global Times* article first pointed that the article did not list which centres were shut down, then offered counter-evidence that many centres are still in normal operations. As for the reasons for those closures, a Chinese professor was quoted to

The global cultural terrain of struggle   109

say they are mostly due to "internal reasons" and "does not have much to do with the Chinese government". Another professor commented that the media sensationalise those closures to "provide legitimacy for them to suppress the CI".[14]

Apart from voicing counter-discourse in China's own media, another important channel is the inclusion of paid inserts, such as the eight-page *China Watch*, prepared by Chinese state media in leading Western newspapers, such as the *Wall Street Journal*, the *Washington Post*, the *Daily Telegraph* and other non-English newspapers in Germany, France, Belgium and Spain, because "it is more effective to use established media institutions" in a host country as they "have more credibility with local audiences than Chinese media" (Benner *et al.*, 2018: 22). As Anderson pointed out:

> Most newspaper readers are 'pre-prejudiced' in so far as they prefer to buy the newspaper that most suits their political viewpoint. From this point of view, the written and online news media most generally reflect and reinforce rather than re-shape their audience's view of the world.
>
> (Anderson, 2007: 84)

This is consistent with the psychological theory of perception (and misperception). As explained by Wang, "psychologists have long noticed that people do not treat all incoming information equally. People accept information that is consistent with their existing perceptions much more than they do information that is contradictory" (2005: 83). It suggests that the multiplied quantity of overseas distribution of the Chinese media does not necessarily mean the influence they can exert also multiplied; the role played by Chinese media in this global terrain is still rather limited for various reasons discussed above. Use CCTV as an example, Qian's research in 2002 found that 90 per cent of CCTV viewers lived in China, only 4 per cent of whom were foreigners; and 80 per cent watched to develop their understanding of English. Rawnsley argued that:

> CCTV International is confident about the size of its *potential* audience – those who merely live in target areas or who subscribe to satellite and cable packages that includes access to the station. However, it is more likely that the *actual* audience remains small and consists mostly of Chinese who wish to improve their English.
>
> (Rawnsley, 2012: 132)

China Daily is another example, the Audit Bureau of Circulations (ABC) result of its 2014 circulation indicates that 94 per cent of their copies reached their audience via monitored free distribution, delivered to hotels, businesses, schools, airport lounges, airlines and other travel points "for free pick up" (ABC, 2015: 1). As pointed out by Creemers (2015: 310–311), "there is a difference between identifying audiences that have access to particular content and audiences that will actively seek out – and even pay for – the same content", which was echoed by Mattimore (2011),

110 *The global cultural terrain of struggle*

> The ultimate arbiter of the value of that media will be the market. That will be the truth test. If international consumers want the Chinese media products because they come to trust them or believe the media represent a valuable alternative to other perspective, that will be a good thing for the world and for China.
>
> (Mattimore, 2011 cited in Hartig, 2018: 135)

So far, Chinese media's government control and laudatory style are the biggest barriers to establishing such international legitimacy. For example, Yang and Hsiao (2012) found that "international sources reflect deliberation, doubts, and debates over the CI phenomenon, while domestic sources concerning CIs are always filled with praises and compliments". An interesting thing worth mentioning here is that in domestic mainstream media, the sentence that "the *New York Times* has acclaimed the CI as "the best and most fantastic export from China so far, it is an important measure for China to implement its strategy of peaceful diplomacy and improve soft power" [孔子学院被 《纽约时报》 评论为 "迄今为止中国最好最妙的一个出口产品，是中国实施和平外交战略，提升国家软实力的重要措施"], since its first appearance in the online portal of the state media people.com.cn in 2008,[15] has been relayed by people.com.cn again in 2009,[16] then by Xinhuanet,[17] Guangming Daily[18] in 2010, and by Chinanews. com as well, but quoted as a comment made by Joseph Nye,[19] then in China National Radio cnr.cn in 2011,[20] and other websites until 2015.[21] No date or link was ever given to the original *New York Times* article that made the alleged statements, nor was it captured in my search or the research of Lueck, Pipps and Lin (2014) quoted in Chapter 2. This may suggest two things, one is the professional standard of journalist reporting in China (with no reference given to quoted reports), one is that they do value the approbation of Western mainstream media and use it as an important evidence to show its domestic audience and the rest of the world to build both domestic legitimacy and international legitimacy.

Before its international legitimacy is established, the laudatory style and government rhetoric pervaded in Chinese media did little in helping the CIs by offering any counterevidence of those accusations, instead, they were often quoted as evidence of the CI's official links and political overtone. Despite that the Chinese media retorted such thinking as "Cold War mentality", the mainstream Western media still dominate the information order and are exerting direct influence on the general public of the host country, who are the main target audiences of China's cultural diplomacy.

The general public in host countries as the target audiences

In a 2001 report produced by the China National Tourism Administration, it was mentioned that when China was promoted as a tourist destination, a frequently asked question is: "China is a socialist country, can American citizens travel to China?" (cited in Zheng, 2015: 100). Of course, the level of understanding/ knowledge about China held by an average member of the general public in the

The global cultural terrain of struggle   111

host country has improved tremendously in the past decades, but it is still lagging. As explained by UKSC2, "for foreigners who have never been to China, their impression of the country is the one conveyed by the media, which is very tarnished in many countries". UKLH1 elaborated this with an example:

> Most people in the local community have a completely outdated knowledge and understanding about China. What is even worse is those who have never been to China but think they know a lot about China. Most of their perceptions of China are based on media reports, such as about China's one child policy and child trafficking, Tibet riots, etc, and use this as their judgement of the whole country.

Or, as UKD1 said:

> For some people they based their whole understanding of China on the only book they've read – Wild Swans; as for contemporary China, again they based their knowledge on the only media reports they've read or watched – about China's environmental problems or human rights issue.

This is why UKD3 believed the CI's role is to "show them a China that is not shown in local media". In other words, the CI can offer a new counter-discourse, to influence the general public and CI students with people-to-people contacts, to teach people Chinese so that they can get access to vastly more sources of first-hand information about China, and to correct some of the mystified or imagined 'knowledge' about China. One such example was given by UKLH1: "one primary school pupil said to her parents that the teacher told them 'Chinese people eat dogs'. Kids at that age never question what the teacher says, but now they have got a Chinese teacher there to double check". She then said quiz is often used as a means of knowledge transfer to school students and teachers: "the 'true or false' statement would help to some extent dispel the common misconceptions by explaining the correct answers".

If the above represents the average knowledge level about China among the general public, it does not actually fall far short of that among the educated elites on a university campus. UKD3 admitted in the interview that "when I was young, I was taught only British and European history, music and art, and know nothing about Chinese history or Asian culture"; he also gave examples of a Europe-centric view of one little town in Britain claiming to be "the first gunpowder factory in the world" – "it may well be the first one in Europe, but Europe is not the world".

Even for students in today's world, their knowledge about China is still haunted by the phantom of the 'otherness': The Chinese cultural image seems to be either antiquated or tinted with ideological colour. SKSC2 gave an example when she asked a Spanish student about the image of Chinese people in his mind before visiting China, the answer she got was "men wearing long pigtail hair and robes" – images from Chinese Gongfu movies but dated before China as a

112 *The global cultural terrain of struggle*

modern state. This offers an interesting comparison with another answer given by UKLH3: "people are very regimented and disciplined" – an image of modern China that lacks freedom. This confirms the view that the receiving end of China's counter-discourse is not a vacuum chamber, but a receptor that was already occupied or even embedded with 'accepted forms of knowledge' shaped through media and the flux of ideologies, or films. It means the counter-discourse the CI is trying to provide does not go through a one-way conduit; rather, it is a two-way interplay with the discourse already produced by the others in the destination, as shown in Figure 1.1 in Chapter 1.

However, no one can ignore a significant aspect of contemporary China as the second largest economy and the largest trading nation in the world, an indisputable rising power on the economic front. This adds an extremely important dimension to the general public's perception of China. According to UKSC4 interviewed, most of the CI students do not feel the rising China as a threat in their life, instead, "the more developed Chinese economy is, the more attractive China becomes, as more and more people would be interested in studying China to find out how it can achieve such growth". It is interesting to note that 'China' is mentioned as the subject of study here, not just Chinese language. This perspective was also shared by answers from SKD2 and SKD4, who both confirmed that because they are so close to China, they see the huge opportunities offered by China's booming economy:

> Korean people nowadays are very interested in going to China for various activities, be it trade, educational or cultural exchanges, so there are more and more people learning Chinese. Over the past 10 years, we offer more and more opportunities for our students to go to China, there are also more and more students and tourists coming from China. For big shops and tourist information centre they all hire staff speaking Chinese, this means more job opportunities for Chinese-speaking skills.
>
> (SKD2)

SKD4 also gave examples of students changing major from Japanese to Chinese after failing to get any jobs with their Japanese skill set, and in the Business School, it is compulsory for students to take a second foreign language after English. "Due to the decreasing number of students taking Japanese, they simply closed the course, and between Russian and Chinese, the majority of students chose to learn Chinese".

Of course, it is important to remember that all the interviewees are people either working for the CI, or those who are already interested in China: students who choose to learn Chinese out of their own wills, and members of the general public attracted by the CI outreach activities in the community, so in a way, this is a China-friendly circle, but nevertheless, they represent a huge potential for cultural diplomacy to play a constructive role. As explained by Carter, cultural diplomacy aims at "producing publics more knowledgeable about and better disposed towards our nation. This, as it were, is the 'national interest' test that such

The global cultural terrain of struggle   113

programs have to pass" (2015: 479). Therefore, as the target audience in the host country where the CI is based, the general public represents the group of players with the largest number and least vested interest in this terrain, they are very responsive to China's changing power position in the world as well. They may have been influenced by the local media and the 'othering' discourse about China, but can also be influenced by the new counter-discourse and first-hand information offered by the CI, and more importantly, the chances to visit China or study in China, which helps correct some of the mystified or imagined 'knowledge' about China.

Step three: epitomising the complexity of the multiple interactions among various players with some actual examples in the field

From the above we can see none of the groups of players are monolithic; they all contain internal dynamics or even some conflicts to a certain degree. There is simply no way to delineate this pervasive and dynamic complexity with five groups of actors at play. In practice, there is no clear-cut division in which some players stay on the hegemonic side while others stay on the counter-hegemonic side: their relationships and positions are more shaped by the interactions with other players in the terrain, making the relationship both circular and interweaving. In Foucault's words (1982: 793), the interactions are "actions upon actions of the others", taking place both horizontally and vertically in this uneven terrain that is imbalanced and hierarchical: with the culturally hegemonic side holding positional superiority over China, and the Chinese government vertically above the home institutions and the Chinese media. The following section illustrates this with some chained interactions from the actor of Chinese government all the way back to it to close the action cycle.

A snapshot: Chinese government → Hanban → CI → China-related Scholars → media → Chinese government

Hu Jintao's speech at the 17th National Congress in 2007 about building cultural soft power carried implicit policy prescriptions for China's cultural diplomacy. As explained earlier, Hanban is such an organisation committed to the claimed mission of developing cultural pluralism and contributing to the construction of a harmonious world, while the CI was considered as a key project to implement this strategy.

However, scholars such as Seiichi (2008) has argued that government involvement in cultural diplomacy is liable to be seen as "meddlesome intrusion" and can cause reflexive backlash. The complexity of the interplays among all stakeholders can be epitomised by one such incident of backlash that happened during the annual meeting of the European Association of Chinese Studies (EACS) held in Portugal in July 2014, when Xu Lin ordered four pages about the Chiang Ching-kuo Foundation (CCKF) to be torn out from the printed

114 *The global cultural terrain of struggle*

conference materials. Actually, both Hanban and CCKF are sponsors of this conference: Xu's overbearing and arbitrary manner shocked the 300 participants who were present there and then, and later, through media reports, it shocked a far wider audience. The president of the Association, Professor Roger Greatrex from the University of Lund, publicly criticised Xu's action as "totally unacceptable" as "providing support to a conference does not give any sponsor the right to dictate parameters to academic topics or to limit open academic presentation and discussion, on the basis of political requirements"; This was "the first time in the history of EACS that its conference materials had been censored", and "censorship of conference materials cannot and will never be tolerated by the EACS".[22]

This incident involves all the five forces listed above as it happened right among the China scholars, and an academic conference held abroad is probably the worst possible platform to stage China's censorship. When freedom of speech and press are protected by law in many European countries, Hanban is showing that a Chinese government decree can override academic freedom, just like Mr FitzGerald, Australia's inaugural ambassador to Beijing in 1972, commented on the Sydney China Yearbook incident cited earlier: "The Chinese position was that its right should override any rights we had – in these cases China's right being to direct how it is seen, presented and understood in Australia" (Garnaut, 2013). But the vertical line of Chinese government over university and media do not translate across the border. On the contrary, in many Western countries, universities and media are at the very centre of the greatest challenges to governments. While the incident was reported in the Western media (the *Wall Street Journal*, BBC News, the *Diplomat*, EACS website) as an outrage, it was lauded as an act of patriotism in the Chinese press *Global Times* under the headline of '*There is no shame in Hanban tearing up overseas conference program*'.[23] In the report, the blame was put on the EACS, who "should not lack clarity over the gravity of the Taiwan problem for China. The reference to the CCKF in the program should not have appeared in the first place", but CCKF has been funding the conference for the past two decades. The opposite media reactions this incident received inside and outside China shows the potentially conflicting interface between domestic and international contexts faced by the Chinese media. When they are written for a domestic readership to feed the national pride in China's growing power, in how China is becoming tougher in safeguarding its national interests, this can be used by the Western media as an alarming proof of China's hard edge.

Then during the BBC interview, Xu emphasised that the content she removed was "not academic but political", a remark made in defence of her action and against accusations for the CI as a threat to academic freedom, but disproved CI's innocence from its political missions. The *Wall Street Journal* reported it under the headline 'Madam Xu's Party Line, Beijing confirms that Confucius Institutes subvert Western academic freedom': "after vehemently denying for years that the CIs have any kind of censorship agenda, Beijing has now tacitly acknowledged that this was false".[24]

The global cultural terrain of struggle 115

More frictions were disclosed in an article written by the BBC interviewer of Xu Lin in December 2014. The starting line reads as the following:

> For starters she accepted a request for a BBC interview. Admittedly she came quickly to regret it, demanding that we delete a large section of our recording.
>
> After we had finished the recording, along with her deputy and her press officers, she kept us for well over an hour, insisting that she had been misled into agreeing to the interview and demanding that we erase, there and then, the section about Portugal.... We refused to delete our tape.
>
> (Sudworth, 2014: n.p.)

These two incidents were quoted together as examples of the Chinese government's "very heavy-handed and very public attempts at censorship" (Scotton, 2015). They embody a few problems in the line of interactions that involves government, academia and the media: the Hanban "demanding" that a foreign media organization "delete" a section of an interview recording, and then having the "demand" "refused" indicates how the relationship between government and the media differs drastically in China and the UK. Actually, there are other examples of Chinese government control spreads to foreign journalists and academic publishers as well. Melissa Chen, an American journalist working for the English-language arm of Al-Jazeera was denied renewal of her visa and press credentials in 2012, which was widely reported as "being expelled from China" by the *Washington Post*,[25] the *Guardian*[26] and Al-Jazeera English. In 2017, Britain's Cambridge University Press initially succumbed to Chinese pressure to remove online access to hundreds of scholarly articles relating to Taiwan, Tibet and the 1989 Tiananmen protests, but later restored them due to pressures from the academics at home, indicating which 'pressure' matters more to an academic publisher in the West.

Similarly, the relationship between government and universities is also completely different in nature cross the two sides: universities hold a strong power of discourse as independent constituents of academia in many host countries, while in China, they are subject to the leadership of the Ministry of Education and the ideological control exercised by the Party State, which again casts shadows over China scholars abroad as well. According to the 2008 report submitted by the US–China Economic and Security Review Commission (USCC):

> This takes the form of providing both positive rewards to 'friendly' scholars – such as preferred access to interviews and documents – as well as taking punitive actions such as denying visas for academics who anger Beijing. These rewards and punishments offer the Chinese government leverage over the careers of foreign scholars and thereby encourage a culture of academic self-censorship.
>
> (USCC, 2008)

116 *The global cultural terrain of struggle*

Self-censorship is also described as an effective tactic employed by the Chinese government in Parton's report:

> The CCP's preferred method is to create dependencies and induce self-censorship and self-limiting policies.... Chinese funding for UK universities, access to research in China and paid invitations to think tank events in China all create obligations which may encourage UK academics to shade the truth or avoid the awkward.
>
> (Parton, 2019: 16)

Apart from the conflicting relationship between Hanban and academia, the EACS incident is particularly detrimental in that Taiwan has always been part of the Chinese nation, the only consensus that has been reached across the Taiwan Straits since 1949. Therefore, its culture should be considered part of the cultural diversity in China, yet it was rejected by Beijing's cultural diplomacy. Xu's action actually discredited the intension of separating the CI's agenda of cultural and language promotion from any political missions. It showed the counter-productive effect the state-run approach could produce and exemplified the contradictions existing between the cultural goals of the Chinese government and the current political system's ability to deliver progress towards those goals: when government control or "agenda setting" influence is extended beyond the border of China in such an explicit manner, it will not be compatible or acceptable in the international domain, but the state-run nature of China's cultural diplomacy determines that a stern domestic approach would definitely prevail when such incompatibility occurs, even at the cost of causing conflicts. When this counter-hegemonic endeavour was driven by an authoritarian government, it may have backfired and be felt as if it was imposing hegemonic influence as well, especially when Xu's action would appear to be a denial, not a defence, of the image of a harmonious China advocating cultural pluralism that the Hanban is so keen to project. It may be a bad coincidence, but this incident happened just before the CI was about to celebrate its first ten-year anniversary and turned out to be a fuse for the first wave of CI closing downs.

Actually, before it hits the ten-year milestone, Hanban has been actively reflecting and responding to address the three common concerns shared by CIs, namely recruitment and control of academic staff; choice of curriculum and texts; and restriction of debate. Some noticeable adjustments have been made over the years, including:

1   In 2009, Hanban established 'Confucius Institute Scholarships' to recruit overseas students on the MA course of Teaching Chinese to Speakers of Other Languages in China, followed by scholarships granted to CIs all over the world in 2010 to train locally hired Chinese teachers. In April 2013, a Hanban directive was distributed regarding jointly setting up positions of CI head teachers who are locally hired by the host institution but paid by Hanban fund. In other words, Hanban is paying for the salary of CI head

The global cultural terrain of struggle   117

teachers who are appointed by the host institution following their own recruitment procedures, as long as the host institution grants the position a formal employment contract and pledges to maintain this position over the long-term. According to Hanban's 2017 *Annual Development Report*, forty-five positions of CI head teachers had been established at thirty-one CIs in sixteen countries, including the USA, UK and Germany.[27]

These measures were adopted as a response to feedback from the front-line and can kill two birds with one stone: while relieving the pressure of teacher supply from the home institutions, and the worries of reduced academic discourse in the host institution, it will offer students equal access to different voices on the debatable questions, and help improve the quality of provision as well.

2   In the *Eight-Year CI Development Plan 2012–2020*,[28] "to formulate rules regarding the exit mechanism of CIs" was listed under the first 'Major Task'.

3   Increased international cooperation in developing Chinese language teaching materials was reported in the CI's 2014 Annual Development Report, with international publishers such as Cambridge University Press, Mandarin Matrix Press, and Espaces et Signes Press of France, etc.[29]

4   More recently, according to UKD5, at the CI Annual Conference held in 2018, there are focused discussions on how to set up a new evaluation scheme that involves a third authoritative party from the locality as it is currently done internally in the CI and lacks transparency. A task force has been formed and a proposal has been made and presented for feedback.

If points 1) and 3) are responsive measures, 2) and 4) are very pro-active and forward-thinking: the exit mechanism was proposed in 2012, before any of the CI closures took place. Other changes include deleting the reference to Falun Gong participation in its recruiting criteria after it led to the closure of the CI at McMaster University in 2012, which has caused very negative media reports.

However, these changes did not receive all positive responses. Both the actions taken by the counter-hegemonic side and the reactions received from the hegemonic side were subject to interpretations that can be poles apart: they could be considered as a positive sign of China learning its lessons, as suggested by Michael Nylan, professor of Chinese history at the University of California at Berkeley, the Chinese government is becoming "less heavy-handed" and learned from its "early missteps", such as insisting that universities adopt a policy that Taiwan is part of China and attempting to block guest speakers critical of China from campus events (PRI Staff, 2012); or they could be negatively labelled as measures of expediency to exchange for long-term gains according to Mosher (2012), who interpreted them as gestures that do not necessarily mean that Hanban has abandoned its political mission, only that they have become subtler about it.

Whichever interpretation is correct, these responsive actions taken by Hanban close the loop line of interactions from the government level feeding back to the

118 *The global cultural terrain of struggle*

government level. To summarise all these interactions, one thing that needs to be emphasised is its dynamic and responsive nature – every interaction could be both a cause and an effect of a change, just as Foucault (1982: 789) put it: "when faced with a relationship of power, a whole field of responses, reactions, results and possible inventions may open up". Therefore, they should not be examined in isolation but studied in an integrated manner. Perhaps, this "terrain of struggle" can be best described in Said's remarks that it is a struggle between the "relationship of power, of domination, of varying degrees of a complex hegemony" (1978: 5).

Conclusion

This chapter has charted the "global cultural terrain of struggle" that China's CIs are launched into by examining the deployment of all the actors at play. The process considers the following questions: how was the global cultural terrain constructed in history; what power dynamics underpin the formation and shifting of the terrain conditions; and how has the relationship among different actors been affected by the flow of people and ideas in the inter-cultural connections? It has developed an argument that this is an uneven terrain both in terms of unbalanced powers with strong resistance from the hegemonic side, and also a hierarchical one influencing the interactions among many players. We can see there are vertical interactions mixed with horizontal ones, and more delicate interplays taking place at every sub-level. Vertically, the topography of this "terrain of struggle" is characterised by the hegemonic side maintaining the superior position and dominating the academia as the source of legitimate knowledge, with Western media holding the power of discourse; on the other hand, the Chinese government hierarchy is also exerting top-down influence over CI's home institutions and the Chinese media; whilst horizontally, there are cultural encounters across different types of cultural boundaries, and constant interactions both between the two partner institutions, and between the CIs and their target audiences in the host destinations.

This perspective has allowed us to gain a three-dimensional view over the massive amount of data collected. While China's growing economic power challenges the US economic domination, the American power of discourse also challenges China's political values. Communism appeared to be the lens China was envisioned, which has further resulted in China being imagined as the opposing force in the "terrain of struggle", and anti-Communism lies at the very heart of many of the speculations and criticisms of the CI, becoming the biggest stumbling block for its setbacks in some Western countries. As the strategic planner and sponsor of China's cultural diplomacy, the government's counter-hegemonic stance was plain to see, which shows that a stronger China today is ready to become more defiant in the fighting against Western hegemony. However, as Castells has argued, power is derived from networks. It is constituted by a "specific configuration of global, national and local networks in a multidimensional space of social interaction" (2009: 19). Therefore, in this terrain, "the state becomes just one node (however important) of a particular network" (Castells, 2009: 19). Any national government, no matter how powerful, has but limited power over how information is received, as their voices will be in competition and interaction with the others in this terrain. Promoting cultural pluralism and constructing a harmonious world is the rhetorical goal of China's cultural diplomacy set by the highest level of Chinese government, but it does not seem to lend enough power to the ongoing battle of 'isms' taking place in the current contested terrain, the drive to this claimed goal was disrupted in the conflict-ridden interactions among players from different sides at various levels that reflect social, economic, political and cultural encounters on a global scale.

According to the British political think-tank Demos, "cultural exchange gives us the chance to appreciate points of commonality and, where there are differences, to understand the motivations and humanity that underlie them" (cited in ICD, 2014: 10). I argue that mutual understanding can only be fostered through open-minded communications between the cultures involved and respect of respective values. This contested terrain shows a struggle between Eurocentric cultural hegemony versus a Sinocentric counter-hegemony, with some rigid Hanban practice even showing signs of running against the defined goal of its cultural diplomacy. I believe a global cultural terrain should be viewed in a flat and de-centred way. This may be the first step to achieving the ultimate goal of cultural diplomacy.

The next chapter will continue to employ the lens of "terrain of struggle" to reveal the hidden barriers existing in this terrain by engaging in analytical comparisons between the CI and its Western counterparts. Once these barriers are exposed, they would shed light on understanding the most fundamental differences in the terrain conditions between the two. It will also look at what factors in the terrain would drive some of the CI partnerships to an end.

Notes

1 They include the General Office of the State Council, the Ministry of Education, the Ministry of Finance, the Ministry of Foreign Affairs, the Ministry of Commerce, the Ministry of Culture, the State Administration of Radio, Film and Television, the State Press and Publications Administration, the State Council Information Office, the State Language Committee, the Overseas Chinese Affairs Office of the State Council and the State Development and Reform Commission.
2 See 2014 Special Issue of the Confucius Institute, pp. 12–15. Full speeches are available at: www.cim.chinesecio.com/hbcms/f/journal/journalDetail?id=8456d5e4155447 bba65a2063798b3216.
3 John Garnaut, China's Criticism of Uni Report Angers Academics. *Sydney Morning Herald*, 4 January 2013, available at: www.smh.com.au/national/chinas-criticism-of-uni-report-angers-academics-20130103-2c794.html.
4 The Debate Over Confucius Institutes, A China File Conversation, China File, 2014. available at: www.chinafile.com/conversation/debate-over-confucius-institutes.
5 Cecily Liu, China to up investment in Confucius Institutes, *China Daily*, 8 June 2012, available at: www.chinadaily.com.cn/world/2012-06/08/content_15484207.htm.
6 See Benner *et al.*, Authoritarian Advance: Responding to China's Growing Political Influence in Europe. Global Public Policy Institution, February 2018, available at: www.gppi.net/media/Benner_MERICS_2018_Authoritarian_Advance.pdf.

120 *The global cultural terrain of struggle*

7 WKU ends agreement with Confucius Institute, West Kentucky University, Bowling Green, KY, 22 April 2019, available at: www.wku.edu/news/articles/index.php?view=article&articleid=7622.

8 Ibid.

9 Xinhua, Xi stresses sound environment for public opinion, *China Daily*, 7 November 2016, available at: www.chinadailyasia.com/nation/2016-11/07/content_15522513.html.

10 Reporters Without Borders, 2018 World Press Freedom Index, available at: https://rsf.org/en/ranking.

11 Shobhan Saxena, How to be a Cultural Superpower, *Times of India*, 22 November 2009, available at: http://timesofindia.indiatimes.com/home/sunday-times/deep-focus/How-to-be-a-cultural-superpower/articleshow/5256363.cms?.

12 See Why is Washington so Scared of Confucius, *Global Times*, 25 May 2012, available at: http://english.peopledaily.com.cn/203691/7826665.html.

13 Q. Liu, 美国为何忌惮孔子学院? *Meiguo weihe jidan Kongzi Xueyuan?* [Why is the USA so Scared of the Confucius Institutes?]. *Financial Times*, 2019, available at: www.ftchinese.com/story/001081989?full=y.

14 See 美媒炒作在华美国文化中心被关闭，但事实又一次并非如此 *Meimei chaozuo zai hua Meiguo wenhua zhongxin bei guanbi, dan shishi youyici bingfei ruci* [American Media Sensationalise the American Culture Centres in China "Being Shut Down", But Again, Not True]. *Global Times*, 2019, available at: https://new.qq.com/omn/20190103/20190103A05ID0.html.

15 See People.com.cn, available at: http://culture.people.com.cn/GB/87423/8522972.html.

16 Available at: http://paper.people.com.cn/rmrbhwb/html/2009-11/26/content_391531.htm.

17 Xinhuanet: Confucius Institute, China's Best Export Product, Won the Chinese Award 24 March 2010, available at: http://phtv.ifeng.com/hotspot/huarenshengdian2009/meitibaodao/201003/0324_9773_1585491.shtml.

18 Available at: http://archive.wenming.cn/sjwm/2010-11/09/content_21343489.htm.

19 *China News*, 9 November 2010, available at: www.chinanews.com/cul/2010/11-09/2644020.shtml.

20 17 May 2011, available at: http://news.sohu.com/20110517/n307683133.shtml.

21 See cwzg.cn, available at: www.cwzg.cn/politics/201506/21436.html.

22 Letter of Protest at Interference in EACS Conference in Portugal, July 2014, European Association for Chinese Studies (1 August), available at: http://chinesestudies.eu/?p=585.

23 T. Li, 环球时报：汉办主任在海外"撕书"，不丢人! *Hanbna zhuren zai haiwai sishu, bu diuren!* [There is no Shame in Hanban Tearing up Overseas Conference Programme!], 2014, available at: http://gd.people.com.cn/n/2014/0804/c123932-21876308.html.

24 Wall Street Journal, 'Madam Xu's Party Line: Beijing confirms that Confucius Institutes Subvert Western Academic Freedom', 25 December 2014, available at: www.wsj.com/articles/madam-xus-party-line-1419375797.

25 Keith B. Richburg, China Expels Al-Jazeera Reporter as Media Relations Sour, *Washington Post*, 2012, available at: www.washingtonpost.com/world/asia_pacific/china-expels-al-jazeera-reporter-as-media-relations-sour/2012/05/08/gIQAlip49T_story.html?utm_term=.68c471d57633.

26 J. Watts, Al-Jazeera closes Beijing bureau after reporter expelled. *Guardian*, 8 May 2012, available at: www.theguardian.com/world/2012/may/08/al-jazeera-closes-beijing-bureau.

27 According to Hanban website, www.hanban.org/report/2017.pdf.

28 See Confucius Institute Development Plan, 2012–2020, available at: https://wenku.baidu.com/view/688c6b10a8114431b90dd88e.html.

29 The Confucius Institute Annual Development Report 2014 is available at: www. hanban.org/report/2014.pdf.

References

ABC (Audit Bureau of Circulations) (2015). *Consumer Magazines Combined Total Distribution Certificate, July to December 2014, China Daily European Weekly.* Berkhamsted: Audit Bureau of Circulations.

Anderson, P. (2007). Speaking the East, Framing the East or Shaping the East? *European Studies: An Interdisciplinary Series in European Culture, History and Politics*, 25 (September): 83–102.

Barr, M. (2011). *Who is Afraid of China? The Challenge of Chinese Soft Power.* London: Zed Books.

Bauman, D. (2018). Amid Fear of Foreign Influence, Colleges: Confucius Institutes Face Renewed Scepticism. *The Chronicle of Higher Education*, 28 February. Available at: www.chronicle.com/article/Amid-Fear-of-Foreign/242687.

Benner, T., J. Gaspers, M. Ohlberg, L. Poggetti and K. Shi-Kupfer (2018). *Authoritarian Advance: Responding to China's Growing Political Influence in Europe.* Produced by GPPI and Merics. Available at: www.merics.org/sites/default/files/2018-02/GPPi_MERICS_Authoritarian_Advance_2018_1.pdf.

Carter, D. (2015). Living with Instrumentalism: The Academic Commitment to Cultural Diplomacy. *International Journal of Cultural Policy*, 21(4): 478–493.

Castells, M. (2009). *Communication Power.* Oxford: Oxford University Press.

Chan, G. (1999). *Chinese Perspectives on International Relations: A Framework for Analysis.* London: Macmillan Press.

Chartrand, H.H. and C. McCaughey (1989). The Arm's Length Principle and the Arts: An International Perspective – Past, Present And Future. In M.C. Cummings Jr. and Mark Davidson Schuster (eds), *Who's to Pay For the Arts?: The International Search For Models of Arts Support.* New York: American Council for the Arts.

China File (2014). The Debate Over Confucius Institutes: Part II. Available at: www. chinafile.com/conversation/debate-over-confucius-institutes-part-ii.

CPHRC (2019). China's Confucius Institutes: An Inquiry by the Conservative Party Human Rights Commission. Conservative Party Human Rights Commission Report. Available at: www.conservativehumanrights.com.

Creemers, R. (2015). Never the Twain Shall Meet? Rethinking China's Public Diplomacy Policy. *Chinese Journal of Communication*, 8(3): 306–322.

Deng, Y. (2005). Better Than Power: "International Status" in Chinese Foreign Policy. In Yong Deng and Fei-ling Wang (eds), *China Rising: Power and Motivation in Chinese Foreign Policy* (pp. 51–72). New York: Rowman & Littlefield.

Ding, S. and R.A. Saunders (2006). Talking Up China: An Analysis of China's Rising Cultural Power and Global Promotion of the Chinese Language. *East Asia*, 23(2): 3–33.

Eck, D.L. (2006). What is Pluralism? The Pluralism Project, Harvard University. Available at: http://pluralism.org/what-is-pluralism/.

The Economist (2011). Rectification of Statues, Confucius as Soft Power, but the Message gets Confused at Home. 20 January. Available at: www.economist.com/node/17969895.

Epstein, E. (2018). How China Infiltrated U.S. Classrooms, *Politico Magazine*, 16 January. Available at: www.politico.com/magazine/story/2018/01/16/how-china-infiltrated-us-classrooms-216327.

122 *The global cultural terrain of struggle*

Foucault, M. (1980). *Power/Knowledge.* Brighton: Harvester.

Foucault, M. (1982). Subject and Power. *Critical Inquiry,* 8(4): 777–795.

Fukuyama, F. (1989). The End of History? *The National Interest* (Summer): 3–18.

GAO (2019). China: Agreements Establishing Confucius Institutes at U.S. Universities are Similar, but Institute Operations Vary. Publicly Released: 27 February. Available at: www.gao.gov/assets/700/696859.pdf.

Garnaut, J. (2013). China's Criticism of Uni Report Angers Academics. *Sydney Morning Herald,* 4 January. Available at: www.smh.com.au/national/chinas-criticism-of-uni-report-angers-academics-20130103–2c794.html.

Gramsci, A. (1971). *Selections from the Prison Notebooks of Antonio Gramsci.* Quinton Hoare and Geoffrey N. Smith (eds). New York: International Publications.

Guibernau, M. (1996). *Nationalisms: The Nation-State and Nationalism in the 20th Century.* Cambridge: Polity Press.

Guo, Y. (2017). The Impact of Chinese National Identity on Sino-US Relations. *Joint U.S. Korea Academic Studies,* (August): 146–158.

Guttenplan, D. (2012). Critics Worry About Influence of Chinese Institutes on U.S. Campuses. *New York Times,* 4 March. Available at: www.nytimes.com/2012/03/05/us/critics-worry-about-influence-of-chinese-institutes-on-us-campuses.html.

Hartig, F. (2015). Communicating China to the World: Confucius Institutes and China's Strategic Narratives. *Politics,* 35(3–4): 345–358.

Hartig, F. (2018). China Daily – Beijing's Global Voice? In Daya Kishan Thussu, Hugo de Burgh and Anbin Shi (eds), *China's Media Go Global.* London: Routledge.

Hoover Institution (2018). Chinese Influence and American Interests, Promoting Constructive Vigilance: Report of the Working Group on Chinese Influence Activities in the US. Available at: www.hoover.org/sites/default/files/research/docs/chinese influence_Americaninterests_fullreport_web.pdf.

Howarth, C. (2011). Representations, Identity And Resistance in Communication. In Derek Hook, Bradley Franks, and Martin W. Bauer (eds), *The Social Psychology of Communication* (pp. 153–168). London: Palgrave Macmillan.

Hubbert, J. (2019). China in the World: An Anthropology of Confucius Institutes, Soft Power and Globalization. Honolulu, HI: University of Hawaii Press.

Hughes, C.R. (2014). Confucius Institutes and the University: Distinguishing the Political Mission from the Cultural. *Issues & Studies,* 50(4): 45–83.

Huntington, S.P. (1998). The Clash of Civilizations and the Remaking of World Order. London: Touchstone.

ICD (Institute for Cultural Diplomacy) (2014). Available at: www.scribd.com/document/25418458/Institute-for-Cultural-Diplomacy

Jacobs, A. and J.M. Yu (2014). Another U.S. University Severs Ties to Confucius Institute. *Sinosphere: New York Times,* 2 October. Available at: http://sinosphere.blogs.nytimes.com/2014/10/02/penn-state-severs-ties-to-confucius-institute/.

Lam, W. (2009). Chinese State Media Goes Global: A Great Leap Outward for Chinese Soft Power?' *China Brief,* 9(2), 22 January. Available at: www.jamestown.org/single/?tx_ttnews%5Btt_news%5D=34387&no_cache=1#.VZvXm_lViko.

Levenson, J. (1968). *Confucian China and its Modern Fate, A Trilogy.* Berkeley, CA: University of California Press.

McCord, E. (2014). Confucius Institutes: Hardly a Threat to Academic Freedoms. *Diplomat,* 27 March. Available at: http://thediplomat.com/2014/03/confucius-institutes-hardly-a-threat-to-academic-freedoms/.

Melissen, J. (2005). The New Public Diplomacy: Between Theory and Practice. In J.

The global cultural terrain of struggle   123

Melissen (ed.), *The New Public Diplomacy: Soft Power in International Relations* (pp. 3–27). New York: Palgrave Macmillan.

Messner, M. (1988). Sports and Male Domination: The Female Athlete as Contested Ideological Terrain. *Sociology of Sport Journal*, 5: 197–211.

Mosher, S.W. (2012). Confucius Institutes: Trojan Horses with Chinese Characteristics. Testimony Presented to the Subcommittee on Oversight and Investigations House Committee on Foreign Affairs presented 28 March, at 2.30 pm. Available at: http://pop.org/content/confucius-institutes-trojan-horses-chinese-characteristics.y.

Nakagawa, U. (2011). Confucius Controversy. *Diplomat*, 7 March. Available at: http://thediplomat.com/new-emissary/2011/03/07/confucius-controversy/.

Osgood, K. and B.C. Etheridge (eds) (2010). *The United States and Public Diplomacy, New Directions in Cultural and International History.* Leiden: Martinus Nijhoff Publishers.

Parton, C. (2019). China–UK Relations Where to Draw the Border Between Influence and Interference? *RUSI Occasional Paper*, February, Royal United Services Institute for Defence and Security Studies. Available at: https://rusi.org/sites/default/files/20190220_chinese_interference_parton_web.pdf.

Perlez, J. and L. Ding (2018). China Thwarts U.S. Effort to Promote American Culture on Campuses. *New York Times*, 30 December. Available at: www.nytimes.com/2018/12/30/world/asia/china-American-centers-culture.html; a Chinese version is available at: https://cn.nytimes.com/china/20190103/china-American-centers-culture/.

Peterson, R. (2017). Outsourced to China, Confucius Institutes and Soft Power in American Higher Education, A Report by the National Association of Scholars. Available at: www.nas.org/images/documents/confucius_institutes/NAS_confuciusInstitutes.pdf.

Peterson, R. (2018). Opposing Communist Chinese Spies Isn't Racist. *National Association of Scholars*, 4 December. Available at: www.nas.org/articles/opposing_communist_chinese_spies_isnt_racist.

PRI Staff (2012). *Confucius Institutes: Trojan Horses with Chinese Characteristics. Testimony Presented to the Subcommittee on Oversight and Investigations House Committee on Foreign Affairs* 28 March. Available at: www.pop.org/confucius-institutes-trojan-horses-with-chinese-characteristics/.

Qian, W. (2002). *Zhengzhi, shichang he dianshi zhidu, guanyu Zhongguo dianshi zhidu de yanjiu* [*Politics, Market and the Television System – Study on Changes in China's Television System*]. Henan: Henan People's Press.

Rawnsley, G. (2012). Approaches to Soft Power and Public Diplomacy in China and Taiwan. *Journal of International Communication*, 18(2): 121–135.

Redden, E. (2012). Confucius Says … *Inside Higher ED*, 4 January. Available at www.insidehighered.com/news/2012/01/04/debate-over-Chinese-funded-institutes-American-universities.

Redden, E. (2014). Confucius Controversies. *Inside Higher Ed*, 24 July. Available at: www.insidehighered.com/news/2014/07/24/debate-renews-over-confucius-institutes.

Sahlins, M. (2013). China U. *The Nation.* Available at: www.thenation.com/article/china-u/.

Sahlins, M. (2015). *Confucius Institute: Academic Malware.* Chicago, IL: Prickly Paradigm Press.

Said, E. (1978). *Orientalism.* London: Penguin Books.

Said, E. (1993). *Culture and Imperialism.* New York: Random House.

Schmidt, P. (2010). At U.S. Colleges, Chinese-Financed Centers Promote Worries About Academic Freedom. *Chronicle of Higher Education*, 57: A8–A10.

124 *The global cultural terrain of struggle*

Scotton, J. (2015). Confucius Institute and China's "Soft Power". Available at: https://blogs.nottingham.ac.uk/chinapolicyinstitute/2015/07/01/confucius-institutes-and-chinas-soft-power/.

Seiichi, K. (2008). Wielding Soft Power. In Yasushi Watanabe and David McConnell (eds), *Soft Power Superpowers: Cultural and National Assets of Japan and the United States* (pp. 191–206). New York: M.E. Sharpe.

Shepherd, J. (2007). Not A Propaganda Tool. *Guardian*, 6 November. Available at: www.theguardian.com/education/2007/nov/06/highereducation.internationaleducationnews.

Sudworth, J. (2014). Confucius Institute: The Hard Side of China's Soft Power. BBC News, 22 December. Available at: www.bbc.co.uk/news/world-asia-china-30567743.

Tomaselli, K.G (1987). A Contested Terrain: Struggle Through Culture. *Communicatio*, 13(2): 54–66.

USCC (2008). Report To Congress of the U.S.–China Economic and Security Review Commission. Available at: www.uscc.gov/sites/default/files/annual_reports/2008-Report-to-Congress-_0.pdf.

Wang, H. (2005). National Image Building and Chinese Foreign Policy. In Yong Deng and Fei-ling Wang (eds), *China Rising: Power and Motivation in Chinese Foreign Policy*. New York: Rowman & Littlefield.

Wang, Y. (2014). 文化的困境在于不知不觉，– 独家对话国家汉办主任、孔子学院总干事许琳 [An Exclusive Interview with Xu Lin, Director of Hanban]. Available at http://newspaper.jfdaily.com/jfrb/html/2014-09/19/content_17605.htm.

Watkins, T. (2015). Useless Fuss Over Confucius Institutes. *China Daily*, 13 January. Available at: http://usa.chinadaily.com.cn/opinion/2015-01/13/content_19303807.htm.

Williams, R. (1982). *The Sociology of Culture*. New York: Schocken Books.

Wong, E. (2016). Xi Jinping's News Alert: Chinese Media Must Serve the Party. *New York Times*, 22 February. Available at: www.nytimes.com/2016/02/23/world/asia/china-media-policy-xi-jinping.html?_r=0.

Yang, A.H. and M. Hsiao (2012). Confucius Institutes as Trojan Horses for Chinese Hegemony. *Asia News*, 18 July. Available at: www.asianews.it/news-en/Confucius-institutes-as-Trojan-horses-for-Chinese-hegemony-25322.html.

Zhao, K. (2015). The Motivation Behind China's Public Diplomacy. *The Chinese Journal of International Politics*, 8(2): 1–30. Available at: www.researchgate.net/publication/276111714_The_Motivation_Behind_China's_Public_Diplomacy.

Zhao, Q. (2007). Better Public Diplomacy to Present a Truer Picture of China. *People's Daily*, 30 March. Available at: http://en.people.cn/200703/30/eng20070330_362496.html.

Zheng, Q. (2015). Crisis Management, Tourism and the Three Gorges Dam, China. Available at: http://clok.uclan.ac.uk/11808/1/Zheng%20Qiying%20Final%20e-Thesis%20(Master%20Copy).pdf.

4 So similar, so different, so Chinese

Analytical comparisons of the Confucius Institute with its Western counterparts[1]

> If something looks very similar, take a second look; If something looks very different, take a third look: at A, at B, then at A and B.
>
> (Xin Liu)

As discussed in Chapter 1, a clear difference in purpose can be seen from the definitions of cultural diplomacy and public diplomacy, with the former aims at "fostering mutual understanding" (Cummings, 2009: 1) and the latter intends "to advance the interests and extend the values of those being represented" according to Paul Sharp (cited in Melissen, 2005: 11), however, the Chinese attempt at using the Confucius Institute (CI) as a vehicle of cultural diplomacy, or simply as a language institute, is often interpreted as a tool for public diplomacy. This mismatch between its own intentions and the perceived goals seems to be unique to the CI compared with its Western counterparts. Although the CI is neither comparable in history with the Alliance Française, which has operated for over 130 years and has more than 800 establishments;[2] nor in impact with the British Council, which administers three million IELTS (International English Language Testing System) tests every year, whose results are accepted by more than 10,000 organisations globally,[3] comparisons are frequently made between the CI and these organisations in both the media and academic literature. This chapter, however, tries to show how a different picture can be revealed by adopting the lens of a global "cultural terrain of struggle" and the alternative analytical framework introduced in Chapter 1. It also goes a step further in revealing the 'differences in similarities' and 'similarities in differences', as well as the reasons behind them. It presents the comparisons in three layers of *why*, *how* and *what*: the purposes, operating models and scope of activities of these organisations.

Purposes

Similar yet different: a mixture of pride and prejudice

If we look at the British Council, Alliance Française, Goethe-Institut and the Instituto Cervantes, it is not hard to see that all these countries engaged in

126 *So similar, so different, so Chinese*

cultural diplomacy are trying to achieve a similar goal, namely, to improve their international status and the position of their cultures in the global multicultural spectrum through the promotion of their languages. For example, at the founding of the British Council in 1934, the Prince of Wales clarified that:

> We are aiming at something more profound than just a smattering of our tongue. Our object is to assist the largest number possible to appreciate fully the glories of our literature, our contribution to the arts and sciences, and our pre-eminent contribution to the political practice. This can best be achieved by promoting the study of our language abroad.
>
> (Cited in Pennycook, 2013: 147)

Similarly, the Goethe-Institut, Alliance Française and Instituto Cervantes have all suggested that learning the language is only a means to the end of appreciating cultural diversity. China with its CI is no exception here: "As China's economy and exchanges with the world have seen rapid growth, there has also been a sharp increase in the world's demands for Chinese learning".[4]

> Confucius Institutes devote themselves to satisfying the demands of people from different countries and regions in the world who learn the Chinese language, to enhancing understanding of the Chinese language and culture by these peoples, to strengthening educational and cultural exchange and cooperation between China and other countries, to deepening friendly relationships with other nations, to promoting the development of multiculturalism, and to construct a harmonious world.[5]

However, a delicate difference in wording is worth noting in that the British Councils' website says: "the British Council aims to bring high-quality English courses and materials to every learner or teacher who wants them around the world".[6] The word "want" actually reveals its superior position in the cultural terrain: "demand" could be driven by practical needs, while "want" is driven by voluntary desire. Other non-English-speaking countries such as France, Germany and Spain all refer to the goals as "(to) promote" their languages and "spread" the culture, but the Confucius Institute Constitution (quoted above) carefully refers to offering the service to "satisfy demands" and "enhance understanding". These deliberations reveal at least two differences in the purposes of these organisations:

1   To "satisfy demands": instead of actively "promoting" its language or "spreading" its culture, the CI put itself in the position of "responding" to the growing demand for learning the Chinese language brought by "the unprecedented China fever" and "Chinese language fever" that was encouraged by the economic rise of China (Hanban website);

2   To "enhance understanding": this indicates there is insufficient understanding of the Chinese language and culture at present, or rather, even

So similar, so different, so Chinese 127

some distorted understandings as argued by the then Chinese Foreign Minister Yang (2011) and scholars like Zhu (2012), setting a different priority for the CI in comparison to its Western counterparts.

These differences show a mixture of "pride and prejudice": in the domestic context, there is a dose of national "pride" when China gains strength again, for almost the very first time in its modern history, a sense of cultural pride ascends. The "rapid growth" of the economy and the "sharp increase" in the demand for learning Chinese not only justifies what the CIs are trying to do, but signifies the growing influence of China, which is articulated and communicated through the new leadership vision of the China Dream of national rejuvenation to domestic audiences. When the rising China today needs a symbol to fill the ideological void and unify the nation, Confucianism brings state nationalism, popular nationalism and cultural nationalism together and provides the basis for the idea of building a "harmonious world", which is written into the mission statement of the CI. While constructing domestic legitimacy, it is a proud task to be called on to "satisfy the demands" for learning Chinese language and understanding Chinese culture.

In the international context, however, there is a need to counter the existing "prejudice", or misconceptions that discursively defined China outside its borders. This was pointed out by its Director, when the State Council Information Office was first established in 1991:

> Some (foreign countries) have prejudices or have wrongly believed rumours, therefore what they think about China is not the true image of China. We will try every means to present a comprehensive and real picture of China to the outside world so that you can see the true image of China.
>
> (cited in Wang, 2005: 73)

To "enhance understanding" is therefore the other task set for the CI with the hope of also constructing global legitimacy. As one scholar noted, "the founding of the CI is, by and large, an image management project ... to promote the greatness of Chinese culture while counterattacking public opinion that maintains the China threat" (Guo, 2008: n.p.). However, using Confucius as the brand image may not be a sound approach to counter prejudice in a world where "national identity is marketed for political spin" (Louie, 2011: 99), so the name itself has become an embodiment of a mixed interpretation of "pride and prejudice". From the Chinese perspective, choosing Confucius as the namesake is an indicator for the revival of traditional Chinese culture, the idea of building a "harmonious world" is essentially a Confucian idea, it proudly reminds the world that China is not so much 'rising', but reasserting its status while reinforcing the peaceful nature of its resurgence. Nakagawa's article (2011) titled "Confucius: What's in a Name?" applauded this name in quoting Starr's two contentions: first, the decision to use the philosopher's name is almost something that unites the Chinese diasporas as well, it is not divisive as a name such as 'China Foundation' may

128 *So similar, so different, so Chinese*

be; and second, Confucius is one of the few global brands the Chinese have. They argue that for many in the West, Confucius is usually associated with learning and general wisdom, so it works with the institute and its purpose in terms of branding. Liu (2017: 237) established a direct link between "the scholarly image of Confucius" and its function to "serve the purpose of dispelling claims and quelling anxieties to the China Threat while promoting the status of China as a friend to the world", echoing Howard French's points made in 2006:

> Among other things, using the name of the country's oldest and most famous philosopher avoids reference to the official ideology, which remains Marxism. Confucius, who was an educator and quasi-religious figure, also stands for peace and harmony, values that China insistently proclaims today, hoping to disarm fears about its rapid rise.
>
> (French, 2006)

This was recognised by Nancy Jervis, vice president of the China Institute, a non-profit Chinese-language study group that became home to a CI in New York City: "They are using Chinese culture to create a warmer, more positive image of Chinese society" (cited in French, 2006: n.p.).

It seems that for these two parts in its mission statement, if what the CI did is just to "meet the demand", that won't cause much controversy, even when it went further to "expand and stimulate the demand" as pointed by BGD1:

> Compared with its Western counterparts, the CI has a more ambitious aim to bring Chinese into the national curriculum system of the host country and a credit-bearing course at the host university. Actually, China has made a gesture of reciprocity of adding French, Spanish and German to the national entrance exam paper of foreign languages in 2019 alongside English, Japanese and Russian.
>
> (BGD1)

However, when the CI tries to accomplish the second aim of "enhancing understanding", it is tied with the complication that Confucius is more than just a cultural icon of wisdom and learning, and Confucian values do not just lie at the core of traditional Chinese culture, they were also given an ideological function in maintaining political order and has had tremendous influence on the statecraft of China throughout history. Besides, the translation of '*Rujia sixiang*' as Confucianism established a narrow link between Confucius himself and the complex system of moral, social, political, philosophical, ethical and quasi-religious thought and value systems that were developed over thousands of years after him; and the multifaceted connotations of Confucianism are often reduced to only represent authoritarian and hierarchical rule in the "political spin". So in a way, the name itself is like a label that implies being the 'cultural other' and 'ideological other'. The inherent constraint that puts many of the Confucian ideas in conflict with modernity tends to be challenged by some Western

So similar, so different, so Chinese   129

scholars, for example, Louie (2011: 78) simply argued that "Confucius as 'brand China' may be an accurate reflection of an ideologically confused country", his views were succinctly summarised in his paper titled "Confucius the Chameleon: Dubious Envoy for 'Brand China' ":

> Domestically, the advocacy of Confucianism will in practice lead to the promotion of very conservative and inconsistent values. Internationally, if such values are to be paraded as the best of "Chinese" essences, China's contribution to world culture will be a confused and regressive one.
>
> (Louie, 2011: 100)

True, throughout China's long history, the vicissitudes Confucianism has experienced could be "confusing" and "inconsistent" to an outsider. It was banned by the first emperor of Qinshihuang who endorsed Legalism as the ideology and ordered many Confucian texts to be burnt. Then during the Han, Tang and Song dynasties, which were widely considered to have been splendid periods of great cultural, intellectual, economic and political achievements, the periods of glory that the China Dream of national rejuvenation aims to restore, Confucianism was established and enshrined as an essential element of the statecraft and education. Conversely, in more recent history when China was the most vulnerable and precarious politically and economically, culture and tradition was blamed by radical reformers as standing obstacles in the way of building a modern China. It is not that long ago when Confucianism and its rigid hierarchical character were treated as the personification of China's 'feudal' traditions that caused China's backwardness during the New Culture Movement in 1912; then denounced by Communist leaders during the 1973 campaign of "down with Confucius" in the Cultural Revolution, when Confucian teachings were censured as "rubbish that should be thrown into the ash heap of history". Today, however, Confucianism survives all the attempts at its destruction, carried out either in the name of democracy (the New Culture Movement) or revolution (the Cultural Revolution), and revives with resurgence in popularity in recent years. So, when the sage is recast as the promoter of peace and harmony, and rebranded as "a symbol of the new China: educated, orderly, harmonious, respectful, unified" (Barr, 2012: 91); when much of China's success is attributed to Confucian thoughts of discipline, hardworking, ethic of mutual obligation, and the value attached to education, it would naturally give rise to the question: how can the same Confucian values holding a society back from modernisation for hundreds of years suddenly propel it onto the path of modernisation over a few decades?

From an insider's point of view, looking through the historical lens allows us to see that when China gains strength again, a sense of cultural pride ascends, making it feel closer to the heyday in history when Confucianism prevails. The leadership wants to replicate the golden age of peace and prosperity, and Confucianism is considered the recipe for centralised order and stability, with no radical reforms encouraged. But one point often overlooked by Western scholars is that the recent revival of Confucianism is actually being promoted more by

130 *So similar, so different, so Chinese*

academics and civil society rather than being government-led. Seeing that Confucianism continues to be entrenched in the Chinese society today, Zaharna (2014) added that the name has conveyed an extra goodwill to symbolise the longevity of the Chinese culture, as well as the longevity envisioned for the initiative. I argue that the resurgence of Confucianism signals both its relevance in the vertical time dimension of today's China rooted in ancient philosophy, and also its worthy place in the horizontal space dimension as a counterbalance to Western values. As Professor Gosset (2013) puts it, the name of the organisation is a reminder that China's modernisation is more about the reinterpretation of the Chinese tradition than a passive Westernisation. However, this was immediately seen as a challenge to Western hegemony by some scholars such as Huntington, who argued that: "East Asia attributes their dramatic economic development not to their import of Western culture but rather to their adherence to their own culture.... The revolt against the West is now legitimated by asserting the superiority of non-Western values" (1998: 93). During my interview, UKD4 lamented that: "our understanding of the name Confucius is purely cultural related, but in the West, it was interpreted as cultural infiltration, and that means brainwashing". We can see the arbitrary equation adopted here between "cultural pride" and "value superiority", and a further speculation that the mission of the CI is to promote Confucian values, thus a potential revolt against Western democratic values and a justification of China's authoritarian rule, resulting in accusing China's attempt at "cultural promotion" as "brainwashing". This is obviously a transmutation that seeks to de-legitimise any alternative perspective by putting on an ideological label, but the Western power of discourse at the knowledge centre has allowed such accusations to be recycled again and again.

The above analysis shows that the CI's purpose was somehow caught between a "cultural pride" internally and a "value prejudice" externally, which helps further explain the question of why, unlike its Western counterparts, the CI's intentions are often questioned with suspicions of ideological infiltration, particularly by some academics and media in Western countries. This question was also asked by a *China Daily* article in 2010: "perhaps no one will call Goethe Institute, Alliance Franchises or Cervantes Institutes propaganda vehicles or tools of cultural invasion. So why all the fuss over China's Confucius Institute, which share the same goals?" (Liu, 2010). Disappointingly, the article did not really answer, or even attempt to answer this question; instead, it just gave its own answer to explain the title: "No Need to Fuss Over Confucius Institute". I argue this question must be answered through both theoretical reflections and empirical investigations to contextualise the operation of the CI so that both the overt and covert differences can be revealed.

The overt and covert differences

Chapter 3 has exposed the biggest hidden difference between the Confucius Institute and its Western counterparts: it is the same competition, but not a level playing field and they occupy completely different positions in this terrain of

So similar, so different, so Chinese   131

struggle dominated by Western cultural hegemony. When the CI emerged as a new force in the terrain, it was recognised as a challenge that needs to be resisted, and some Western countries simply used their power to determine what *they* think the CI's goal is by highlighting the ideological connotations in the concept of culture, and further, use the power of discourse to turn their voices into 'knowledge' and disseminate such 'knowledge' to justify the type of resistance they want to generate. Foucault (1980) has argued that knowledge impregnated in power is no longer an objective reflection of truth, but is presented and accepted as truth with power in practice. China's cultural diplomacy aims to achieve a dialogue between cultural contestants: it does not seek to negate the hegemonic culture, nor to replace it with a new hegemony as its appeal of cultural pluralism means they do not view this struggle as a zero-sum game. In other words, if China is perceived as a threat, it is an unintentional one, thus trying to use its culture to both gain respect from, and give reassurance to the rest of the world its peaceful nature of the rise, and the harmless nature of the CI. However, some Chinese government rhetoric may even 'lend hilt' to the politicised interpretations, for example, Liu Yunshan, China's Ministry of Propaganda has said in 2010:

> Coordinate the efforts of overseas and domestic propaganda, further create a favourable international environment for us.… With regard to key issues that influence our sovereignty and safety, we should actively carry out international propaganda battles against issues such as Tibet, Xinjiang, Taiwan, Human Rights, and Falun Gong. Our strategy is to proactively take our culture abroad.… We should do well in establishing and operating overseas cultural centres and Confucius Institutes.
>
> (cited in Sahlins, 2015: 6)

Then during my 2014 interview, it was echoed by a Chinese Director, commenting on the differences between the CI and its Western counterparts:

> We have to have a firm stand about the "five poisons" – Tibet, Taiwan, Xinjiang, Falun Gong and democratic movement, there are principles that we must stick to as government-sponsored teachers, this is one of the differences between the CI and Goethe Institute and British Council, we are state-sponsored, so the minimum we should do is not to harm national interest. This is the bottom line.
>
> (UKD4)

Even a seconded teacher talked about "national interest" in the interview:

> After all, I'm sent here by the Chinese government, of course I would not say anything negative about China. I would safeguard China's national interest; this is my personal view anyway as I am very patriotic. To see the country image tarnished is like ruining my own image.
>
> (UKSC5)

132 *So similar, so different, so Chinese*

Such open rhetoric about the CI being state-sponsored and how they would safeguard national interest exacerbates beliefs held by some Western scholars such as Hughes (2014: 54) that the Chinese government is using "culture as a tool for the preservation and promotion of the CCP power", and Mosher claimed that the seemingly benign purpose of the CI leaves out a number of purposes both salient and sinister, namely, "sanitising China's image abroad, enhancing its soft power globally, and creating a new generation of China watchers who are well-disposed towards the Communist dictatorship" (2012: n.p.). But what is "sinister" is actually the wording that describes China as a "dictatorship" that attempts to "sanitise" its image, not the purpose itself, as shaping preferences in attitudes towards a particular country is actually named as the very goal of public diplomacy by its founding father Gullion (Melissen, 2005); and Paschalidis simply pointed that: "the culture projected abroad has always been a sanitised culture, that excludes all the embarrassing or controversial elements.… The moment of a nation's cultural projection is that of its most polished, sublimated, and hence, artificial representation" (2009: 287).

Besides, the political dimension in cultural diplomacy is not a unique "Chinese characteristic" either. As a matter of fact, as Belanger argued, "cultural diplomacy has never been apolitical, even if in general, and quite naturally, it claims to be so" (1999: 678). Taylor puts it more blatantly: "Cultural diplomacy is very much a political activity designed to serve national interests in an ostensibly cultural guise" (1997: 80). Mulcahy also argued that: "public diplomacy initiatives can never be completely separated from creating a favourable impression of a country's policies and way of life, there is inevitably a tendency to engage in international lobbying" (2017: 35). This shows the political undertone exists in all countries' cultural diplomacy, only to different extents and in different forms: while lobbying is a synonym for persuasion that makes the political purpose look more innocent under the cultural guise, the Chinese way of explicit propaganda makes the purpose easily unveiled and seen as a special attribute, to the effect that what 'we' do is called cultural diplomacy, what 'they' do is making political inroads. Therefore, UKD3 commented that: "Chinese intention is not sinister in itself, it is only read as sinister because Chinese is seen as the 'other', and therefore different motivations".

As observed by Paschalidis, "the world map of Cultural Institutes at the beginning of the twenty-first century continues to bear a disturbing resemblance to the imperial system of the early twentieth century" (2009: 287). Now that this map is being shifted by the rapid expansion of the CIs, triggering fear, worries and resistance. Most criticisms so far have focused on the fact that it operates within established universities, institutions and schools around the world, with Hanban providing funding, teachers and educational materials. Despite Hanban's repeated clarification that the CI's mission is language teaching rather than values-promotion as specified in its Constitution, by-laws and partnership agreements, this model has raised concerns over finances, academic freedom, legal and ethical issues, as well as ideological concerns about improper influence over teaching and research (Chey, 2008; Golden, 2011; Guttenplan, 2012; Hubbert, 2014; Hughes, 2014; Sahlins, 2015).

So similar, so different, so Chinese   133

Therefore, despite the similar missions of these organisations, the actual journey and 'road conditions' of getting there are very different that makes the uphill struggle of the CI more arduous. As Paschalidis has observed, the once dominant bilateral model of cultural relations is "characterised by asymmetric, uni-directional flows" (2009: 284). For Western organisations who share the same political values, their mission is simply language and cultural promotion that is not conflict-ridden, and the hegemonic position they occupy helps to shape this process into a natural flow from high to low, while for the CI, its similar intention was interpreted as challenging the current culture hegemony by spreading China's own ideologies, thus induce resistance from the hegemonic side who already occupies the vantage points. However, these fundamental differences that put the CI in an extremely disadvantaged position in the terrain were hidden barriers that are rarely mentioned in the Western media or academic literature, instead, they tend to seize upon other differences at a more visible level, namely the CI's operating model and government background. The next section takes a closer look at these overt differences.

Operating models

What is the CI model?

As a 'latecomer', the CI does not hide its intention to learn from the successes of its 'forerunners', as is made clear on its official website:

> Benefiting from the UK, France, Germany and Spain's experience in promoting their national languages, China began its own exploration through establishing non-profit public institutions with an aim to promote Chinese language and culture in foreign countries in 2004: these were given the name of Confucius Institute.[7]

Therefore, it is a ready acknowledgement that the CI tries to follow in the footsteps of the UK's British Council, France's Alliance Française, Germany's Goethe-Institut and Spain's Instituto Cervantes, but it does not mean that it will copy their models. According to DPEC who participated in the initial discussions of setting up CIs, Hanban has studied carefully the operation models of all the above-mentioned organisations, and came up with its own model design. The biggest difference is that the CI is not an institute set up by China – not by Chinese government or Chinese universities; but set up by the local university in the host country as an international collaboration programme. Therefore, its legal status is a local organisation with the host university as the sole legal representative. The procedure begins with an application proposal from a foreign organisation (usually a university), which must demonstrate a strong demand for Chinese language instruction in the university/local community; and second, the willingness of the applicant to contribute (both fiscally and physically) to the establishment and the growth of the CI. While Starr (2009) has summarised this model

134 *So similar, so different, so Chinese*

merit as sharing establishment and operation costs and the prestige derived from association with host universities, this fact is often used by Hanban as the strongest counter-argument for the Chinese infiltration theory: the CIs are invited by their host universities overseas, not imposed on. Although they wouldn't mention that the overture was often made by the Chinese side in the early years, particularly to approach prestigious universities, such as Stanford and Columbia Universities in the USA. Similarly, at home, Hanban would also approach and urge some prestigious universities to go out and set up CIs as disclosed by UKD4 and BGD1: "In a way, we were entrusted with such a task by the Ministry of Education and are obliged to carry it out as a way of supporting the Ministry's work". But as Kahn-Ackermann (2014) has clearly pointed, the CI is not an overseas arm of a Chinese organisation but a local organisation at the host institution, this is "a basic fact" that distinguishes it from the Goethe-Institut. A very insightful correction of a common misrepresentation was made by BGD2: "It is therefore inaccurate to say how many CIs have been established by the Chinese government all over the world, rather, it is how many overseas universities have accepted Hanban funding in setting up CIs on their campuses."

It is fair to say that this process is based on consent, like the marriage metaphor used earlier: the partnership is out of mutual agreement, but the matrimonial home will be based on overseas campus. Once the application is approved, both institutions receive financial benefits: every Chinese home university receives 200,000 RMB (about US\$30,000) from Hanban as the supporting matching funds for each CI that it sets up, and the overseas host university also receives generous funding from Hanban, including start-up funds of between US\$100,000–150,000, and an average annual operational fund of US\$50,000 (Xu, 2011). Some prestigious universities such as the Chicago University received a US\$200,000 start-up fund, (Sahlins, 2013) and Penn State University was even awarded US\$1 million grant according to its website.[8]

Although the host university is nominally requested to match funding, it is generally provided in kind with little in the way of out-of-pocket expenses. As a result, some question if the CI can represent a soft-power strategy. According to Nye's definition, soft power is the ability to attract and co-opt, contrasted with "hard power", which is the use of coercion and payment (Nye, 2004). This model may not rely on coercion, but it does rely on payments, which "may be attractive for financially stretched educational authorities facing a growing demand for Chinese language instruction" (Hughes, 2014: 69). Although meeting such "growing demand" is the CI's remit, the controversies come from its means to meet the demand. For example, the CI's model has raised scepticism and concerns with strings attached. The "'strings' associated with accepting money may be fairly loose" (Paradise, 2009: 662), but there are still worries that those who pay the piper may call the tune. The common list of censored topics includes the "three Ts" (Tibet, Taiwan and Tiananmen), human rights, China's military build-up and factional fights inside the Chinese leadership (Chey, 2008; Golden, 2011; Mosher, 2012; Sahlins, 2015). In other words, it is the government's role as sponsor and censor that lie at the core of such worries.

So similar, so different, so Chinese   135

Chinese rationale behind the CI model

As explained above, the CI model is an innovation after studying its Western counterparts. In the CPHRC Report on the CI published in 2019, Dr Terence Russell of the University of Manitoba was quoted to say "many nations seek to promote their native cultures and political agendas abroad. However, only the Chinese government has targeted universities as the preferred location for their influence project".[9] As a strategy of "creating alternative institutions and alternative intellectual resources within existing society" (Cox, 1983: 165), this deliberate move using university as nodes is a modern-day annotation of Gramsci's term of "war of position", expanding its scope of analysis from domestic politics to international relations. From China's point of view, its rationale can be found in the following three points.

First, the significance of establishing CIs in overseas universities can be revealed in the de facto existence of China as no longer the external 'other', but part of a living matrix of 'us'. This is a vitally important move following the knowledge–power nexus given that:

> new knowledge is not an evolutionary improvement on what precedes it; rather, new knowledges enter adversarial relationships with older, more established ones, challenging their position in the power play of understandings, and in such confrontations new insights can be provoked.
> (Fiske, 1989, cited in Kramsch, 1993: 238)

And just like Gramsci has pointed out,

> knowledge is not an established body of data and ideas possessed by a culturally superior entity; rather, knowledge is itself the product of the "conversation" between teacher and student, and 'truth' is understood as the inter-subjective' product of the interaction.
> (cited in Fontana, 1993: 151)

By being there and telling its own stories, and influencing students with people-to-people contacts, the Confucius Institute is able to play its subtle role in generating new knowledge.

This was endorsed by Hubbert's ethnographic research findings that "the more personal contacts students had with CI teachers, the less China appeared the epitome of an authoritarian state" (2014: 348). Also, since the majority of the educated people in the host countries do not read Chinese, their understanding of China mainly relies on second-hand information in English, which tends to be infiltrated with Western hegemonic perspectives and Orientalist representations. Actually, it is not rare for programmes of China Studies offered in Western countries to be taught in English and by academics or sinologists who cannot speak or read the Chinese language. With this in mind, I think the contribution the CI can make to is to start tipping the balance by letting as many Westerners

136 *So similar, so different, so Chinese*

understand China in Chinese language as the educated Chinese population can speak and read in English. Only when this change occurs can we begin to lay a foundation for a possible equal dialogue and a more balanced mutual understanding, the identified purpose of cultural diplomacy.

Second, using universities as a vanguard would give cultural diplomacy a non-official face. Universities can be driven by their own motivations to pursue exchanges and cooperation, and thus play the roles of autonomous 'diplomats' to aim for win–win partnerships. The benefits for the CI were enormous as explained by Hughes:

> When universities allow the activities of CIs to appear on their websites and to use their logos, they provide them with a degree of legitimacy in the eyes of students and the public who expect such brands to guarantee high standard of academic integrity.
>
> (Hughes, 2014: 71)

This was supported by comments of UKD2: "Hanban is very smart in creating this model, it utilises the good platform provided by British universities to build creditability and trustworthiness. It also helps with long term development". UKLH2 echoed the point: "It gives public more faith in your product, to see it based on a university"; the point was also supported by the example given by UKSC2:

> It helps with identity building and recognition, for example, when we run an event and CI's brand is new to the local community, the university logo which also appears on the banner or stand would help establish trust and status.

Third, according to the three layers of public diplomacy suggested by Cowan and Arsenault, the CI model is actually leading the move from "monologue" to "dialogue", then further to "collaboration", which was defined as "initiatives that feature cross-national participation in a joint venture or project with a clearly defined goal" (2008: 10). It is a much more effective model because "nothing creates a sense of trust and mutual respect as fully as a meaningful collaboration". When working together, participants can learn from each other, respect each other by not viewing difference as a barrier but a source of synergy that can form more lasting relationships, and generate knowledge and insight that neither had before. The CI model was also used by Zaharna (2014: 9) to exemplify a "network collaborative approach", with "relational structures and relational dynamics" as its pivotal features. It can help "extend the reach and sustainability of the communication" by "transforming the target audience into stakeholders". This "stakeholder perspective is reinforced through co-created narratives and shared identity as well as shared ownership of the initiative" (Zaharna, 2014: 32).

The rationale seems to make sense in theory, and according to my interview findings, the model appeared to be working in practice as well. A long list of

So similar, so different, so Chinese   137

advantages were mentioned for this model, for example, both the MOD and MXD mentioned the "the speed and scope the CI has managed to achieve so far, it is very efficient". Both BGD1 and BGD2 also recognised the efficiency of the CI model in comparison with that of the CCC, which only allows one to be set up in each country. What is more important than efficiency is the sustainability built through transforming the host university into stakeholders, which also include local community as illustrated by UKD3 with an example:

> It requires the local community to make a positive commitment, a partnership with a university or local school gives you a partner who has already made that first step, they are more likely to act as the bridge.... If we were based in city centre, we could encourage local universities to offer a Chinese degree course, but why would they want to listen to us? I doubt it would have any influence on our curriculum at all. I cannot believe they would have been able to persuade the Pro Vice Chancellor and colleagues to include Chinese as part of our degree to improve student experience, and build Chinese studies into the research, while because CI is part of the university, we now have achieved this.
>
> (UKD3)

The merit of "learning from each other" argued by Cowan and Arsenault's (2008) was also endorsed by SKD4: "Having a host university means more solid support, it facilitates mutual learning and cooperation between Chinese and overseas universities". Perhaps the most hidden but potentially biggest benefit for China from this model was revealed by UKD1:

> Hanban can assemble hundreds of university presidents/vice chancellors from all over the world to Beijing every year to listen to them, if the effects are not to 'brain wash' them, at least to tame them not to "sing an opposite tune".
>
> (UKD1)

Also, in attendance in this annual conference are a wide spectrum of "honourable delegates", from academia to media, from officials to business, and senior advisors/consultants of various cultural organisations including the British Council, Goethe-Institut and Instituto Cervantes. It has created a multilevel face-to-face engagement across sectors, leveraging the knowledge and power equation. Therefore, both theory and practice seem to suggest that this model is a smart strategy in the "war of position".

However, everything changes colour through the tinted glasses of ideology, just like Xi Jinping noted in a speech given to the Australian parliament in 2014: "there are people who find fault with everything China does" (cited in Hartig, 2016: 1). When China was trying to do the same thing, it was perceived differently by the other side in this uneven terrain of struggle. Its potential constraints, both endogenous and exogenous, come to the fore during interactions with the

138 *So similar, so different, so Chinese*

hegemonic side. By endogenous constraints, I mean factors from within the CI structure, while the exogenous constraints are caused by factors outside the structure. The next section looks at these two sets of constraints in order.

Endogenous constraints of the CI's operating model

Compared to Alliance Française's identity as being "a local not-for-profit organisation operating autonomously with no political or religious commitments",[10] the CI does not claim to be independent from the government. In fact, the CI has a double identity, as pointed out by Kahn-Ackermann (2014), the first Director of the Goethe-Institut in Beijing and currently advisor to Hanban. Its headquarters Hanban is a government organisation, while the CI exists as a local organisation overseas as part of a host university. This double identity corresponds to both the first and third forms of cultural diplomacy prescribed by the Institute of Cultural Diplomacy (cited in Pan, 2013: 24):

1   state-sponsored cultural diplomacy, which is often used by governments for distinct political purposes;
2   independent or semi-independent cultural diplomacy institutions, such as the British Council and the Goethe-Institut, which take an informative and exchange-based approach to the promotion of national culture; and
3   potential cultural diplomacy channelled by academic institutions or individual artists, academics or professionals involved in academic exchanges and cooperation.

These two irreconcilable identities could produce a clash of missions according to Hughes:

> There is a big difference between organising a conference with a Chinese university or working with academic colleagues from China on the one hand, and allowing an institution that has the mission of promoting the values and interests of the CCP to have a long-term base on campus and to share in the prestige of the university by having a page on its website and use of its logo, on the other.
>
> (Hughes, 2014: 57)

The most sensational way to describe this double identity is a "Trojan horse" (Mosher, 2012). The Hanban Director, Xu Lin, directly refuted this accusation, saying that "CIs are definitely not Trojan Horses, since we are holding no weapons in our hands" (cited in Qu, Zhao and Cheng, 2012), but according to Mosher, this difference is so vital that it invalidates the whole comparison of the CI to its Western counterparts:

> Unlike Alliance Française, the Confucius Institutes are not independent from their government; unlike the Goethe Institute establishments, they do

So similar, so different, so Chinese 139

not occupy their own premises. Instead, participating universities agree to provide office space in exchange for funding, and to cede academic control to the United Front Work Department of the Chinese Communist Party.

(Mosher, 2012: n.p.)

Jocelyn Chey (2008: 42), a former diplomat and expert in Australia–China relations, also disagreed with the view of the CI as a counterpart to the Goethe-Institut or Alliance Française, as the close links between the institute and the Chinese Communist Party "could lead at best to a 'dumbing down' of research and at worst could produce propaganda".

This double identity also led to an inconsistent stance of Hanban about the CI's function in increasing China's soft power: in 2007, Xu Lin proudly claimed that the CI is the "brightest brand for China's soft power", which was made the title line in the Xinhua report;[11] this was addressing CI's mission in the first identity. However by 2010, she emphasised that CIs "are not projecting soft power, nor aim to impose Chinese values or Chinese culture on other countries ... just hopes to be truly understood by the rest of the world" (cited in Yang, 2010: 243), speaking of the CI in its third identity. Meanwhile, an interesting contrast can also be spotted in my own interviews, while all CI directors acknowledged the role of the CI in China's cultural diplomacy back in 2014, interviewees in 2019 simply negate this connection between the CI and any 'diplomatic' activities, regarding serving the national interests as something way beyond their remits. As this double identity is embedded structurally, I think the conflict of mission would always be lurking. For example, on the CI Conference held in 2017, it was called on to be a "key player in the implementing of the Belt and Road Initiative", and making "new contributions to the 'community of common destiny'" (cited in Shimbun, 2018: n.p.). This was interpreted as "the Confucius Institute is expected to serve the initiative through the role of expanding China's influence and ideology internationally at the forefront of this campaign". A survey result showed that the CI held only seven events for the purpose of promoting the BRI in 2015, but by 2017, the number had grown to 37 events (Shimbun, 2018).

CI's double identity could explain why some of the advantages in the Chinese eyes would turn into disadvantages in the critics' eyes, such as the "quick expansion" it facilitates was seen as leading to fears of China as a threat when the word "alarming speed" (Dale, 2014) was used by the Western media. Its location on university campus was commented as an advantage by UKSC2: "It stands at the centre of knowledge dissemination, to have access to students and faculty, it is better targeted as university students are elite groups and backbone of the country". Again, this exact point was perceived as a potential problem that can lead to worries of reduced academic freedom and ideological infiltration as well as procedure issues as the CI teachers are not appointed by the host universities. As pointed out by UKD3: "In universities that uphold academic freedom, this could pose 'potential concerns' or 'occasional cultural frictions'", as "what we're looking at is a conflict between the structure of the large organization of CI on

140   *So similar, so different, so Chinese*

overseas campus and its goals of seeking to achieve and promote a favourable picture of China".

These "potential concerns" that "could" be caused were often turned into judgemental assumptions by those who shut the doors to the CI. What we can see here is an important difference between the discussions of advantages and disadvantages of the CI model: all the advantages were raised by the interviewees with facts of what has happened, while the disadvantages are mostly potential constraints that were supported by little evidence but speculations or worries that things *may* happen if we had a CI. For example, those who raised the teacher concern seem to be unaware that many CIs also use locally hired teachers. According to BGD2, their teaching team is composed of both teachers seconded from China and locally hired teachers and volunteers at Hanban funding, but recruited by the host university as per their own selection criteria and procedures. UKLH3 used herself as an example: "I was locally hired by the host institution as a full-time staff and has never been brainwashed by the Chinese government. I went through a rigorous recruitment process. We also have locally hired office administrators and language instructors". UKLH1 is also locally hired and expressed her frustration that these accusations are not coming from people who have connections with the CI, nor students or the general public, but "professors who refuse to have any dealings with the CI and just believes that the CI's remit is to promote communism".

Interestingly, with regards to the negative aspect of the CI model, although all the 25 interviewees pondered over it during the first two phrases of the research (2013–2014), there was only one answer provided by the MXD, in comparison with the Goethe-Institut:

> CIs could be very uneven in quality, unlike the Goethe Institute that has a standard, the CI is restrained in its ability to follow the Goethe Institute model, both in terms of getting approval to register overseas and in management expertise.

However, in the 2019 rounds of interviews, all the four CI directors have provided their own answers. For example, according to UKD5,

> CI's long-term development is very volatile as it largely depends on individual personal factors. To be honest, many teachers were not entirely clear of what the CI job entails, they applied mainly for the overseas experiences; and for key positions, a change of person could largely affect the performance of the whole CI. For example, a very successful one that was awarded 'CI of the Year' could quickly downgrade to below-average standard following the change of key staff.
>
> (UKD5)

This "human factor" was mentioned as "factors of uncertainty" by UKD6, while it was also mentioned by other interviewees, probably not recognised as a

So similar, so different, so Chinese   141

constraint of the model. An example was given by UKLH4 to show how this change of Director has a direct effect on the CI's day-to-day work:

> At the time when our Director was the Head of School, the CI was in close working relations with the host school, but since the new Director took over, the CI is on its own tracks with little convergence with the host school, even on Open Days, we have our own stand, kept a distance from the school stand, we also teach different students with no overlapping groups. It seems each side feels that we do not need each other.
>
> (UKLH4)

An interesting comment made by a UKD on another awardee of 'CI of the Year' is that "they are very lucky as their Director is the Pro Vice Chancellor whose wife is Chinese, he just loves China. That makes a huge difference". In other CIs however, a change of staff could even have a direct bearing on the CI's fate. Take the Stockholm University as an example, the decision was already announced in 2008, under the previous Chancellor, to remove the CI from its campus due to concerns of undue influence,[12] but the termination was not executed due to strong support and influence from its Director, Professor Torbjörn Lodén, until his retirement in 2014, when the CI was closed as "its usefulness had been outlived" (Fiskesjö, 2015), meaning its function of opening contacts with China has been served. The other case of the LCI closure also had to do with the change of Chinese Director, which will be looked at in more details later in this chapter.

True, a different Director behind the wheel of the same CI could mean taking different directions and paths, as each CI has a clear hallmark of the Director's personal style, competence and perceptions of China. For example, some Chinese Directors do not speak good English or the language of the host country; and some foreign Directors may not speak a word of Chinese while his/her predecessor/successor could well be an overseas Chinese hired by the host institution. However, on the other hand, the individual personal factor could not prevail over the decision made by the host university as a whole. The recent incidents of CI closures have all shown that the CI's life can come to an end for various reasons related to the host university, from financial constraints to a change of domestic political climate. Therefore, the CI's partnership model means that the marriage relationship could be ended by 'the other half', and an international marriage could face a potentially higher 'divorce rate' due to the double-edged nature of being engaged in a cross-cultural collaboration as explained by Kahn-Ackermann (2014): The two CI directors from the host and home universities have to work together collegially. It sounds wonderful when both sides are in harmony, but in reality, all kinds of misunderstandings, disagreements and even conflicts could arise in this process. Many of the examples given in Chapter 3 prove such constraints could be real problems in practice.

The other point raised by Kahn-Ackermann (2014) is in comparison with the Goethe-Institut, whose headquarters guides and supervises its worldwide

142 *So similar, so different, so Chinese*

networks to maintain standards, train and develop their own staff, and some Institute Directors are given lifetime appointments. The CI, meanwhile, does not have "its own people" on site: both the Chinese Director and teachers are seconded on a short-term basis, they are not trained adequately to conduct intercultural communications, let alone become experts in this field, which requires knowledge, skills and experience. This is also a key difference compared with the British Council according to DPEC:

> The British Council holds substantial expertise in international operation, they have a perfect command in combining government, non-government and commercial elements, and manages a local team of 800 Chinese employees in China, allowing the BC to adapt very well to local conditions.
>
> (DPEC)

UKSC4 raised a similar point in her comparison of the CI model with Alliance Française:

> I think there are two main differences compared with Alliance Française. First is that they hire local people to do it, second and more importantly, they charge for their language services, there is an element of prestige and quality with their classes. Here, when we offer many activities for free, it actually makes people suspect if there is any hidden intentions.
>
> (UKSC4)

The CI's hiring practice is actually a common cause of concerns according to UKD3:

> Hanban reserves the right to select the tutors, no British university would ever make an appointment. There is a potential clash as the university demands that it makes its own appointment. At the moment, this hasn't become a conflict, but we know it is there lurking when the appointment is made.
>
> (UKD3)

Although UKD1 explained that the host university could interview the candidates, they had no role to play before these candidates were vested and recommended by Hanban. In other CIs, these kinds of frictions have already escalated into conflicts. If we look at the few CIs that have decided not to renew their agreements with Hanban, we can see that they are all connected, in one way or another, with this arrangement of having Hanban select and train teachers before sending them over to the CIs, which invites the suspicion of compromising academic freedom on campus. Host institutions were asked "why risk the reputation for academic freedom and integrity by subcontracting teaching and research from a Chinese government that has repeatedly shown itself to be inimical to these values?" Some host institutions were criticised that accepting such appointments is to "ignore or

So similar, so different, so Chinese   143

dismiss the unsavoury political aspects of Confucius Institutes so long as they get a good deal" (cited in Sahlins, 2015: 62).

On the Hanban side, the recruitment issue is more reflected as a problem in quality assurance mechanism. The CI's quick proliferation in the past ten years has made it hard to keep up with staffing. Actually, at home university level, the supply of full-time professional teachers for secondee positions is a real challenge, many home institutions lack understanding of the needs of their foreign partners and local conditions, and also lack expertise of teaching Chinese as a second language according to Li (2008). The high turnover rate of the CI tutors (two-year contract based) makes it harder to maintain standard and continuity of teaching, or to expect long-term commitment from the teachers. As a new measure to tackle this problem, Hanban has modified the contract term to three years as from September 2013. While it may help relieve the concern of teaching continuation and student experience overseas, it may make things even harder at home for Chinese universities to find enough willing and qualified candidates, especially for countries that are not considered attractive destinations in many parts of the world. Many of the interviewees have mentioned the "sacrifices" they have to make for such overseas postings: interrupted career ladder, family separation and children's education are the three major restraining factors, making the CI jobs often end up with attracting teachers who do not have such worries, but applied for the job more as a chance to travel abroad. Even for attractive destinations like the UK, most of the UKSCs interviewed still complained about delayed promotions, and difficulties in getting visas for their children to join them and study in the UK. The challenge is much more salient for CIs in Africa. For example, after two years' service, the MRD's conclusion is:

> I don't think the government should try very hard to establish CIs in remote and poor parts of Africa, as the conditions are too harsh for the teachers, it is difficult to send people there, no quality staff means no quality provision, and therefore no impact produced, it would be a waste of money and effort. The teachers have to sacrifice a lot, both in term of their personal life and health, while the impact it can produce is very limited, it's just not worth it.
>
> (MRD)

This was supported by Hartig's (2014: 57) research focusing on CIs in Africa, which identified "lack of skilled teachers who are willing to go to Africa" as "one of the most crucial issues". The Ministry of Education estimated that 100 million people outside China would be learning Mandarin by 2010 (Peters and Zhang, 2011), and the gap of teacher shortage worldwide was five million in 2014 according to Chen and Yu (2016), which means many CIs have to use MA students in their gap years or high school teachers as volunteers. Actually, all the three secondees I interviewed in South Korea fall into this category. Though eligibility for becoming a volunteer has raised the bar from "any applicant with a HE diploma, including retired Chinese subject teachers from university, secondary and primaries schools", to "Bachelor degree or above and standard

144 *So similar, so different, so Chinese*

Mandarin" and "Qualified to teach Chinese language teaching in the country (region) or with certain experience and skills in Chinese language teaching",[13] it still raised concerns about teaching quality, especially when qualified locally hired teachers were turned away because of the free staffing from Hanban. When locally hired teachers from Taiwan were replaced by Hanban-sponsored less experienced teachers, it also took on a political overtone.

All the above exemplified that some of the CI model's merits can also have adverse side effects, just as some of its advantages and disadvantages are like mirror images. These can be understood as *endogenous* constraints that are results of factors from within the CI structure, while the next section looks at *exogenous* constraints caused by factors outside the structure.

Exogenous constraints of the CI's operating model

Though operating as the Cultural and Educational Section of the British Embassy, the British Council is a "stand-alone organization" according to its chief executive Martin Davidson, who believed the CI is "not comparable" because "they are being embedded in university campuses". He pointed out the real question has to be one of independence and self-censorship that come with the government funding: "I doubt they have to say, 'we'll only give you this money if you never criticise China'" (cited in Guttenplan, 2012). Actually, according to Hanban Director Xu Lin (French, 2006) "The British Council spends over 3 billion pounds a year", and China is spending only about $12 million on the CIs.

How can the British Council, who gets more funding from the government and also has a double identity – explicitly shown on its sign in two lines: British Council/ the Cultural and Education Section of the British Embassy, accuse the CI of lacking independence when it is based on a university campus? A distinction must be made here between government connection and affiliation. Hanban does not just get money from the government: it is under the leadership of the government, while the British Council defines its role as focusing on "developing people-to-people links and complementing government-to-people and government-to-government contact" (British Council website). Its role is to "complement" government contact, not to "implement" government aims, which may represent the "degree of separation" that sets the CI apart from its Western counterparts. The Goethe-Institut even claims to enjoy 'autonomy' in its Director Mr Anders' words:

> We are a world-wide structure and I'm very happy to have the autonomy. After the WWII, we were very concerned about propaganda, the political instrumentalization of culture, it was written into the German constitution that arts and culture has to be autonomous, it is not a field of government influence. Therefore, the freedom of art is upheld. We're getting our money from the Foreign Ministry, but as an association, not a state organisation. the GI is not affiliated to the ministries or housed inside the embassies, and the GI Director is not part of the diplomatic mission.
>
> (Mr Anders)

So similar, so different, so Chinese   145

Kahn-Ackermann (2014) used the term "small difference" in describing the connections to government of the CI and Goethe-Institut. They both rely on government funding and support, which is of "tremendous help but also a burden", and both institutes have to walk the same tightropes between the "political and cultural realms". However, I argue there is a "big difference" in the "political realm" that gives the CI model its exogenous constraints. In the USA, there is no resistance to the activities of Alliance Française, which claims to represent "a defensive action to battle against Anglo-Saxon hegemony" and "resistance to Americanisation'" (Mulcahy, 2017: 34) when "American popular culture made the concept of 'cultural imperialism', originally applied to the developing world, a rallying cry for European as well" (Paschalidis, 2009: 283), yet why the CI met with such strong resistance when it positions itself as just teaching Chinese to "meet the growing demand" of its own people?

The answer is in the top three factors contributing to the negative reports about the CI according to Li and Dai's research (2011): communism, propaganda and threat/danger, which are inter-related between one another. Hubbert (2019: 194) has pointed bluntly that: "the trope of communism often functions to frame the programs politically regardless of the curricular content of the Chinese language courses themselves or the teachers' identifiable political ideologies and practices." In Germany, critics and sinologists fear that the influence of the Chinese state on the CI would put "German universities at risk of becoming mouthpieces for the Chinese Party" (Ricking, 2012). Here we can see a tacit "equation" of the Chinese government and the Communist Party, which in turn is synonymous with authoritarian rule and a threat to democracy.

Therefore, people who dislike the Chinese political system tend to see state involvement in the CI as "dangerous communist propaganda". In other words, being the 'ideological other' is a more salient label, and this one big difference that "springs from the authoritarian nature of the Chinese political system" (Hartig, 2012: 70) overrides the similarity in government funding and the purpose of language and cultural promotion.

On the other hand, the Chinese government's presence, which tends to be much more 'in the limelight' compared with Western governments' backstage role, fosters such speculations. A lot of the CI's media exposure is because of high-profile official visits from state leaders. Images of visiting officials are often used in negative Western media reports about the CI. For example, when reporting the closure of Chicago University's CI in 2014, the BBC used a picture of Xi Jinping unveiling a CI plaque in Melbourne in 2010, while the *Telegraph* used a picture of Liu Yandong, Vice-Premier and Council Chair of the CI Headquarters, speaking at George Washington University's CI in 2013. A picture of Xi attending a function at the Stockholm CI in 2010 was also used by the *South China Morning Post* in its 2015 report on this CI's closure. A reading of the *Milestones in 2014* in the CI's *Annual Development Report* shows 16 high-profile official visits to CIs by senior Chinese leaders in a year, including six from Xi himself.[14] These visits seem to make the implicit connection with government more

146 *So similar, so different, so Chinese*

explicit. In comparison, pictures of state leaders are rarely found on the websites of the CI's Western counterparts.

If the government's presence is an overt demonstration of the CI's affiliation with government, censorship within China is a covert indication, even if it is not directly about what the CI can or cannot do, its existence in the domestic environment could be considered a source of exogenous constraints as well. The effects of inconsistency between China's international appeal and domestic practice was well articulated by Li:

> The domestic political values, institutions and political system are important considerations for a state's soft power because all these things demonstrate how the ruling elite in that state uses power on its own people. Such use of power in the domestic context can resonate in the international arena because people outside see and observe how foreigner rulers treat their own nationals and associated that practice with their dealings with the international community.
>
> (Li, 2009: 9)

Since home institutions are part of the CI partnership, what is happening in the Chinese universities has a natural 'spillover' effects on the CIs operating abroad. For example, in the CCP directive issued to local party committees in May 2013, discussions of the following seven topics were banned in universities and the media on the grounds that they were "dangerous Western influences": universal values, freedom of speech, civil society, civil rights, the historical errors of the Chinese Communist Party, crony capitalism and judicial independence (Liou and Ding, 2015: 138). The Chinese journalist Gao Yu, who was accused of leaking this 'state secret' to Western media, was initially sentenced to seven years in prison and then reduced to five years after her appeal in November 2015, which was widely reported by all the mainstream Western media such as BBC and CNN.

The speech given by Xi Jinping in December 2014, calling for tighter ideological control in universities, was also put under international media spotlights, including the BBC, *Guardian, Daily Mail* and *Reuters*. Following the speech, the then Chinese Education Minister, Yuan Guiren, called for a ban on textbooks that promote Western values, and warned against "remarks that slander the leadership of the Communist Party of China and smear socialism" in the classroom.[15] When Western values and textbooks are banned in Chinese universities, such acts are not recognised as counter-hegemonic actions, but countering its own principle of "harmony in diversity" claimed as the very goal of China's cultural diplomacy, it also runs against the definition of cultural diplomacy per se by reducing "mutual understanding" to one-way explanation.

What is worth noting is that the same Minister told a government advisory panel four years previously that restricting the use of Western teaching materials was wrongheaded. This stark reversal revealed the growing tension between academics and party control on the one hand, and the power of bureaucracy on the other hand. If the Ministry of Education can change direction like a weathercock,

So similar, so different, so Chinese   147

Hanban and universities under its direct auspices just have to trim their sail to the wind, echoing UKD4's first mandate as not to "get into any trouble", as they are working for the position, not the mission.

A recent example was a Tsinghua Professor was suspended from teaching after criticising the party leadership in March 2019, which was reported by both *Financial Times*[16] and the *New York Times*,[17] but the reports were censored inside China, including the Chinese versions on their Chinese portals. Actually, UKT2 found it hard to believe when he noticed that there are CCTV cameras inside university classrooms, he asked if this is to record the lesson to put onto e-Learn to benefit the students, but was told that "No, these are for the teachers, to make sure they don't say things inappropriately".

> So blunt! When this was proposed in the UK, as a way to make use of tech-nology to benefit students, it was strongly resisted by staff due to concerns of monitoring the lecturers and affecting academic freedom, but here they don't even bother to pretend this is for the students.
>
> (UKT2)

During my interview with Mr Anders at the Goethe-Institut, even a blacklist published by the MOC in 2015 about 120 pop songs that are not allowed to be aired anymore could raise concerns, let alone silencing academics:

> This act raised a lot of questions in the Western context and immediately made problems for the CI, as they are the representative of Chinese cultural organisation in the host country, people would ask: what is going on in your country? From this you see a heavily censored country, one must be aware everything happening here (in China) has an influence in the outside world.

A professor of political science at the University of Waterloo that hosts a CI called this "unintended consequences of their close alignment with Beijing" (cited in Little, 2010). Compared with the 'hidden hand' approach in the USA and Europe, there is a 'visible hand' at play in China, and Fallows (2016: n.p.) has commented this as "oversteps": "nearly everyone I spoke with agreed that China's oversteps have generated ill will far greater than the goodwill fostered by its foreign aid and Confucius Institutes". China now tries to learn its lessons and apply an approach called "square inside but round outside" (*neifang waiyuan*), which means while keeping a stern and firm stance domestically, adopt a gentle and smooth stance internationally to reduce criticisms. In my own interviews, UKD5 mentioned "there is no change of tone" in the directives they received from Hanban following the tightening of ideological control at home. When asked to comment on the 'spillover' effect of domestic censorship on the CI, most of the foreign Directors have expressed their views with a rhetorical ques-tion: "There are so many other things we can do, why must we touch the 'mine-field' when the fund for the CI operation is provided by the Chinese government?" (UKD1). However, such a response indicated the existence of self-censorship,

148 *So similar, so different, so Chinese*

which is always an inherent danger that may or may not operate at a conscious level. Examples were mentioned in the interview that some proposed topics for lectures and conferences by the host institution were vetoed by CIs themselves, not being disproved by Hanban, such as a conference on China's Human Rights.

Other UKDs used the British Council as an example in defence as "they wouldn't want to talk about IRA either". UKSC2 cited the example of "foreign teachers who came to China to teach 20–30 years ago, some of them have a missionary background and would infill religious influence in their teaching, but it does not mean their students will be converted to Christianity". UKD2 simply retorted: "No one would claim if you study in the US and taught by Americans, you'll be in danger of indoctrination, or being guided by the American government. Why would you start saying this about China?"

This 'double standard' is obviously built on the Western hegemony in this "terrain of struggle", but just as Gramsci believed, the fight for hegemony and struggle for power is ceaseless; if the hegemon starts to worry about losing the hegemonic position, the sense of crisis would be translated into an urge to fight on to maintain that position. So, when Chinese UKD4 commented rather sensibly that "they are very alert, which is understandable", this "understandable alert" tends to be escalated into alarms on the hegemonic side based on their speculative assumptions that the CI's remit is to "promote Communism". UKD2 has used himself as an example to disable such alarms:

> I do not think the CI is trying to sell political ideology, I myself am not even a Communist party member. It is not listed as a criterion to select the CI directors or teachers. What we want to do is cultural promotion, and in today's information era, it is impossible to brainwash people, local people have full access to a wealth of information.
>
> (UKD2)

This was supported by Parton's findings:

> The threat to UK values posed by a skewed presentation of China in teaching materials is not serious: for those who advance from language study to a degree on China, there are copious materials which convey a more balanced picture; and those of us educated through Mao-era material have not ended up as Maoists.
>
> (Parton, 2019: 18)

The discussions so far have revealed the imprint of centralised Chinese political culture on its cultural diplomacy practices. Despite the merits of the CI model, it also comes with both exogenous and endogenous constraints that fall into two categories summarised by Starr (2009): "insiders" with practical concerns and "outsiders" with ideological concerns. As a way to overcome these constraints, the CI model has another level of difference: its flexibility and non-uniformity. Compared with its Western counterparts that mostly follows a standard operating model all

So similar, so different, so Chinese 149

over the world prescribed by their headquarters, the CI's model has more room for flexibility to fit into local conditions. The next section elaborates on the last aspect of the comparison: the provisions of the CI activities.

Scope of activities

According to the 2007 version of the Confucius Institute's Constitution and by-laws, Confucius Institutes provide the following services overseas: (1) Provide Chinese language teaching; (2) Train Chinese language instructors and provide Chinese language teaching resources; (3) Hold the Chinese proficiency test (known as HSK in Chinese acronym) and tests for the certification of Chinese language teachers; (4) Provide information and consultative services concerning Chinese language education and China's culture, economy and society; and (5) Conduct research on contemporary China (Ren, 2010).

Therefore, the CI mainly focuses on language teaching, with the word "language" repeated in the top three services. Culture, meanwhile, was only mentioned as an area of its consultative services (point 4). It is unknown when the change was made, but at least after 2012, the last item was changed to "5) Conduct language and cultural exchange activities between China and other countries" (Hanban website), replacing the term "research" in the old version. I now compare these two aspects of provision in conducting cultural activities and research with the Confucius Institute's Western counterparts.

Cultural activities: the "what" and "how"

Despite the centralised input from Hanban and the globalised outreach of the CI, no standard 'recipe' can be found for CIs across the world. Each CI has its own focus in provision, which is allowed and encouraged by Hanban, and determined by the specific conditions at the home and host institutions. Sometimes, they even provide services other than what is shown in the Constitution, such as advertising jobs with Chinese companies to local students. The ratio between language and cultural provision also varies from CI to CI, depending on the host institutions. If hosts do not offer Chinese language programmes, the CI can add great value in running Chinese modules or even setting up a degree course. Otherwise, the CI will add value more in the form of cultural provisions, both for the host university and to the wider community. Penn State University is an example of the latter, since it already has a "very robust Chinese-language program":

> We did not use Chinese teachers from Hanban at Penn State, and did not use Hanban pedagogical material, this meant that much of the work the CI could do was restricted to a fairly narrow range of activities within the university – cultural activities and events by visiting Chinese troupes promoted by Hanban for instance, and then some other activities outside the university (support for community events).
>
> (Redden, 2014)

150 *So similar, so different, so Chinese*

Among these cultural activities, the most popular one is China Day at schools. Activities include calligraphy and brush painting, Chinese food and tea tasting, Taiji (Tai Chi), shuttlecock, Chinese knot and lantern making, language tasters, quiz and lectures, just to name a few. Such cultural activities are often criticised for reducing the diversity of China's cultures to a "uniform, quaint commodity" characterised by Taiji and Chinese dance performances, it tends to become a "taxidermised" version of Chinese culture, or a product of "culturetainment" according to Lionel Jensen, an associate professor of East Asian Languages at the University of Notre Dame, meaning "the abridgment of Chinese civilisation in the name of digestible forms of cultural appeal can be readily shipped overseas" (cited in Redden, 2012: n.p.). This commodity concept is actually closely related to the CI's new nickname of "spiritual high-speed train": it may go very far very quickly, but the impact it can produce may be short term. This was echoed by UKD1's comments that "most of these are superficial stuff", UKD3 also pointed out that:

> One of the dangers of CI is that it can project a slightly folk culture, like using thatched cottages to represent England, they do exist in a few places, but they are not really what England is about; traditional Chinese dance is important, but it does not really capture the real rich modern range of Chinese culture.
>
> (UKD3)

During my interview with the Director of Goethe-Institut China in his Beijing office, Mr Anders enunciated that:

> The main and obvious difference is our understanding of culture is much broader than those held by the CI concerning cultural activities. Their notion of culture is very traditional, also in a way very repetitive, meaning they are very much focused on calligraphy, Chinese cooking etc. These aspects of life are important, but it would be more successful to open up discussions of contemporary society, to engage with the discourses of the country where they are. The CIs are very close to the academic world, they are easily linked up to the other departments of the University, or bring in somebody from China, this would be a more interesting role to play.
>
> (Mr Anders)

On the one hand, Anders' remarks seem to support Shambaugh's (2013) observation of China's cultural "footprint" of being increasingly broad across the globe, but not particularly deep. On the other hand, it shows the dilemma for the CI: since it is based on a university campus, it has the stage to play a bigger role, but the controversies it has caused suggest it is safer simply repeating those harmless, traditional cultural activities. Therefore, it is up to the individual CI's position and vision to use the scope available, either in a more trailblazing

So similar, so different, so Chinese   151

manner, or a more 'play it safe' mode. The second difference mentioned by Mr Anders was the approach of the Confucius Institute:

> Our approach is to develop everything we do together with our partners in the respective countries, for example, we work closely with ministries and the academic world in China to promote professionalization of German teacher training, while my observation is that the Chinese approach is very much focused on themselves: talking about the significance of Chinese tradition and culture, emphasizing the difference of the Chinese way, of course, it is right there are differences and that's why we're here, to discuss the differences, but we felt the different approach is they want to promote themselves, and we promote the partnership.
>
> (Mr Anders)

> This point is a little ironic as the CI model itself is actually a partnership. Nothing is more critical than getting the partner on board in order to make a partnership work. But it is worth mentioning that Hanban has adopted a very positive learning attitude. In the 9th CI Conference held in December 2014, one of the presidents' forums was committed to discussing the CI function of cultural exchange and academic research, and this forum was chaired by Kahn-Ackermann, former Director of the Goethe-Institut (China) and currently senior consultant for the CI headquarters. The annual conference is a useful scheme for CIs all around the world to listen to each other and the advisors, to reflect and act on improvements.
>
> (Mr Anders)

Research: a unique element associated with the CI model

A quick comparison between the services offered by the Confucius Institute and its Western counterparts also shows one distinct element that is only on the menu of the CI: research, which may have to do with its unique model of being based on university campuses. Compared with the deletion of "economy and society" from its scope of consultative services in point 4, the complete change of content in point 5 of its Constitution is very intriguing, while the explanation for the reasons behind the removal of "research" is nowhere to be found (none of the interviewees was even aware of the change). It may suggest that Hanban wishes to avoid controversial activities that might make the cooperation difficult and lead to some frictions, or even closures.

However, despite the removal of the word "research" from the list, research activities were not abandoned. In the directive Hanban issued in 2011, it asked each CI to conduct research on Chinese culture and "foster a new generation of sinologists" (cited in Kluver, 2014). Then in November 2012, Hanban launched the new 'Confucius China Studies Program' to take on more of a facilitator's role in channelling research from overseas campus to China. This programme is a series of research projects including generous scholarships for 'PhD in China

152   *So similar, so different, so Chinese*

fellowship', 'Young Leaders in China Fellowship' as well as 'Understanding China Fellowship' that serves to support academics from foreign universities to "undertake research with Chinese researchers in China" (Hanban website). This could be considered a clever move of 'stepping backward is actually moving forward' in the battle for the power of discourse by inviting foreign scholars to study the 'other' with the 'other' in the 'other's' land, also being consistent with the CI's mandate: "let more foreigners come to experience China first hand" (UKLH3); but it has also attracted scepticisms from some critics who viewed this as cultivating a new generation of "China watchers who are well-disposed toward the dictatorship" (Mosher, 2012). This view was refuted by UKD2: "but no one would say if you to study in the US with a full scholarship, you'd be polluted and anything you wrote would automatically be in favour of America".

However, this programme was mentioned as a direct reason leading to the closure of the Lyon Confucius Institute (LCI) in 2013. It was rarely reported until "The Debate Over Confucius Institutes" was published on China File following the AAUP's report submitted in June 2014. Gregory Lee, Chair of the LCI Board, participated in Part II of the debate and explained that since a "new director taking his instructions directly from Beijing arrived in Sep 2012", he "insisted strongly on a deeper integration of the LCI in the University itself" through participating in teaching of the University degree programmes and partnership with the university research centres on the Confucius China Studies Program to send PhD students to study in China (China File, 2014). As disclosed in a BBC report titled: *Investigation: Behind the Closed Door of LCI*, the Chinese Studies program at Lyon 3 University also offers courses in Min Nan Dialect (spoken in Taiwan) and Taiwan studies. The CI's new move was perceived as gaining leverage over independent research, and when this "interference" was deemed to be "inappropriate since it would put in doubt our academic freedom" thus refused by the LCI Board, Xu Lin, the Hanban Director, demanded the resignation of the LCI Board chair and announced without warning the suspension of Hanban's annual fund allocated to LCI. As a result, one locally hired teacher was fired, and the LCI eventually ceased its activities in September 2013, becoming the first CI closed down due to research controversy.[18] Both sides felt hitting a bottom line that could not be compromised.

If we look into the reasons behind the Penn State University CI's closure, a similar dose of "research" can be detected. This CI is one of the few that have specified "research" in its mission statement. When asked to elaborate on the ways in which their goals differ from that of Hanban that led to the termination of the agreement, the former CI Director said via email:

> I will say that in my experience as CI director one of the major frustrations with the relationship was that we consistently had more ambitious ideas for the ways CI funding could be used – mainly to support research not only in the humanities or on Chinese culture, but also on science, politics, the environment, and a variety of other topics – that the Hanban regularly

So similar, so different, so Chinese   153

rejected as too far outside the official CI remit (which they would tell us was mainly 'cultural')…. Had they been flexible, it would have helped Confucius Institute succeed here.

(cited in Jacobs and Yu, 2014: n.p.)

Hanban may have learned its lesson and indeed become more flexible, or here is another example of CIs being different from one another: According to UKD6 interviewed in 2019, research is one of the three-pronged activities they provide along with language teaching and cultural promotion, and since their partner is a science and technology institution in China, a key research area is environmental technology. If the Chinese programme mainly benefits the language department and the cultural programme benefits the student body and local community, the research programme is the most beneficial part to the university as a whole as it helps with both reputation and research funding. The collaboration area fits in both with the partner's expertise and a global theme while avoiding the sensitive political complications.

An interesting comparison can be made between the LCI's case, where it is Hanban's demand for the CI to offer sinology PhD scholarships in China through its partnerships with the university research centres that caused the relationship to stumble; and the Penn State's case, where they wanted to utilise the CI's resources to support more activities in humanities research, but these ideas were rejected by Hanban for being too far outside the official remit of the CI. These two cases may seem to contradict each other, but if we look at the actual "war of position", we will see it is the same fight for power: the significance of the Confucius China Studies programme is that China's contribution to research is not just in the form of funds, but more in terms of 'knowledge' production, while just providing funds to the host university to do research that the CI has no direct participation and control does not contribute to gaining positions of influence. However, in the current terrain where the USA and Europe hold and try to maintain their 'positional superiority', it seems no matter whether the CI wants to be actively engaged in research or passively refuses to get involved, they can all lead to discords in the partnerships.

We can see from these examples that research can be a flashpoint in the interactions between China scholars, host universities and the Chinese government. A deeper investigation is thus worthwhile to look at a more influential Confucius Institute closure, the one at the University of Chicago (CIUC), which also identifies itself to be "research oriented". Of all the CI closures that have taken place so far, if we look at the sheer number, the tiny proportion of thirty-five out of 532 may be rightfully considered a sign of 'success' of the CI, however, if we look at their calibres and locations, we will note the fact that all the closures after 2013 took place in North America and Europe, the most targeted areas where perceptions of China have been the most unfavourable, thus received the most concentrated CI spreads: according to statistics released by Hanban in June 2019, the USA alone is home to the biggest number of CIs (88 in total) in the world, while Europe has the most concentrated coverage (184 in total).[19]

154 *So similar, so different, so Chinese*

All the Hanban-sponsored student summer camps and school principal visits, nine in total in 2014, were all from these two regions only.[20] Besides, a great number of the host universities that have closed down their CIs are prestigious institutions: McMaster is rated No. 4 among all Canadian universities and the highest among all the thirteen that host a CI in Canada; Stockholm University was the first in Europe to host a CI, its closure left a big gap in Norway, Sweden and Denmark where no major universities now host a CI; Leiden is the oldest university in the Netherlands; both Chicago and Michigan University are among the most prestigious host universities in the USA, and the CIUC closure has created the biggest sensation by announcing not to renew its agreement when Hanban was celebrating CI's first ten-year anniversary in September 2014. Then in the same week, Penn State University also made the closing announcement, making a big impact through wide media coverage (reported by BBC, Reuters, *The Economist*, *Times High Education*, *New York Times*, *Wall Street Journal*, *Forbes*, *Telegraph*, *South China Morning Post*, to name a few).

The CIUC's closure was then referred to when the Stockholm University announced its decision to close its CI in December 2014, and further in June 2015, when the Stuttgart Media University decided to "scuttle" its plans to establish a CI as per its contract signed with Hanban in August 2014. Its ripple effect is also long lasting when more American universities shut down their CIs in 2018 and 2019, making CIUC a very illustrative case to show the challenges faced by China's cultural diplomacy. Besides, the University of Chicago only came to this decision after lengthy negotiations with Hanban, which can function like a micrograph of the terrain of struggle that merit a detailed investigation into. The section below will take a closer look at this closure, because its decision "mirrors controversies over the CI's perceived threats to western academic freedom that in turn reflect wide-ranging perceptions of China as a general threat to global well-being" (Hubbert, 2014).

To be, or not to be – a tale of the CIUC closure

The 'Trilogy': three key documents and their subtexts

To set the scene for this investigation, three key documents that led up to the final announcement will be presented in a timeline: the Chicago University petition, the AAUP report and the Chicago University statement, followed by a close reading and subtext analysis that continues to employ the lens of "terrain of struggle" to decipher the messages conveyed and examine different players' roles in driving the CIUC to its closure step by step.

i The Chicago University petition

In April 2014, 108 professors, including seven department chairs from the Chicago University, signed on a petition to "urge the Council of the Senate to

So similar, so different, so Chinese 155

terminate the contract with the Confucius Institutes".[21] Among the reasons presented, the four points below were highlighted (with emphasis added):

- The fact that Hanban is an *agency of the Chinese government*, whose global agenda is set by high officials of the *Party-State*, makes it a dubious practice to allow such an external institution to staff academic courses within the University and approve funding for its research proposals.
- It subjects the University's academic programme to the *political constraints on free speech and belief* that are specific to the People's Republic of China. The Executive Director of the Canadian Association of University Teachers (CAUT) was quoted that Canadian colleges and universities were compromising their own integrity by allowing Hanban *"to have a voice in a number of academic matters such as curriculum, texts, and topics of class discussions"*.
- It was established in the McMaster case and has since been corroborated as well in an American Confucius Classrooms that the Hanban teachers are trained to *ignore or divert* questions on issues that are politically taboo in China, such as the status of Taiwan, Tiananmen, the pro-Democracy movement, etc.
- Although the University of Chicago *has ignored the provisions in the Agreement specifying that Hanban will supply texts and course materials for Chinese language instruction*, the University of Chicago is hosting a CI under privileges not available to many other schools, the effect is that, mindful only of its own welfare, the University is participating in a worldwide, politico-pedagogical project that is contrary in many respects to its own academic values.

The wording of "dubious practice" and the quotes emphasised in italics suggest a logic that because Hanban is "an agency of the Chinese government", which is a party-state, therefore, to submit research proposals to them for approval is dubious practice, as it is to subject the University's academic programme to the "political constraints on free speech and belief". However, there was no evidence given except the 'counter' evidence that the University of Chicago "has ignored the provisions in the Agreement specifying that Hanban will supply texts and course materials for Chinese language instruction", and as quoted earlier, Penn State University also "did not use Chinese teachers from Hanban at Penn State, and did not use Hanban pedagogical material", which means this *did not* happen due to their "privileges", and all these are no more than speculative assumptions. Actually, the choice of not using Hanban supplied textbooks is not such a rare "privilege", according to Xu Lin, "only 12.5% of the institutes used textbooks published in China, the others used teaching materials composed in foreign countries" (Qu, Zhao and Cheng, 2012). This was supported by the GAO report:

156 *So similar, so different, so Chinese*

No school officials we interviewed at case study schools stated they felt they did not have full control over their curriculum. Additionally, none of the 10 case study schools offered credit-bearing courses through the institute or used Hanban-supplied materials for credit-bearing courses offered through the school's language department.

(GAO, 2019a: 25)

The McMaster case was cited as evidence, which is about one individual tutor who hid her faith in Falun Gong in order to get the job, and based on one individual case, the CAUT's statement made a blanket assertion and appealed for *all* Canadian universities not to compromise their own integrity by "*allowing Hanban to have a voice in a number of academic matters such as curriculum, texts, and topics of class discussions*". Hanban was clearly treated as a source that would impose inappropriate influence over such academic matters as it is identified as a government organisation. But not using 'teachers from Hanban' is a deceiving change of concept here: Hanban as a government organisation has no teachers, all teachers were recommended and sent by the home universities in China. If teachers from Chinese universities are considered as not fit for teaching Chinese abroad, then it is no longer a covert, but an overt claim for the sole legitimacy of '*us*' to teach about '*the other*' under the hoisted banner of academic freedom. What is more, if Chinese university teachers cannot "have a voice" in "topics of class discussions", isn't this self-contradictory in criticising censorship by censoring voices from China? Hubbert has pinpointed that:

What might constitute "real" freedom of speech in this case is an acknowledgement of the limiting nature of our own discourses of power and recognition of others' ability to speak as equally human and modern subjects when their politics diverge from those of our own social and political worlds.

(Hubbert, 2019: 144)

As for its accusation that: "*Hanban teachers are trained to ignore or divert questions on issues that are politically taboo in China*". This is again paradoxical: if the CI teachers are accused of "ignoring or diverting" such questions, are they encouraged, or even allowed, to engage in these discussions and disseminate the Chinese views? No better explanation of what freedom of speech means than the one given in the book *The Friends of Voltaire*: "I disapprove of what you say, but I will defend to the death your right to say it".

True, my own interview findings did confirm that during the pre-departure trainings, the CI tutors were advised to avoid or divert discussions of politically sensitive issues. The teachers are on a mission to teach Chinese language and do not have to "introduce into their teaching controversial matter which has no relation to their subject". This is to borrow a line from the AAUP's definition of academic freedom: "teachers are entitled to freedom in the classroom

So similar, so different, so Chinese 157

in discussing their subject, but they should be careful *not to introduce into their teaching controversial matter which has no relation to their subject*".[22] A fine line needs to be noted here: if the 'subject' is Chinese language teaching, then "politically sensitive issues" can be argued to be "controversial matter which has no relation to their subject". If this is the definition endorsed as the core principle by more than 200 national scholarly and educational associations, then it is another classic example of double standard when the CI teachers doing exactly the same thing would be accused of interfering in "academic freedom". This is not a definition of freedom but one of hegemony in essence.

Of course, the CI teachers are not a homogenous body: they come from various backgrounds and are delivering various content of teaching in various styles. They are a rather heterogeneous group of teachers in this sense, yet both sides seem to refer to this group as one monolithic: both in the accusations against "Hanban teachers" in the petition and the defence against "the CI teachers" given by Hanban, though both sides could be referring to an actual minority in this group in their arguments. The common thing shared in this group is that they are the commanders of classrooms. Said has commented on the power of classroom discourse with a punch: "One is taught to be patriotic, to understand certain, carefully selected aspects of history of this country, and so on. *It's very powerful*" (1993: 206). Because it is so powerful, it can help maintain hegemony by not only deciding on what can be said and what cannot, but also who can say it and who cannot.

The other common trait of the CI teachers is that most of them are sent by the home universities in China, which reflects back to the McMaster case where both the discriminatory hiring and the fact that host university cedes hiring decision entirely to Hanban was at the core of the disagreement. Actually, in the negotiation process between Hanban and the University of Chicago as disclosed by Redden (2014), an ad hoc committee charged with evaluating the CI function issued a report proposing some significant changes, including "replacing the three instructors hired through the Confucius Institute and Hanban with instructors hired directly by the East Asian languages department". The report concluded that "a permanently renewable and adequately large group of locally hired, trained, and supervised Chinese language instructors would be preferable to these temporary, 'outsourced' teachers". Hanban is willing to consider this and actually has already initiated changes on this practice in 2013, because it is quite aware of the issues about teaching quality and expertise as discussed earlier. However, the negotiation process was aborted suddenly as disclosed in the university's statement, which will be looked at later following the timeline.

ii The AAUP report

Then in June 2014, the American Association of University Professors (AAUP) submitted a report *On Partnerships with Foreign Governments: The Case of*

158 *So similar, so different, so Chinese*

Confucius Institutes, calling on American universities to rethink their relationship with the CIs (the full text can be found in Appendix 4), claiming that:

> Confucius Institutes function as an *arm of the Chinese state* and are allowed to *ignore academic freedom.* Their academic activities are under the supervision of Hanban, a Chinese *state agency* which is chaired by a member of the Politburo and the vice-premier of the People's Republic of China.

The report compared the CI with the British Council, the Goethe-Institut, and Alliance Française, and pointed out that:

> These latter three entities are *clearly connected to imperial pasts, ongoing geopolitical agendas, and the objectives of 'soft power'*, but none of them is located on a university or college campus. Instead, their connections to national political agendas and interests require that they be established in sites where they can fulfil their mandates openly without *threatening the independence and integrity of academic institutions in host countries.*

The report concluded that AAUP joins CAUT in recommending that universities cease to permit CIs to advance a state agenda in the recruitment and control of academic staff, in the choice of curriculum, and in the restriction of debate.

From the above we can see the report very much echoed the key points in the petition: the "protection of academic freedom" was hoisted as the banner at the very start, allying with CAUT to make the appeal for the whole North American campuses to cease their involvement in the CIs. The CI's function is again interpreted as "an arm of the Chinese state" under the supervision of Hanban, which is chaired by a member of the Politburo and the vice premier to "advance a state agenda". Three days after the AAUP report was released, the official Chinese news agency Xinhua responded with an angry editorial titled "China Voice: Fear, ignorance behind calls to stem Confucius Institutes" (Ren, 2014), saying that the claims made by the report actually "expose not so much communist propaganda as their own intolerance of exotic cultures and biased preconceived notions to smear and isolate the CPC". As a counter-argument, the Xinhua article emphasised the role of the CI Board and management committee that consists of both Chinese and foreign scholars, including many professors and university presidents of the host institution, who have their direct say in decision-making.

It is interesting that the AAUP report also put the CI in comparison with its Western counterparts, and even recognised that these Western institutions "*are clearly connected to imperial pasts, ongoing geopolitical agendas, and the objectives of soft power*", but the "imperial pasts" was brushed off lightly as a passing comment, ignoring that this "past" is 500 years of colonialism and capitalism that created today's West-centred world in terms of culture, economy and politics; it is a past with lingering influence of Orientalism and Western cultural hegemony that still shapes today's global cultural terrain, and puts them in an superior position in pursuing the "ongoing geopolitical agendas and the objectives of soft power".

So similar, so different, so Chinese   159

Their centre of attention is that today's China has established over 500 CIs world-wide, but its Western counterparts has established a global cultural influence for over 500 years: English is spoken in more than 100 countries in the world, French in more than forty and Spanish in more than twenty countries. However, this fundamental difference in cultural power *position* was dismissed as an understate-ment, while putting an overstatement on *location* as the critical difference as the sites of the CIs "threaten the independence and integrity of academic institutions in host countries".

iii The Chicago University statement

Then after five months' negotiations, a statement was made regarding the CI on September 25, 2014 by the University of Chicago,[23] stating that "the University and Hanban have engaged in several months of good faith efforts and steady progress toward a new agreement. However, recently published comments about UChicago in an article about the director-general of Hanban are *incompatible with a continued equal partnership*". It then quoted the article[24] saying Xu Lin wrote a letter to the college president containing only one sentence: "If your school has made the decision to pull out, then I agree".

Surprisingly, in this final CIUC statement announcing the University's deci-sion to suspend negotiations for the renewal of the agreement, the repeated accu-sations of "academic freedom" disappeared and only one reason was mentioned: the state-backed *Jiefang Daily*'s article, which sang an eulogy to Xu Lin in showing how powerful she is: "That attitude of hers made the other side anxious, and they quickly replied that they'd continue to operate the Confucius Institute" (Wang, 2014) – the University of Chicago is the 'they', who finds Xu's attitude "incompatible with a continued equal partnership". As explained in Chapter 3, there is a vertical hierarchy between Ministry of Education/Hanban and home universities in China as well as between Chinese government and the state media, meaning that the Hanban Director can talk to a Chinese university in such a commanding manner, and there are often laudatory-style media reports about government officials in China. However, here Hanban is dealing with an Amer-ican University that cherishes its reputation as independent from government influence, and is already under intense internal questioning of jeopardising such a reputation. It also regards itself as holding a superior position and finds Hanban's imposing stance 'hegemonic', thus resisted it with full pride. *The Eco-nomist* (2014) article of 'Confucius Institute: About Face' called Xu Lin's state-ment a "boastful challenge", and the *Business Spectator* also criticised the hard-line behaviour of officials like Xu, "who still think and act like party ideologues who like to assert their authority and bully people into submission" (Cai, 2014). As commented by a professor at University of Chicago on the lengthy negotiations, "the Chinese officials were heavy-handed, condescending and difficult" (cited in Redden, 2014). In a way, this feeling of not being treated as an "equal partnership" left them with no choice but to end the relationship altogether.

160 *So similar, so different, so Chinese*

The above shows the counter-productive role played by Hanban as the third party, which was fatal in terminating the partnerships of both LCI and Penn State University CI, and now CIUC. It gives further evidence that government-led approach can have deadly effects. We can see the knock-on effects from this chain of events, especially when the first CI closure at McMaster was cited in the petition, and the Chicago University's closure was further referred to in the following closures. The CIUC case has offered us a lot of food for thought: Gramsci has viewed the "education relationship as a political relationship" (Fontana, 1993: 145), and the closure revealed such hidden power relations at the core of these interactions. Just as Foucault once pointed out, "at every moment the relationship of power may become a confrontation between two adversaries", and "a relationship of struggle between two adversaries is the result of power relations with the conflicts and cleavages they engender" (1982: 794–795). The closure of CIUC is an example of such a cleavage. When the CI was trying to be engaged in a "war of position", it found itself being dragged into a "battle of location", the hegemonic side holding vantage positions can easily manoeuvre a blocking action based on the CI's location on campus: it is both accused for "political censorship" when the CI teachers avoided discussing contentious topics, and "ideological infiltration" when those issues *were* discussed. It was these dual accusations that brought it to a deadlock, raising the classic question of 'to be, or not to be': it seems for the CI, to discuss, or not to discuss those sensitive topics, they are equally accusable of violating "academic freedom", which is a recurring key word in most of the criticisms against the CI.

Through the repetition of the same discourse, this perception of the CI is manufactured as generally accepted 'knowledge' for all the CIs, despite their multifarious provisions and activities – all those report recommendations, from CAUT to AAUP, from NAS to CPHRC, were made to *all* the universities hosting CIs, though Parton has rightly advised, it is better to "look at individual issues on their own merits" as the accusations are made "justly in some cases but with exaggeration in others where transparency and proper practice prevails" (2019: 3–4). In BGD1's words,

> because the CIs are based on two partner universities, they are as different from each other as one university is from another in the world: yes, they are all universities, but obviously universities come in various calibres and pro-files and serve different student bodies. The Goethe-Instituts are more similar in standard and function as they are designed that way.
>
> (BGD1)

This actually forms one of the key differences between the CI and its Western counterparts, its gigantic scale combined with multifarious provisions defies the validity of any conclusion regarding "all CIs". 'Blind men feel the elephant' is a Chinese idiom: one blind man felt the tail and said that the elephant is like a rope; another blind man felt its ear and said that the elephant is

So similar, so different, so Chinese   161

like a fan. The CI is like the elephant, but we should know better than the blind men.

The GAO's reports (2019a; 2019b) have fully recognised this feature: after reviewing 90 CI agreements, interviewing ten case study schools, and speaking to officials about benefits and concerns related to the institutes, their findings highlighted that "Confucius Institute Management, Operations, and Agreements Vary by School". As for the concern that the presence of CIs could constrain campus activities and classroom content by avoiding hosting events on topics that could include criticism of China, such as Taiwan or Tibet, school officials they interviewed "offered examples to illustrate that these concerns did not apply to their institutes, noting institutes had sponsored events on such topics" (GAO, 2019b: 5). This was also supported by my own interview findings. BGD2 said the majority of their CI budget is used to support research and academic activities. From the list I was given, I can see a wide range of research themes, including seminars and conferences on some sensitive topics, such as the Taiwan Issues and EU–China relations, South China Sea Issues, the 19th Party Congress, the USA and China – A New Cold War in Asia? and also on China's Public Diplomacy and the CI. BGD2 also emphasised that: "we rarely organise lecturers, but more in the forms of seminars, workshops and conferences, because lecture is one person speaking with one view, while seminars and conferences are forums for discussions to take place and exchange of views".

GAO's reports finished with some suggestions for improvement of the CI, including "removing the confidentiality section of the agreement and make it publicly available online", which would "dispel questions and concerns over their contents", and several representatives of higher education institutions "believed the confidentiality language in agreements was unnecessary" (2019b: 10). This is a very reasonable suggestion if you look at each individual agreement, which more or less follows the same template provided by Hanban, all content are normal clauses one can find in any partnership agreement, but again, it is the non-uniformity between CIs that could explain the necessity of the confidentiality: although the majority receive a similar amount of funding and support from Hanban, some host universities have stronger bargaining powers than the others, which is reflected in the different treatments they received as prescribed in the agreements.

Conclusion: so similar, so different, and so Chinese

This chapter has continued to employ the lens of "terrain of struggle" to examine what distinguishes the CI from its Western counterparts operating in the same terrain. It has applied theories of Orientalism, cultural hegemony and the knowledge–power nexus to make analytical comparisons that address a much broader and deeper dimension beyond the superficial differences in government background and operating models. The results can be summarised as being "so similar, so different, and so Chinese":

162 *So similar, so different, so Chinese*

- The missions are very similar, one can even venture to say government involvement is also a similarity, which are all in conformity with the definition of cultural diplomacy;
- What is visibly different is the deliberate wording of the CI's purpose, its specific operating model and the unique element of research in the scope of provisions. But when placed in different historical, cultural and ideological contexts, a largely hidden and vital difference is revealed: the uneven condition in this terrain dominated by Western cultural hegemony, and the ensued different power *positions* occupied by the CI and its Western counterparts, not the actual *locations* of where the CI is based, lie at the root of the perceived differences in the CI's intentions and government involvement.
- Another not-so-visible difference is the side effects of being called the Chinese version of its Western counterparts: there is no standard formula in the provision of CIs; they are not just different from their Western counterparts, but also different from each other.
- The Chinese government's presence both "behind the stage" and "on the stage" is a distinguishing Chinese characteristic. It brought the government "background" to the "foreground", and thus was easily seized upon by the hegemonic side to generate resistance.

The comparative case studies drove the differences from the surface to the very core. Through the lens of a "terrain of struggle", we can see how some of the similarities between the CI and its Western counterparts were converted into differences: the similar purpose of language and culture promotion was interpreted with political connotations, turning the CI into an imagined propaganda vehicle; the similar funding sources from government were also interpreted as "strings attached" for the CI because of the different ideology of the Chinese government. This lens revealed that the most fundamental difference is not in the organisation itself, but in power relations with others, as was sharply pointed out by Foucault, "the fundamental point of anchorage of the relationships, is to be found outside the institution" (1982: 791). If we detach the organisation from the terrain of struggle it is placed into, we distort and inhibit the possibility of a comprehensive analysis.

As Chan has insightfully put it: "All perceptions are culturally biased and specific in time and space" (1999: x). A specific example is the CI's purpose, for we can see a clear disjunction between Hanban's aspirations and the external perceptions of it. Of course what matters is not how the CI sees its own intentions, but how it is perceived by others, just like the famous Henry Kissinger quote: "It is not a matter of what is true that counts but a matter of what is perceived to be true", by the hegemonic side, I shall add, and the power they hold transforms this perception into accepted 'knowledge'. While the difference in operating models is surely a major factor that distinguishes the CI from its Western counterparts, it is also an oversimplification that does not challenge the Orientalist grounds or the "positional superiority" the hegemonic side has occupied in this

So similar, so different, so Chinese   163

terrain of struggle. Instead, this difference was magnified through the lens of ideology, to the extent of negating the comparability of the CI to its Western counterparts. The way they over-interpret the difference in location while shifting attention away from the difference in position is actually a strategy of struggle. As Foucault (1982: 794) pointed out indeed, "between a relationship of power and a strategy of struggle, there is a perpetual linking and a perpetual reversal", which drives to the same point: the real difference rests in power relations and hegemony is maintained by the "locking together of power relationship with strategy and the results proceeding from these interactions" (Foucault, 1982: 795).

However, no matter which lens was adopted, it all pointed to one shared finding regarding the Chinese government's presence: both "behind the stage" and "on the stage" of cultural diplomacy, which was arguably counterproductive as a major source for attracting scepticisms. It seems not hard to understand why the authoritarian nature of the Chinese Party-state, and the blurred boundary between state involvement and the social cultural realm would generate cautions in reception. This chapter also dissects some cases of CI closures to reveal the lessons that can be learned. From Hanban's point of view, in a sense, it looks up to the CI's Western counterparts as role models to learn from and targets to exceed. As Lo and Pan commented, if "outcomes are measured solely in terms of quantitative leaps ... the achievements of the CI project are very remarkable" (2014: 12). However, the government presence as both the sponsor and censor becomes a major source attracting scepticism and sets the CI apart from its Western counterparts.

With its counter-hegemonic stance, the CI is fighting a 'defensive' battle under Western hegemony, but through 'offensive' expansions into overseas educational institutions. It's a state-led approach, whose "scale, speed, resources and strategic thinking" adds to the apprehension (Hughes, 2014: 75). Its status as the flagship project makes the CI an easy target that attracts mixed responses from applause to speculation, from doubts and fears to different interpretations. Reflections from the cases of CI closures demonstrate the tension and potential damage that the endogenous and exogenous constraints of the CI model can produce. Perhaps, there are better ways of using government input to move the CI model to a more constructive collaboration and equal partnership. How to improve the model and draw on more non-government-initiated programmes will be discussed in the following chapters.

Notes

1 This chapter is derived, in part, from an article published in *Journal of Asia Studies Review*, summer 2019, available at: www.tandfonline.com/doi/full/10.1080/10357823 .2019.1584602.
2 Alliance Française's website: www.alliancefr.org/en/who-are-we.
3 British Council website. Take an Exam, available at: https://takeielts.britishcouncil. org/choose-ielts/what-ielts.
4 Confucius Institute/Hanban: http://english.hanban.org/ (English); http://hanban.edu.cn (Chinese).
5 See Hanban website, at: http://english.hanban.org/node_7880.htm.
6 See British Council website, at: www.futurelearn.com/partners/british-council.

164 *So similar, so different, so Chinese*

7 See Hanban website, at: http://english.hanban.org/node_7716.htm.
8 "Confucius Institute", Penn State News, 2011, available at: http://news.psu.edu/tag/confucius-institute.
9 Conservative Party Human Rights Commission Report. (2019). *China's Confucius Institutes: An inquiry by the Conservative Party Human Rights Commission.* Available at: www.conservativehumanrights.com.
10 See Alliance Française website, at: www.afkampala.org/about.html.
11 Xinhua (2007). Confucius Institute becomes the Brightest Brand of China's Soft Power. *Xinhua*, 10 April 2007, available at: http://news.xinhuanet.com/politics/2007-04/10/content_5955253.htm.
12 Lise Richter, Svensk universitet lukker Kina-institut, *Information*, 1 October 2018, available at: www.information.dk/indland/2008/09/svensk-universitet-lukker-kina-institut.
13 See Hanban website, at: http://english.hanban.org/node_9806.htm.
14 The Confucius Institute Annual Development Report 2014 is available at: www.hanban.org/report/2014.pdf.
15 Xinhua, *Yuan Guiren: Gaoxiao laoshi bixu shouhao zhengzhi, falv, dade sandao dixian* [Yuan Guiren: University Teachers Must Abide by Political, Legal and Moral Bottom Lines], 29 January 2015., available at: http://news.xinhuanet.com/2015-01/29/c_1114183715.htm.
16 Christian Shepherd, Chinese academic stopped from teaching after criticising party leadership. *Financial Times*, 25 March 2019, available at: www.ft.com/content/8af0cfdc-4f11-11e9-b401-8d9ef1626294.
17 A Chinese Law Professor Criticized Xi. Now He's Been Suspended. *New York Times*, 26 March 2019, available at: www.nytimes.com/2019/03/26/world/asia/chinese-law-professor-xi.html.
18 BBC (2015). *Diaocha: Faguo Liang Kongzi Xuyuan guanbi de beihou* [Investigation: Behind the closure of the Lyon Confucius Institute], available at: www.bbc.com/zhongwen/simp/china/2015/01/150126_congfuciousinstitute_france.
19 See Hanban website, About Confucius Institute, available at: www.hanban.org/confuciousinstitutes/node_10961.htm.
20 The Confucius Institute Annual Development Report 2014 is available at: www.hanban.org/report/2014.pdf.
21 The full text is available at: www.insidehighered.com/news/2014/04/29/chicago-faculty-object-their-campuss-confucius-institute.
22 See AAUP website, at: www.aaup.org/report/1940-statement-principles-academic-freedom-and-tenure.
23 Statement on the Confucius Institute at the University of Chicago, 25 September 2014, available at: http://news.uchicago.edu/article/2014/09/25/statement-confucius-institute-university-chicago.
24 The full article in question can be found at: http://newspaper.jfdaily.com/jfrb/html/2014-09/19/content_17605.htm.

References

Barr, M. (2012). Nation Branding as Nation Building: China's Image Campaign. *East Asia*, 29: 81–94.
Belanger, L. (1999). Redefining Cultural Diplomacy: Cultural Security And Foreign Policy in Canada. *Political Psychology*, 20(4): 677–699.
Benner, T., J. Gaspers, M. Ohlberg, L. Poggetti and K. Shi-Kupfer (2018). *Authoritarian Advance: Responding to China's Growing Political Influence in Europe.* Produced by GPPI and Merics. Available at: www.merics.org/sites/default/files/2018-02/GPPi_MERICS_Authoritarian_Advance_2018_1.pdf.

Cai, P. (2014). Hard Times for China's Soft Power. *The Australian*, 29 September. Available at www.theaustralian.com.au/business/business-spectator/hard-times-for-chinas-soft-power/news-story/f8470e915b0fcd400cdaab5d9e087e62.

Chan, G. (1999). *Chinese Perspectives on International Relations: A Framework for Analysis.* London: Macmillan Press.

Chen, Y. and Z. Yu (2016). *Kongzi Xueyuan Hanyu jiaoshi duiwu fazhan xianzhuang ji cunzai de wenti* [Problems and Suggestions Regarding Teacher Shortage of the Confucius Institutes]. *Journal of World Education*, 10. Available at: www.360doc.com/content/16/0624/07/12810717_570300790.shtml.

Chey, J. (2008). Chinese "Soft Power" – Diplomacy and the Confucius Institute. *Sydney Papers*, 20(1): 32–46.

China File (2014). The Debate over Confucius Institutes: Part II. Available at: www.chinafile.com/conversation/debate-over-confucius-institutes-part-ii.

Cowan, G. and A. Arsenault (2008). Moving from Monologue to Dialogue to Collaboration: The Three Layers of Public Diplomacy. *Annuals of the American Academy of Political and Social Science*, 616(1): 10–30.

Cox, R. (1983). Gramsci, Hegemony and International Relations: An Essay in Method. *Millennium*, 12(2): 162–175.

Cummings, M.C. (2009). *Cultural Diplomacy and the United States Government: A Survey*. Washington, DC: Centre for Arts and Culture. Available at: www.Americansforthearts.org/sites/default/files/MCCpaper.pdf.

Dale, H. (2014). China's Confucius Institutes Could Threaten Academic Freedom. *Daily Signal*, 17 January. Available at: http://dailysignal.com/2014/01/17/chinas-confucius-institutes-threaten-academic-freedom/.

The Economist (2014). Confucius Institutes: About-Face. 26 September. Available at: www.economist.com/blogs/analects/2014/09/confucius-institutes.

Fallows, J. (2016). China's Great Leap Backward. *The Atlantic*, December. Available at: www.theatlantic.com/magazine/archive/2016/12/chinas-great-leap-backward/505817/.

Fiskesjö, M. (2015). Stockholm University Terminating its Confucius Institute. *H-Asia*, 1 January. Available at: http://networks.h-net.org/node/22055/discussions/56521/stockholm-university-terminating-its-confucius-institute.

Fontana, B. (1993). *Hegemony and Power: On the Relation between Gramsci and Machiavelli.* Minneapolis, MN: University of Minnesota Press.

Foucault, M. (1980). *Power/Knowledge*. Brighton: Harvester.

Foucault, M. (1982). Subject and Power. *Critical Inquiry*, 8(4): 777–795.

French, H.W. (2006). Another Chinese Export is all the Rage: China's Language. *New York Times*, 11 January, p. A2. Available at: www.nytimes.com/2006/01/11/world/asia/another-chinese-export-is-all-the-rage-chinas-language.html.

GAO (2019a). China: Agreements Establishing Confucius Institutes at U.S. Universities are Similar, but Institute Operations Vary. Publicly Released: 27 February 2019. Available at: www.gao.gov/assets/700/696859.pdf.

GAO (2019b). China: Observations on Confucius Institutes in the United States and U.S. Universities in China. Testimony Before the Permanent Subcommittee on Investigations, Committee on Homeland Security and Governmental Affairs, U.S. Senate. Publicly Released: 28 February. Available at: www.gao.gov/assets/700/697156.pdf.

Golden, D. (2011). China says no Talking Tibet as Confucius Funds U.S. Universities. *Bloomberg*, 2 November. Available at: www.bloomberg.com/news/articles/2011-11-01/china-says-no-talking-tibet-as-confucius-funds-u-s-universities.

166 *So similar, so different, so Chinese*

Gosset, D. (2013). Confucius Institutes More Than Language. *China Daily*, 6 September. Available at: http://europe.chinadaily.com.cn/epaper/2013-09/06/content_16948709.htm.

Guo, X. (2008). *Repackaging Confucius.* Stockholm: Institute for Security and Development Policy. Available at: www.isdp.eu/images/stories/isdp-main-pdf/2008_guo_repackaging-confucius.pdf.

Guttenplan, D. (2012). Critics Worry About Influence of Chinese Institutes on U.S. Campuses. *New York Times*, 5 March. Available at: www.nytimes.com/2012/03/05/us/critics-worry-about-influence-of-chinese-institutes-on-us-campuses.html.

Hartig, F. (2012). Confucius Institute and the Rise of China. *Journal of Chinese Political Science*, 17(1): 53–76.

Hartig, F. (2014). *Kongxi Xueyuan hequ hecong*? [The Future of the Confucius Institute]. *China Daily*, 29 December. Available at: http://ent.chinadaily.com.cn/2014-12/29/content_19194541.htm.

Hartig, F. (2016). *Chinese Public Diplomacy: The Rise of the Confucius Institutes.* London: Routledge.

Hubbert, J. (2014). The Anthropology of Confucius Institutes. *Society for East Asian Anthropology*, 5 May. Available at: http://seaa.Americananthro.org/2014/05/the-anthropology-of-confucius-institutes/.

Hubbert, J. (2019). *China in the World: An Anthropology of Confucius Institutes, Soft Power and Globalization.* Honolulu, HI: University of Hawaii Press.

Hughes, C.R. (2014). Confucius Institutes and the University: Distinguishing the Political Mission from the Cultural. *Issues & Studies*, 50(4): 45–83.

Huntington, S.P. (1998). *The Clash of Civilizations and the Remaking of World Order*. London: Touchstone.

Jacobs, A. and J.M. Yu (2014). Another U.S. University Severs Ties to Confucius Institute. *Sinosphere: New York Times*, 2 October. Available at: http://sinosphere.blogs.nytimes.com/2014/10/02/penn-state-severs-ties-to-confucius-institute/.

Kahn-Ackermann, M. (2014). *Kongzi Xueyuan xuyao tingzhi kuozhang qu zhua zhiliang* [Confucius Institute Should Shift Focus from Expansion to Quality]. Available at: http://cul.qq.com/a/20141204/014701.htm.

Kluver, R. (2014). The Sage as Strategy: Nodes, Networks and the Quest for Geopolitical Power in the Confucius Institute. *Communication, Culture & Critique*, 7(2): 192–209.

Kramsch, C. (1993). *Context and Culture in Language Teaching*. Oxford: Oxford University Press.

Li, K. and Z. Dai (2011). Evaluation of Confucius Institute's Media Environment in the US. *World Economy and Politics*, 7: 76–93.

Li, M. (2008). Soft Power in Chinese Discourse: Popularity and Prospect. *RSIS Working Paper, 165*. S. Rajaratnam School of International Studies, Nanyang Technological University.

Li, M. (ed.) (2009). *Soft Power: China's Emerging Strategy in International Politics*. Plymouth: Lexington Books.

Liou, C.-S. and A. Ding (eds) (2015). *China Dreams: China's New Leadership and Future Impacts*. Singapore: World Scientific Publishing.

Little, M. (2010). Confucius Institutes: Getting Schooled by Beijing, Chinese Regime uses Academic Institutes to Expand its Soft Power. *Phayul.com*, 16 July. Available at: www.phayul.com/news/article.aspx?id=27757.

Liu, C. (2010). No Need to Fuss Over Confucius Institutes. *China Daily*, 14 August. Available at: www.chinadaily.com.cn/cnddy/2010–08/14/content_11152936.htm.

Liu, T.T. (2017). Exporting Culture, the Confucius Institute and China's Smart Power Strategy. In Victoria Dutter, Toby Miller and Dave O'Brien (eds), *The Routledge Handbook of Global Cultural Policy* (pp. 233–246). New York: Routledge.

Lo, J.T. and S. Pan (2014). Confucius Institute and China's Soft Power: Practices and Paradoxes. *Compare: A Journal of Comparative and International Education*, 46(4): 512–532.

Louie, K. (2011). Confucius the Chameleon: Dubious Envoy for "Brand China". *Boundary 2*, 38(1): 77–100.

Melissen, J. (2005). The New Public Diplomacy: Between Theory and Practice. In J. Melissen (ed.), *New Public Diplomacy: Soft Power in International Relations* (pp. 3–27). New York: Palgrave Macmillan.

Mosher, S.W. (2012). Confucius Institutes: Trojan Horses with Chinese Characteristics. Testimony presented to the Subcommittee on Oversight and Investigations House Committee on Foreign Affairs presented 28 March. Available at: http://pop.org/content/confucius-institutes-trojan-horses-chinese-characteristics.

Mulcahy, K.V. (2017). *Public Culture, Cultural Identity, Cultural Policy: Comparative Perspectives*. New York: Palgrave Macmillan.

Nakagawa, U. (2011). Confucius: What's in a Name? Confucius Institutes have Little to do with the Ancient Philosopher after which They're Named. But does it Matter? *Diplomat*, 28 Febraury. Available at: https://thediplomat.com/2011/02/confucius-whats-in-a-name/.

Nye, Jr, J.S. (2004). *Soft Power: The Means to Succeed in World Politics.* New York: Public Affairs.

Pan, S.Y. (2013). Confucius Institute Project: China's Cultural Diplomacy and Soft Power Projection. *Asian Education and Development Studies*, 2(1): 22–33.

Paradise, J. (2009). China and International Harmony: The Role of Confucius Institute in Bolstering Beijing's Soft Power. *Asian Survey*, 49(4): 647–669.

Parton, C. (2019). China–UK Relations Where to Draw the Border Between Influence and Interference? *RUSI Occasional Paper*, February, Royal United Services Institute for Defence and Security Studies. Available at: https://rusi.org/sites/default/files/20190220_chinese_interference_parton_web.pdf.

Paschalidis, G. (2009). Exporting National Culture: Histories of Cultural Institutes Abroad. *International Journal of Cultural Policy*, 15(3): 275–289.

Pennycook, A. (2013). *The Cultural Politics of English as an International Language*. New York: Routledge.

Peters, M. and C. Zhang (2011). Confucius Alive. *China Daily*, 25 September. Available at http://usa.chinadaily.com.cn/china/2011-09/25/content_13786782.htm.

Qu, Y., H. Zhao and Y. Cheng (2012). Confucius Institutes Go Beyond Borders. *China Daily*, 2 December. Available at: www.chinadaily.com.cn/china/2012-12/02/content_15978436.htm.

Redden, E. (2012). Confucius says…. *Inside Higher Ed*, 4 January. Available at: www.insidehighered.com/news/2012/01/04/debate-over-Chinese-funded-institutes-American-universities.

Redden, E. (2014). Confucius Controversies. *Inside Higher Ed*, 24 July. Available at: www.insidehighered.com/news/2014/07/24/debate-renews-over-confucius-institutes.

Ren, Z. (2010). Confucius Institutes: China's Soft Power? George Washington University, *Rising Powers Initiative*, June. Available at: www.risingpowersinitiative.org/wp-content/uploads/policycommentary_jun2010_confuciusinstitute.pdf.

Ren, Z. (2014). China Voice: Fear, Ignorance Behind calls to Stem Confucius Institutes. CCTV, 24 June. Available at: http://english.cntv.cn/2014/06/24/ARTI1403568561698629.shtml.

168 *So similar, so different, so Chinese*

Ricking, C. (2012). Critics Fear Influence of Chinese State on Confucius Institute Affiliates. *DW News*, 25 January. Available at: www.dw.de/critics-fear-influence-of-chinese-state-on-confucius-institute-affiliates/a-15688977.

Sahlins, M. (2013). China U. *The Nation*. Available at www.thenation.com/article/china-u/.

Sahlins, M. (2015). *Confucius Institute: Academic Malware*. Chicago, IL: Prickly Paradigm Press.

Said, E. (1993). *Culture and Imperialism*. New York: Random House.

Shambaugh, D. (2013). *China goes Global: The Partial Power*. New York: Oxford University Press.

Shimbun, S. (2018). [History Wars] Confucius Institute Pushes China's Belt and Road Ambitions in Europe. *Japan Forward*, 28 August. Available at: https://japan-forward.com/history-wars-confucius-institute-pushes-chinas-belt-and-road-ambitions-in-europe/.

Starr, D. (2009). Chinese Language Education in Europe: The Confucius Institutes. *European Journal of Education*, 44(1): 65–82.

Taylor, P.M. (1997). *Global Communications, International Affairs and the Media since 1945*. London: Routledge.

Wang, H. (2005). National Image Building and Chinese Foreign Policy. In Yong Deng and Fei-ling Wang (eds), *China Rising: Power and Motivation in Chinese Foreign Policy* (pp. 73–102). New York: Rowman & Littlefield.

Wang, Y. (2014). *Wenhua de kunjing zaiyu buzhi bujue, dujia duihua guojia Hanban zhuren, Kongzi Xueyuan zongganshi Xulin* [An Exclusive Interview with Xu Lin, Director of Hanban]. *JF Daily*, 19 September. Available at: http://newspaper.jfdaily.com/jfrb/html/2014-09/19/content_17605.htm.

Xu, L. (2011). Report of the 2012 Work and 2013 Plan of the Confucius Institute Headquarters. Beijing: Hanban. Available at: www.hanban.org/report/2012.pdf.

Yang, J. (2011). Promoting Public Diplomacy. *China Daily*, 2 September. Available at: http://usa.chinadaily.com.cn/opinion/2011-09/02/content_13603197.htm.

Yang, R. (2010). Soft Power and Higher Education: An Examination of China's Confucius. *Globalisation, Societies and Education*, 8(2): 235–245.

Zaharna, R.S. (2014). China's Confucius Institutes: Understanding the Relational Structure & Relational Dynamics of Network Collaboration. In J. Wang (ed.), *Confucius Institutes and the Globalization of China's Soft Power* (pp. 9–32). Los Angeles, CA: Figueroa Press.

Zhu, C. (2012). *Zhongguo wenhua "zouchuqu" weihe kunnan chongchong*? [Why is the "Going Global" of Chinese Culture Beset in Difficulties?]. *Zhongguo Wenhua Chanye Pinglun [Review of Chinese Cultural Industry]*: 2: 84–104.

5 The last three feet

Where citizen diplomacy can dissolve the perception of Chinese sharp power

> The key to sound relations between states lies in the affinity between their peoples.
>
> (Han Feizi (280–233 BC), an ancient Chinese philosopher)

What is the "last three feet" and why it matters

"The last three feet" is a term coined by Ed Murrow: "the real crucial link in the international exchange is the last three feet, which is bridged by personal contact, one person talking to another" (cited in Clack, 2006: 2). People-to-people contacts have expanded cultural diplomacy beyond the professional diplomat's sphere to include more initiatives developed by everyday citizens engaged in cross-border activities. In 2007, a U.S. Centre for Citizen Diplomacy (USCCD) was formally established and defined citizen diplomacy as "the concept that every global citizen has the right, even the responsibility, to engage across cultures and create shared understanding through meaningful person-to-person interactions".[1] As argued by Holden, in today's global environment, the role played by the general public is becoming increasingly crucial as "people-to-people cultural contacts set the tone and sometimes the agenda for traditional state-to-state diplomacy" (2013: 3). A more detailed definition of citizen diplomacy was given by Bhandari and Belyavina:

> Citizen diplomacy is a concept that involves two seemingly disparate ideas: private citizens engaging in individual endeavours that serve their own interests; and diplomacy, which includes a framework for cooperation between countries. Taken together, citizen diplomacy refers to an array of actions and activities that individuals can partake in that contribute to deepening ties between individuals and communities and to advancing the goals of public diplomacy. Citizen diplomacy is thus an integral part of public diplomacy.
>
> (Bhandari and Belyavina, 2011: 3)

In the context of China, probably only the term of "citizen diplomacy" is relatively new, while people-to-people diplomacy or "track two diplomacy" ("track

170   *The last three feet*

one" refers to government-to-government diplomatic efforts) has been an instrument often utilised by the Chinese government since Mao Zedong's time. The Chinese People's Institute of Foreign Affairs (CPIFA) was founded in December 1949, the first of its kind devoted to people-to-people diplomacy, on the initiative of the late Premier Zhou Enlai. Then the Chinese People's Association for Friendship with Foreign Countries (CPAFFC) was established in 1954 as "a national people's organization engaged in people-to-people diplomacy of the People's Republic of China" and has "established relationship of friendly cooperation with nearly 500 NGOs and institutions in 157 countries".[2] Ping-pong diplomacy may be the most classic example to show the tremendous role it can play by paving the way for the normalisation of the relationship between China and the USA.

In the last few decades, along with China's miraculous economic development, unprecedented growth in two-way cross-border traffic is evident in the increase of people-to-people contacts across the border: hugely improved international mobility of Chinese citizens give rise to the year-on-year sharp increase of Chinese students, tourists, entrepreneurs and investors venturing abroad; reciprocated by substantial increase in the number of 'foreigners' coming to China, attracted by its generous offer of scholarships, booming economy and job opportunities, diverse tourism resources as well as proliferating international forums and conferences. It is fair to argue that China is now in a better position than ever before to close the cultural encounter to the "last three feet" through people-to-people interactions, be it among short-term visitors, or long-term migrants, diasporas, expatriates, returnees, or their use of internet and engagement on social media. George H.W. Bush once proclaimed that: "no nation on earth has discovered a way to import the world's goods and services while stopping foreign ideas at the border" (cited in Campbell and Ratner, 2018: n.p.). Not giving credits to the Great Fire Wall of China as such a way to try stopping foreign ideas at the border while importing the world's smart phones and computers, as the Chinese government actually blocked Google's services including YouTube in 2010 as well as Apple's iTunes movie and iBooks services and apps in 2016; I wish to modify this statement into that "no nation on earth has discovered a way to stop foreign ideas at the border when people exchange visits across the border".

People-to-people diplomacy also frequently appears in government rhetoric both domestically and internationally. For example in 2012, people-to-people exchanges was proposed to be the third pillar of EU–China relations by setting up the EU–China High Level People-to-People Dialogue as the overarching mechanism to accommodate joint initiatives in this field, complementing the other two pillars – the High Level Economic and Trade Dialogue and the Strategic Dialogue. In 2013, in addressing the 100-year anniversary of the Western Returned Scholars Association, Xi Jinping encouraged both Chinese diaspora and overseas Chinese students to tell Chinese stories in ways that the audience "can hear, can understand and would listen" to gain "better understanding of and more support to China",[3] and in 2014, he specified in a speech that "people-to-people diplomacy represents the most profound force in promoting inter-civilisation exchanges and mutual learning".[4]

When China's political system often becomes a barrier to the full effects of government-led cultural diplomacy, citizen exchange at the grassroots level becomes all the more important. According to Anholt (2006), "nation branding" is the umbrella concept whereas public diplomacy is considered a subset that focuses on the political brand of a nation. It can be inferred that cultural diplomacy is the subset that focuses on the cultural brand of a nation. However, a nation's brand and image hinges on the overall sum across six areas of national competence, namely a nation's cultural, political, commercial and human assets, investment potential and tourist appeal (please refer to Figure 2.1 in Chapter 2). We have already discussed the two areas that China got the highest and lowest rankings: a strong ranking for "culture and heritage" and a very low ranking for "governance", but the "people" dimension is where its utility is still much under-employed. Too often, a Chinese person travelling abroad hears their international companions say, "I do not like your government, but I love Chinese people". Actually, a common statement made by almost all the reports evaluating the CI is to separate Chinese government from the Chinese people. For example, in Parton's report, he wrote "criticism in this paper is not aimed at the Chinese people. The Party is adept at turning criticism of itself into a charge of being anti-Chinese and thereby racist" (2019: 1). Then, in Peterson's paper (2018), a very similar statement was made:

> We must distinguish between the Chinese government and the Chinese people, and recognize that criticizing one does not mean denigrating the other. The PRC regime has repeatedly tried to blur this line, using its citizens as a shield for its political agenda.
>
> (Peterson, 2018)

And finally, in the CPHRC report to investigate the CI, it says:

> We must realise that the present Chinese government is an authoritarian one-party, quasi-police state. It is not China. China, its cultural tradition and its people, is infinitely greater than the Beijing government. To be seduced by the prestige and perceived financial benefits of cooperating with Beijing; to allow the Chinese government to co-opt the legitimacy of our universities; not only compromises the moral and intellectual integrity that we have worked so hard to maintain, it is a travesty, and an insult to the people and cultural legacy of China.
>
> (cited in CPHRC Report, 2019: 18)

This may help explain why, despite the closure of the CIUC, the University of Chicago Centre in Beijing continues to "enhance and strengthen the University's traditionally strong ties to Chinese thought and culture".[5] This is also the reason why Copenhagen University in Denmark rejected to have a CI in 2006 as they "prefer to collaborate directly with Chinese academics at Chinese universities, rather than collaborating directly with the Chinese government" (cited in

172 *The last three feet*

Sahlins, 2015: 51). Such comments reiterate the importance of reducing government presence in cultural diplomacy efforts. There is a tendency for top-down approach in China by hosting high-profile international events or launching state-sponsored projects. While for domestic audiences they proudly displayed China's national achievements, they may be perceived more cynically internationally. The "highly scripted" Hanban-sponsored Bridge summer programme is another example of such, that students had come to "view these experiences with disbelief and distrust.... These students equated the 'real' China they were being shown with image control" (Hubbert, 2019: 81). Even if Hanban is trying really hard at "telling better Chinese stories", the explicit government role simply means they cannot be as good storytellers as ordinary citizens. As Hubbert's ethnographic evidence shows, "the more our hosts provided material examples of China's modernity that were meant to stress China's rightful position on the global stage, the more their efforts were met with scepticism from the students, confirming negative stereotypes" (Hubbert, 2019: 83). She even drew an analogy between these organised trips and the Potemkin village, staged to "guide the foreigners through a 'cultural show'" (David-Fox, 2011: 98, cited in Hubbert, 2019: 82), and commented that "while the historical eras and global hierarchies of power are different, China's efforts to fashion a particular image through cultural exchange reflect Soviet–US/European cultural exchanges in the period between the two world wars" (Hubbert, 2019: 81). What Bellamy and Weinberg (2008: 56) said about the USA is equally applicable to China, if not more so: since "the US government is less trusted", hence "the messengers cannot be people who are perceived as spokespersons for US foreign policy", and "creating a successful strategy for public diplomacy will require rethinking some fundamental assumptions". Cultural diplomacy being state-led is one of such fundamental assumptions being made in China, and its side effects can be revealed in the "sharp power" perception for its "soft power" efforts.

The debatable sharp power[6]

Since China openly engaged in projecting soft power, its endeavours have been constantly facing challenges. When China's investment on soft power exceeds the combined government spending of the USA, UK, France, Germany and Japan (Davidson, 2017), cultural diplomacy blurs into the area of money diplomacy, and inducement combined with intimidation were often considered to be the "hard edge" of China's soft power. To some, the edge has become so hard that it is deemed to have changed the nature of soft power as argued by Christopher Walker and Jessica Ludwig from National Endowment for Democracy (NED), a Washington-based think-tank funded largely by the US Congress. They coined the new term of "sharp power" in 2017 to refer to the "authoritarian soft power", as it "pierces, penetrates, or perforates the political and information environments in the targeted countries" through the use of "outward-facing censorship, manipulation and distraction" (Walker and

Ludwig, 2017: n.p.). They used China and Russia as typical examples, and stated that "what we have to date understood as 'soft power' when speaking of authoritarian regimes might be more properly labelled as 'sharp power'" (Walker and Ludwig, 2017: 13). It is interesting to see that they did not shy from using the word "labelled", making it clear that their definition of sharp power is more about 'who' does it rather than 'how' it is done – even if China and Russia are doing the same thing, it becomes a different thing because "although Russia and China undertake some activities that can credibly fall into the category of normal public diplomacy, the nature of these countries political systems invariably and fundamentally colour their efforts", which gave the authoritarian projects a "malign and aggressive nature" (Walker and Ludwig, 2017: 13). They even used "cultural events like Chinese New Year celebration" (Walker and Ludwig, 2017: 16) and "people-to-people exchanges" (Walker and Ludwig, 2017: 19) as examples of sharp power, which were echoed by Singh (2018) who also included "tourists" in his article.

Since the term was created to safeguard the concept of soft power from being misused or even contaminated, Nye's comments bear particular significance. In his article "How sharp power threatens soft power", published in January 2018 as a direct response, Nye clearly articulated that "sharp power, the deceptive use of information for hostile purposes, is a type of hard power". To him, the difference between soft power and sharp power is also in nature, only that it lies in the 'how' and 'why': if power is used in this way and for this purpose, then it is hard power, and the USA had done it before during the Cold War (secret funding for anti-Communist parties in the 1948 Italian election and the CIA's covert support to the Congress for Cultural Freedom). When the term is simply directed against 'who', then it is nothing more than "a new term that describes an old threat" (Nye, 2018: n.p.). He also elaborated that "government backing does not mean they are necessarily a sharp power threat", citing a more controversial example than the Chinese New Year celebration and people-to-people exchanges: "Chinese soft power programs, such as Confucius Institutes, do not slip into 'sharp' power", "only when a Confucius Institute crosses the line and tries to infringe on academic freedom (as has occurred in some instances), should it be treated as sharp power" (Nye, 2018: n.p.). By contrasting the examples of CIA and the CI, Nye has made the focus quite sharp in the 'how' rather than 'who' to distinguish "sharp power" from "soft power".

For other scholarly exchanges, Nye has explained that:

> The United States has long had programs enabling visits by young foreign leaders, and now China is successfully following suit. That is a smart exercise of soft power. But when visas are manipulated or access is limited to restrain criticism and encourage self-censorship, even such exchange programs can shade into sharp power.
>
> (Nye, 2018: n.p.)

However, although in discussing countermeasures, *The Economist* article (2017) has warned that "calls from American politicians for tit-for-tat 'reciprocity' over

174   *The last three feet*

visas for academics and NGO workers, would be equally self-defeating", in April 2019, the *New York Times* carried a report about FBI bars some Chinese scholars from visiting the USA:

> In the four decades since China and the United States normalized relations, Washington has generally welcomed Chinese scholars and researchers to America, even when Beijing has been less open to reciprocal visits.... Now, that door appears to be closing, with the two nations ramping up their strategic rivalry and each regarding academic visitors from the other with greater suspicion – of espionage, commercial theft and political meddling.[7]

Despite Nye's clear articulation and China's counter-rhetoric, "sharp power" as a term and perception seem to be spreading very quickly, China needs to look at how to dissolve it at the same time of refuting it. If "smart power" is the right mix or a successful "combination of the hard power of coercion and payment with the soft power of persuasion and attraction" (Nye, 2011: xiii), I think "sharp power" is better understood as a result of unsuccessful combination of the two. In other words, I disagree with both Walker and Nye but believe that the perceived "sharp power" is not soft power nor hard power, it is the product of an unskilled mixing of the two, or put it simply, the "unsmart power". This is not to coin a new term, but rather, to make the point that no new term is needed as this is an old challenge China has been facing, however, it *is* something different from the three established concepts of soft, hard, and smart power. It describes the outcome of an unsmart approach, as Li has argued, "soft power does not exist in the nature of certain resources of power, but rather it has to be nurtured through a soft use of power" (2009: 3). Therefore, it is the 'how', not the 'who' or 'why' that defines the difference: how can tourists, Chinese New Year celebration and people-to-people exchanges mean to serve a hostile purpose? All states' soft power efforts can have good intensions, but the effects can sometimes be distorted by the application of hard methods.

Gilboa (1998: 58) describes this as the distinction between providing "civilised persuasion" and distortions and half-truths, while Parton's (2019) argument of the border between "legitimate influence" and "unacceptable interference" can be understood as another way to distinguish "soft power" from "sharp power". In the case of the Confucius Institute, Parton's conclusion is that "if kept transparent and out of a university's operational affairs, CIs can be confined to the influence end of the spectrum; without that proviso, they constitute interference" (Parton, 2019: 18). He further explained that: "a major tool of interference is to create dependency on Chinese funding (or to imply that it may be withdrawn). Often this promotes self-censorship and self-limiting policies, to avoid losing financial support" (Parton, 2019: 10). For example, China put the University of Calgary on the blacklist of study destinations for government scholarships to deprive it of Chinese student revenue after it hosted Dalai Lama's visit. The CIA also reported that: "the CCP provides 'strings-attached' funding to academic institutions and think-tanks to *deter* research that casts it in a negative light. It has used this tactic to *reward* pro-China viewpoints and *coerce* Western academic publications and conferences to self-censor" (Johnson, 2018: n.p.). This is where the boundary blurs between the use of soft power and hard power resources, and it is the overuse or misuse of the latter that gives it a sharp edge.

A further tactic for sharp power is "elite capture", referring to the "appointing of former politicians, civil servants, businessmen, or high-profile academics/think-tank personnel who retain influence in their home countries on positions in Chinese companies and think-tanks or on affiliated posts in Chinese universities" (Parton, 2019: 10). This was identified as one of the 'how's that give the attribute of "sharp power" as they are directed at "key individuals" (politicians, journalists, academics and think-tank researchers) according to Walker and Ludwig (2017: 19). For China, this approach contains a cultural element that is unintentional to be "sharp": *guanxi*, a Chinese cultural concept that has been elaborated by plenty of writings, is no longer an alien notion to many Westerners, yet how powerful and pervasively embedded it is in the Chinese way of doing things is perhaps beyond genuine understanding. In fact, there are often inaccurate understandings that this concept is mostly business-related, a must-know if you want to do business with China; it is actually underpinning everyone's everyday life in the Chinese society, including government behaviour. For example, using personal relations as an ice-breaker or a messenger is a common practice in China's foreign relations. "Chinese people's good friends", Edgar Snow and Henry Kissinger, have all played such roles in different stages of Sino-US relations. Similarly, summit meetings between state leaders are also attached greater importance in China in the hope that a close personal relationship can help warm bilateral relations.

This may help understand China's official response to the Chinese way being labelled "sharp": Wang Guoqing, the spokesperson for Chinese People's Political Consultative Conference, said in March 2018 on a press conference that "the new expression has been concocted [by the West] to vilify China", and the accusations that China "infiltrates" in the political and information environments of other nations are "filled with prejudice, discrimination, and hostility" as "some Westerners may have physically entered the 21st century, but are mentally stuck in the Cold War era".[8] Xinhua also carried an article calling the term "no more than a language trap, coined and manipulated by some Western countries with 'zero-sum' mentality and cultural hegemony".[9] Wang's official remarks were captured by international media, such as *Reuters*,[10] *Newsweek*[11] and *South China Morning Post*,[12] as an aggressive move against Western discrimination; and by domestic media such as *Xinhua*[13] and *China Daily*[14] as a counter-attack to the smearing of China. I do not think China should blame the coinage of the term, as one cannot dictate the target audience's reception and reaction to one's message, the sharp power rhetoric is a true reflection of the perception held by some receivers. If this is a *misperception* due to "fear and misunderstanding" as the spokesman has put it, or due to an overdose of hard resources, then China needs to look at how to dissolve them by adjusting the recipe. As Confucius said, "when it is obvious that the goal cannot be reached, do not adjust the goals, adjust the action steps". This should be the smart move for China, as creating smart power is the ultimate goal.

176 *The last three feet*

This adjustment may include doing more of one thing and less of another. While people-to-people exchanges are named as examples of sharp power, as they are directed at "key individuals" (Walker and Ludwig, 2017: 19), I believe citizen diplomacy is where such perceptions can be neutralised in a just way, as ordinary citizens are perceived to be authentic messengers between whom the two-way communications and personal contacts take place in a most 'unauthoritarian' manner, thus are often far more effective generators of soft power than official efforts. This was supported by the research findings shared by Bellamy and Weinberg (2008: 59) in "the ability of face-to-face interactions to break through national stereotypes", as "people communicate through verbal and non-verbal signals that tend to be accepted by the listener as authentic and honest. There is less questioning, more acceptance, and more rapid change in perceptions", and I hope, the changes produced would also be longer lasting. Hubbert's (2019: 121) contrasting ethnographic findings offered compelling evidence: while Hanban-sponsored Bridge summer school produced paradoxical effects in that "the more Hanban's instrumentalization of culture became apparent – the less 'authentic' and more 'authoritarian' it was perceived – the more it fed into students' worst perceptions about China's structures of governance and control" (Hubbert, 2019: 93), back at home inside the Confucius Classrooms,

> it was these personal relations with the CC teachers more than anything else that decreased students' and parents' negative perceptions about the Chinese state ... the more intimate contact that the students had with CC teachers made them begin to see China less as the epitome of an authoritarian state.
>
> (Hubbert, 2019: 121)

From the above we can see that the sharp power perception is based on a circular reasoning: China cannot be seen to project soft power because of its authoritarian nature of state, and on the China's side, the sharp power accusation simply feeds a growing spiral of anti-West sentiment. Citizen diplomacy can help break this vicious and enclosed cycle of misperceptions. Its value has been underestimated till today, when it has become all the more important than ever before to untap its huge potential to maximise its value. The next section is going to look at a case study of a non-government-initiated student exchange programme to see how citizen diplomacy and people-to-people interactions can help improve effects of cultural diplomacy in shaping perceptions.

The value of citizen diplomacy – a case study of a student exchange programme

While Kurlantzick (2007) argues that mass media and cultural exchange programmes are the two strongest image shapers that influence public perceptions of a country in the modern world today, Bellamy and Weinberg (2008) have referred to cultural and education exchanges as a synonym for citizen diplomacy, and the increase of people-to-people contacts between China and the rest of the world is particularly phenomenal in student numbers. In 2014, China overtook the USA and UK as the top destination for anglophone African students.[15] Between China and the UK, Chinese already constituted the largest single source of overseas students in the UK according to the 2016/17 statistics released by the UK Council for International Students Affairs, "the number of Chinese students far exceeds any other nationality; almost one third of non-EU students in the UK is from China. This is the only country showing a significant increase in student numbers" (UKCISA, 2018).[16] When Xinhua News reported the 17 per cent increase in the number of visas granted to Chinese students to study in Britain compared with 2015/2016, the Home Office Minister Baroness Williams was quoted to say "We absolutely recognise the cultural and financial contribution that they make to this country",[17] showing that "cultural contribution" was fully recognised and highlighted. Meanwhile, the number of British students studying in China has also increased by 60 per cent since 2013. As reported in 2016, the number of UK residents seeking degrees or work exchanges in China has more than tripled within the past ten years (Pells, 2016). The British Council promotes the 'Generation UK' programme, which aims to bring 80,000 UK students to China between 2016 and 2020, with a view to help them understand China better and become more competitive globally. The British government is also encouraging young people to go to China. During her first official visit to China in February 2018, the former Prime Minister May signed an education deal to "enable more children and more young people than ever to share their ideas about our two great nations",[18] which gave further impetus at government level to keep the momentum going.

On the other side of the Western world, Fallows has commented that:

> U.S. universities depend on Chinese students who pay full freight; the culture of each country is enriched by its exposure to the other. Millions of people on each side enjoy, respect, and love people they have met and the encounters they have had in the other country.
>
> (Fallows, 2016: n.p.)

When addressing the 40th anniversary of USA–China Relations in 2019, Shambaugh (2019: n.p.) has started with:

> Forty years ago there were no students exchanged – today there are 363,341 Chinese students studying in American universities and an estimated 80,000 in American secondary schools, while there are approximately 12,000 American students studying in China.... Four decades ago only a few of American tourists visited China, while none travelled to the United States. During 2018 an estimated 3.24 million Chinese tourists will have visited America, with approximately 2.25 million Americans going to China. Approximately 250 direct flights per week traverse the Pacific between the two countries. These people-to-people ties are buttressed by more than 201 sister city and 44 sister state-province relationships.

178 *The last three feet*

Then in the speech given by Harvard University President at Peking University in March 2019, he mentioned that "Chinese is the second-most widely studied foreign language at Harvard", and in 2019 alone, over 1,000 students and more than 1,000 scholars have joined Harvard from China – the largest cohort from any nation. He also mentioned there are over 2,500 alumni from China. And most importantly, it doesn't stop at these impressive numbers, because

> each interaction that unfolds, each relationship that blossoms on our campuses depends on both humility and hope – a willingness to say to others "I don't know", to look in the same direction with them, and to imagine success – and risk failure – in the joint pursuit of knowledge.[19]

Students, teachers, scholars and alumni could all act as citizen diplomats during their time in the host countries, and produce ripple effects to change perception when they return to their home countries – a miniature of the mutual process illustrated in Figure 1.1, embodying country A and B as individuals from A and B. Paradise's research (2012: 203) indicate that students who have studied in China will return with at least a "measure of good will" towards China, which was confirmed by Hong's research (2014: 166) on EU–China Education Diplomacy and Bislev's (2017: 105) research on Student-to-Student Diplomacy. Even when students study Chinese in their own country, but with teachers expatriated from China, such an effect of changing perception is also taking place at individual level as cited earlier in Hubbert's research (2019).

This case study will explore the role citizen diplomacy can play via student exchange programmes, and evaluate its impact on local people's perception to a country through people-to-people interactions and access to first-hand knowledge and experience. It is based on a student collaboration programme between China and the UK, "Journey to the East", initiated by a British university in 2013 and inspired by *Journey to the West* – a classic novel in Chinese literature. The programme aims to bring together great student talents from both countries and put them into groups of four (to simulate the four characters in the original story) to work together as a team. Each team will be given a specific task to complete proposed by an expert panel, who will select the winning team at the end. The awards include scholarships for Chinese students to study in the UK (sponsored by the British University) and paid internship opportunities in China for British students (sponsored by corporate participants). It provides opportunities for students to encounter and engage peers from vastly different backgrounds by having in-depth social interactions both inside and outside campus, experiencing a shared sense of community as simply students, not just *Chinese* students and *British* students. For UK students in particular, it allows them to embark on a journey of discovery to better understand China, find out what opportunities are made possible to young people by its economic rise, and become more competitive globally. So far, 11 Chinese universities have hosted Journey to the East. The programme has received wide coverage in the local newspapers in China, and was shortlisted by UK Trade and Investment for its final education award for the greater China region in 2015.

Data and method

The focus of the study will be more on British students' visits to China and their experience as the case study aims to test the value of people-to-people interaction in improving the general public's perception of China. As English is part of the curriculum taught in China at primary school level and above, and the UK has been a populous destination for Chinese students and tourists, British culture is more accessible to average Chinese citizens through literature, film and other forms of popular culture such as music and football. In contrast, when the exchange programme first started in Lancashire in 2013, awareness of China among the general public was quite limited. Nearly all of the participants, including teachers, are seeing China with their own eyes and experience university life there for the first time.

A combined quantitative and qualitative data were collected through questionnaires and semi-structured interviews. The questionnaire was designed to be completed in two parts: five questions before the students left for the visit and five at the end, to facilitate the purpose of comparing and identifying changes in their perceptions of China. For example, two sets of questions of using key words to describe China and Chinese people are deliberately repeated pre and post visits to compare the answers. Other than this, before the trip, students were asked about what they were 'most looking forward to' and their 'biggest worry"; after the trip, they were asked about their 'highlights of the trip' and 'biggest surprise'. The full questionnaire can be found in Appendix 6.

Thirty questionnaires were distributed and twenty-eight were returned from three groups of students joining the 2019 'Journey to the East' trip to three different destinations, Beijing/Inner Mongolia, Xiamen/Chongqing and Qingdao. They are from three different schools, the School of Business and Enterprise, School of Education and School of Sports, and the majority of them have never learned any Chinese language. Along with the returned questionnaires, a surprise 'bonus' is a student's 1,870-word blog. Six semi-structured interviews were then carried out to three teachers and three groups of student representatives from each destination. The pool of eighty-four key words (28×3) produced in each set to describe their perceptions of China and Chinese people were then processed using word cloud software to show the most frequently used, and to contrast the top five before and after the trip. Similar words were grouped into one representation to focus on semantic meaning rather than varied expressions, for example, "big", "vast", "large" and "massive" are all represented by "big" to describe the country, and "reserved", "shy", "quiet", "mild" are all represented by "reserved" to describe the people.

Bigger sample size and a more comprehensive evaluation of the impact of exchange programmes would be desirable by applying the framework created by Wang and Nisbet's research (2018) in examining the five categories of "capital" that such exchange may impact: Knowledge Capital, Cultural Capital, Social Capita, Civic Capital and Economic Capital. It is also desirable to have a comparison group who did not join the trip and were not exposed to interpersonal

180 *The last three feet*

contacts with Chinese people. However, due to the limited scope of the book, this case study focuses on using empirical evidence to support the assumption that ordinary citizens can contribute to the aim of cultural diplomacy of enhancing mutual understanding in their own terms, and non-governmental initiatives may be a more effective tool for China to dissolve the sharp power perception than government-organised ones, compared with the empirical research findings of Hubbert (2019).

Data analysis and discussions

Figures 5.1–5.4 below show the results from the twenty-eight questionnaires regarding their impressions of China and Chinese people pre and post visits. The key words were processed with word cloud to show the difference at a glance:

Figure 5.1 Key words to describe China before the trip.

Figure 5.2 Key words to describe China after the trip.

Figure 5.3 Key words to describe Chinese people before the trip.

Figure 5.4 Key words to describe Chinese people after the trip.

Figures 5.1 and 5.2 represent students' descriptions of China before and after the trip, while Figures 5.3 and 5.4 represent their descriptions of Chinese people before and after the trip.

As we can see, the top five key words used to describe China before the visit are "busy", "big", "modern", "cultural" and "populated"; while the top five key words (with a tie for the fifth place) after the visit in the same order of frequency are: "busy", "big", "technologically advanced", "cultural", and "traditional"/ "beautiful". What appears in both lists are "busy", "big" and "cultural", representing a consistent general impression of the country. Compared with "busy" and "big", which are more fact-based, "cultural" is a key feature defining China,

182   *The last three feet*

which is consistent to the highest-ranking dimension in China's brand hexagon depicted earlier. What has shifted are "modern" being replaced by "technologically advanced" and "traditional", and "populated" being replaced by "beautiful". These are interesting changes as "modern" could be an impression based on pictures while "traditional" is more based on seeing people's lifestyle, and "technologically advanced" is what they experienced through daily life; while "populated" is more fact-based, "beautiful" is again more experience-based. The other two striking differences include the wider range of vocabulary used to describe China afterwards, showing that people may be impressed by different aspects of the country, depending on the region they visited and the activities they were involved in; and overall, more positive words are used than negative ones such as "repressive", "suppressed" "regimented", "fearful", which were used to describe China before the trip have either disappeared or reduced in use. The full list of key words can be found in Appendix 7.

A similar pattern is shown in the contrast of key words to describe Chinese people: from "reserved", "polite", hardworking", "intelligent", and "friendly" before the trip, to "friendly", "welcoming" "polite" "hardworking" and "family-oriented" after the trip. Again, three key words were repeated: "polite", "hardworking" and "friendly", but in a different order, with "friendly" ascending from the fifth position to the top one, followed by "welcoming", which has a similar meaning, but can only be felt once experienced the Chinese hospitality. Like one student commented under "surprise": "I didn't expect people working in small shops further away from the university to be so warm and friendly and helpful to a foreigner". The other student simply put "the biggest surprise was how friendly and nice the Chinese people were in Qingdao".

The biggest change is the top word "reserved" disappeared and replaced by a new entry of "family-oriented". "Reserved" can be a feeling from the distance while "welcoming" is the feeling from actual interactions that build friendship. This is supported by the interview findings, when a few have mentioned that "they (the Chinese students) were shy and quiet at first, but once they come out of the shell, we had a lot of laugh together, and we were treated very nicely". As for the new entry of family-oriented, an example was given by UKSG3:

> It's a common scene to see a family of three generations going out together, in the restaurant or at tourist spots – I see a grandma in wheelchair, pushed by her daughter with her young children next to them. We don't see that a lot in this country.
>
> (UKSG3)

Regarding "highlights of the trip", most responses mentioned "people". For example, one response reads "meeting many new friends"; one says "walking around the grounds meeting the local people and exploring"; one says "meeting the many students, who are inquisitive about culture in the UK"; another says "seeing China through my own eyes, mixing with Chinese people and seeing their ways, how they go about their studies and how they are with foreigners".

The last three feet   183

One answer gave more details: "definitely meeting the students and getting to know them and realising we like the same things, for example, fashion brands. I still speak to some of the students on WeChat". This was confirmed in the interview of UKSG1:

> Before I went, I thought China is so different that I might find it hard to adapt. After the trip I realised that despite all the differences between the two countries, we are all very similar to each other as students: we like the same things, we talk about the same things, fashion, football, they love Manchester United and Liverpool, and we become friends very easily.
>
> (UKSG1)

This was echoed by another response from UKSG1: "At first, you see all the differences, then I am surprised to see how similar we are as people". This confirms what Bellamy and Weinberg stated that: "the change often reflects an emerging view that similarities far outweigh differences and that remaining differences can be viewed as enriching rather than threatening" (2008: 59). Both interviewees of UKSG1 mentioned that they already have friends from China on UK campus, which arouses their interests in China and enthusiasm of joining the trip. They also mentioned one of their classmates, who does not have any Chinese friends, did not sign up on the trip as he just felt China is too different for him to cope. His decision is driven by his pre-perception of the country that depicts the differences as "threatening", while the two interviewees were warmed up to the idea of visiting this different country by their friendship with Chinese students that help them perceive the differences as "enriching".

UKSG2 is from a different school and none of them had any Chinese friends on the course, nor was there any pre-departure cultural briefing, they were not exposed to much interpersonal contacts with Chinese people or pre-perceptions of China either, so their understanding of the country is more like a 'blank paper'. They have all chosen to go to China over the other option of the USA, as "the culture is so different", and they get the chance to "teach in a local school": these two are the biggest attractions that made the China trip an "once-in-a-life" opportunity, and came back with some "life-changing decisions" – some are seriously considering working in China upon graduation, and their teaching experiences in China are the common answers to the 'highlights'. They talked about how this experience is a booster in their CVs, which echoes the purpose designed for the trip – to become more competitive globally with stronger cross-culture awareness.

Some very interesting answers came up to the question of "what surprised you most". A few (UKT3 and UKSG3) mentioned how "capitalist" China seems to be rather than a communist country, "only the apartment blocks remind me of Russia and East Berlin, but there are Western fashion brands everywhere". "People are talking about how expensive it is to buy an apartment and send their children to private schools, I think it is more capitalist than the UK, and I feel I am the one from a middle-income country". UKSG1 commented that:

184   *The last three feet*

On the one hand, China is so developed in modern technology that all you need is a mobile phone, much more advanced than the UK; but on the other hand, there is no paper in the toilets, it's happening at the same time – a cashless society and paperless toilets!

(UKSG1)

These are like first-hand footnotes to what Weiss (2019) described "a nominally Communist state that embraced capitalism", and what Rudd (2012) described "it is like the English Industrial Revolution and the global information revolution combusting simultaneously and compressed into not 300 years, but 30". The outcome is thus a big complexity with a very mixed picture. For example, most of UKSG2 who have little exposure to China beforehand actually used "modern" to describe China before the trip, and one used "futuristic" to describe the airport and the bullet train after the trip. However, one commented that "the city was not as modern looking as I expected" as a "surprise", and one added: "I expect many more people to be able to speak English, and I thought I would see more foreigners who are Caucasian and African ethnicity as it is a capital city". This was echoed in the blog written by a student from UKSG3:

I was indeed surprised that Beijing, as a capital city of such a world leading country of technology as China, is deceivingly rustic in its manner. I thought it would carry along with it a Western vibe, but I was told by the Chinese students that is to be found in another renowned city of China, Shanghai, that I'd like to visit next time.

(UKSG3)

Another interesting example shows how first impression could be a 'false picture':

When I first came, I see security people everywhere, I think of "police state" in my mind or I might be in a high-crime area, so I am a bit worried and fearful. But then by talking to people, I realised their presence is meant to make people feel safe. Not all people wearing uniforms are police, they are just security people for the campus or apartment compound, or traffic warden to help make the road safer, and most important thing is, it's a big country with a lot of people, this is to make sure everyone has a job!

(UKSG3)

This example struck me in particular in the two contrasts it offers: one is UKSG3's initial "fearful" impression compared with many other interviewees' comments on how "safe" they actually feel at Beijing, one student wrote "I feel really safe everywhere I went", and another one even mentioned it under the "surprise": "for such a huge international city, I am actually surprised at how safe it is when I go out in the evening and come back in late hours". The second contrast is to the student's own understanding later on by talking to people, she

The last three feet   185

not only felt safe, but actually saw how it made sense to employ so many people in uniforms, it benefits the individual citizens and the society as a whole. A similar perception is shared by another student's blog:

> The sheer amount of people that pour onto the trains each day is astonishing, and naturally there are vigorous security checks that come with the scale of travellers. Whilst there is quite an emphasis on security, at times to the superfluous extreme, there is a tremendous sense of community within the people, and whilst this may be seen through rose-tinted tourist sunglasses, it is endearing nonetheless.
>
> (UKSG3)

To me, the most interesting finding is the contrast of the absence of 'political element' in student interviews and its presence in staff interviews. Although communism/communist were mentioned in Part 1 of the questionnaire completed prior to the trip, it disappeared from Part 2 completed after the trip, and no political element was mentioned at all in each of the three student group interviews. This forms a sharp contrast to Hubbert's (2019: 81) research findings about Hanban-sponsored trips, which were "being experienced by students as forms of censorship and control that reinforced common Western perceptions of China's authoritarian political life" (Hubbert, 2019: 93). British students seem to get a completely different story, when I pushed a bit in asking: "do you see the government influence on ordinary people's life in any way?", one student said: "I thought Chinese people always have to follow certain ways, very regimented with rules, but actually they have a lot of freedom. They can study abroad and travel abroad just like us". Another student complemented that he found "Beijing not as tense politically as imagined: I am not being watched, I can go to places freely and talk to people on the street freely". UKSG3 from a different group also agreed: "I don't see many restrictions in people's life. I went to visit my Chinese friends' family and had a home meal with them, and we went out together, no one seems to be worried about anything".

But lack of freedom was mentioned by both UKT2 and UKT3. One observed that: "there seems to be not many restrictions to where *you can go*, but the government knows *where you are going* as there are CCTV cameras everywhere. It still feels like 'big brother' watching". UKT3 said he "read a few books and a dozen journal articles about China before the trip", and found the trip "reinforced many of the perceptions" he has. The first example he gave is Tiananmen. He deliberately asked the question about Tiananmen incident in 1989 when they visited there, and reported that "one student turned back to ignore this question, and the guide (a University staff) told me this question cannot be discussed in public", so "it is still a very repressive country". To me, this is like a test to collect evidence to support a certain pre-perception. But UKT3 followed this with another example of the same guide engaging him with another political conversation: UKT3 is browsing a magazine in a school library with Xi Jinping on the cover page, and the guide told him (without being asked) about the constitutional amendment to scrap term

186 *The last three feet*

time limit, and "frowned upon the idea"; but before UKT3 is due to give a presentation to the school students, the guide quickly "warned" him not to say "anything political", which is not intended or relevant to his talk on British culture anyway. There are several other occasions like during the coach journey, "some conversations are exchanged that touches on some political issues, I see people can talk about them between individuals, but just not in public".

The year 2019 marks the 30th anniversary of the Tiananmen incident, which also means that the young generation in China today was born post-1989. When a mature student from UKSG3 asked a Chinese student about the Tiananmen incident, she was told "they were terrorists", referring to the terror attack happened there in 2013,[20] not the 1989 incident. The young student did not get the question because they themselves know very little about what happened back then, especially for people from other parts of China, but the terror attack in 2013 is not censored news and they don't shy from talking about it. After all, how many young people in Britain and Northern Ireland today know about the Bloody Sunday happened in 1972? Even after the Saville's investigation report was made public in 2010 and the then British Prime Minister made a formal apology on behalf of the UK government? As UKSG3 herself commented: "There are bad things happened in very country, but they don't get to be revisited and revisited all the time, kept being brought up like the Tiananmen incident".

China has transformed so much in the last three decades for its own people, but for Westerners who have never been to China to experience the change, their perceptions were entrenched in Tiananmen as a political symbol for anti-democracy. A typical conversation was described by Zhang and Baker: A foreigner journalist asked an ordinary Chinese people: "how could you be really free if you could not go to Tiananmen Square and start yelling, 'Down with the Communist party' or 'Free Tibet?'" The Chinese interviewee looked at him quizzically and said: "Why on earth would anyone ever want to do that?!" (Zhang and Baker, 2008: 42). This is a completely honest answer and reaction as that question has never crossed the Chinese person's mind, let alone the urge suggested in the question. Actually, one British student's entry to the "highlight of the trip" in the questionnaire is intriguing: "in Tiananmen square, imagining everything that happened there whilst it seemed so tranquil and beautiful when I was standing there".

These data can tell us at least three things. First, they confirm the role of pre-perceptions in leading people to look for 'evidence' consciously to prove or disapprove their pre-perceptions if they already hold some, or use their pre-perception as a frame or lens to view China. For example, "the night market with snacking on unidentified creatures roasted on a stick" was what American students perceived to be a "form of Chinese authenticity" according to Hubbert's (2014) recounts of the Chinese Bridge Summer Camp. In my own interviews, UKT1 said he was surprised to find that "people, especially the older generation, seem to hold reverence and gratitude for Mao Zedong, quite different from what we thought he did to his country and his people", and looking at the same scene of school students doing interim exercises on the playground, one student was amazed at its "beautiful movement in uniformity", and applauded the positive

The last three feet 187

side of this practice as students "get to enjoy the fresh air during break-time, and they all look very happy", while the other saw "indoctrination that stifles individual expression" in the same exercise. It was also reflected in students' answers to their "biggest worry" before the trip, one student wrote:

> I worry that they might be too polite and reserved to talk to me and I will not get to know anyone or talk to anyone. That I might get arrested for using a VPN! That I might get stopped and asked for ID a lot, that I would be followed and watched and questioned a lot. That I would get ill due to insect bites or the water. I had heard that most Chinese might be prejudiced again me due to my darker skin colour!
>
> (UKSG2)

Of course, after the trip, the student wrote: "I did not get ill or even the suggestion of it. I didn't get arrested or stopped and asked for my passport, and I made many new friends". Another student wrote in his blog:

> A lot is said in the news about China, often filled with information that seeks to scaremonger those native to the West. It is as though this should be a place that we are weary, if not slightly fearful of. I always considered China to be presented as a fierce and mysterious country far in the East that shared little commonality with the way life is lived in the West.

After the trip, he wrote:

> China is an extraordinary place, and also a hospitable one, and whilst it is not without its faults, it has within it a deep-rooted appreciation for its antecedent and wealth of history. It is something that I believe is a defining predicate in the character of Beijing. In terms of whether my original thoughts on China have changed, I would say that without exception any conditioned idea the media would have us believe before visiting is no more than a small facet of what is a rousing country.
>
> (UKSG3)

The data also show a contrast between the older generation who are exposed to more pre-perceptions of a communist China as a polity, and who have gone through the Cold War themselves, and the young students' appreciation of China as a vibrant economy and society, their understanding of communism is less ideologically and historically specific. They are more open to allow their first-hand experience to shape their understandings of China on a blank paper with no embedded presumptions, and they welcome the opportunity brought by China's development. This more or less echoes Hubbert's research finding in that:

> Students engagement with it (China), through their concomitant desire for Chinese and their reduction of China to a tool of their own power, may

188 *The last three feet*

suggest an evolving perception of China away from the ideological nemesis that has to date predominated in US relationships with the Chinese nation-state.

(Hubbert, 2019: 83)

Second, they all feel they've seen the 'real' China. They recognised that what they've seen is "the best selected class and the best performance, but who wouldn't? If I have guests coming from afar, I would tidy my house and show them the best I can" (UKSG3). During and after class, they can talk to the students and staff, and in the evening, they can walk around the hotel area, see local people doing TaiChi and dance to the music in the park, they get the chances to see, to explore, and to interact with local people, they get honest answers even if sometimes they confirm the view of a 'not-so-free' China. There is no attempt at covering things up and "no hidden agenda" (UKSG3). At the end of the trip, in disregard of all the issues or negative aspects of China they reported in the questionnaires and/or interviews, such as the "unhygienic toilets", "chaotic traffic", "smoggy days", "large contrast between modern city and deprived areas", and people's "rude" behaviours in "jumping the queue", "pushing and shouting in stations", "taking pictures without asking permission", and "leaving theatre before the show ends", the majority of them said they would like to go back again, either to visit or to work. Actually, many unexpected discoveries were made when they visited tourist spots. For example, two observant remarks were made by UKT1:

> When we were in Beijing zoo, we noticed that the pandas enjoy a great enclosure, which is understandable as they are considered the 'national treasures' and they are shown to the world, but for other animals, the conditions are much poorer, there is a big difference in standards ... I am also surprised to see those museums we were taken to are all very empty, they are very new, huge and modern, but there are more staff inside than visitors.
>
> (UKT1)

UKT2 and UKSG3 also mentioned the 'zoo effect' when they were taken to visit a zoo in a different city, to see the lovely pandas, but students were left with the same impression, appalled to see the conditions for most other animals that were kept in a very confined space and pet shops. I think this is the true picture of the 'real China', probably different from the version that the government is very keen on showing the world – a 'real' China with picture-perfect pandas and modern museums, yes, they are real, but cropped from the background that shows the overall view. I think China just needs to embrace a simple fact: no one is perfect, and no one expects you to be perfect. A real China is a big complexity that contains all the contradictory features: traditional and modern, rich and poor, developed and underdeveloped, advanced and backward, polite and rude people ... but they do not detract from its attraction as an ancient civilisation and contemporary powerhouse. Due to the

The last three feet 189

complexity, a real China can only be fully discovered by experiencing it first-hand, when there are local people around to explain the differences. Let ordinary citizens answer the question of "why China is different". There is no standard answer, but there is no wrong answer either, and each answer represents a tiny piece to the giant puzzle of 'the real China'. Just like what happened to the students and teachers during the trip, let the conversation begin with the differences, begin with the questions and answers of 'why', and that is the beginning of gaining mutual understanding in the last three feet. At the end of the trip, in the closing speech, UKT1 shared with me his proud punch line said in Chinese: As Confucius said, "in a party of three, there must be one whom I can learn from" (*san ren xing, bi you wo shi*).

Third, the cultural traits reflected on people, such as family-oriented, respectful to the elders and teachers, hardworking to improve themselves, sense of community, and the actual people-to-people interactions, have only produced positive effects on people's perception of the country. For example, one of UKT2's answers to "what surprised you most" is about the people: "they are a lot happier than I thought. You would think it is a miserable country to live in with a repressive government and a poor standard of human rights, but people are actually enjoying their lives". The other one wrote: "I am surprised at how organised and efficient the subway was and also how friendly the locals were". In the interview, UKSG3 talked about the flag-raising ceremony on an early Monday morning,

> I was impressed by the sense of pride and nationalism I see in the large crowd, watching the national flag going up with the national anthem, we don't do such things here, and it's not an organised event, those people were there because they wanted to be there.
>
> (UKSG3)

The best summary I can give to the benefits of such trips is to borrow a paragraph written by the students:

> The trip is adventurous and educational, it is very different from a holiday trip as we get to do things with students there, it really helps in knocking down perceptions and gaining empathy. We appreciate more how much effort Chinese students are making in studying in this country, and I am impressed by their desires to improve their life for themselves and their families through hardworking.
>
> (UKSG2)

Conclusion

Cultural diplomacy is a very complex and slow undertaking, it requires a bottom-up approach to succeed, and ordinary citizens convey much longer-lasting and more accessible images of a country than government-sponsored events. The

190   *The last three feet*

power of people-to-people diplomacy is hugely under-utilised in China's current practice of cultural diplomacy. Walker and Gaynor (2014) found that: "citizen exchanges reveal that despite differences in language, religion and culture, the world's brightest young minds have far more common interests than most would ever expect". The data shows that these exchanges have directly underpinned significant advances in mutual understanding by providing them access to first-hand experience and information about China, which increased their knowledge of the host culture, reduced susceptibility to stereotypes, helped correct some of the mystified or imagined 'knowledge' about China, expand cross cultural networks while building lasting friendships and relationships that one can learn and grow from. Therefore, a more effective cultural diplomacy should look to its own people as the best place to start.

More often than not, citizens have more power than they often believe when it comes to both supporting the state-sponsored efforts and creating their own initiatives. The students on these trips do not consider their activities in any way political, nor do they recognise that they are engaging in citizen diplomacy, they simply see their travel as a chance to make new friends and share experiences and learn from each other while working together. But it is exactly this autonomy from any political involvement and agenda that is its greatest strength. According to UKT1, in the pre-departure briefing, the students were called as "ambassadors of the university". In the term of citizen diplomacy, such advice can be translated as fulfilling the proposed role as "citizen diplomats" on their country's behalf as each individual involved is part of an equation that builds a general reputation of a country and it often starts with a handshake and a conversation in the last three feet.

More recognition and utilisation of the valuable contributions made by non-state actors are needed, they provide a vibrant landscape of cross-cultural engagement and two-way communications that have generated remarkably positive and effective impacts by fostering affinity and facilitating mutual learning. Increasing grass-roots citizen diplomacy initiatives can make a real difference, as people are the best assets and agents; they are the primary sources and secret ingredients in the recipe of a successful cultural diplomacy.

Notes

1 Why is Citizen Diplomacy Important?, Center for Citizen Diplomacy, available at: www.centerforcitizendiplomacy.org/.
2 See CPAFFC (Chinese People's Association for Friendship with Foreign Countries) website, available at: http://en.cpaffc.org.cn/introduction/agrintr.html.
3 See the Central Commission for Discipline Inspection website, available at: www.ccdi.gov.cn/toutiao/201711/t20171113_126275.html.
4 Speech by H.E. Xi Jinping President of the People's Republic of China at China International Friendship Conference in Commemoration of the 60th Anniversary of the Chinese People's Association for Friendship with Foreign Countries. 15 March 2014, available at: http://en.cpaffc.org.cn/content/details25-47426.html.
5 See the University of Chicago Centre in Beijing website, available at: www.uchicago.edu/research/center/center_in_beijing/.

The last three feet 191

6 This section is derived, in part, from a blog What Sharp Power? It's Nothing But "Unsmart" Power, published on Centre on Public Diplomacy, 15 November 2015, available at: www.uscpublicdiplomacy.org/blog/what-sharp-power-it%E2%80%99s-nothing-%E2%80%9Cunsmart%E2%80%9D-power.

7 Jane Perlez, F.B.I. Bars Some China Scholars From Visiting U.S. Over Spying Fears, *New York Times*, 14 April 2019, available at: www.nytimes.com/2019/04/14/world/asia/china-academics-fbi-visa-bans.html.

8 China News, *Wang Guoqing huiying "rui shi li" shuo: paozhi xinci "hei" Zhongguo* [Wang Guoqing Responds to the Term of "Sharp Power": Coining New Words to Vilify China]. 2 March 2018, available at: www.chinanews.com/gn/2018/03-02/8458485.shtml. See also in Manya Koetse, On 'Sharp Power' & the China Threat 3.0: "The West Is Mentally Stuck in Cold War Era", What's on Weibo, 5 March 2018, available at: www.whatsonweibo.com/on-sharp-power-the-china-threat-3-0-the-west-is-mentally-stuck-in-cold-war-era/.

9 S. Liu, Spotlight: Who's Behind the Term "Sharp Power"? *Xinhua News*, 13 February 2018, available at: www.xinhuanet.com/english/2018-02/13/c_136972986.htm.

10 Ben Blanchard, China Kicks Off Parliament Season with Attack on the West, *Reuters*, 2 March 2018, available at: www.reuters.com/article/us-china-parliament/china-kicks-off-parliament-season-with-attack-on-the-west-idUSKCN1GE1IP.

11 Tom O'Connor, China Quotes Martin Luther King Jr. to attack U.S. Cold War "Discrimination". *Newsweek*, 2 March 2018, available at: www.newsweek.com/china-attacks-us-cold-war-discrimination-using-martin-luther-king-jr-829073.

12 Sarah Zheng, Beijing Blasts Western Critics who "Smear China" with the Term Sharp Power, *South China Morning Post*, 2 March 2018, available at: www.scmp.com/news/china/diplomacy-defence/article/2135516/beijing-blasts-western-critics-who-smear-china-term.

13 Xinhua, "Sharp Power" a New Version of "China Threat" Rhetoric, *Xinhua News*, 2 March 2018, available at: www.xinhuanet.com/english/2018-03/02/c_137011743.htm.

14 Y. Zhang, Sharp Power' Accusations seen as Unfair Ploy to Tarnish China's Image. *China Daily*, 3 March 2018, available at: www.chinadaily.com.cn/a/201803/03/WS5a99d7e6a3106e7dcc13f43d.html.

15 Victoria Breeze and Nathan Moore, China has Overtaken the US and UK as the Top Destination for Anglophone African Students, *QuartzAfrica*, 30 June 2017, available at: https://qz.com/africa/1017926/china-has-overtaken-the-us-and-uk-as-the-top-destination-for-anglophone-african-students/.

16 UKCISA, International Student Statistics: UK Higher Education, 2018, available at: www.ukcisa.org.uk/Research–Policy/Statistics/International-student-statistics-UK-higher-education.

17 Xinhua, Huge Rise in Chinese Students Heading to Study in Britain, 12 October 2017, available at: www.xinhuanet.com/english/2017-10/12/c_136672931.htm.

18 Theresa May Unveils Education Deal at Start of China Visit. BBC News, 30 January 2018, available at: www.bbc.co.uk/news/uk-politics-42865133.

19 See President Lawrence S. Bacow Affirms Academic Freedom in Peking University Speech, Fairbank Center for Chinese Studies, 20 March 2019, available at: https://fairbank.fas.harvard.edu/president-lawrence-s-bacow-affirms-academic-freedom-in-peking-university-speech/.

20 CNN, Five Arrested in Tiananmen Square Incident: Deemed a Terrorist Attack, 31 October 2013, available at: https://edition.cnn.com/2013/10/30/world/asia/china--tiananmen--arrests/index.html.

192 *The last three feet*

References

Anholt, S. (2006). Public Diplomacy and Place Branding: Where is the Link? *Place Branding*, 2(4): 271–275.

Bellamy, C. and A. Weinberg (2008). Educational and Cultural Exchanges to Restore America's Image. *Washington Quarterly*, 31(3): 55–68. Available at: www.tandfonline.com/doi/pdf/10.1162/wash.2008.31.3.55.

Bhandari, R. and R. Belyavina (2011). Evaluating and Measuring the Impact of Citizen Diplomacy: Current Status and Future Directions. Institute of International Education (IIE), June. Available at: http://peaceandjusticesig.pbworks.com/f/Impact+of+Citizen+Diplomacy+Report.pdf.

Bislev, A.K. (2017). Student-to-Student Diplomacy: Chinese International Students as a Soft-Power Tool. *Journal of Current Chinese Affairs*, 46(2): 81–109.

Campbell, K. and E. Ratner (2018). The China Reckoning, How Beijing Defied American Expectations. *Foreign Affairs*, March/April. Available at: www.foreignaffairs.com/articles/china/2018-02-13/china-reckoning.

Clack, G. (ed.) (2006). *Edward R. Murrow: Journalism at its Best*. Washington, DC: Department of State. Available at: http://iipdigital.usembassy.gov/media/pdf/books/murrow.pdf.

CPHRC (2019). China's Confucius Institutes: An inquiry by the Conservative Party Human Rights Commission. Conservative Party Human Rights Commission Report. Available at: www.conservativehumanrights.com.

David-Fox, M. (2011). *Showcasing the Great Experiment: Cultural Diplomacy and Western Visitors to the Soviet Union, 1921–1941*. New York: Oxford University Press.

Davidson, M. (2017). China's Soft Power: A Comparative Failure or Secret Success? *2017 Soft Power*, 30: 70–72. Available at: https://softpower30.com/wp-content/uploads/2017/07/The-Soft-Power-30-Report-2017-Web-1.pdf.

The Economist (2017). What to do About China's "Sharp Power". 14 December. Available at: www.economist.com/news/leaders/21732524-china-manipulating-decisionmakers-western-democracies-best-defence.

Fallows, J. (2016). China's Great Leap Backward. *The Atlantic*, December. Available at: www.theatlantic.com/magazine/archive/2016/12/chinas-great-leap-backward/505817/.

Gilboa, E. (1998). Media Diplomacy: Conceptual Divergences and Applications. *Harvard International Journal of Press/Politics*, 3(3): 56–75.

Holden, J. (2013). *Influence And Attraction: Culture and the Race for Soft Power in the 21st Century*. London: British Council.

Hong, N.Y. (2014). EU–China Education Diplomacy: An Effective Soft Power Strategy? *European Foreign Affairs Review*, 19: 155–172.

Hubbert, J. (2019). *China in the World: An Anthropology of Confucius Institutes, Soft Power and Globalization*. Honolulu, HI: University of Hawaii Press.

Johnson, N. (2018). CIA Warns of Extensive Chinese Operation to Infiltrate American Institutions, Intel Report: Beijing Provides "Strings-Attached Funding" to "Coerce" Self-Censorship. *The Washington Free Beacon*, 7 March. Available at: https://freebeacon.com/national-security/cia-warns-extensive-chinese-operation-infiltrate-American-institutions/.

Kurlantzick, J. (2007). *Charm Offensive: How China's Soft Power is Transforming the World*. Cambridge, MA: Yale University Press.

Li, M. (2009). Soft Power: Nurture Not Nature. In M. Li (ed.), *Soft Power: China's Emerging Strategy in International Politics* (pp. 1–18). Lanham, MD: Lexington.

Nye, J.S. (2011). China's Soft Power (speech given to Carnegie Council for Ethics in International Affairs in 2011). Available at: www.youtube.com/watch?v=RmW1gZPqFDs.

Nye, J.S. (2018). How Sharp Power Threatens Soft Power, The Right and Wrong Ways to Respond to Authoritarian Influence. *Foreign Affairs*, 24 January. Available at: www.foreignaffairs.com/articles/china/2018-01-24/how-sharp-power-threatens-soft-power.

Paradise, J. (2012). International Education: Diplomacy in China. *The Brown Journal of World Affairs*, 19(1): 195–205.

Parton, C. (2019). China–UK Relations Where to Draw the Border Between Influence and Interference? *RUSI Occasional Paper*, February. Royal United Services Institute for Defence and Security Studies. Available at: https://rusi.org/sites/default/files/20190220_chinese_interference_parton_web.pdf.

Pells, R. (2016). Number of British Students Choosing to Study in China Soars. *Independent*, 14 September. Available at: www.independent.co.uk/student/study-abroad/number-of-british-students-choosing-to-study-in-china-soars-a7307261.html.

Peterson, R. (2018). Opposing Communist Chinese Spies Isn't Racist. *National Association of Scholars*, 4 December. Available at: www.nas.org/articles/opposing_communist_chinese_spies_isnt_racist.

Rudd, K. (2012). The West Isn't Ready for the Rise of China. *The New Statesman*, 11 July. Available at: www.newstatesman.com/politics/international-politics/2012/07/kevin-rudd-west-isnt-ready-rise-china.

Sahlins, M. (2015). *Confucius Institute: Academic Malware*. Chicago, IL: Prickly Paradigm Press.

Shambaugh, D. (2019). The 40th Anniversary of U.S.–China Relations: Looking Back and Looking Forward. *Foreign Policy*, 9 January. Available at: www.chinausfocus.com/foreign-policy/the-40th-anniversary-of-us-china-relations-looking-back-and-looking-forward.

Singh, M. (2018). From Smart Power to Sharp Power: How China Promotes her National Interests. *Journal of Defence Studies*, 12(2): 5–25.

Walker, C. and J. Ludwig (2017). From "Soft Power" to "Sharp Power", Rising Authoritarian Influence in the Democratic World. National Endowment for Democracy. Available at: www.ned.org/wp-content/uploads/2017/12/Sharp-Power-Rising-Authoritarian-Influence-Full-Report.pdf.

Walkers, J. and D. Gaynor (2014). Smarter Diplomacy: Doubling Down on People-to-People. *Diplomat*, 14 March. Available at: www.centerforcitizendiplomacy.org/resource/smarter-diplomacy-doubling-people-people/.

Wang, J. and E. Nisbet (2018). Reimagining Exchange: The Local Impact of Cultural Exchanges. Centre on Public Diplomacy. Available at: https://uscpublicdiplomacy.org/blog/reimagining-exchange-local-impact-cultural-exchanges.

Weiss, J.C. (2019). No, China and the U.S. Aren't Locked in an Ideological Battle. Not Even Close. *Washington Post*, 4 May. Available at: www.washingtonpost.com/politics/2019/05/04/no-china-us-arent-locked-an-ideological-battle-not-even-close/?utm_term=.1f334ef68637.

Zhang, H. and G. Baker (2008). *Think Like Chinese*. Sydney: Federation Press.

6 Cultural diplomacy with Chinese characteristics[1]

> When China is viewed from an insider's perspective, one sees its "national conditions", from an outsider's perspective, one sees its "Chinese characteristics", it is now time for China to view itself from an outsider's perspective.
>
> (Xin Liu)

The phrase "with Chinese characteristics" was Deng Xiaoping's invention to define socialism in the Chinese context in the early 1980s, with a view to putting ideological contention between capitalism and socialism on the backburner and focusing on economic development. This term was then used to explain the 'uniqueness' of Chinese conditions in almost everything that has the same name but different nature or practice in China, such as "democracy with Chinese characteristics", "free market with Chinese characteristics", "human rights with Chinese characteristics", "legal system with Chinese characteristics"; and the list is getting longer all the time. For some, "Chinese characteristics" tends to be used as a shield to fend off criticisms: if you do not agree, then you will be deemed as not getting China, or not understanding its unique 'national conditions' (*guoqing*). Or, it is used as a looking-glass through which a non-Western phenomenon can only be meaningfully explained by non-Western terminology and from a Chinese point of view. This book, however, represents a journey to make sense of the unique challenges faced by China's cultural diplomacy, and to fill some gaps of understanding by taking both an insider and an outsider's perspective.

This is a concluding chapter that aims to build on previous chapters that explicate how the changing power position and unchanging power struggle determine the purpose and the timing for China to be engaged in cultural diplomacy. When carrying the shadows of 'otherness' and delivered in a trademark state-run method – coupled with its long-established party-state and propaganda system and its vastly different political values compared with the dominant Western model – it makes this classic suffix of "Chinese characteristics" indispensable for an accurate understanding of China's cultural diplomacy. It will achieve a diagnostic description of the prominent features of China's cultural diplomacy by examining the trajectory of China's global cultural footprints made through its recent expansion of the Confucius Institutes (CIs). The four

Cultural diplomacy with Chinese characteristics   195

features correspond to the four themes of the research carried out, that is, *why* China wants to launch cultural diplomacy, *what* is the vehicle, *who* is the agent, and *how* it is carried out in the field. The chapter will also discuss what will make this 'cultural leap outward' truly 'great'.

To this end, one thing that must be borne in mind is that China's cultural diplomacy aims to engage with the entire world, so no generalised conclusions would be tenable given the uneven conditions in the global cultural terrain, argued in Chapters 3 and 4. Therefore, a comparison and contrast of the primary and secondary data collected in the UK, USA, Belgium and South Korea will be undertaken first before any conclusion is drawn. The comparative data suggests that if the sustainable and effective operation of the CI is the dependent variable (DV), then its ability to localise the product and process is the independent variable (IV), and the interactions between the CI and its target audiences in different cultural spheres further suggest a number of other extraneous variables (EVs), including ideology, nationalism, media environment of the recipient country, bilateral relations and the nature of cultural boundary in between, as well as the mediating variable (MV) of people-to-people interactions, that all play a role in affecting the DV. The complexity of all the variables at work will be mapped out in a chart in Figure 6.1.

One mission statement, two different priorities

We've looked at the Confucius Institute's twofold mission in Chapter 4: satisfying the demands of people who learn the Chinese language and enhancing their understanding of the Chinese culture. Based on the empirical data collected from the UK and South Korea, there seems to be a general consensus among all interviewees concerning its purpose, with a few directors emphasising the careful wording of "*introducing*" Chinese culture instead of "*promoting*" it, to be sensitive to the concerns or fears of China's 'cultural invasion' in the recipient country (SKD1 and SKD4). However, despite the unanimous understanding, a clear difference in terms of priority setting can be observed from the responses gathered from the UK and South Korea.

In South Korea, where the geographical vicinity, cultural closeness and economic and business connections with China mean that many people have been to China already, or have plenty of opportunities to interact with Chinese people, language teaching was made a clear central task of the CI, as pointed by SKD2:

> China is our neighbour, the closest country to us, historically we were heavily influenced by Chinese traditions, Chinese literature and other aspects, so Korean people nowadays are very interested in going to China for various activities, be it trade, educational or cultural exchanges, there are more and more people, both old and young, learning Chinese, we have tens of thousands candidates sitting the HSK tests every year, the largest group in the whole world.
>
> (SKD2)

196 *Cultural diplomacy with Chinese characteristics*

Nowadays, the influence of China on its neighbouring countries is often linked to trade and business opportunities, generating a bigger demand for learning its language. A *New York Times* article reported that "in South Korea, an American ally that fought alongside the United States in a war against China's troops a half century ago, Chinese has reportedly outstripped English as the most popular foreign language among students" (French, 2006: 2). In Xu Lin's own words, "the launch of this program (the CI) is in response to the Chinese language craze, especially in neighbouring countries" and "Chinese is as popular in Korea today as English is in China" (cited in French, 2006: 2). This may help explain why the very first CI in the world was established in Seoul, where the host organisation has been promoting the Chinese proficiency test (HSK) in South Korea since 1993. South Korea has been the No. 1 source country of international students learning Chinese in China since 2000, with over 50,000 Korean students studying in China in 2018;[2] and there are 120 universities offering Chinese degree courses in South Korea.[3] All the three South Korea directors interviewed are consistent in commenting that CIs in South Korea have focused a lot on selling HSK exams and offering scholarships to school students to study in China.

This may have to do with the South Korean education system and the employment market that attaches greater value to certificates and exam results. The priority of language teaching was echoed by a blunt statement from SKSC1:

> They (Korean students) are very pragmatic, not interested in the cultural aspects, they only care if they can master the language or not, and Chinese is now included as one of the subjects they can choose to sit in their entrance examinations to go to university.
>
> (SKSC1)

SKD1 even commented that:

> There is really not much need for the CI to 'promote' Chinese language and culture here, in fact, there is such a high demand and inner drive to master the language that more and more Koreans are voluntarily learning the language in the hope to use it as a tool to tap into opportunities offered by this next-door neighbour. As for culture, some of the traditional Chinese cultural practices were kept better in South Korea than in China.
>
> (SKD1)

Because of this, SKD4 mentioned that many CIs operating in Asia (especially in Japan, South Korea and Singapore) do not request operating funds from Hanban:

> Some universities offer Chinese as compulsory degree modules, so they pay for Hanban sponsored teachers' salary into CI's account as their operating fund. This is not a significant amount of money for the university to bear. This would gain them more freedom than requesting operating fund from Hanban.
>
> (SKD4)

This forms a stark contrast to most CIs in other parts of the world that are attracted by Hanban's funding to nurture the language programme, both in Africa (Hartig, 2014) and the USA (Sahlins, 2015). The attraction for learning the language is much less in the UK compared to South Korea. According to Young (2014), being born a native English speaker is both a blessing and a curse as 39 per cent hold the perception that "most people speak English". When commenting on the fact that the number of UK students choosing to study foreign languages at university level has been in steady decline for the past seven years, Worne (2015), Director of Strategy at the British Council, used "can't, won't, don't" to sum up the British national view on speaking foreign languages. This was confirmed by responses received from the interviewees: UKLH2 commented that: "Chinese is not yet a language popular enough that would automatically attract students to learn, actually, it still has the reputation of one of the hardest languages to learn". Therefore, in UKSC5's words, "trips to China are the 'appetiser', culture is the 'main course', and language teaching is the 'side order'".

Unlike South Korea, study tours to China were the highlight events for all the other CIs interviewed. They all mentioned the visitors' excitement or even shock to see 'the real China' with their own eyes compared to their imaginative impressions. For example, in the UK, in a local school's pre-departure briefing meeting for their first trip to China, UKLH1 was asked if £200 is enough to buy a house in China. In Morocco, where China has always been pictured as a developing country and their own as a developed country, students simply could not believe or even accept that the airport in Beijing is much more modern than their own at home. Therefore, UKD1 believes "it is very important for us to offer students the starting opportunity to walk into China". These organised tours (both for school principals and students) played very positive roles in significantly changing their perceptions through first-hand experiences, many school partnerships were formed and an exchange of visits resulted following the agreement. In addition, many degree students decided to go to China for MA courses on CI scholarships after graduation. Its significance was also enunciated by UKLH3:

> When the CI can offer opportunities like this to someone who does not have much expectation, or even some negative expectations of China, to see China with his own eyes and see the difference from media image, Hanban has already achieved its initial purpose. They gain one more person who likes China and wants to speak for China.… When the guest speaker is a dignitary 'foreigner' to talk about China, Chinese culture and Chinese economy, the effects are much better than a Chinese speaker. They play a very constructive role in helping enhance understanding of China, they are not blowing trumpets for China like propaganda, but have a very fair tone.
>
> (UKLH3)

The above explains the rationale for why CIs in the UK focus on "enhancing understandings", as for Chinese language teaching, UKLH3 believes the CI's main job is:

198 *Cultural diplomacy with Chinese characteristics*

to nurture and keep students' interests in China as our main goal is to correct misunderstandings of China held by foreign countries. Once they are interested, they would want to know more, and once they know more, they would have more objective views.

(UKLH3)

This was echoed by UKSC2, who explained the "ripple effect" this can generate:

To start with, we need to get more foreigners interested in China, then after getting some knowledge and understanding, they may want to go to China and see it for themselves, then they can come back to influence more people, to generate a ripple effect. It takes a long time to work the infiltration.

(UKSC2)

Citing figures from China's Ministry of Education, Lampton (2008) highlighted the fact that over thirty former students who undertook studies in China hold ministerial positions back in their own countries; more than ten have served as their country's ambassadors to China; thirty hold high-level positions in their country's embassies in China; 120 are associate professors or professors and hundreds more serve in cultural, economic and trade entities involved with China. Now with the CIs reaching out into 155 countries in the world (by June 2019), this potential benefit can only build up over time.

The above appears to reveal a pattern of "one mission statement, two different priorities" delivered by the CIs in different destinations. Regional differences are clear and allow for localised priorities: language teaching is the core function of the CIs in the East Asian cultural sphere like South Korea, where traditional China enjoys a very respectable culture image and modern China offers new opportunities; while in Western countries like the UK and USA, where vestiges of Orientalism and the Cold War mentality are amplified by the distances in culture and space, Chinese cultural introduction and enhancing local people's understanding of contemporary China is given more weight, with trips to China functioning as a particularly effective tool.

While this section shows that the CI's ability to localise its product to adapt to and meet the different needs of the target audiences should be the IV, it also reveals other EVs involved in this process that results in the "two different priorities". Aside from understanding the local road conditions and driving practice, it is as important to have adequate local knowledge about the target audiences, especially about what they already know about China and how they acquire that knowledge. These will be examined in the sections below.

See China and read China: first-hand knowledge versus third-hand stories

The study tours and scholarships for university students to learn about China first-hand may be an effective remedy in relieving the symptoms of holding

Cultural diplomacy with Chinese characteristics   199

misperceptions of China, but they do not address the root cause for such misperceptions, which lie in where people get their preconceptions from. The example below from the author's direct observations shows how deeply embedded preconceptions can be.

In a talk about "China, the New Land of Opportunities" given to a local British high school, the Confucius Institute teacher asked if any students in the audience had been to China before – only one student raised his hand. So the teacher said she would show them a two-minute video clip first called *China China*,[4] and then asked students to share their impressions of China with some key words after watching it. There is only a one-word narrative 'China' in the video, repeating itself numerous times throughout the video with thousands of different snapshots from China, from varied landscapes to a wide variety of wild animals, from diverse food to different ethnic groups, wearing different costumes and following different life styles in rural and urban China. The message is quite strong and clear: This is *all* China, a country of vast diversity. Yet, when the floor was given to students, the first answer (not from the one who had been to China before) of the key word was 'communism'. Even the British teacher present there was surprised: where did he get that from? There is not even a glimpse of a red flag during the video, nor any images of Chinese leaders or the government.

So where do people get preconceptions from? Manzenreiter simply attributes the responsibility for people's misperception to the mainstream media that: "rather than preparing the space for a dialectic exploration of alternative modes and views, the media contribute to the reinforcing of national stereotypes" (2010: 43). This echoes Said's argument from back in 1978 that one aspect of the electronic postmodern world is that there has been a reinforcement of the stereotypes by which the Orient is viewed: "so far as the Orient is concerned, standardisation and cultural stereotyping have intensified the hold of the 19th-century academic and imaginative demonology of the 'mysterious Orient'" (1978: 26). As pointed out by Morley and Robins,

> we are all largely dependent on the media for our images of non-local people, places, and events, and the further the 'event' from our own direct experiences, the more we depend on media images for the totality of our knowledge.
>
> (Morley and Robins, 1995: 133)

Willnat and Metzgar's (2012) research finding on "American Perceptions of China and the Chinese: Do the Media Matter?" seems to support this. It is based on the content analysis of 886 news stories about China published in the *New York Times* throughout 2010 and on a national online survey conducted in early 2011. The findings show significant associations between respondents' media use and their views of China's economic, political and military power. Their findings generally support the assumption that the American public is influenced primarily by media agenda setting and framing processes, and that "respondents

200 *Cultural diplomacy with Chinese characteristics*

with more news exposure hold more negative perceptions of Chinese foreign and economic policies" (Willnat and Metzgar, 2012: 24–25). Similar research was done by a Chinese scholar Zhang (2007) by undertaking a thorough analysis of the China-related reports in American mainstream media outlets including the *New York Times*, *Washington Post*, *Los Angeles Times* and CNN. Zhang also found that the US press seldom constructed a favourable image of China: they tend to adopt a negative angle even in reporting developments achieved in China, such as the Olympic successes or the breakthroughs China made in exploring outer space; and the reporting is persistently constructed in an anti-communist frames and Cold War mentality.

It is at this point that we need to consider the impact of Western media on 'the Rest', and the impact of representations of 'the other' on Western audiences, some of whom may be 'ignorant' about China to a certain extent, but instead of making them 'educated' and 'informed', some media influence has only made them 'biased'. Examples of this were shown in Chapter 5 and in the ossified image of China planted in that student's mind, which can become so deeply embedded that if it does not generate resistance, at least it forms an inertia to embrace a new understanding of China. For example, SKSC3 said that: "many students thought China is a similar country to North Korea before they visited it, because of ideology". Such preconceptions were "culturally constituted", as Hubbert explains, "by U.S culture and the ideologies of democracy that shaped their conceptions of Chinese state intentions and practices", making communism a "product of both historical discourse and contemporary analysis that take the nature of communism for granted" (2014: 340).

This is why UKD3 believed that "China is a much misunderstood country", and the CI's role is "to provide a window into China, for those who would otherwise live with their prejudices and ignorance with China", or be "denied access to balanced information" (Cull, 2008: 117). In the speech given by Harvard University President Lawrence Bacow to Peking University in March 2019, he said, "we must embrace the difficult task of being quick to understand and slow to judge".[5] I believe, however, perhaps a better piece of advice would be of "being *slow* to understand and even *slower* to judge" China in all its complexities and the preconceived perceptions. We all need to take the time to truly understand what is beyond and beneath the constructed knowledge to avoid situations that we thought we understood. Events that people experience first-hand can counter the most sophisticated strategic narratives. This was elaborated by UKLH3 who works in a different CI:

> In advanced class, all our students have been to China, they are able to understand China in the Chinese way and more willing to accept the difference, and they would express the difference in a more respectable way. If people do not have the knowledge, they tend to take the opposite stand.... Therefore, the scholarship we offer is a great thing, for foreigners to study and stay in China for a period of time. No matter how much we try to teach, or tell them about China here, it will never match the first-hand experience.

Cultural diplomacy with Chinese characteristics 201

After having a positive experience of China, the students would come back to talk up China, no need for us to make a painstaking effort. It is much more convincing than what we want to feed their mind.

(UKLH3)

In comparison, there were also similar researches done in South Korea concerning China-related media coverage. One study titled "Chinese News in Korean Media" was carried out in 2005 by Yoo, who analysed 632 randomly selected articles from one of the major Korean newspapers, *Joong Ang Ilbo*, from January 2000 to November 2004, just before the first Confucius Institute was set up. The study found that overall attitudes of the *Joong Ang Ilbo* towards China were neutral (54.7 per cent), but that 33.3 per cent remained unfavourable. It also found a few recurring themes constructing positive images of China: the economic growth of China and the development of China in technology, cultural and diplomatic fields. Another more recent study done by Xu (2010) focused on a case study of *Chosun Ilbo* from 2007–2008: it found that it had more reports on China than other developed countries such as the USA and Japan. Of these China-related reports, 59.4 per cent were neutral and 20.5 per cent were favourable; in other words, 79.9 per cent of the reports were not negative, showing an overall friendly media environment towards China in South Korea. In January 2015, a seven-episode documentary *Super China* was aired by KBS TV in South Korea, which completely shook China: even the Chinese media could not believe this had been made by 'foreign media': instead of showing the dark side of China ridden with environmental and human rights issues, it projected the 'superness' of China in a very positive light. It was so positive that many Chinese audiences commented that it had done a better job than China's own central television CCTV.

Research about specifically Confucius Institute-related reports also show a stark contrast between the USA and South Korea: Liu's (2014) research in the *New York Times* found that 35.3 per cent reports were negative, 31.4 per cent were neutral and 27.5 per cent were positive. This is on the whole consistent with Li and Dai's (2011) research findings about the overall American media environment for the Confucius Institute; sampling thirty-three media including newspapers, journals, television, radio and websites, they concluded that 50 per cent were negative reports, 15 per cent were neutral and 35 per cent were positive. On the other side of the globe, Jin (2013) sampled five mainstream newspapers and three television channels, namely, KBS, MBC and SBS in South Korea, and collected their reports of the Confucius Institutes from November 2004 to November 2012. Jin's research found that for the first two years since the very first Confucius Institute in the world was established in South Korea in 2004, the main content of CI-related reports was mostly 'positive', about the academic and cultural exchanges as well as the opportunities to learn the Chinese language provided by the CIs. Then, since 2006, "soft power strategy" has become the most frequently mentioned theme in the Confucius Institute-related reports (Jin, 2013: 239). Owing to the deeply rooted influence and understanding

202 *Cultural diplomacy with Chinese characteristics*

of Confucian thought in South Korea, the fact that the Confucius Institute was identified as a tool of enhancing Chinese soft power did not lead to more criticism of or opposition to it; instead, they are more focused on the revelations this may have for South Korea. Even in other Asian countries with less amicable media environments than South Korea, the 2015 Pew reports found that "overall, despite historical and territorial frictions, Asia-Pacific publics tend to view their regional neighbours in a positive light", and "Asia-Pacific views of China are far more positive than the perception held by Americans". That is largely due to geographical vicinity, historical connections and cultural affinity, and more people from Asian countries such as South Korea have already been to China or have watched Chinese films and television series at home, and most importantly, have had opportunities to interact with Chinese people in shops, universities or companies. While in Western countries such as the UK and USA, where fewer people benefit from the direct experience in visiting China, both the geographical and cultural distances can expand the perception gap between first-hand knowledge and third-hand stories. Even when presented with an 'air of authority' such as mainstream media, and even when the reporter is reporting live or writing the report *in situ*, the audience can only see or read what is edited (intentionally or unintentionally) by the reporter; this can, at best, be classed as second-hand information, while editorials written by commentators with second-hand information can only be taken as 'stories' that may not enable the audience to get to know the whole truth. Within media studies, the relationship between the representor and the represented has been addressed in terms of "media imperialism". For example, in the works of Schiller (1992), Mattelart, Delcourt and Mattelart (1984) and Tunstall (1977), there has been considerable analysis of the complex process which the media plays a vital role in having influence over their audiences, and the cultural consequences of the West's long-exercised control over the world's media systems.

This shows different media environments in different destinations function as one of the EVs that justify the different foci at different Confucius Institutes. The focus is more on language teaching in East Asia, while in Western countries such as the UK and USA, a better understanding of China and Chinese culture is considered as important as mastering its language. There, offering first-hand knowledge is used as an effective tool to combat third-hand media bias, hence, the Confucius Institutes focus more on providing opportunities for people to visit China and more chances for local people to have face-to-face interactions with Chinese people. This further helps to explain the uneven distribution of Confucius Institutes all over the world: USA and UK are the home to the biggest number of Confucius Institutes in the world and in Europe respectively, while 649 out of the 1,193 Confucius Classrooms (over 54 per cent) in the whole world are located in these two countries alone.[6] In contrast, in the whole of Asia (126 CIs and 114 Confucius Classrooms in total) where the demand for Chinese language learning is arguably higher, and the whole of Africa (59 CIs and 41 Confucius Classrooms in total) where the demand for Hanban funding in expanding

Cultural diplomacy with Chinese characteristics   203

Chinese provision is arguably stronger, their greater desire and interest only made them less prioritised target destinations of the CI. This is because the Chinese government wants to use the Confucius Institutes to "correct misunderstandings of China" (Lo and Pan, 2016), which are more prevalent in those areas dominated by Western media.

This section discusses the media's role as an EV in shaping or even solidifying people's pre-perceptions, thus affecting the media environment in which the Confucius Institute operates. However, what underpins the media framing is ideology, which can ferment tensions in bilateral relations that could have fatal effects on the DV of CI's sustainable development. Chapters 3 and 4 have provided abundant evidence-based discussions, and the next section will further elaborate on this with the recent wave of CI closures in the USA.

Messages from the Confucius Institute closures

Although just a language and cultural programme, the Confucius Institute is a barometer of the changing temperatures in the Sino-US economic and political climate. For example, in September 2015, after Xi Jinping visited the USA, the then American president Barack Obama announced the "One Million Strong Initiative" that seeks to increase the number of students learning Chinese in America from 20,000 to 100,000 by 2020 (cited in Liu, 2017: 240). There were no CI closures in the USA from 2015–2018. However, "after a year of escalating trade disagreements between the U.S. and China", according to the latest Gallup news released in March 2019, "Americans' views of the country have dropped sharply to their lowest levels since 2012. Currently, 41% of Americans say they have a favourable view of China – down 12 percentage points from last year" (McCarthy, 2019). Accompanying this slip of positive views of China, there were also fifteen Confucius Institutes closed in the USA from 2018–2019. But it is worth mentioning that not just was the CI programme affected by the recent tensions between the two countries, but also a bigger programme at the national level, 'the thousand talent program' (*qianren jihua*), "a high-profile, state-backed recruitment drive set up in 2008 to attract overseas Chinese students and academics – particularly those in the science and technology field – with cash grants to fund their research and living costs"[7] was "overshadowed by mistrust as conflicts over tariffs and politics poison well of goodwill" (Mai and Huang, 2019).

Redden's (2019a) article "Closing Confucius Institutes" has suggested the casual connections between the CI closures and the intensified "political pressures", "as universities grapple with calls from Washington". Kahn-Ackermann commented very incisively back in 2014 during the first wave of the closures:

> This decision (of closing down the CI) has nothing to do with the CI, it is made by people who dislike the Chinese government and their policies and simply use the CI to show their discontent.... Cultural Centres are very easily made a target to show such resentment, the Goethe Institute has

204 *Cultural diplomacy with Chinese characteristics*

encountered similar problems, when it was shut down in Iran following the Iranian Revolution.

(Kahn-Ackermann, 2014: n.p.)

Similar things have also happened to the British Council in Russia. In 2007, all the British Council offices outside Moscow were shut down as "clearly a political reprisal after the expulsion by Britain this summer of four Russian diplomats in connection with the murder of the Russian dissident Alexander Litvinenko".[8] In 2018, the British Council was ordered to cease operations in Russia following the diplomatic dispute over a nerve agent attack on a former spy in Britain. The following statement was released on the British Council website: "We are profoundly disappointed at this development. It is our view that when political or diplomatic relations become difficult, cultural relations and educational opportunities are vital to maintain on-going dialogue between people and institutions".[9]

Now, if we look at the recent tide of CI closures in the USA, we can see there are three main reasons behind them. First is the political influence of some anticommunism congressmen, such as the University of Texas A&M System according to Redden's (2018a) report: "Closing a Confucius Institute, at Congressmen's Request". The first paragraph disclosed the reason:

The chancellor of the Texas A&M system said the university would terminate its agreement to host Confucius Institutes – centres for Chinese language teaching and cultural programming funded by the Chinese government – in response to the urging of two congressmen who described the institutes as threats to national security.

(Redden, 2018a)

Redden also mentioned that: "this appears to be the first time a university has explicitly cited a recommendation from elected officials as its reason for terminating a Confucius Institute agreement" (2018a). The closing down of North Carolina State University Confucius Institute was reported with the question: "NC State is Closing its Chinese backed Confucius Institute. Is Politics Behind Decision?"[10] One quoted answer was "it might have been an economic decision driven by the political climate" as both the Congressmen's influence and the National Defence Authorization Act were mentioned, with the latter being the second reason that led to other CI closures. As explained by GAO and on the NAS website:[11]

The federal government currently funds Chinese language programs at American colleges and universities, in part through the National Defence Authorization Act. The 2019 authorization bill would require that in order for colleges and universities to access that funding, they must not have a Confucius Institute or must demonstrate that the Confucius Institute and its staff play no role in the federally funded Chinese language program.

(GAO, 2019: 28)

Cultural diplomacy with Chinese characteristics   205

This triggered the closing down of the Confucius Institutes at the University of Rhode Island, San Francisco State University, the University of Oregon, and Western Kentucky University, with more expected to follow (Redden, 2018b; 2019b). The statement below, made by Oregon University, was very explicit:

> Closing the Confucius Institute was necessary in order to protect the Chinese Language Flagship program, which has received nearly $3.8 million in grants from the Defence Department since the 2016–17 academic year. According to Oregon, the Defence Department has withheld $343,000 in funding for Oregon students to study or intern in China pending the Confucius Institute's closure.
>
> (Redden, 2019b)

This reason was also behind the Confucius Institute's closure at the University of Minnesota, according to *Minnesota Daily*: "University administrators say the closure was due to shifting priorities and new federal policy".[12] On its university website, the announcement is quite positive about the Confucius Institute's achievements:

> After a successful 10 years of outreach to the K-12 Chinese language community, the Confucius Institute at the University of Minnesota will wind down operations and close at the end of the 2018–19 academic year.
>
> We are extremely proud of the role CIUMN and our partners have had in advancing Chinese language and culture in the greater Minnesota community. During the tenure of the Confucius Institute, the number of students enrolled in Mandarin language classes in Minnesota grew more than 125%, and thousands of students have been introduced to Chinese culture.[13]

The third reason falls into the category of a 'normal termination of agreement', such as the University of Illinois-Urbana Champaign, which was closed "four months before the FBI director warned universities across the country and announced dozens of Confucius Institutes were under close federal watch".[14] The interim University Provost John Wilkin said he didn't think "the University's Confucius Institute was in any way politically involved"; "The institute was shut down when the University's funding was not substantial enough to maintain it, but the University is exploring the opportunity to re-establish the institute on campus".[15] As mentioned in Chapter 3, "the exit mechanism of CIs" was already formulated in the *Eight-Year CI Development Plan 2012–2020*[16] to explain the procedure of such normal terminations of the agreement, which is signed for a term of five years. As in all types of cooperation, it is up to the two partners to decide whether they wish to have the agreement renewed, depending on their own considerations and circumstances.

However, these different cases were all grouped together to make sensational news that the Confucius Institutes were closing down. They did not distinguish between the political climate, federal funding policy changes and institutional

206 *Cultural diplomacy with Chinese characteristics*

budgetary constraints, but simply announced the "call on *all* colleges and universities to close their Confucius Institutes at once".[17] Using discerning eyes, we can see all the three EVs at work here: ideology, media and bilateral relations.

Meanwhile, when commenting on these closures, BGD2 also believed that some universities have been blind in applying for setting up their Confucius Institutes in the first place. It could have been an impulsive decision without giving full considerations to their own circumstances, or weighing carefully the costs and benefits, and "it is only normal for some marriages to end up in divorces after five or ten years". "Very normal" is a recurring remark made by all my interviewees in 2019, which was also used to describe Hanban's reaction: "at first, they tried to renegotiate and see if they can keep some of the outgoing ones, now they no longer make such an effort, it is not necessary" (BGD1); "Actually, since it is based on a mutual agreement, the Chinese side could also choose to close down some CIs if they do not perform satisfactorily" (BGD2). UKD5 also mentioned that:

> On the 2018 CI Conference, Hanban has only stressed on the importance of improving quality provision of the CI as a language institute. One of the agendas was proposing to put in place new evaluation schemes of involving an independent third party as it has only been done internally so far.
>
> (UKD5)

These Chinese reactions suggest a continuation of seeing the Confucius Institutes' role as a 'cultural wheel' only, and trying to focus more on *what they can do* to improve its primary function of language teaching, while ignoring what seems to be out of their control by avoiding any political complications.

If the variable of souring bilateral relations tends to be more related with CIs operating in a more ideologically charged environment, the next section will look at other EVs that affect CIs operating in a less ideologically charged environment, that is, nationalism and the cultural boundary.

Soft cultural boundary and hard nationalism boundary

Entering the twenty-first century, our world is beset by a growing sense of global connections, which transcends national and regional borders and boundaries, and nowhere is it more evident than in the economic and cultural realms. As the movement of people and capital accelerates, the cultural boundaries have become more fluid and more contested than ever. Among scholars of boundary studies, Newman and Paasi (1998) argue that boundaries and identity are different sides of the same coin, with the former creating and being created through the latter. Chan and McIntyre define boundary as "the interface between two entities; it marks the end of one and the beginning of another" (2002: xv). Therefore, the world is marked by various boundaries: cultural, social, territorial, political, racial and psychological. Wallman (1978) talks about how boundaries mark members off from non-members in a similar way to the identity creation

Cultural diplomacy with Chinese characteristics 207

ability of nationalism, thus dividing the world into "us" and "them" (Ozkirimli, 2005). Shapiro has argued that cultural governance grows out of Foucault's understanding of power as a productive force that is generated by social relationships, aiming at "making territorial and national/cultural boundaries coextensive" (2004: 34). According to Duara, "every cultural practice is a potential boundary marking a community. These boundaries may be either soft or hard" (1996: 49). Groups with soft boundaries between them do not view mutual boundary breaches as a threat, while communities with hard boundaries tend to privilege their differences and develop an intolerance and suspicion towards other cultures.

In contrast to the territorial and national boundaries, the most important attribute of cultural boundary is that it is always in flux: soft boundaries can harden, and hard boundaries can soften as well. It is dynamic in nature as a relative concept that must have a reference object. Duara (1996) used the example of changing cultural boundaries between the Manchu and Han in Chinese history, while I believe this narrative has contemporary and global relevance when mutual transformations can find perfect demonstrations in looking at China's cultural boundaries with South Korea and the UK respectively.

China's cultural boundaries with these two countries are at different marks in the spectrum as evidenced by the cross-case data presented in the previous chapters: the level of cultural understanding, historical connections, people exchange and media influence as well as their relative positions in the global cultural terrain all contribute to the differences. The cultural boundary between China and the UK is arguably a harder one of the two as Europe is where Orientalism was bred and the UK was in a different ideological camp from China during the Cold War era, so China has been held as both a 'cultural other' and an 'ideological other' in the past. If the lack of understanding of Chinese culture was partly a result of a lack of interest from the hegemonic side, the recent economic rise of China in the globalised era, along with the trans-border exchanges and people mobility can help generate and stimulate such an interest in understanding China. As early as 1848, the then prime minister, Henry John Temple, made the famous statement that no allies or enemies are eternal, but only national interests are perpetual. Common national interests in working together can create an agent in softening the traditional boundaries. For example, following the launch of the first UK–China Year of Cultural Exchange in January 2015, the UK became the first Western country to join the China-led Asia Infrastructure Investment Bank (AIIB) in March – a decision over which the USA made clear its displeasure in no uncertain terms and said: "We are wary about a trend toward constant accommodation of China".[18] Soon after that, the former Prime Minister Cameron hailed the UK as China's "best partner in West" as he signed £40 billion deal[19] during Xi Jinping's visit in October 2015, which kicked off the 'golden era', indicating a softening of the ideological stance by economic interests.

As Chan and McIntyre state, "boundaries are in a constant state of flux, being created, maintained, elaborated, contested, eroded and deconstructed" (2002: xv).

208   *Cultural diplomacy with Chinese characteristics*

Oommen (1995) applied the contradictory trends of 'isms' to describe such changes in today's world:

> It is a world of 'endisms' (end of history, ideology, nation, geography), 'postisms' (postindustrial, postcapitalist, postmodern) and 'beyondisms' (beyond the nation-state, beyond the Cold War). Endisms represent the disappearance of boundaries, postisms signify the emergence of new boundaries and beyondisms allude to the elongation of boundaries.
>
> (cited in Chan and McIntyre, 2002: xiv)

Oommen then concluded that the construction and deconstruction of different types of boundaries, including cultural boundaries, make up the very story of human civilisation and of contemporary social transformations. As argued earlier, this shows what carves the boundary and drives its change is actually power, and cultural diplomacy can potentially play a role in moving the boundaries along with the power shift. The new knowledge of "not the end of history" and "beyond the Cold War", and the flow of people across established boundaries facilitated by cultural diplomacy can help to move the relatively hard cultural boundary between China and the UK towards the softer side.

Meanwhile, the role nationalism plays could potentially move the relatively soft cultural boundary between China and South Korea towards the harder side as well. Its ability to create a sense of national identity is constructed against 'the other', thus it entails cultural resistance and sensitivity to cultural invasions. Robinson has commented on cultural nationalism in colonial Korea, saying that:

> As the idea of nationalism rose among Korean intellectual at the turn of the century, the Confucian tradition came under attack as an obstacle to the creation of a strong national identity. Subservience to foreign ideas and cultural norms inhibited the development of a unique, self-conscious Korean identity. Nationalist, therefore, work to exhume the Korean past as a repository of nationalist symbols smothering under a mantle of excessive veneration for Chinese culture.
>
> (Robinson, 2014: 161)

This indicates a delicate balance to strike for the Confucius Institute as explained by SKD4:

> There are aspects of *Sadaejuui*,[20] or admiration and worship of China from history; there are also components of contempt. Because Korea had been a tributary state to China for thousands of years in history, that some of the Confucian traditions or rituals that we carry out here in South Korea was already extinct in China, for example, our wedding and funeral ceremonies are more particular about rituals; and we never say "Traditional Chinese Medicine" here, it is known as "Traditional Korean Medicine".... Actually we (the CI) are being very careful in using the word "introducing" Chinese

Cultural diplomacy with Chinese characteristics   209

culture instead of "promoting" it, we always have to clarify that we are only providing opportunities, not serving the Chinese interests.

(SKD4)

The carefulness in avoiding the wording of "promoting Chinese culture" was also shared by SKD1 from China, saying that: "the Koreans are very sensitive to 'cultural invasions' from China, they would accuse you of doing this if you do too much". Meanwhile, a number of scholars (Forsby, 2011; Li, 2008; and Yan, 2011) have argued that there has been a Sino-centric tendency to direct attention inwardly towards the distinctness of Chinese identity. This is most conspicuously demonstrated by the rise of nationalist rhetoric from the 1990s and onwards. Sino-centrism signals an identity shift towards an increasingly self-centred China more attuned to its distinct civilisational history. This gives its neighbouring countries very mixed feelings.

On the one hand, countries in Asia, especially in East Asia, are familiar with Confucianism and Confucian values, which carry universal meanings in this region on a par with freedom and democracy in the West. According to the constructivist understanding of identity formation, the historical past is highly significant in forming the identity of the present. Anderson has pointed to this in his famous book *Imagined Communities* that: "nationalism has to be understood by aligning it, not with self-consciously held political ideologies, but with the large cultural systems that preceded it, out of which – as well as against which – it came into being" (1991: 12). Therefore, China's civilisation and historical legacies have the potential to summon common interests and orientations among those who share its legacy, and to be reconstructed and reinvented to help create an "imagined" Asian identity and values (Cho and Jeong, 2008). On the other hand, China's cultural diplomacy needs to tread a fine line between not appearing to be too imposing when promoting the traditional aspects of its culture, and not appearing to be too aggressive when showcasing the contemporary side of China that is involved in territorial disputes with a number of its neighbours. For example, one Indonesian official made it clear that "the problem the Indonesian has is not that China is Communist, it is that China is nationalistic" (cited in Lampton, 2008: 144). SKLH mentioned the distaste of local people when seeing Chinese national flags dotted around their city centre squares for the Confucius Institutes' China Day events, giving them a feeling of a "Chinese takeover". Another example given by SKD4 was the difficulty in selling traditional Chinese dance performances: "they are not exotic enough for the Korean audience, we're very familiar with these art forms, and we also have *our* own folk dances". If Orientalism may be blamed for the lack of popularity of such performances in Western countries such as the UK and the USA, in East Asia, it was regarded as crossing a boundary that they wish to maintain as their own. It is fair to argue that in countries of the same Confucian cultural sphere, the cultural boundary is more carved by cultural nationalism, which "aims to regenerate the national community by creating, preserving or strengthening a people's cultural identity when it is felt to be lacking, inadequate or threatened" (Yoshino, 1992: 1). While

210 *Cultural diplomacy with Chinese characteristics*

cultural nationalism provides the driving force for China to pursue its dream of national rejuvenation, it also offers defence in the recipient countries in protecting their own national identities.

On the other hand, China suffers from a similar 'loss of identity' in such cultural encounters when aspects of culture that China takes pride in its distinctiveness and splendour, tend to be blurred into a general Oriental culture in Western countries. Like UKSC4 shared:

> Sometimes I cannot help feeling disheartened that after some painstaking efforts in explaining cultural traits of China, the students just said, well, it's very similar to Japanese culture, not much difference it seems. Like once, after one hour into a paper cutting session held in a shopping centre to celebrate Chinese New Year, a participant asked if this is from Japan.
>
> (UKSC4)

SKSC3 also mentioned that in terms of contemporary art and culture, it is China that is in the weak position and copying everything from the South Korea, not the other way round. These mutual feelings show that nationalism is working as a two-way process, especially between China and other Asian countries that are familiar with and influenced by traditional Chinese culture. This 'us-centred' nature of nationalism acts like a 'double-edged sword' that could harden the soft cultural boundary when one group privileges their cultural practices.

In summary, the analytical angle of cultural boundary showed us that on the one hand, "the normal response to foreign influence is to build walls" (Pool, 1990: 66), so boundaries do exist, and disputes over and about them involve sovereignty and nationalism, often resulting in conflicts. Also, a soft cultural boundary may coexist with a hard nationalism boundary and vice versa, which means that the CI has to navigate very carefully with these EVs in consideration, drawing on the different attractions of its offerings. On the other hand, we now live in an age where human movements across national borders are happening on an unprecedented scale, delivering new conflicts and new anxieties, but also new knowledge and new communities. This would allow cultural diplomacy to play a more conducive role in facilitating flows of people, ideas, and cultures between China and the rest of the world. In a way, cultural boundaries reconfigure themselves and become more dynamic in the process of cultural diplomacy, which will transfer the traditional way of viewing different cultures as barriers, to a new way as different perspectives, thus contributing to new knowledge generation.

People-to-people interaction as a moderating variable

Along with the all the external variables (EVs) discussed above, people-to-people interaction functions as a moderating variable (MV) in this process. What the CI offers can considerably contribute in this aspect: by bringing teachers from China to the host institutions, facilitating student exchange programmes between the two partner institutions, organising study tours, and providing

Cultural diplomacy with Chinese characteristics 211

scholarships and chances to study in China. All these helps correct some of the mystified or imagined 'knowledge' about China, it could also create a multiplier effect as elaborated by Xu Lin:

> The CI sends over 10,000 tutors and volunteers a year abroad, each of them would teach a minimum of 200 students, and there are another 200 families behind these students. Through them, foreigners would see the amazing changes taking place in China, and the good qualities of Chinese people.
>
> (cited in Wang, 2014: n.p.)

On its tenth anniversary, the CI received a congratulatory letter from Xi Jinping, who has commended its contribution to creating "people-to-people, heart-to-heart communication".[21] As elaborated in Chapter 5, in a way, everyone involved in cross-cultural communications can be considered informal ambassadors in cultural diplomacy, as people-to-people interactions can help combat the unbalanced media influence and enhance mutual understanding, thus constitute a MV that can contribute to the CI's effective operation.

Global vision versus localised practice

China's cultural diplomacy aims to engage with the entire world, but the world is one big place. If China was the "sleeping dragon", and its waking "will shake the world" as Napoleon once predicted, needless to say, this shaking would be perceived differently in different regions of the world: some communities with hard cultural boundaries may feel more threatened, especially if they depict the dragon as an evil monster in their own cultures; while others with soft cultural boundaries, who are more familiar with the dragon, may be more willing to learn how to live with it, or even 'dance with it'. As Gries put it, "who do we see? A cuddly panda or a menacing dragon? Westerners interpreting Chinese foreign policy, like subjects staring at inkblots during a Rorschach test, frequently reveal much more about themselves than they do about China" (2005: 235).

After revealing both the symptoms and root cause of people's misperception of China, this chapter offers a therapy to expand the three crucial questions for an effective public diplomacy strategy proposed by Melissen (2005), namely *what* messages are sent under *what* circumstances, *who* received them, and *how* the messages are interpreted. I argue *who sends the messages, how the messages are sent, along with how these messages interact* with the messages produced by others in the destination and *how soft/hard the cultural boundary* is in between all have direct bearings on how they are interpreted. This explains why despite the centralised input from Hanban and the globalised outreach of the CI, no standard 'recipe' can be found for all the twelve CIs interviewed, and stark differences can be observed in their day-to-day activities. As the CI case study has clearly shown, the number of variables explicate the need to tailor the 'end products' to each destination rather than having one unified model as a fit for all. Goonatilake has stated that:

212   *Cultural diplomacy with Chinese characteristics*

We are seeing today, in the field of culture, two contradictory though inter-twined historical processes that are operating simultaneously: a globalising tendency, where the economies and cultures around the world are being embedded increasingly in more and more pervasive global webs; and a localising tendency, expressed in its extreme form by a number of insurgen-cies on the basis of ethnic, religious and other local identities.

(Goonatilake, 1995: 225–226)

Localisation, for both the products and the process of cultural diplomacy, should be the key word for a global vision initiated by a centralised approach to work, as the same message sent would be received and perceived differently in the process of interacting with different ideologies, cultural spheres, historical con-texts and media environment of the destinations. The current approach, albeit with different foci in offering, tends to be Sino-centric and treat the target audi-ences just as receivers of the messages rather than stakeholders with whom to engage. Particularly for CIs based in a host country with a relatively hard cul-tural boundary with China, the relationship between Hanban and the host institu-tions could pose more problems. Many such problems are due to general cultural differences or different ways of doing things, such as the decision-making process, notice time, efficiency and procedure, but occasional cultural frictions would also occur. An example was provided by UKD3 who considered the Hanban proposal of having a global CI Day to celebrate its tenth anniversary in September 2014 "a bad idea":

Because of the misunderstandings of China, people need to be persuaded in a more subtle way to take China seriously, they need to watch a good film, a wonderful cultural show, then they feel, Oh gosh, China is good, but having a China Day in town is something like, an unfriendly analogy, having a Jehovah's Witnesses Day, a kind of Day that a set of people with a par-ticular interest, it doesn't fit into British culture, we don't have other days – we don't have a Germany Day, or US Day, a China Day is in a way almost reinforces the sense that China is quite a different culture.

(UKD3)

In terms of the logistics side of delivering it on a centrally allocated date, UKD3 also commented quite candidly:

I think it's a terrible mistake, it hasn't taken into account the different cul-tures in different countries, and different cultures of different kinds of universities. In the UK, it's way too early to organize such a big event in mid-September. The timing is quite wrong, most students would only arrive on campus for induction. It's also on a Friday, a holy day for Muslims, any Muslims in the country wouldn't be here. This is the kind of drawback. I think Hanban needs to recognize that we all have the same objectives, and follow the same kinds of plans, we recognise their leadership, we recognise

Cultural diplomacy with Chinese characteristics 213

the importance of all working towards the same goals, but we should also recognise cultural differences around the world, in exactly the same way we want people around the world to recognise Chinese culture. It is a two-way process, we need people in Britain to recognise other cultures, and we also need the Chinese authority to recognise there are different cultures.

(UKD3)

This is an extremely important message for Hanban to listen to, as it is not from the media but from the CI Director, who made the application to have a CI set up in the first place, and run it on a daily basis to help accomplish the purpose of China's cultural diplomacy. If they also think some practice runs counter to exactly what cultural diplomacy is about, promoting "mutual understanding" of "cultural diversity", they would lose faith in the CI. When such opinions were fed back to Hanban, it was handled in the Chinese way: listen to the majority's voice, but UKD3 argued that:

Democracy doesn't always work. In the discussion of the CI Day proposal, there were probably four people in the room who felt exactly the same way, other people from other countries are all right because they have a different timetable. In a way, it looks like most people are happy, we are the minority, just a small number of awkward British people, but that's because our culture is different, it is not about what the majority want, it is about how to make it work in individual areas.

(UKD3)

As a pro-China scholar himself, what UKD3 suggests is exactly what the CI claims to be trying to promote: "harmony in diversity"; however, its centralised approach defies its own goal. Hanban needs to become a better listener in these communications, and realise that sometimes, only a localised approach can make a global venture work.

Map out the variables

This chapter has found that there are a number of variables at work in the process of China's cultural diplomacy, and each variable also contains internal dynamics and there are intertwining interactions going on between these variables, thus there is simply no way to delineate and reflect this complexity with one static diagram, however, the diagram below represents an attempt to chart them all out in action.

The DV of the CI's effective operation is mainly determined by the IV of its ability to localise its product and process to suit different target audiences, meanwhile, a number of EVs also play important roles, including ideology, nationalism, the media environment in the destinations, bilateral relations and the nature of cultural boundary in between. In addition, since we now live in an age where human movements across national borders are happening on an unprecedented

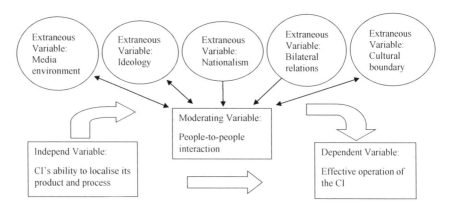

Figure 6.1 Chart of variables.

scale, people-to-people interactions become an important mediator that enables cultural diplomacy to play a more subtle role in facilitating mutual understanding. This chart demonstrates the close interconnections between culture, ideology and power that mark the complexity of cultural diplomacy. As an effort aiming to facilitate culture flows across established boundaries, its strategy needs to be recalibrated carefully against the recipient countries by taking all the variables into consideration. When China is viewed from an insider's perspective, one sees a lot of "national conditions" (*guoqing*), from an outsider's perspective, one sees its "Chinese characteristics", it is now time for China to view itself from an outsider's perspective, as cultural diplomacy is not a one-way dissemination but a two-way interaction between two sets of identities: the sender's view of China and the audiences' perception of China. While the former may shape the Chinese characteristics, it is the latter that determines whether this cultural leap outward is a 'great' one or not.

The great leap outward?

China's expanding global presence goes hand in hand with its deeper engagement with the world across cultural, economic, and diplomatic realms of international affairs. As China becomes a major economic and military power and its diplomacy becomes more assertive, Beijing is trying hard to win friends and understanding, and to transfer its global presence into stronger global influence with its cultural diplomacy. However, it has not been a smooth journey. Its short-term goal is to increase 'the two-way traffic' to reverse the huge 'cultural deficit', while the long-term goal is to show the world merits of its culture and advocate cultural pluralism, believing that no culture is only an exporter or importer. However, in practice, cultural diplomacy is a completely different endeavour from international trade, it needs to aim at long-term effects rather

Cultural diplomacy with Chinese characteristics   215

than short-term results, and what really mattered is whether the increased traffic generates increased volume of impact in its destinations, and that, to a large degree, depends on the variables discussed above.

In the case of the CI, the goal of letting Chinese culture 'go global' is set by the central government with a clear vision and ambition to promote cultural pluralism. It is communicated as a national strategy with abundant financial support channelled down to Hanban as the implementer at the forefront, who tends to reduce the vision somehow to building more CIs as a measurement of its success, counting the number of flags in the world map as China's increased soft power. This number driven mentality risks rendering the CI into a kind of vanity project. During the interviews, Chinese directors both in South Korea and the UK have mentioned it as a "box to tick": the Chinese university wants the CI as a proof of 'internationalisation' and university prestige. As UKD2 disclosed, "the home institution only cares about this result to show their achievement and get the ¥200,000 matching fund, but does not care much about the process and quality of the end product".

A historical lesson should be learned from the Great Leap Forward: just as it is dilettante to measure economic power with a single dimension of steel output, quantified measurement will not only fail to measure the effects of soft power, but may encourage the forming of a 'hard shell' with excessive input of resources. From the impressive circulation number of *China Daily* overseas to the number of CIs and CCs all over the world, the figure of financial input was never presented in the picture of output, which is always about growth in numbers. Both the criteria of evaluating a Model CI in Europe and CI of the Year also set a series of numerical thresholds: How many students were enrolled? How many cultural activities were staged? How many people particip-ated in the China Day/CI event? These quantifiable measures of outputs tell us little about the impact: Does the student enrolled in a taster session continue to study Chinese? Does the number of cultural activities mean any internalised knowledge? Does participating in a China Day show better understanding of China? Obviously, the answers cannot be found in those specious numbers, but as told by UKLH2 during the interview, "I think Hanban is still number-driven, they just want to know how many activities have been carried out in how many schools". UKD2 also expressed his concern that the CI tends to go a bit "too far, too fast", because "this suits the taste of the Chinese decision makers: they want to see things happen quickly. It is the Chinese speed". But speed can kill. Ryan Allen, an assistant professor of educational studies at Chapman University, said that even absent the political pressures, he would expect to see some CIs closing: "They expanded so fast and so quickly that it's almost like throw everything at a wall and see what sticks – of course some of things are going to fall down" (cited in Redden, 2019a). Cultural diplomacy can only work the magic like a trickle feed, slower but going deeper with longer effects.

However, at the top level, when there were comments about CIs being exported faster than China's high-speed trains, Liu Yandong, Vice-Premier and Chairperson of the Council of the CI Headquarters, simply adopted the new

216 *Cultural diplomacy with Chinese characteristics*

nickname of "soul high-speed train" in her speech commemorating the CI's tenth anniversary.[22] This analogy was actually used by Shambaugh (2013) in criticising China's unsophisticated approach to cultural diplomacy as constructing high-speed rail – by investing money and expecting to see development. After all, the greatness of a cultural leap outward needs to be measured not by how big the stride is or how extensive the footprints are, but by how deep the footprints are and how long-lasting the impact is. As Zhang argued:

> The critical question is … not how popular China has become in certain parts of the world, but how much China's improved image has increased the trust of the international community in China's growing power and the moral authority and legitimacy of China's domestic and international politics. The evidence in this regard is at best patchy.
>
> (Zhang, 2009: 55)

A decade on, instead of celebrating with more such evidence, new terms of "sharp power" and "new Cold War" were brewed against China amidst its remarkable growth of cultural exports, and the global cultural terrain remains highly contested.

Prominent features of China's cultural diplomacy

To conclude the research findings, four statements are summarised as the prominent features of China's cultural diplomacy. A comparative perspective plays a critical role in this process; the words of "Western" and "Eastern" countries are used below as historical, political and cultural constructs rather than a geographical one. Still, no conclusion can be globally inclusive and hence conclusive of local diversities and cultural specificities.

1 China's cultural diplomacy faces different challenges in different cultural spheres. In Western countries with relatively hard cultural boundaries, China's cultural diplomacy was staged with Orientalism in the background, and anti-communism in the foreground, giving it a dual aim of reshaping China's image from being the 'cultural other' and the 'ideological other'; In Eastern countries with relatively soft cultural boundaries, the softness can be hardened by the double-edged nature of nationalism, which provides the driving force for China to launch its campaign of cultural diplomacy domestically, and the defending force for the recipient countries to safeguard their own national cultural identities.

2 The vehicle of China's cultural diplomacy carries the mission on two wheels: one 'cultural wheel' to advocate cultural pluralism and the other 'political value wheel' to counter the perception of China as a threat. The different cultural boundaries between China and the recipient countries, and the different media environments justify different priorities in delivery to different target audiences.

Cultural diplomacy with Chinese characteristics 217

3   The state-led approach to implementing cultural diplomacy is generating some side effects with its sponsorship, censorship and presence on the front seat. Such side effects appear to be shared concerns across different cultural boundaries, and have a paradoxical effect of taking on an ideological overtone when it wishes to separate it from the cultural dimension.

4   The globalised outreach of China's cultural diplomacy is sustained by a centralised input with a non-uniform model to allow reflexive adaptation to local conditions, but more sophisticated localisation is needed to engage different target audiences.

Developed from and sharpened by the analysis and discussions of the previous chapters, these four statements summarise the prominent features of China's cultural diplomacy. Although they are mostly drawn from the comparative case study of the CIs, they also apply to other forms and fronts of cultural diplomacy, such as internationalisation of the Chinese media and artistic exchanges to name a few. These features are generalised construction that may not reflect particularised forms of cultural diplomacy as different fronts may face different challenges, but it is the same contested terrain that China's cultural diplomacy is launched into, and by similar state-led approach that features concentrated state power and quantified measurement for effects.

These features were drawn from the four perspectives that framed this research project at the very beginning: the different historical, international and domestic contexts interweave the complex backgrounds for China's cultural diplomacy, meaning that the vehicle of the CI needs to carry the shared mission but deliver different priorities in different parts of the cultural terrain; the government as the agent should not just focus on speed but needs to be aware of the side effects produced by government sponsorship and censorship; and the actual driving practice of the vehicle also needs to be adapted to suit different road conditions. A clearly contrasting feature is shown in the first two statements between countries of relatively soft and hard cultural boundaries, while the latter two statements apply to both cultural boundaries. Overall, a dual character can be traced as a permeated feature: Western domination over the power of discourse has rendered China as being both the 'ideological other' and 'cultural other', with the domestic undercurrent of double-edged nationalism at play, Chinese cultural diplomacy needs to gain external rapport and internal recognition at the same time, thus its purpose must be understood within both the international and domestic contexts. An historical perspective is also indispensable where the 'Occident' and 'Orient' dichotomy; 'us' and 'other' camps divided by ideology and nationalism all underpin the tensions and challenges for China to achieve its dual aims of countering the China threat perception and advocating cultural pluralism. Chinese culture and political values function as the two wheels of the vehicle for cultural diplomacy, which takes an offensive and defensive stance respectively. Perhaps no other country's cultural diplomacy would be etched with such a level of complexity.

218 *Cultural diplomacy with Chinese characteristics*

All the dual characters described above can be found in the CI, the most well-known and controversial project of China's cultural diplomacy. Multiple competing forces and different power relations in the terrain were teased out through the comparative case studies of the CI. It shows the challenges of making this 'cultural leap outward' truly great, and suggests that China's cultural diplomacy must differentiate its approaches and foci in the field as the terrain conditions vary substantially by region and countries, and its policy-making process needs to respond to both international and domestic contexts. As d'Hooghe pointed out:

> The content and conduct of China's public diplomacy are suffering from structural problems that cannot simply be 'fixed' by intensifying and expanding current activities in the field of soft power projection. Beijing needs to rethink its strategy as a whole.
>
> (d'Hooghe, 2011: 19)

Now that the prominent features of China's cultural diplomacy have been refined, it is hoped to shed some useful light on how to rethink its strategy and how to improve the actual practice in the field: How can China better translate its cultural resources into desired policy outcomes? How can the side effects produced by China's 'prescription' of cultural diplomacy be managed? And how can the 'China model' of cultural diplomacy be improved? The next section will look at the implications of the research findings in the same order as the four statements, and what initiatives can be taken to bring about changes that can help elevate the subtleness and sophistication of cultural diplomacy in practice.

Implications of the prominent features on the practice of China's cultural diplomacy

Purpose: can be achieved better by better understanding the target audiences

The analysis of the different terrain conditions in Statement 1) suggests that China's cultural diplomacy must recalibrate itself carefully against the cultural boundaries with the recipient countries, because it is the target audience who will decide whether and how they accept, internalise and act upon the messages, depending on a range of internal and external influences, such as education, family, media and travel (Rawnsley, 2013), which all affects and determines their responses. As recommended by Ang, Isar and Mar, the role of audiences needs to be taken into account as "active meaning makers when they consume cultural diplomacy products: there is no guarantee that the way they read, interpret or understand such products will be in line with the original intentions of cultural diplomacy" (2015: 375).

For example, the 2008 Beijing Olympics Slogan of "One World, One Dream" is a nice catchphrase transmitting the Confucius idea of "harmonious world"

Cultural diplomacy with Chinese characteristics   219

according to Beijing, but in the edited book titled *Owning the Olympics: Narratives of the New China* (Price and Dayan, 2008), three chapters play with the phrase in their titles to show how it is read by the USA at least, if not the rest of the world: *Whose World, What Dream?, One World, Different Dreams*, and *Dreams and Nightmares*. Then in the opening ceremony of the Games, there were 2008 drummers performing and people acting as movable type printing blocks while forming the Chinese character "he" (peace and harmony), however, "the image of massive numbers of efficient Chinese performers in perfect rows and columns drumming in perfect unison" was commented as "Authorit-awesome" by the *Daily Show* with Jon Steward, and interpreted as an all-powerful state that would "take over the world" and "bring down America" in the episode of "The China Problem" in *South Park*[23] (cited in Gries, Crowson and Sandel , 2010: 231). Although these are comedy programmes with a focus on satire, this is a classic case that the original message of China's peaceful rise being interpreted in the opposite way of China as a threat. It reminds us of the importance in understanding that the messages are not sent to a vacuum chamber, but a receptor that was preoccupied or even embedded with pre-perceptions about the 'other', besides, the receiving destinations are also in a different and changing power relations with China in a world of unchanging power struggle. All these dynamics and complexities must be taken into account as variables for an effective strategy.

At the classroom level, more questions need to be asked to find out students' pre-perceptions in Western countries, and choose teaching materials that can engage their interest or address their misperceptions. Films, documentaries and television programmes can be drawn on more as teaching materials to learn the language in the cultural and social setting, thus help student understand ordinary people's lives, appreciate their different life styles but common aspirations. In terms of content delivery in the classroom, more debates can be held in Western universities as debating is a much more welcomed teaching method than one-way input. By staging both sides' arguments, students are exposed to alternative views to those dominating their own education and media environment while finding the process intellectually stimulating. Most importantly, teacher–student interactions should play a bigger role in enhancing mutual understandings as people-to-people, not just instructor and learner.

In Asian countries where their cultural understanding of traditional China is much better, more focus can be put on improving teaching quality while more sensitivity should be given to recipient countries' national cultural identity, especially those who were tributary states to China in history. The promotion of Chinese language and culture should aim at celebrating cultural differences and compatibilities.

In summary, a more effective cultural diplomacy has to aim at achieving a balance of the variables that best frame the production of knowledge and understanding of China for the target audiences, and more importantly, not treating them as passive *audiences* who receive messages, but *stakeholders* with whom to engage.

220 *Cultural diplomacy with Chinese characteristics*

Vehicle: promoting Chinese culture as an internalising process rather than a product

The 'culturetainment' trend of reducing the diversity of Chinese culture to a uniform commodity needs to be addressed. For example, Hanban sponsors tours of university art troupes all over the world. In Asian countries that are much more familiar with Chinese folk dance, such tours can be reduced and the fund redirected to more activities engaging the target audiences while enabling internalisation of cultural appreciation. For example, using the fund as awards to encourage students' participation, such as student-organised Chinese cultural events, drama acting, video-making competition, or even business proposals, that students are the main initiators and active creators; the awards can be trips to China or scholarships to study in China.

Cultural boundaries should also be considered in altering some of the sweeping offerings carried by the vehicle across the globe hitherto. For example, Hanban allocates a large number of teaching materials and book gifts to each CI (3,000 volumes as specified in most of the agreements), even though it is not a Hanban mandate and only 12.5 per cent of the institutes actually used textbooks recommended by Hanban according to Xu Lin (Qu, Zhao and Cheng, 2012), such donations are often used as evidence of government control, or at least its' 'top-down, parachute' model in some host countries. Therefore, the choice of not using Hanban-sanctioned textbooks can be used as a strong counterargument to those accusations, and such wasteful donations can stop going to those CIs where they are left gathering dust on the shelf (of course, they can continue to go to other parts of the world where they are needed and actually used). Instead, the saved funding can be used for book orders in the host country, this would be a much more effective way of utilising the fund, by again engaging the receiver as the stakeholder and active participant.

Just like the metaphor used in statement 2), the vehicle must make necessary changes to its configuration to suit different road conditions, and adapt itself to different driving practices in 'left-driving' and 'right-driving' countries. And most importantly, it is the journey that counts.

Agent: playing down the roles and presence of the government

As argued throughout Chapters 3 to 4, in the prescription of cultural diplomacy, the dose of government defining, planning, funding and leading is one of the ingredients that are causing side effects, particularly for China, whose identity as a polity reduces the cultural appeal of its identity as a civilisation. The authoritarian nature of the Chinese government may cause its challenge to Western cultural hegemony to rebound as being challenged. Many criticisms of the CI are not about what CIs did, but about what the Chinese government *did not allow* them to do, resulting in a least desirable outcome mentioned in Chapter 2: the negative perception based on what *did not* happen could wipe out the positive effects of what *did* happen. Therefore, the implied advice from

Cultural diplomacy with Chinese characteristics 221

Statement 3) is to play down the roles and the presence of Chinese government across both types of cultural boundaries, while non-state agents should be engaged to play bigger roles.

In the case of the CI, this can be done by putting the two partner institutions more in the limelight for CI events, especially for academic conferences and forums, Hanban can continue with the role of 'helping build the stage' with funding support, but not as actors appearing on the stage as well, nor as producers making decisions on the lines of the play. As insightfully expressed by BGD2, Hanban needs to correctly understand its role as an equal partner with "cooperative relationship" with the host university, and not regard the CI as a tool at its disposal to project China's influence: "the CI is not the subject but object of China's influence, in other words, Hanban can only influence the target audience in the host country by influencing the CI". More trust and autonomy should be delegated to the two partner institutions, and less government presence should be made in CI opening ceremonies and major events. The roles played by the Board of Advisors should be made more visible through media communications and more voices should be given to people-in-the-know who can offer substantial counterevidence and more convincing persuasion than government defence. Meanwhile, the CI can be used as an infrastructure to leverage more non-governmental exchanges, such as to facilitate exchange of visiting scholars between the two partner institutions.

At the same time, more awareness of the side effects of government presence is needed when considering some pragmatic solutions. For example, it is commendable to see a number of very responsive and pro-active new practices were initiated and actioned by Hanban, however, some measures in store may cause some 'side effects' while only addressing the 'symptom' of teacher shortage problem: according to the MOD, some embassies have now proposed to allow spouses of diplomats to fill in positions of the CI teachers through competitive examinations. This only applies to CIs that are close enough to Embassies and mostly located in non-English speaking counties that suffer from a more serious teacher shortage. The benefits are to help with teacher supply and offer job opportunities for embassy staff's spouses at the same time, but the drawbacks are obviously stronger government colour attached to the CI, which may override the benefits.

Apart from reducing government presence, a more important change should be made from its top-down approach to a bottom-up one to engage more non-state agents. As recommended in the British Council report, "governments cannot and should not seek to control culture or cultural contact, but they can nonetheless play a constructive role by facilitating the cultural work of other actors in civil society" (Holden, 2013: 35). For example, Hanban or the Ministry of Culture and Tourism can create a bidding system with transparent procedures that is open to all organisations: regardless of whether it is privately or government-owned, Chinese or foreign, as long as the bidding party can come up with an initiative that serves the purpose of promoting Chinese language and culture and enhancing mutual understanding, it can win government funding to

222 *Cultural diplomacy with Chinese characteristics*

generate the desired output. The CI and CCC may continue to be the flagship projects, but more initiatives should be created utilising private fund and organisations. As discussed earlier, the multi-agent view and engagement of non-state actors represent the future development of cultural diplomacy, as it can mobilise and unleash more nodes to activate a whole network. When the government is functioning just like one node in this network, the desired elevation of sophistication in cultural diplomacy can be achieved.

Implementation: localisation through engagement and capacity building

Both my own research and GAO's report (2019) suggest that the CIs are more likely to be controversial if the host university entirely relies on the CI to deliver the whole Chinese language and studies programme. If the host university has their own course team or locally hired lecturers, and only use CI's expertise on language teaching and cultural activities, the risk would be largely reduced and more manageable. Specifically, I would suggest keeping the CI as a separate arm to the body of university offering with locally hired lecturers and/or researchers. It allows the host university to take advantage of Hanban's generous support for expansion of the language programme and enrichment of cultural activities, without restricting freedom of inquiry for students to investigate potentially sensitive topics, while adding the benefits for students to have access to diverse international points of view.

For host universities that do not have their own Chinese team, changes can be easily made through expanding the head teacher scheme that Hanban already set up in 2013: they are hired locally by the host institution following their own recruitment procedures but paid by the Hanban fund. The blend and cooperation between Hanban secondees and locally hired teachers would help nurture a healthy balance and create a more "equal partnership" that both parties can benefit from while minimising the worries of reduced academic discourse on campus. However, the current criteria to apply for this scheme is that each CI that has been running for over two years and has a total registered number of students of over 200 can get one quota for such a position. In other words, the scheme only goes by 'numbers' in its global implementation. I argue that locally hired teacher should become a part of the standard CI model, and the cultural boundaries also deserve special considerations: probably an enlarged quota would be beneficial for CIs in countries with relatively hard cultural boundaries with China. These positions will give the host institutions the "relational structures" and "shared identity" proposed by Zaharna (2014), making them feel like a stakeholder in a truly collaborative entity. It is interesting to note that according to *Methods of Evaluating a Model CI in Europe*, one of the criteria (point 10.3) is "the ratio of local Chinese teachers and secondees from China should reach 1:1", indicating that this is the exemplary model.

As discussed in Chapter 4, the quality gap needs to be narrowed when the CI is compared to its Western counterparts, which can be achieved through capacity building. Specifically, pre-job training provided by the host university

Cultural diplomacy with Chinese characteristics   223

should become systematic and mandatory before the CI teachers start teaching, to ensure quality and align the CI teachers with the academic standard required by the host university. This is of vital importance that I argue for it to be included in the CI agreement under the "Obligations of the Host University". So far, there are only pre-departure trainings offered by Hanban before teachers leave China, usually they are very general in nature as it is the same training for teachers being sent to different countries. Pre-job training in situ is currently not compulsory and very sporadic: making it a compulsory duty of the host university will again give them the "relational structures" and "shared identity", and benefit the tutors themselves, the student body, and the CI as a whole.

Statements 1), 2) and 4) all suggest a strong need to localise the practice of the CI. As discussed earlier, flexibility is already a unique feature of the CI model and there is no standard formula prescribed for the CI provisions all over the world, but localisation needs to go a step further in offering an individualised diet that best matches each CI's conditions and the needs of the target audiences. When we consider the initiatives recommended in the above four aspects, we can see a common theme in making the 'the receiver' a stakeholder rather than a passive receiving end or inactive nodes: from engaging the target audience, to engaging the host university and seconded staff from home university, and more non-state actors as agents of cultural diplomacy. If a lesson can be learned from reflecting on the CI closures, the most important message is to respect the cooperation as an equal partnership by both sides. Mutual trust is at the core, and it can be built by working together. The implementation of cultural diplomacy should evolve from a vertical approach that is government-centred to a horizontal one that is network-based, which can facilitate more collaborations and generate synergy. As commented by Seiichi (2008: 191): "cooperative interaction is what distinguished public diplomacy from propaganda". And most importantly, a change of stance is needed from "promoting" to "engaging", as "promotion" is something you do *to* someone, while "engagement" is something you do *with* someone, for mutual benefits.

Notes

1 This chapter is derived, in part, from an article published in *Journal of Contemporary China* on 26 December 2018, available at: www.tandfonline.com/doi/abs/10.1080/10 670564.2018.1557951?journalCode=cjcc20.
2 Ministry of Education Released the 2018 International Students Statistics in China, 13 April 2019, available at: www.sohu.com/a/307635576_206494?sec=wd.
3 The Evolution and Current Status of Chinese Teaching and Research in South Korea, *Education Office of the Chinese Embassy in South Korea* website, 2017, available at: www.chinaedukr.org/publish/portal109/tab5123/info92047.htm.
4 China China, available at: www.youtube.com/watch?v=_etl_qkelX0.
5 See the full speech, President Lawrence S. Bacow Affirms Academic Freedom in Peking University Speech, Fairbank Center for Chinese Studies, 20 March 2019, available at: https://fairbank.fas.harvard.edu/president-lawrence-s-bacow-affirms-academic-freedom-in-peking-university-speech/.

224 *Cultural diplomacy with Chinese characteristics*

6 See Hanban website, About Confucius Institute, available at: www.hanban.org/confuciousinstitutes/node_10961.htm.

7 Laurie Chen, China's Thousand Talents Plan fuels US Suspicions about Overseas Students, Warns Leading Ex-Harvard Academic Wei Yingjie, *South China Morning Post*, 7 March 2019, available at: www.scmp.com/news/china/diplomacy/article/2189083/chinas-thousand-talents-plan-fuels-us-suspicions-about-overseas.

8 Luke Harding, Russia tells British Council to Shut Offices, *Guardian*, 12 December 2007, available at: www.theguardian.com/uk/2007/dec/12/russia.world.

9 Statement from the British Council on Russia. 17 March 2018, available at: www.britishcouncil.org/contact/press/statement-british-council-russia.

10 Jane Stancill, NC State is closing its Chinese-backed Confucius Institute: Is Politics Behind Decision? *The News and Observer*, 21 November 2018, available at: www.newsobserver.com/news/local/article221985800.html.

11 Defence Bill Limits Funding for Colleges with Confucius Institutes, National Association of Scholars, 3 August 2018, available at: www.nas.org/articles/defense_bill_limits_funding_for_colleges_with_confucius_institutes.

12 Helen Sabrowsky, China-Funded Institute Set to Close, *Minnesota Daily*, 21 February 2019, available at: www.mndaily.com/article/2019/02/n-china-funded-institute-set-to-close.

13 Confucius Institute at the University of Minnesota, available at: http://confucius.umn.edu/.

14 Haipei Wu, University Confucius Institute Closed Months before FBI Monitoring, *Daily Illini*, 3 March 2018, available at: https://dailyillini.com/news/2018/03/03/university-confucius-institute-closed-months-fbi-monitoring/.

15 Ibid.

16 See Confucius Institute Development Plan, 2012–2020, available at: https://wenku.baidu.com/view/688c6b10a8114431b90dd88e.html.

17 Defence Bill Limits Funding for Colleges with Confucius Institutes, National Association of Scholars, 3 August 2018, available at: www.nas.org/articles/defense_bill_limits_funding_for_colleges_with_confucius_institutes.

18 Nicolas Watt, Paul Lewis and Tania Branigan, US Anger at Britain Joining Chinese-Led Investment Bank AIIB. *Guardian*, 13 March 2015, available at: www.theguardian.com/us-news/2015/mar/13/white-house-pointedly-asks-uk-to-use-its-voice-as-part-of-chinese-led-bank.

19 Phillip Inman, Cameron Hails UK as "Best Partner in West" as He Signs £40bn China Deal, *Guardian*, 21 October 2015, available at: www.theguardian.com/business/2015/oct/21/china-and-britain-40bn-deals-jobs-best-partner-west.

20 *Sadaejuui* (lit. "serving-the-Great-ism", Hangul: 사대주의, Chinese: shi da zhu yi) is a Korean term which evolved in the mid-twentieth century from a more widely used historical concept. According to Wikipedia, *Sadae* literally means "dealing with the great" or "serving the great" and is interpreted as "loving and admiring the great and powerful"; *Juui* means "ideology" and it is conventionally translated as "-ism". The Chinese term is sometimes translated as Flunkeyism in English; I think it is more accurate to keep the Korean expression here.

21 Xi Jinping, A Letter to Congratulate the Confucius Institute on its 10th Anniversary and the First Global Confucius Institute Day, dated 25 September 2014. *Confucius Institutes Magazine*, Special Issue, 35(2014): 12–13. Available at: www.confucius-institute-magazine.com/revistas/english35/.

22 The full speech is in the 2014 Special Issue of the Confucius Institute, pp. 17–19, available at: www.cim.chinesecio.com/hbcms/f/journal/journalDetail?id=8456d5e4155447bba65a2063798b3216.

23 See Olympic Nightmare: The Opening Ceremonies of the 2008 Summer Olympics in China Terrorize Cartman, clip from Season 12 South Park episode, "The China Problem", available at: www.southparkstudios.com/clips/187263.

References

Anderson, B. (1991). *Imagined Communities*, revised edn, London: Verso.

Ang, I., Y.R. Isar and P. Mar (2015). Cultural Diplomacy: Beyond the National Interest? *International Journal of Cultural Policy*, 21(4): 365–381.

Chan, J. and B. McIntyre (eds) (2002). *In Search of Boundaries, Communication, Nation States and Cultural Identities*. Westport, CT: Ablex Publishing.

Cho, Y.N. and J.J. Ho (2008). China's Soft Power: Discussions, Resources, and Prospects. *Asian Survey*, 48(3): 453–472.

Cull, N. (2008). The Public Diplomacy of the Modern Olympic Games and China's Soft Power Strategy. In Monroe E. Price and Daniel Dayan (eds), *Owning the Olympics: Narratives of the New China.* The New Media World series, Ann Arbor, MI: University of Michigan Press.

Duara, P. (1996). De-Constructing the Chinese Nation. In Jonathan Unger (ed.), *Chinese Nationalism.* New York: East Gate Book.

Forsby, A. (2011). An End to Harmony? The Rise of a Sino-Centric China. *Political Perspectives*, 5(3): 5–26.

French, H.W. (2006). Another Chinese Export is all the Rage: China's Language. *New York Times*, 11 January, p. A2. Available at www.nytimes.com/2006/01/11/world/asia/another-chinese-export-is-all-the-rage-chinas-language.html.

GAO (2019). China: Observations on Confucius Institutes in the United States and U.S. Universities in China. Testimony Before the Permanent Subcommittee on Investigations, Committee on Homeland Security and Governmental Affairs, U.S. Senate. Publicly Released: 28 February. Available at: www.gao.gov/assets/700/697156.pdf.

Goonatilake, S. (1995). The Self Wandering Between Cultural Localisation and Globalisation. In Jan Pieterse and Bhikhu Parekh (eds), *The Decolonisation of Imagination, Culture, Knowledge and Power.* London: Zed Books.

Gries, P. (2005). Social Psychology and the Identity-Conflict Debate: Is a "China Threat" Inevitable? *European Journal of International Relations*, 11(2): 235–265.

Gries, P., M. Crowson and T. Sandel (2010). The Olympic Effect on American Attitudes Towards China: Beyond Personality, Ideology, and Media Exposure. *Journal of Contemporary China*, 19(64): 213–231.

Hartig, F. (2014). The Globalization of Chinese Soft Power: Confucius Institutes in South Africa. *Confucius Institutes and the Globalization of China's Soft Power* (pp. 47–63). Los Angeles, CA: Figueroa Press.

Holden, J. (2013). *Influence And Attraction: Culture and the Race for Soft Power in the 21st Century.* London: British Council.

d'Hooghe, I. (2011). The Expansion of China's Public Diplomacy System. In J. Wang (ed.), *Soft Power in China: Public Diplomacy through Communication* (pp. 19–35). New York: Palgrave Macmillan.

Hubbert, J. (2014). Ambiguous States: Confucius Institutes and Chinese Soft Power in the U.S. Classroom. *Political and Legal Anthropology Review*, 37(2): 329–349.

Jin, X. (2013). *Hanguo meiti guanyu Kongzi Xueyuan de baodao yu pinglun* [Media Reports and Commentaries Concerning the Confucius Institutes in South Korea]. In Zhang Lihua (ed.), *Zhongguo Wenhua Yu Waijiao* [*Chinese Culture and Diplomacy*]. Beijing: Intellectual Property Publishing House.

Kahn-Ackermann, M. (2014). *Akeman: Kongzi Xueyuan xuyao tingzhi kuozang* [Kahn-Ackermann: Confucius Institute Should Shift Focus from Expansion to Quality]. Available at: http://cul.qq.com/a/20141204/014701.htm.

226 Cultural diplomacy with Chinese characteristics

Lampton, D.M. (2008). *The Three Faces of Chinese Power: Might, Money, and Minds.* London: University of California Press.

Li, K. and Z. Dai (2011). Evaluation of Confucius Institute's Media Environment in the US. *World Economy and Politics*, 7: 76–93.

Li, M. (2008). Soft Power in Chinese Discourse: Popularity and Prospect. *RSIS Working Paper*, No. 165, S. Rajaratnam School of International Studies, Nanyang Technological University.

Liu, T.T. (2017). Exporting Culture, the Confucius Institute and China's Smart Power Strategy. In Victoria Dutter, Toby Miller and Dave O'Brien (eds), *The Routledge Handbook of Global Cultural Policy* (pp. 233–246). New York: Routledge.

Liu, Y. (2014). *Guojia wenhua shiyu xia de shehua yunlun yanjiu, yi Niuyue Shibao dui Kongzi Xueyuan baodao de neirong weili.* [Research on China-Related Media from the Perspective of National Cultural Security – A Case Study of Confucius Institute Reports in New York Times], *Xueshu Jiaoliu [Academic Exchange]*, 4: 202–205.

Lo, J.T. and S. Pan (2016). Confucius Institutes and China's Soft Power: Practices and Paradoxes. *Compare: A Journal of Comparative and International Education*, 46(4): 512–532.

Mai, J. and K. Huang (2019). US–China Trade War Suspicions have had Chilling Effect on Beijing's Thousand Talents Plan. *South China Morning Post*, 6 March. Available at: www.scmp.com/news/china/diplomacy/article/2188919/us-china-trade-war-suspicions-have-had-chilling-effect-beijings.

Manzenreiter, W. (2010). The Beijing Games in the Western Imagination of China: The Weak Power of Soft Power. *Journal of Sport and Social Issues*, 34(1): 29–48.

Mattelart, A., X. Delcourt and M. Mattelat (1984). *International Image Markets.* London: Comedia.

McCarthy, J. (2019). Americans' Favorable Views of China Take 12-Point Hit. Available at: https://news.gallup.com/poll/247559/Americans-favorable-views-china-point-hit.aspx.

Melissen, J. (2005). The New Public Diplomacy: Between Theory and Practice. In J. Melissen (ed.), *The New Public Diplomacy: Soft Power in International Relations* (pp. 3–27). New York: Palgrave Macmillan.

Morley, D. and K. Robins (1995). *Spaces of Identity, Global Media, Electronic Landscapes and Cultural Boundaries.* London: Routledge.

Newman, D. and A. Paasi (1998). Fences and Neighbours in the Postmodern World: Boundary Narratives in Political Geography. *Progress in Human Geography*, 22: 186–207.

Oommen, T.K. (1995). Contested Boundaries and Emerging Pluralism. *International Sociology*, 10: 251–268.

Ozkirimli, U. (2005). *Contemporary Debates on Nationalism: A Critical Engagement.* New York: Palgrave.

Pew Research Centre (2015). How Asia-Pacific Publics See Each Other and Their National Leaders. Available at: www.pewglobal.org/2015/09/02/how-asia-pacific-publics-see-each-other-and-their-national-leaders/.

Pool, I.S. (1990). *Technologies Without Boundaries: On Telecommunications in a Global Age.* Cambridge, MA: Harvard University Press.

Price, M. and D. Dayan (2008). *Owning Olympics: Narratives of New China.* Ann Arbor, MI: University of Michigan Press.

Qu, Y., H. Zhao and Y. Cheng (2012). Confucius Institutes go Beyond Borders. *China Daily*, 2 December. Available at: www.chinadaily.com.cn/china/2012-12/02/content_15978436.htm.

Cultural diplomacy with Chinese characteristics 227

Rawnsley, G. (2013). Limits of China's Cultural Diplomacy. *CPI Analysis*, 23 October. Available at: https://cpianalysis.org/2013/10/23/limits-of-chinas-cultural-diplomacy/.

Redden, E. (2018a). Closing a Confucius Institute, at Congressmen's Request, *Inside Higher ED*, 9 April. Available at: www.insidehighered.com/news/2018/04/09/texas-am-cuts-ties-confucius-institutes-response-congressmens-concerns.

Redden, E. (2018b). University of Rhode Island Closes Confucius Institute. *Inside Higher HE*, 18 December. Available at: www.insidehighered.com/quicktakes/2018/12/18/university-rhode-island-closes-confucius-institute.

Redden, E. (2019a). Closing Confucius Institutes. *Inside High Ed*, 9 January. Available at: www.insidehighered.com/news/2019/01/09/colleges-move-close-chinese-government-funded-confucius-institutes-amid-increasing.

Redden, E. (2019b). Three More Universities Close Confucius Institutes. *Inside High Ed*, 1 May. Available at: www.insidehighered.com/quicktakes/2019/05/01/3-more-universities-close-confucius-institutes.

Robinson, M.E. (2014). *Cultural Nationalism in Colonial Korea, 1920–1925*. Seattle, WA: University of Washington Press.

Sahlins, M. (2015). *Confucius Institute: Academic Malware*. Chicago, IL: Prickly Paradigm Press.

Said, E. (1978). *Orientalism*. London: Penguin Books.

Schiller, H. (1992). *Mass Communications and American Empire*, 2nd edn. Boulder, CO: Westview Press.

Seiichi, K. (2008). Wielding Soft Power. In Yasushi Watanabe and David McConnell (eds), *Soft Power Superpowers: Cultural and National Assets of Japan and the United States* (pp. 191–206). New York: M.E. Sharpe.

Shambaugh, D. (2013). *China Goes Global: The Partial Power*. New York: Oxford University Press.

Shapiro, M.J. (2004). *Methods and Nations: Cultural Governance and the Indigenous Subject*. New York: Routledge.

Tunstall, J. (1977). *The Media are American*. London: Constable.

Wallman, S. (1978). The Boundaries of "Race": Processes of Ethnicity in England. *Man*, 13(2): 200–217.

Wang, Y. (2014). *Wenhua de kunjing zaiyu buzhi bujue, dujia duihua guojia hanban zhuren, Kongzi Xueyuan zong ganshi Xu Lin* [An Exclusive Interview with Xu Lin, Director of Hanban, 2014], *Jiefang Ribao*, [*Jiefang Daily*], 19 September. Available at: http://newschapter.jfdaily.com/jfrb/html/2014-09/19/content_17605.htm.

Willnat, L. and E. Metzgar (2012). American Perceptions of China and the Chinese: Do the Media Matter? Chapter presented at the 65th Annual Meeting of the World Association for Public Opinion Research, Hong Kong, June. Available at: https://wapor2012.hkpop.hk/doc/papers/ConcurrentSessionsI/IB/IB-3.pdf.

Worne, J. (2015). Language Learning in the UK: "Can't, Won't, Don't". *Telegraph*, 27 January. Available at: www.telegraph.co.uk/education/educationopinion/11369703/Language-learning-in-the-UK-cant-wont-dont.html.

Xu, Y. (2010). *Hanguo Meiti Zhong de Zhongguo Guojia Xingxiang, yi Chaoxian Ribao Weili* [China's National Image in Korean Media: A Case Study of Chosun Ilbo]. Available at: http://media.people.com.cn/GB/22114/206896/207970/13294052.html.

Yan, X. (2011). *Ancient Chinese Thought, Modern Chinese Power*. Princeton, NJ: Princeton University Press.

Yoo, Y. (2005). China News in Korean Media. Available at: http://ntur.lib.ntu.edu.tw/handle/246246/58325.

228 *Cultural diplomacy with Chinese characteristics*

Yoshino, K. (1992). *Cultural Nationalism In Contemporary Japan: A Sociological Enquiry.* London: Routledge.

Young, H. (2014). Do Young People Care About Learning Foreign Languages? *Guardian* 7 November. Available at: www.theguardian.com/education/2014/nov/07/-sp-do-young-people-care-about-learning-foreign-languages-data.

Zaharna, R.S. (2014). China's Confucius Institutes: Understanding the Relational Structure & Relational Dynamics of Network Collaboration. In J. Wang (ed.), *Confucius Institutes and the Globalization of China's Soft Power* (pp. 9–32). Los Angeles, CA: Figueroa Press.

Zhang, J. (2007). *Meiguo zhuliu meiti shehua baodao fenxi* [China-Related Report Analysis in American Main Stream Media]. *Guoji Guancha* [*International Review*], 1. Available at: www.rcgpoc.shisu.edu.cn/c1/d4/c3504a49620/page.htm.

Zhang, Y. (2009). The Discourse of China's Soft Power and its Discontents. In Mingjiang Li (ed.), *Soft Power: China's Emerging Strategy in International Politics* (pp. 45–60). Lanham, MD: Lexington.

Conclusion

The gentleman aims at harmony, and not at uniformity.
The mean man aims at uniformity, and not at harmony.

(Confucius (551–473 BC))

Summary of the key findings

This book combines the richness of substantial empirical data and scholarly debates with new insights developed in conceptualising China's cultural diplomacy from multiple theoretical perspectives. It has organised its arguments around the purpose, vehicle, agent, and field practice of China's cultural diplomacy. Its central argument is that China's cultural diplomacy, as a political response and even a moral claim on cultural pluralism, has to be understood from crossovers of the historical grandeur of Chinese culture, Western cultural hegemony in modern history, China's recent economic rise amidst global power shift, and the undercurrents of nationalism at home. It argues that an accurate understanding of China's new image needs to be framed in the historical, international and domestic contexts, which are constantly interacting with each other, thus cannot be looked at in isolation from one another. Both the internal dynamics of change and the external geopolitical and economic shifts of power, as well as the historical contexts are examined in exploring how the old Chinese discourse of anti-imperialism has returned in the new discourse of anti-cultural hegemony, and how the formation of China's international image is fused with the creation of new identities within China itself, whose vision today is shaped by its own historical experiences. Throughout the book, the alternative analytical frameworks have been employed to deepen and enrich our understandings of the global cultural terrain of struggle. Under these multiple intertwined contexts, there is a non-alignment between the picture shown through the lens of 'soft power' and the empirical reality constructed through the author's field study. Under the new perspectives, cultural diplomacy is not just an articulation of the Chinese soft power, but serves a grand strategy to bring these contexts together in realising China's "national rejuvenation" politically, economically and culturally.

230   *Conclusion*

The book also identifies the structural limits and operational challenges faced by its flagship project, the Confucius Institute (CI). It pinpoints that the main challenge of China's cultural diplomacy lies in how to counter the old perceptions of 'otherness' with China's own self-representations, particularly with its state-led approach. Grounded in substantiate field studies that explore transregional and transnational cultural encounters and interactions, the comparative CI case studies show contrasting pictures between different cultural spheres: in Western countries with relatively hard cultural boundaries to China, the disputes that the CIs have caused serve as a reminder that language teaching and cultural activities can be ideologically charged; whereas in East Asia where shared cultural roots underpin the relatively soft cultural boundaries, the national identities are shored up through cultural nationalism. Soft or hard, cultural diplomacy does not necessarily cross cultural boundaries intact, and that's exactly where the crucial point is in making the 'leap outward' truly 'great'.

After presenting what forms the prominent features of China's cultural diplomacy, the book then discusses the multiple challenges it faces that are rooted in the unbalanced contested terrain of struggle, the current position of Chinese culture and its approach of cultural promotion. What the CI is expected to do is to leverage the growing attention China's rise gets, and translate that into growing attraction of Chinese language and culture, which can then serve to build growing influence of China as a new power. The question of how to improve the implementation strategy is discussed by proposing some new variables to consider and new initiative to take. In one word, the greatness needs to be measured not just by how large the stride is or how extensive the footprints are, but more importantly, by measuring how deep the footprints are and how long lasting the impact is. It is a 'Great Leap Outward' only if the leap is well landed and well received.

The road forward: some open issues

Due to the limited scope of the book, it has focused more on the effects of China's cultural diplomacy on the receiver's end. Given that the endeavour of cultural diplomacy aims at "fostering mutual understanding" (Cummings, 2009: 1) by connecting the two sides through exchanges, its effects should also be evaluated from both sides. So far, very little evaluation has been done from the reflexive perspective of the Chinese partners; and even from the receiving side, it has been limited to measuring the change of China's national image or the success of building 'soft power'. Paradise's research (2009) found that people in the education field do not like the idea of 'soft power', believing that power per se is aggressive. They prefer instead to think of the CI as a vehicle for academic exchange and mutual understanding. Therefore, Paradise challenged the grounds of judgment, contending that the standpoint of expanding Chinese 'soft power' may be the wrong standard for measuring the CI's success. Pan (2013) also argued that the increasing number of international students studying in China gain Chinese universities improved international image. Indeed, as China

Conclusion 231

attempts to bolster its innovation and scientific capability, increased communications and exchanges with foreign academic institutions facilitated by the CIs is a huge benefit. I believe these views are extremely useful in evaluating the CI's impact. At least, one good positive output produced by the CI programme is that it is both an endeavour to promote Chinese language and culture, and a process of self-reflection, self-development and mutual learning from the collaboration. Adopting a new lens would allow one to see the effects in a different colour. For example, judging the CI according to how Chinese universities view them may reach a completely different conclusion. Questions such as how much the Chinese universities have benefited from their participation in the collaboration, and how successful they have been in playing their roles as 'cultural diplomats' need to be answered. These questions may help open up a wider spectrum of research topics for the possibilities and limitations of China's cultural diplomacy.

Besides, the cultural boundary theory can be applied in further depth to generate a more detailed map of the global cultural terrain. When a culture meets a hard boundary with another culture that holds a hegemonic position, the chances of having a conflict are much greater than two cultures sharing a soft boundary, and the roles played by ideology and nationalism in drawing such boundaries also need to be further elaborated. There is plenty of scope to refine the charting of the global cultural terrain of struggle. What this book has done is identifying a gap or limitations by taking stock of the current body of literature, then filling the gap by developing and employing a new analytical framework, and finally, hoping to move scholarship to more new directions.

Lastly, the value of citizen diplomacy and non-government-initiated exchange programmes is relatively under-researched, the mini case study included in this book can function as a seedling project to develop into more comprehensive comparative studies as it represents an area of enormous gap between China's practice of cultural diplomacy and its Western counterparts, and an area with huge potentials left untapped at the same time. For example, a longitudinal research with a ten-year tracking of those who have studied and worked in China would be desirable to evaluate the long-term impact of citizen diplomacy.

Final thoughts – a new Cold War in the making?

At the beginning of Chapter 1, I started with a saying shared by the two strong powers standing face to face today: "the Pacific is big enough for the USA and China". Now I'd like to finish with another saying quoted by both sides – "we are actually in the same big boat", first said by the US former Secretary of Treasury Tim Geithner at the opening ceremony of the first round of the US–China Strategic and Economic Dialogue in 2009, then repeated by the Chinese Ambassador Cui Tiankai on the Second Session of the 8th US–China Civil Dialogue in 2018: "I believe we are still in the same boat. We still live in this small global village, this planet of ours", echoing China's new strategic narrative of "a community of shared future for humankind".[1] But Cui carried on to say:

232   *Conclusion*

> Some believe that because the US has failed to change China over the past decades, we are no longer in the same boat and should not be in the same boat.... China has its own history, culture, and political and economic systems. Whatever has happened in China is an outcome of China's long history. I don't think that any country can really change China.

It seems that throughout the past four decades, what China has been saying to the USA is: please understand us, but do not try to change us; while the US side has been saying: I cannot understand why you don't want to try our way, it has been proved to be a better way. So there have been mismatched expectations from this relationship, leaving both sides with some bitter feelings, as described by Jimmy Carter (2018) on commemorating the 40th anniversary of USA–China relations: "I hear Chinese elites claiming that Americans are conducting an 'evil conspiracy' to destabilize China. I hear prominent Americans, disappointed that China has not become a democracy, claiming that China poses a threat to the American way of life".

Actually, instead of *being changed*, China *is changing* in its own course, along a more observable route since Xi Jinping took over. This change is well captured and articulated by Guo (2017: 151) in describing the two-pronged strategy at the heart of the China Dream discourse: "political de-Westernisation and cultural re-Sinicisation". As the Chinese folk saying goes: "riding in the same boat requires decades of efforts, while sharing the same pillow, a lifetime". If the China Dream is built on the above-mentioned strategies, it would be hard to persuade the Western world to dream "on the same pillow"; or believe that the China dream will lead to "creating a community of shared future for humankind".

French (2006) has commented that in many respects, China's CIs seem like a throwback to the 1950s and 1960s, when the United States and the Soviet Union were competing intensely for international prestige and influence. When the Confucius Institute was referred to as the new "Sputnik" moment – a start of space race between the USA and the Soviet Union when the latter launched the first artificial satellite in 1957 – French (2006) pointed out that:

> but where Sputnik fed a sense of alarm in the United States and elsewhere about the rise of an aggressive new superpower, the Confucius Institutes are intended to do almost the opposite, elevating the country's prestige while easing anxieties over the arrival of a new power.
>
> (French, 2006, n.p.)

True, this is the Confucius Institute's intension, and it is the very purpose of cultural diplomacy to turn adversaries into partners with mutual understanding, however, the challenge is how to bridge the gap between its intention and effects. As Ambassador Cui mentioned in his remarks,

> Some people believe that the US and China are not in the same boat and should not be in the same boat, because as China develops, it will try to

Conclusion 233

challenge the position of the US and its dominance in the world. But I don't think this is a correct interpretation of China's intention.... Some are scared by the term "new era". I have met with some very serious American scholars who asked me this question – does China's new era mean the end of the American era?

Clearly, those who asked such questions still cannot picture a positive-sum game scenario between the USA and China, and that was before the trade war was in full swing in May 2019. In the same speech commemorating the forty-year anniversary of bilateral relations in 2018, Carter has pointed out:

U.S. government reports declare that China is dedicated to challenging U.S. supremacy, and that it is planning to drive the United States out of Asia and reduce its influence in other countries around the world. If top government officials embrace these dangerous notions, a modern Cold War between our two nations is not inconceivable.

(Carter, 2018)

Shambaugh's remarks on the same anniversary have shed some positive light on this "obviously deeply strained" bilateral relations at the moment:

Yet, beyond the daily headlines of frictions, underneath a quieter set of thick interactions and exchanges endure to tie the two societies together in times of trouble. This is exactly as Carter and Deng envisioned it forty years ago, and is worth remembering today as the two major powers increasingly clash over a range of issues. This is what makes the current U.S.–China competition fundamentally different than the US–Soviet Cold War.

(Shambaugh, 2019: n.p.)

However, this "fundamental difference" does not necessarily mean a 'new type of Cold War' will not break out between the two new powers. In late April 2019, the State Department Director of Policy Planning Kiron Skinner said that her office is working on a new 'Letter X' policy for dealing with China, "a really different civilization and a different ideology" that is "not Caucasian", based on George Kennan's 'X Article' that set forth principles for containing the Soviet Union during the Cold War era (cited in Ward, 2019: n.p.). In contrast, two weeks later on the other side of the Pacific Ocean, Beijing hosted a conference on Dialogue of Asian Civilisations. Xi's keynote speech underscored the inclusiveness of Chinese civilisation since ancient times, noting the entry of ancient Greek civilisation, ancient Roman civilisation, Mediterranean civilisation, as well as Buddhism, Islam and Christianity into the country through the ancient Silk Road, and "there has never been any clash of civilisations or any religious war in China". The Greek President Pavlopoulos also said in Beijing that the "clash of civilisations" argument drummed up by certain people in the international arena was a huge mistake, and "Greece highly

234 *Conclusion*

appreciates the Xi-proposed outlook on world civilisations, the joint development of the Belt and Road Initiative, and the concept of building a community
with a shared future for humankind".[2]

Skinner's attempt at framing the USA–China confrontation as a civilisational
clash and defining China as a racial rivalry have courted a lot of criticisms at
home, such as Ward's (2019) analysis titled 'Because China isn't 'Caucasian,'
the USA is planning for a 'clash of civilizations'. That could be dangerous', but
not much criticism about her remarks of China as a "different ideology". In my
view, even the so-called "trade war" broke out between the two countries is actually an "ideological war" in disguise, as at its core is a conflict of different ways
of governance, supported by different ideologies. The Chinese solution aiming
at "mutual benefits" in trade terms can no longer appease the American quest for
"reciprocity" in rules and systems, marking a turning point for the trade and economic field in the bilateral relations from being a foundation to form a symbiotic
Chinmerica (Ferguson, 2008) to a fierce battlefield.

The Huawei case made this very clear. The Chinese telecom giant was
already banned from the US market due to concerns that its technology could be
used by the Chinese government to spy on other countries, but it did not stop at
the bilateral level. Since Europe's stance has not been as adamantly against
Huawei, with Britain and Germany having accepted its part in the construction
of their networks, the USA decided to "press allies to keep Huawei out of 5G in
Prague meeting"[3] held in early May that was attended by security officials from
the USA and more than 30 EU and NATO countries. The Prague Proposal came
out of the conference warned governments against relying on suppliers of 5G
networks that could be "susceptible to state influence" or based in countries that
haven't signed international agreements on cyber security and data protection.
The U.S. National Security Agency was quoted to say that "allowing Chinese
companies in 5G networks is like handing the Chinese government a loaded
gun".[4] Then on 17 May 2019, Huawei and "67 of its affiliates scattered across 26
countries from Germany to Madagascar" were put on a "blacklist that curtails its
access to critical U.S. suppliers".[5] A subsequent blow immediately came from
Google, which barred Huawei from some updates to the Android operating
system, as it was "complying with the order and reviewing the implications".[6]
The Bloomberg report says:

> The threat is likely to elevate fears in Beijing that Trump's broader goal is
> to contain China, igniting a protracted cold war between the world's biggest
> economies. In addition to a trade fight that has rattled global markets for
> months, the U.S. has pressured both allies and foes to avoid using Huawei
> for 5G networks that will form the backbone of the modern economy.
>
> (Donnan, 2019)

The above shows internationally, Huawei couldn't detach itself from the shadow
of ideology, while back at home, its fate was tired with nationalism, when
"Chinese social media users are rallying behind Huawei. Some say they're

Conclusion 235

switching from Apple",[7] and Huawei boss has to "defend US companies against rising Chinese nationalism" in saying that "One can't be deemed patriotic simply for using Huawei products, or the other way round. Huawei is a commercial business. If you like [the product] then use it. Do not politicise it".[8] Unfortunately, this Chinese company has become another epitome of all the entangled EVs discussed in Chapter 6, a pawn on the chessboard of bilateral relations.

There are obviously multiple and complex reasons for the rising tensions between China and the USA. China was referred to as a "competitor", "challenger", "rival power" and "revisionist power" in the 2017 *National Security Strategy of the USA*, the first national security report issued by the Trump Administration.[9] In May 2019, the US House of Representatives unanimously passed bills reaffirming Taiwan Relations Act (TRA), following its fortieth anniversary in April. It also "backed by unanimous voice vote the 'Taiwan Assurance Act of 2019', which states that Washington should conduct 'regular sales and defence articles' to Taiwan and back Taipei's participation in international organizations".[10] The TRA serves as one of the defining documents authorising US–Taiwan relations, alongside the Three Joint Communiqués issued by Washington and Beijing and the Six Assurances offered from the United States to Taiwan. In the past four decades, Beijing has always been referring to the 'One China' principle laid down in the Three Joint Communiqués while Washington priorities TRA, stating that the communiqué "is not a treaty or an agreement but a statement of future U.S. policy", and "cannot bind any future President".[11] While the USA regards Taiwan as "a vital part of the US free and open Indo-Pacific strategy",[12] Beijing treats Taiwan as its core interest regarding non-negotiable territorial integrity and internal affairs; and while the *Reuters* reported it as a move "amid trade tensions with China", *Asia Times* reported it as "amid PLA drills". This was followed by a *Guardian* report on *US warship sails in disputed South China Sea amid trade tensions*,[13] showing the entangled nature of all fronts in the bilateral relations of the two powers in trade, military, politics and foreign policy.

Both the US rhetoric and the actual actions of proposing China policy change domestically and "pressing allies" against China internationally did give off a familiar smell of the Cold War. However, if a new Cold War *is* in the making, we can see not only the difference between today's China and yesterday's Soviet Union, but also the division within the Western camp. For example, in the same week when Skinner's controversial remarks were contested in the USA, the *Telegraph* carried a report titled "After Huawei, Government turns to China for HS2 line",[14] about the UK government "encouraging China's involvement in the construction of the £56 billion rail line". And following the US ban, European chipmakers including Infineon from Germany and AMS from Austria, are continuing to supply Huawei. When this was reported by Bloomberg, they also mentioned:

> Some companies are even openly optimistic. "As a U.K. headquartered global organisation, with no research and development in the USA, we're in

236   *Conclusion*

a unique position to work with companies around the world", said Woz Ahmed, executive vice president of corporate development at Imagination Technologies.[15]

One after another, all the flagship projects from China, from the Confucius Institute to BRI (Belt and Road Initiative), from Huawei to high-speed rail, be they cultural and academic institutions, semi-private or state-owned enterprises, or state-sponsored infrastructure investments, have all triggered similar debates but have received different receptions all over the world. China's impact on and engagement with the rest of the world, across the East and West, North and South, along with the Trump Administration's "America First" foreign policy that has alienated some of its traditional allies, have all prevented a formation of an unified 'camp' against China. The time is long gone when all the Western powers would "have entered into a holy alliance to exorcise the spectre of communism".[16]

Time for self-reflection

This book has only focused on the cultural dimension, and the "Sputnik" analogy for the Confucius Institute seems to suggest an answer to the question asked at the beginning of the book: whether cultural diplomacy is really a non-menacing platform to showcase China's peaceful rise, or is it actually starting a new battlefield? Guo believes that China's endorsement of cultural nationalism "has facilitated the construction of a new, re-sinicised national identity with far-reaching implications for Sino-US relations" (2017: 147). I will use a simple example here to show this re-sinicised national identity embodied in a two-part poster designed for the Summit of the CPC in Dialogue with World Political Parties,[17] held in Beijing in December 2017, with the participation of over 600 delegates representing nearly 300 political parties and political organisations from more than 120 countries of the world. China's new strategic narratives were made the theme: "Working Together Towards a Community with a Shared Future for Mankind" and "A Better World: Responsibilities of Political Parties".[18] All the other key messages discussed in this book have made their appearances in the *Beijing Initiative*[19] published as the 'fruit' of the conference, including "discarding bi-polar mentality", "mutual respect for each other's choice of paths of development and values", "seeking common grounds while transcending differences in social system, ideology and cultural tradition", "forgoing double standard and the zero-sum-game mentality", "discarding the Cold War mentality and power politics", and "following the spirit of harmony among diversity".

The poster received overwhelmingly positive reviews. I personally agree and applaud the first half as a brilliant idea to use "drinking from the same pool of water" (*gong yin yi hong shui*) to interpret the strategic narrative of "a community with a shared future", as we all live in the same world and take the water of life from the same planet; and the tea even shows a reflection of the

Conclusion 237

world map in the traditional blue and white Chinese tea cup, a shining display of wisdom. However, I believe the second half fails to capture the essence of the same narrative interpreted with a different quotation: "shared appreciation of beauty, harmony with non-uniformity" (*mei mei yu gong, he er bu tong*). Here is why: the concept of harmony can only be established on the basis of differences, which has been the core message of China's counter-narrative to the Western appeal of universal values and model of democracy. The original meaning of the Chinese word 'he' comes from matrimonial harmony between husband and wife, which is then extended to mean that people with different dispositions and views can live peacefully under one roof. If 'under this roof' is China as a host country, then it means that no matter who walks in, he/she should be able to pick a cup he/she likes and choose a drink he/she wants. The idea to use three different cups is superb, which represents different cultural traditions, and different ideologies represented by different political parties for this particular poster, however, they are all filled with the same Chinese tea. If the Chinese, Arabic and Western cups are filled with different tea and coffee respectively, and people sitting around the same table are exchanging ideas freely, then it captures the real essence of "harmony in diversity", showing elevated sublimity of the first part of the message, as different geographical environment and history give birth to different national drinks, which are fit to drink from different cups, and further nourishes different national cultures. This summit, however, allows everyone to "seek common grounds while reserving differences", a motto of China's foreign policy since 1949.

The second message is actually inspired by the original sixteen-character verse by Fei Xiaotong to explain what is "harmony in diversity": "appreciate the beauty of other's culture, as you do with your own; with mutual appreciation, the world would be harmonious as a whole" (*ge mei qi mei, mei ren zhi mei, mei mei yu gong, tian xia da tong*). The word '*tianxia*' in the last phrase is an ancient philosophical and cultural concept in China, translated as the 'world' here. It has two meanings in a modern Chinese dictionary: (1) all land under heaven, refer-ring to the entire territory of China in ancient times; the whole of China; (2) the whole world. The phrase "harmonious world" represents the ideal advocated by Confucianism, which has been reinvigorated as the new strategic narrative of the Chinese government. However, in French's book that is dedicated to elaborating this notion of '*Tianxia*' – *Everything Under the Heavens: How the Past Helps Shape China's Push for Global Power*, it was interpreted to mean "a contention for world leadership" (French, 2018: 4). It even used the word "universality" to describe China's "unshakable conviction in the enduring universality of its values and ethics, its own culture, and its unquestioned centrality" when "the new, Western form of global universality" took shape that was not based on "the presumed natural hierarchy in the world with China at the apex", but based on "the presumed equality" (at least legally and theoretically) (French, 2018: 8). Here, a contrast to put the "Chinese world order" as the opposite end of the "Western world order" is evident; it also suggests when China today wants to restore its former glory, it wants back "its long and mostly unchallenged status

238   *Conclusion*

as the standard-setter of civilisation" (French, 2018: 8). It is such a mirror image that these modifying adjectives French used on China are exactly what China thinks of the USA today, except that the USA is the standard-setter of modernity.

Although the book claims to derive its arguments from examining the long course of Chinese history, the author needs to be reminded that the first world map in Chinese, *"Da Ying Quan Tu"* (literally, Complete Map of the Great World), was only composed by the Italian Jesuit Matteo Ricci in 1584 during the Ming Dynasty, while the classic poetry of "everything under tianxia belongs to the king", or the belief that the emperor possessed a divine mandate to rule "all under heaven", was dated in the Zhou dynasty (1046–256 BCE) – at a time when China believed the Middle Kingdom was the centre of, or even was, the whole world. The tribute system French elaborated as the "Chinese world order" began as far back as the Han Dynasty (206 BCE–CE 220). After two whole millenniums, how much "lingering place of the tribute system" are left "in the Chinese psyche" today? (French, 2018: 10) Has China been isolated in an ivory tower, or has it survived and thrived with interactions with the rest of the world during these two millenniums? As stated in the starting sentence of this book, China is the oldest continuous civilisation on earth – it is the same name, but definitely not the same country after more than 2,000 years. Just like the notion of *'tianxia'* – it is the same word, but not with the same connotation when it is used today. Using 'everything under heaven' to describe the ambitious sphere of influence China wants to exert today is far-fetched, just as the old saying he quoted is out-of-date: "when two emperors appear simultaneously, one must be destroyed" (French, 2018: 10) – it is a totally zero-sum perception. French's book has received an impressive collection of praise, one comments that it "makes it clear China's sense of national superiority is of more than historical significance … Chilling". Another applauds it as "a wonderfully well-researched and elegantly written book about what we might call China's 'sharp memory'". To me, this book about China's "chilling sharp memory" reads like a historical version of the China Threat.

However, as repeatedly argued already, one can refute this as an Orientalised understanding of China, but with the reality that it was acclaimed as "an outstanding font of knowledge and provides compelling insights into how China sees the world and its own destiny", and "a guide to thinking about the next stage in China's evolution, and the positive signs and danger signs to be watching for", let's go back to the second half of the poster, with an outsider's perception this time, and a self-reflecting question in mind: is there anything which China does that has encouraged such views? Does this poster show China's ambition to regain its glory of "having a thousand states come to pay tribute" (*wan guo lai chao*)? Are these delegates here to bow to the Chinese way or to have a 'dialogue'? If they are treated as guests from afar, won't they be asked a simple question first: what would you like to have, coffee or tea? Besides, one of the cups comes with a spoon, which is an awkward mismatch for drinking Chinese tea and gives people an unpleasant association of "being imposed to tea", or "being harmonised by imposition" – both are euphemisms to indicate how different thoughts or dissidents are treated in China. Such representation may fall victim to being identified as a "danger sign" that they are watching for.

When Confucius elaborated the idea of harmony, he said: "the gentleman aims at harmony, and not at uniformity. The mean man aims at uniformity, and not at harmony". To fill different cups with the same kind of tea is in fact to misinterpret "harmony" as "uniformity" or "universality". It shows a 'my way is the way' approach. If it is done unconsciously, then it reveals the subconscious China-centric view. Imagine, if the conference were hosted by a Western country using the same poster, except that all of the three cups, including the traditional Chinese tea cup with a lid, are filled with coffee, how would China feel? Mutual respect can only start with a change of perspective. Confucius again has provided the best advice: do unto others as you would have them do unto you. As a host, the best way to respect your guests is to learn about their cultural traditions, and if they are not known already, asking first before giving. The same holds true in the treatment of your target audiences in the host countries, as cultural diplomacy is a mutual process. After all, providing different cups is just the form; what the cups contain is the essence of cultural pluralism.

Notes

1 Remarks by Ambassador Cui Tiankai at the 8th US–China Civil Dialogue, 26 July 2018, available at: www.china-embassy.org/eng/zmgxss/t1580425.htm.
2 Xi Holds Talks with Greek President, *Xinhuanet*, 14 May 2019, available at: www.xinhuanet.com/english/2019-05/14/c_138058284.htm.
3 Reuters, US will Reportedly Press Allies to Keep Huawei out of 5G in Prague Meeting, *CNBC*, 16 April 2019, available at: www.cnbc.com/2019/04/16/us-to-press-allies-to-keep-huawei-out-of-5g-in-prague-meeting.html.
4 Kara Frederick, The 5G Future Is Not Just About Huawei, *Foreign Policy*, 3 May 2019, available at: https://foreignpolicy.com/2019/05/03/the-5g-future-is-not-just-about-huawei/.
5 Shawn Donnan, U.S. Places Huawei and Scores of Affiliates on Export Blacklist, *The Bloomberg*, 17 May 2019, available at: www.bloomberg.com/news/articles/2019-05-17/u-s-places-huawei-and-67-affiliates-around-world-on-blacklist.
6 Google Suspends Huawei from Android Services. *Financial Times*, 20 May 2019, available at: www.ft.com/content/d8b3d6e6-7aaa-11e9-81d2-f785092ab560.
7 Chinese Social Media Users are Rallying Behind Huawei: Some Say They're Switching from Apple. *CNBC*, 21 May 2019, available at: www.cnbc.com/2019/05/22/chinese-social-media-users-are-rallying-behind-huawei.html.
8 Mimi Lau, Huawei Boss Defends US Companies Against Rising Chinese Nationalism. *The Star* online, 23 May 2019, available at: www.thestar.com.my/news/regional/2019/05/23/huawei-boss-defends-us-companies-against-rising-chinese-nationalism/.
9 National Security Strategy of the United States of America. The White House, 12 December 2017, available at: www.whitehouse.gov/wp-content/uploads/2017/12/NSS-Final-12-18-2017-0905.pdf.
10 U.S. House Passes Pro-Taiwan Bills, Amid Trade Tensions with China. *Reuters*, 8 May 2019, available at: www.reuters.com/article/us-usa-china-taiwan-congress/us-house-passes-pro-taiwan-bills-amid-trade-tensions-with-china-idUSKCN1SE00T.

240 *Conclusion*

11 For detailed background information regarding the TRA and the Three Joint Communiqués, see Determining U.S. Relations with China: The Taiwan Relations Act or the August 17 Communique with Beijing?, Asian Studies Centre, the Heritage Foundation, 30 November 1987, available at: www.heritage.org/asia/report/determining-us-relations-china-the-taiwan-relations-act-or-the-august-17-communique.
12 US House Passes Taiwan Assurance Act amid PLA drill, *Asia Times*, 9 May 2019, available at: www.asiatimes.com/2019/05/article/us-house-passes-taiwan-assurance-act-amid-pla-drill/.
13 Reuters, US Warship Sails in Disputed South China Sea Amid Trade Tensions. *Guardian*, 20 May 2019, available at: www.theguardian.com/world/2019/may/20/us-warship-sails-in-disputed-south-china-sea-amid-trade-tensions.
14 Edward Malnick, After Huawei, Government Turns to China for HS2 Line. *Telegraph.* 4 May 2019, available at: www.telegraph.co.uk/politics/2019/05/04/huawei-government-turns-china-hs2-line/.
15 Stefan Nicola and Natalia Drozdiak, European Chipmakers to Keep on Supplying Huawei After Trump Ban. *Bloomberg*, 20 May 2019, available at: www.bloomberg.com/news/articles/2019-05-20/european-chipmakers-drop-as-huawei-ban-cripples-supply-chain.
16 This is to Borrow the Starting Line in Karl Marx's Manifesto of the Communist Party published in 1848, available at: www.marxists.org/archive/marx/works/1848/communist-manifesto/ch01.htm.
17 The posters are available at: http://news.ifeng.com/a/20171201/53766742_0.shtml.
18 CPC in Dialogue with World Political Parties, *Asia One*, 5 December 2017, available at: www.asiaone.com/business/cpc-in-dialogue-with-world-political-parties.
19 Beijing Initiative, 中国共产党与世界政党高层对话会 [The CPC in Dialogue with World Political Parties High-Level Meeting]. 北京倡议 [Beijing Initiative], *China Daily*, 4 December 2017, available at: http://language.chinadaily.com.cn/a/201712/04/WS5b20d2b9a31001b8257214af.html.

References

Carter, J. (2018). How to Repair the U.S.–China Relationship – and Prevent a Modern Cold War. *Washington Post*, 31 December. Available at: www.cartercenter.org/news/editorials_speeches/jimmy-carter-repair-us-china-relationship.html.

Cummings, M.C. (2009). *Cultural Diplomacy and the United States Government: A Survey.* Washington, DC: Centre for Arts and Culture. Available at: www.Americansforthearts.org/sites/default/files/MCCpaper.pdf.

Donnan, S. (2019). U.S. Places Huawei and Scores of Affiliates on Export Blacklist. *Bloomberg*, 17 May 2019. Available at: www.bloomberg.com/news/articles/2019-05-17/u-s-places-huawei-and-67-affiliates-around-world-on-blacklist.

Ferguson, N. (2008). Niall Ferguson Says U.S.–China Cooperation Is Critical to Global Economic Health. *Washington Post*, 17 November. Available at: www.washingtonpost.com/wp-dyn/content/article/2008/11/16/AR2008111601736.html.

French, H.W. (2006). Another Chinese Export is all the Rage: China's Language. *New York Times*, 11 January, p. A2. Available at: www.nytimes.com/2006/01/11/world/asia/another-chinese-export-is-all-the-rage-chinas-language.html.

French, H.W. (2018). *Everything Under the Heavens: How the Past Helps Shape China's Push for Global Power.* New York: Vintage Books.

Guo, Y. (2017). The Impact of Chinese National Identity on Sino-US Relations. *Joint U.S. Korea Academic Studies*, (August): 146–158.

Pan, S.Y. (2013). Confucius Institute Project: China's Cultural Diplomacy and Soft Power Projection. *Asian Education and Development Studies*, 2(1): 22–33.

Paradise, J. (2009). China and International Harmony: The Role of Confucius Institute in Bolstering Beijing's Soft Power. *Asian Survey*, 49(4): 647–669.

Shambaugh, D. (2019). The 40th Anniversary of U.S.–China Relations: Looking Back and Looking Forward. *Foreign Policy*, 9 January. Available at: www.chinausfocus. com/foreign-policy/the-40th-anniversary-of-us-china-relations-looking-back-and-looking-forward.

Ward, S. (2019). Because China isn't "Caucasian", the U.S. is Planning for a "Clash of Civilizations". That Could be Dangerous. *Washington Post*, 4 May. Available at: www. washingtonpost.com/politics/2019/05/04/because-china-isnt-caucasian-us-is-planning-clash-civilizations-that-could-be-dangerous/?utm_term=.a84c977f3917.

Appendix 1
Gallup Country Ratings: China, 1979–2019

Table A.1 Gallup Country Ratings: China, 1979–2019

	Very favourable %	*Mostly favourable* %	*Mostly unfavourable* %	*Very unfavourable* %	*No opinion* %
China					
1–10 February 2019	8	33	39	18	2
1–10 February 2018	7	46	32	13	2
1–5 February 2017	10	40	35	13	2
3–7 February 2016	8	36	34	18	4
8–11 February 2015	8	36	34	16	5
6–9 February 2014	9	34	35	18	5
7–11 February 2013	-8	35	35	17	5
2–5 February 2012	6	35	36	20	2
2–5 February 2011	6	41	37	13	3
1–3 February 2010	5	37	36	17	5
9–12 February 2009	5	36	34	17	7
11–14 February 2008	6	36	38	17	3
1–4 February 2007	7	41	32	15	6
6–9 February 2006	4	40	35	14	6
7–10 February 2005	5	42	35	12	6
9–12 February 2004	6	35	38	16	5
3–6 February 2003	6	39	34	12	9
4–6 February 2002	6	38	37	12	7
1–4 February 2001	5	40	31	17	7
13–15 November 2000	5	31	39	18	7
17–19 March 2000	6	29	40	16	9
25–26 January 2000	4	29	33	18	16
7–9 May 1999	5	33	38	18	6
12–14 March 1999	2	32	39	20	7
8–9 February 1999	8	31	34	16	11
7–8 July 1998	6	38	36	11	9
22–23 June 1998	5	34	42	9	10
26–29 June 1997	5	28	36	14	17
8–10 March 1996	6	33	35	16	10
26–28 February 1994	4	36	38	15	7
14–17 March 1991	5	30	35	18	12
10–13 August 1989	5	29	32	22	12
28 February–2 March 1989	12	60	10	3	15
22 February–3 March 1985	5	33	35	16	11
September 1979	18	46	18	7	10

Source: https://news.gallup.com/poll/1624/perceptions-foreign-countries.aspx

Appendix 2
Pew Report

Table A.2 Pew Report

Country	2002	2005	2006	2007	2008	2009	2010	2011	2012	2013	2014	2015	2016	2017
Argentina	–	–	–	32	34	42	45	–	–	54	40	53	–	41
Australia	–	–	–	–	52	–	–	–	–	58	–	57	52	64
Bangladesh	–	–	–	–	–	–	–	–	–	–	77	–	–	–
Bolivia	–	–	–	–	–	–	–	–	–	58	–	–	–	–
Brazil	–	–	–	–	–	–	52	49	50	65	44	55	–	52
Bulgaria	–	–	–	44	–	–	–	–	–	–	–	–	–	–
Burkina Faso	–	–	–	–	–	–	–	–	–	–	–	75	–	–
Canada	–	58	–	52	–	53	–	–	–	43	–	39	45	48
Chile	–	–	–	62	–	–	–	–	–	62	60	66	–	51
China	–	88	94	93	95	95	97	95	94	95	96	96	95	–
Colombia	–	–	–	–	–	–	–	–	–	–	38	–	–	43
Czech Republic	–	–	–	35	–	–	–	–	33	34	–	–	–	–
Egypt	–	–	63	65	59	52	52	57	52	45	46	–	–	–
El Salvador	–	–	–	–	–	–	–	–	–	52	48	–	–	–
Ethiopia	–	–	–	–	–	–	–	–	–	–	–	75	–	–
France	–	58	60	47	28	41	41	51	40	42	47	50	33	44
Germany	–	46	56	34	26	29	30	34	29	28	28	34	28	34
Ghana	–	–	–	75	–	–	–	–	–	67	61	80	–	49
Greece	–	–	–	–	–	–	–	–	56	59	49	–	57	50
Hungary	–	–	–	–	–	–	–	–	–	–	–	–	45	38
India	–	–	–	–	–	–	–	–	–	35	31	41	31	26
Indonesia	–	73	62	65	58	59	58	67	–	70	66	63	–	55
Israel	–	–	–	45	–	56	–	49	–	38	49	55	–	53
Italy	–	–	–	27	–	–	–	–	30	28	26	40	32	31
Ivory Coast	–	–	–	92	–	–	–	–	–	–	–	–	–	–
Japan	55	–	27	29	14	26	26	34	15	5	7	9	11	13
Jordan	–	43	49	46	44	50	53	44	47	40	35	33	–	35
Kenya	–	–	–	814	–	73	86	71	–	78	74	70	57	54
Kuwait	–	–	–	52	–	–	–	–	–	–	–	–	–	–
Lebanon	–	66	–	46	50	53	56	59	59	56	53	52	–	63
Lithuania	–	–	–	–	–	–	–	52	–	–	–	–	–	–
Malaysia	–	–	–	83	–	–	–	–	–	81	74	78	–	–
Mali	–	–	–	92	–	–	–	–	–	–	–	–	–	–
Mexico	–	–	–	43	38	39	39	39	40	45	43	47	–	43
Morocco	–	–	–	26	–	–	–	–	–	–	–	–	–	–
Netherlands	–	56	–	–	–	–	–	–	–	–	–	–	47	49
Nicaragua	–	–	–	–	–	–	–	–	–	–	58	–	–	–
Nigeria	–	–	–	–	–	–	76	–	–	76	70	70	63	72
Pakistan	–	79	69	79	76	84	85	82	85	81	78	82	–	–
Palestinian Territories	–	–	–	46	–	43	–	62	–	47	61	54	–	–
Peru	–	–	–	56	–	–	–	–	–	–	56	60	–	61
Philippines	63	–	–	–	–	–	–	–	–	48	38	54	–	55
Poland	–	37	–	39	33	43	46	51	50	43	32	40	37	42
Russia	71	60	63	60	60	58	60	63	62	62	64	79	–	70
Senegal	–	–	–	–	–	–	–	–	–	77	71	70	–	64
Slovakia	–	–	–	45	–	–	–	–	–	–	–	–	–	–
South Africa	–	–	–	–	37	–	–	–	–	48	45	52	41	45

continued

244 *Appendices*

Table A.2 Continued

Country	2002	2005	2006	2007	2008	2009	2010	2011	2012	2013	2014	2015	2016	2017
South Korea	66	–	–	52	48	41	38	–	–	46	56	61	–	34
Spain	–	57	45	39	31	40	47	55	49	48	39	41	28	43
Sweden	–	–	–	43	–	–	–	–	–	–	–	–	37	41
Tanzania	–	–	–	70	71	–	–	–	–	–	77	74	–	63
Thailand	–	–	–	–	–	–	–	–	–	–	72	–	–	–
Tunisia	–	–	–	–	–	–	–	–	69	63	64	–	–	63
Turkey	–	40	33	25	24	16	20	18	22	27	21	18	–	33
Uganda	–	–	–	45	–	–	–	–	–	59	61	65	–	–
Ukraine	–	–	–	–	–	–	–	–	–	–	64	58	–	–
United Kingdom	–	65	65	49	47	52	46	59	49	48	47	45	37	45
United States	–	43	52	42	39	50	49	51	40	37	35	38	37	44
Venezuela	–	–	–	–	–	–	–	–	–	71	67	58	–	52
Vietnam	–	–	–	–	–	–	–	–	–	–	16	19	–	10

Sources: www.pewglobal.org/database/indicator/24/survey/all/ Opinion of China, 2002–2017.

Appendix 3
List of Confucius Institute Closures

Table A.3 List of Confucius Institute Closures

Number	Country	Host Institution	Year of CI Closure
1	Japan (1)	Osaka Sangyo University	2010
2	Russia (2)	Yakutsk Confucius Institute	2010
3		Blagoveshchensk State National Normal University	2015
4	Canada (2)	McMaster University	2013
5		Université de Sherbrooke	2013
6	US (20)	University of Chicago	2014
7		Pennsylvania State University	2014
8		Pfeiffer University	2016
9		Tulane University	2017
10		University of Illinois-Urbana Champaign	2017
11		University of West Florida	2018
12		Texas A&M University System	2018
13		Prairie View A&M University	2018
14		University of Iowa	2018
15		University of North Florida	2018
16		North Carolina State University	2018
17		University of Michigan	2018
18		University of Rhode Island	2018
19		University of South Florida	2018
20		University of Massachusetts Boston	2019
21		University of Minnesota	2019
22		Indiana University	2019
23		Western Kentucky University	2019
24		University of Oregon	2019
25		San Francisco State University	2019
26	France (3)	University of Lumière Lyon 2/ University of Jean Moulin Lyon 3	2013
27		Toulouse 1 University Capitole	2017
28		West Paris Nanterre La Defense University	2018
29	Sweden (3)	Stockholm University	2014
30		Karlstad University	2015
31		Blekinge Institute of Technology	2015
32	Germany (2)	Stuttgart Media University	2015
33		University of Hohenheim	2015
34	Denmark (1)	Copenhagen Business School	2017
35	Netherlands (1)	Leiden University	2019

Appendix 4

The American Association of University Professors (AAUP) report on partnerships with foreign governments: the case of Confucius Institutes

This report was prepared by the Association's Committee A on Academic Freedom and Tenure in June 2014

Globalisation has brought new challenges for the protection of academic freedom and other faculty rights. In the operations of North American universities in other countries, administrators often refer to local customs, practices, and laws to justify practices that the American Association of University Professors (AAUP) and the Canadian Association of University Teachers (CAUT) would not tolerate on North American campuses. In 2009, our two organisations adopted a joint statement – On Conditions of Employment at Overseas Campuses – setting forth appropriate employment standards for overseas campuses of North American universities and stating our commitment to see that those standards are met.

Globalisation has also meant that university administrators have welcomed involvement of foreign governments, corporations, foundations, and donors on campuses in North America. These relationships have often been beneficial. But occasionally university administrations have entered into partnerships that sacrificed the integrity of the university and its academic staff. Exemplifying the latter are Confucius Institutes, now established at some 90 colleges and universities in the United States and Canada.[1] Confucius Institutes function as an arm of the Chinese state and are allowed to ignore academic freedom. Their academic activities are under the supervision of Hanban, a Chinese state agency which is chaired by a member of the Politburo and the vice-premier of the People's Republic of China. Most agreements establishing Confucius Institutes feature nondisclosure clauses and unacceptable concessions to the political aims and practices of the government of China. Specifically, North American universities permit Confucius Institutes to advance a state agenda in the recruitment and control of academic staff, in the choice of curriculum, and in the restriction of debate.

Confucius Institutes appear designed to emulate the cultural ambassadorship and programming associated with, for example, the British Council, the Goethe-Institut, and L'Alliance Française. These latter three entities are clearly connected to imperial pasts, ongoing geopolitical agendas, and the objectives of "soft power", but none of them is located on a university or college campus. Instead, their connections to national political agendas and interests require that they be established in sites where they can fulfil their mandates openly without threatening the independence and integrity of academic institutions in host countries.

Allowing any third-party control of academic matters is inconsistent with principles of academic freedom, shared governance, and the institutional autonomy of colleges and universities. The AAUP joins CAUT in recommending that universities cease their involvement in Confucius Institutes unless the agreement between the university and Hanban is renegotiated so that (1) the university has unilateral control, consistent with principles articulated in the AAUP's Statement on Government of Colleges and Universities, over all academic matters, including recruitment of teachers, determination of curriculum, and choice of texts; (2) the university affords Confucius Institute teachers the same academic freedom rights, as defined in the 1940 Statement of Principles on Academic Freedom and Tenure, that it affords all other faculty in the university; and (3) the university–Hanban agreement is made available to all members of the university community. More generally, these conditions should apply to any partnerships or collaborations with foreign governments or foreign government-related agencies.

(available at: www.aaup.org/report/confucius-institutes)

Appendix 5

Interviewee Information Grid

Table A.5 Interviewee Information Grid

Code	Role of the interviewee	Nationality	Date of interview	Venue of interview	Language of interview
UKD1	CI Director from the British host university	GB	6 June 2013 3 July 2014	Host university in the UK	Chinese
UKD2	CI Director from the Chinese home university	CN	6 June 2013 27 June 2014	Host university in the UK	Chinese
UKD3	CI Director from the British host university	GB	9 July 2014	Host university in the UK	English
UKD4	CI Director from the Chinese home university	CN	14 July 2014	Home university in Beijing	Chinese
UKD5	CI Director from the Chinese home university	CN	26 March 2019	Host university in the UK	Chinese
UKD6	CI Director from the British host university	CN	9 April 2019	Host university in the UK	Chinese
SKD1	CI Director from the Chinese home university	CN	16 July 2013	Home university in Shandong	Chinese
SKD2	CI Director from the South Korean host institution	SK	22 July 2014	Host university in the SK	Chinese;
SKD3	CI Director from the South Korean host institution	SK	22 July 2014	Host university in the SK	Chinese
SKD4	CI Director from the South Korean host university	SK	23 July 2014	Host university in the SK	Chinese
BGD1	CI Director from the Chinese home university	CN	16 April 2019	Interview via WeChat	Chinese
BGD2	CI Director from the Chinese home university	CN	16 April 2019	Interview via WeChat	Chinese
UKSC1	CI secondee from the Chinese home university	CN	6 June 2013	Host university in the UK	Chinese
UKSC2	CI secondee from the Chinese home university	CN	4 July 2014	Host university in the UK	Chinese
UKSC3	CI secondee from the Chinese home university	CN	6 June 2013	Host university in the UK	Chinese
UKSC4	CI secondee from the Chinese home university	CN	26 June 2014	Host university in the UK	Chinese
UKSC5	CI secondee from the Chinese home university	CN	23 June 2014	Host university in the UK	Chinese
SKSC1	CI secondee from the Chinese home university	CN	22 July 2014	Host university in the SK	Chinese
SKSC2	CI secondee from the Chinese home university	CN	23 July 2014	Host university in the SK	Chinese
SKSC3	CI secondee from the Chinese home university	CN	23 July 2014	Host university in the SK	Chinese
UKLH1	CI administrator locally hired by the host university	GB	10 June 2013 26 June 2014	Host university in the UK	English
UKLH2	CI administrator locally hired by the host university	GB	3 July 2014	Host university in the UK	Chinese

Appendices 249

Code	Role of the interviewee	Nationality	Date of interview	Venue of interview	Language of interview
UKLH3	CI teacher locally hired by the host university	GB	23 June 2014	Host university in the UK	Chinese
UKLH4	CI teacher locally hired by the host university,	CN	27 June 2014	Host university in the UK	Chinese
SKLH	CI teacher locally hired by the host institution	SK	22 July 2014	Host university in the SK	Chinese
FRD	CI Director in France from the Chinese home university	CN	28 July 2013	Home university in Beijing	Chinese
MOD	CI Director in Morocco from the Chinese home university	CN	28 July 2013	Home university in Beijing	Chinese
MXD	CI Director in Mexico from the Chinese home university	CN	28 July 2013	Home university in Beijing	Chinese
Mr. Anders	Director of Goethe Institute in Beijing, no code needed as he agreed to have his name revealed in the book.	GM	13 August 2015	Goethe Institute in Beijing	English
DPEC	Senior Diplomat in Education and Cultural Affairs from a Chinese diplomatic mission	CN	9 May 2019	Diplomatic mission	Chinese
UKT1	British teacher joining the Journey to the East	GB	28 March 2019	University in the UK	English
UKT2	British teacher joining the Journey to the East	GB	29 April 2019	University in the UK	English
UKT3	British teacher joining the Journey to the East	GB	2 May 2019	University in the UK	English
UKSG1	British students joining the Journey to the East (two in a group interview)	GB	3 April 2019	University in the UK	English
UKSG2	British student group joining the Journey to the East (five in a group interview)	GB	1 May 2019	University in the UK	English
UKSG3	British student joining the Journey to the East (two individual interviews)	GB	6 May 2019 8 May 2019	University in the UK	English

Appendix 6

Questionnaire for trip to China/Journey to the East

Part 1: prior to the trip

1. Is this your first trip to China?
   If not, when was your last visit, and for how long?
2. Can you use three words to describe your impression of China?
3. Can you use three words to describe your perception of Chinese people?
4. What are you most looking forward to in this trip?
5. What is your biggest worry about this trip?

Part 2: after the trip

6. What is your highlight of this trip?
7. What is your biggest surprise?
8. Can you use three words to describe your impression of China? (please answer "same as Q2" if there was no change after the trip).
9. Can you use three words to describe your impression of Chinese people? (please answer "same as Q3" if there was no change after the trip).
10. Are you happy to be interviewed if you want to elaborate on how this trip has changed your perception of China in any way? If yes, please give your contact email. Thank you very much in advance!!

Appendix 7

Key words to describe China and Chinese people before and after the trips

Table A7.1 Key words to describe China before the trip

Key words	Number of times used
Busy	12
Big	11
Densely Populated	6
Modern	5
Cultural	5
Traditional	4
Different	3
Advanced	3
Private	2
Regimented	2
Mysterious	2
Unique	2
Scenic	2
Hardworking	1
Humid	1
Cloudy	1
Attractive	1
Confusing	1
Far	1
Colourful	1
Up-and-coming	1
Innovative	1
Powerful	1
Progressive	1
Strict	1
Disciplined	1
Rich	1
Technological	1
Historic	1
Cute	1
Hot	1
Welcoming	1
Varied	1
Slightly fearful	1
Stressful	1
Rustic	1
Repressive	1
Suppressed	1

252 *Appendices*

Table A7.2 Key words to describe China after the trip

Key words	Number of times used
Busy	12
Big	6
Technologically advanced	6
Traditional	5
Cultural	4
Beautiful	4
Unhygienic	3
Exciting	2
Intriguing	2
Disciplined	2
Overpopulated	2
Lively	2
Varied	2
Unorganised	2
Hot	1
Growing	1
Unique	1
Regimented	1
Entertaining	1
Respectful	1
Educational	1
Chaotic	1
Friendly	1
Humid	1
Heavily urbanised	1
Convenient	1
Sociable	1
Community	1
Interesting	1
Westernised	1
Cute	1
Welcoming	1
Modern	1
Cool	1
Rich	1
Vibrant	1
Powerful	1
Efficient	1
Extraordinary	1
Futuristic	1
Grey	1
Impressive	1
Lovely	1
Fast-changing	1

Appendices 253

Table A7.3 Key words to describe Chinese people before the trip

Key words	Number of times used
Reserved	8
Hardworking	8
Polite	7
Intelligent	5
Friendly	4
Busy	4
Traditional	3
Small	3
Loud	3
Welcoming	2
Cute	2
Rude	1
Interesting	1
Down to earth	1
Helpful	1
Regimented	1
Caring	1
Loving	1
Independent	1
Organised	1
Family orientated	1
Good at cooking	1
Blunt	1
Calm	1
Happy	1
Humble	1
Focused	1
Serious	1
Technical	1
Communist	1
Thoughtful	1
Well presented	1
Spiritual	1
Rich	1
Fashionable	1
Curious	1
Excitable	1
Kind	1
Repressed	1
Educationally driven	1
Patriotic	1
Innovative	1
Intimidating	1
Fun	1
Mysterious	1
Lovely	1

254   *Appendices*

Table A7.4 Key words to describe Chinese people after the trip

Key Words	Number of times used
Friendly	8
Welcoming	6
Polite	5
Hardworking	5
Family orientated	4
Respectful	3
Loud	3
Helpful	3
Generous	3
Happy	3
Caring	2
Rude	2
Funny	2
Knowledgeable	2
Kind	2
Open	2
Curious	2
Lovely	2
Proud	2
Indirect	2
Busy	2
Different	1
Thoughtful	1
Hospitable	1
Regimented	1
Creative	1
Sociable	1
Intelligent	1
Crazy drivers	1
Heavy drinkers	1
Military	1
Active	1
Traditional	1
Understanding	1
Dedicated	1
Fun	1
Always on their phones	1
Pragmatic	1
Blunt	1
Interested in learning	1

Index

affirmative nationalism 38
aggressive nationalism 38
Agreement on Mutual Establishment of
    Cultural Centres between China and
    host country 64, 68
Ahmad, Jalal al-e 35
Alliance Française 6, 74, 125–6, 133,
    138–9, 142, 145, 158
American Association of University
    Professors (AAUP) 71, 99, 158–9
American cultural diplomacy 64
American devil 36
anti-imperialism 229
"Anti-US propaganda" 37
assertive nationalism 38
Australia–China relations 139

bad actors 28
Beijing Consensus 54
Beijing Initiative 236
Beijing Olympics Slogan of "One World,
    One Dream" 219
Belt and Road Initiative (BRI) 25, 44n10,
    139, 234, 236
bourgeois liberalisation 35
Brand China Hexagon (2008) 62, *63*
British Broadcasting Corporation (BBC)
    104
British Council 125–6, 133, 137, 142, 144,
    158; 'Generation UK' programme 177
Bush, George H.W. 170

California State University 107
Canadian Association of University
    Teachers (CAUT) 155–6, 158, 160
Carter, Jimmy 232–3
Chen, Melissa 115
Chen, X. 28
Chey, Jocelyn 139

Chiang Ching-kuo Foundation (CCKF)
    113–14
Chicago University 101, 106–7, 134, 145,
    154–5, 159–60
China: authoritarian regime of 1;
    censorship 114; as cultural other and
    ideological other 26–9; economy 112;
    endorsement of cultural nationalism
    236; Europe-centred study of 3;
    evolution of image 28; first-hand
    knowledge *vs* third-hand stories
    198–203; foreign media's portrayal of
    105; foreign policy, post-Deng era 7;
    general public's perception of 112;
    'Going Global' strategy 2, 7, 71; image
    problem 9, 22; as military and economic
    threat 4; modern development 1;
    national humiliation 35; new image 229;
    'other' representation of 2; political
    values 52–6; problem for 2; promoted as
    tourist destination 110; ranking of 8–9;
    self-identity and foreign policies 7;
    USA-centred study of 3
China Cultural Centre (CCC) 5, 64;
    comparison of CI and 64–70;
    effectiveness in China's public
    diplomacy 65; in North America and the
    UK 67; similarities between CIs and 69
China Dream of national rejuvenation 22,
    36, 38
China-related scholars 92, 98–103, 113
China's cultural diplomacy 2, 5, 7–8,
    18–20, 24, 38, 42–3, 131, 195, 229–30;
    aim of 74; cultural boundaries 206–10;
    domestic debates on agents of 58–64;
    features of 216–18; foreign influence,
    issue of 51; global vision *vs* localised
    practice 211–13; goal of 90; historical
    and cultural links 51–2; implications of

256   *Index*

China's cultural diplomacy *continued*
218–23; international debates on agents
of 56–8; localisation through
engagement and capacity building
222–3; mainstream view of 61; mixed-
agent view of 61; people-to-people
interaction 210–11; for playing down
government role 220–2; political values
52–6; purpose 218–20; role of the CI in
139; spiritual and popular culture,
aspects of 51; state-run nature of 116;
teacher-student interactions 219;
universalism *vs* relativism 53–6;
variables at work in process of 213–14,
214; as a vehicle for promoting culture
220; against Western media 106; 'what'
(vehicle) 50, 73; 'who' (agent) 50,
56–64, 73
China–US aircraft collision incident
(2001) 33
China–US trade war 37
Chinese characteristics 56, 64, 89, 104,
194, 214
Chinese civilization: abridgment of 150;
complexity of 69; inclusiveness of 233;
perception of 1, 55
Chinese cultural image 111
Chinese exceptionalism 54
Chinese family hierarchy 98
Chinese media 103–10; awareness of 'sans
frontiers' nature 106; censorship and
EACS incident 113–16; *China Daily*
108–9, 130, 215; *China Watch* 109;
Dalai Lama's honorary doctorate, issue
of 107; government control 103–4, 110;
role in global cultural terrain of struggle
109; Western media influence 106
Chinese nationalism 29–42, 91, 235; *aiguo*
32; "Anti-US propaganda"37; changing
face of 37–42; collectivist culture 32;
contemporary Chinese patriotic
nationalism 34; cultural attributes 32–4;
dual characteristics of 38–9; as
emotional investment of individuals 33;
fanshi zhuanyi (paradigm shift) 38; *guizi*
36; '*guojia*' 32; '*jia*' 32; media
campaigns against Western-inspired
liberal ideas 35; *mianzi* 33; military
collision incident and letter of apology
33–4; as new ideology 30–1; Patriotic
Education Campaign 36; political face
of 34–7; three-P incentive structure for
37, 41
Chineseness, notion of 38, 52

Chinese People's Association for
Friendship with Foreign Countries
(CPAFFC) 63, 170
Chinese People's Institute of Foreign
Affairs (CPIFA) 170
Chinese People's Political Consultative
Conference (CPPCC) 105
Chinese representation of Western forces
34
Chinese threat perception 54
citizen diplomacy 12, 64, 169, 176–89,
190, 231
collective identity 27, 28, 30, 31, 90
communism 2, 26, 56, 89, 91, 118, 140,
145, 148, 185, 187, 199, 200, 204, 236
Confucianism 22, 51, 127–30, 209, 237
Confucius Classrooms (CCs) 6, 155, 202
Confucius Institute (CI) 5–6, 8, 10, 64,
195, 230–2; advantages and
disadvantages of 140; in Africa 143;
anti-CI literature 100; in Australia 72;
benefits of having on university campus
100; Board of Advisors 94; in Canada
70; case study on 71–4; challenges with
78–9, 97–8; China-related scholars of
98–103; Chinese rationale on 135–8;
closures 70, 79, 96, 100, 106, 141,
154–61, 163, 203–6, 215; common list
of censored topics 134; comparison of
CCC and 64–70; comparison with
Goethe-Institut 73, 125–6, 134, 137–41,
144; Confucian philosophy of "harmony
without uniformity" 93;
contextualisation of entity 71–2;
contributions of 76, 135–6;
controversies 71; criticism of 132; as
'cultural wheel' 77; Dalai Lama's
honorary doctorate, issue of 107; debate
over 99–100; in Denmark 70; directors
140–2; domino effect of 73; double
identity of 138–9, 144; in Europe and
North America 67; expansion 132;
foreign perception about 95; in France
70, 72; funding of 134; in Germany 70,
72; global expansion of 71; Hanban's
role in 93–4, 97; hiring practice 142–3;
infringement on academic freedom 107;
interaction with home institution 97; in
Japan 70; as a language institute 70–1;
in media 103–10; in Mexico 72; mission
of 95, 97; mission statement 74, 195–8;
in Morocco 72; in the Netherlands 70;
network collaborative approach 136;
objectives 96; operating model 133–49,

230; outreach activities 112; as a partnership between home and host institutions 72; as people-to-people diplomacy 95; promotion of Chinese language and culture 74, 76, 116; in Russia 70; in South Africa 72; in South Korea 72, 78–9, 78–9; in Sweden 70; target audiences of 110–13; teaching and cultural exchange activities 74–80; terminations of agreements 107; three-party partnership 94, 98; transforming China's national image, role in 77–8; triangular partnership 93–8; turnover rate of tutors 143; in UK 72–3, 78, 100; in USA 70–80, 100

Conservative Party Human Rights Commission (CPHRC) 100, 107, 135, 160, 171

contested ideological terrain 87
counter-hegemonic struggle 87
CPC Central Committee 52, 59–60, 77, 104
cultural boundaries 5, 12, 118, 195, 206–10, 212–13, 216–22, 230–1
cultural confidence 40, 108
cultural difference 19–20, 55, 97, 212–13, 219
cultural diplomacy 19–20, 29, 42, 91, 126, 132, 138, 172, 214–15; as a mutual process 20; in UK 58
cultural diplomats 231
cultural diversity 19, 89–90, 116, 126, 213
cultural hegemony 2, 24, 26–9, 38, 41–2, 91, 98, 119, 131, 159, 161–2, 175, 220, 229
cultural nationalism 30, 38, 51, 127, 208–10, 230, 236
cultural other 1, 11, 26–9, 51, 128, 207, 216–17
cultural pluralism 2, 5, 19, 89–91, 93, 113, 116, 119, 131, 214–17, 239
cultural promotion 6, 95, 100, 130, 133, 145, 148, 153, 230
cultural resistance 29, 91, 208
Cultural Revolution 7, 129
cultural soft power 22, 52–3, 61, 92, 113
cultural state 58
cultural struggle 229; China-related scholars and 98–103; global cultural terrain of struggle 88–91; interactions among various players 113–18; media, role of 103–10; stakeholders 92–113; target audiences 110–13
cultural superiority and inferiority 29

culture hegemony 89, 133

Dalai Lama 78, 107, 174
Daoism 22
defensive nationalism 39
Deng Xiaoping 5, 31–2, 56, 194; open-door policy 7
de-Orientalised cultural China 28
dominations, functions of 26

East–West dichotomy 3
Eight-Year CI Development Plan 2012–2020 117, 205
Emory University 107
Erlangen-Nurnberg 75
Etzioni, A. 23
EU–China Education Diplomacy 178
EU–China High Level People-to-People Dialogue 170
EU–China relations 161, 170
European Association of Chinese Studies (EACS) 113–16
explicit propaganda 60, 132
external propaganda 60

Fardid, Ahmad 35
Fei Xiaotong 237
Foreign Affairs (Nixon) 21
Foreign Correspondents' Club of China 104
Foucault, M. 87, 90, 118, 160, 162; power of discourse 98; power relations 24, 26, 29; role of ideology 26; theory of "knowledge is power" 27
Fukuyama, F. 3, 54, 89

Geertz, C. 50
Gilboa, E. 174
globalisation of knowledge and Western culture 27
Goethe-Institut 6, 64, 73–4, 125–6, 133–4, 137–41, 144–5, 147, 150–1, 158, 160, 246
Gongfu movies 111–12
Google's services, blocking of 170
government-sponsored cultural centres 64
Gramsci, A. 26, 91, 135; concept of "cultural hegemony" 27, 29
Greatrex, Roger 114
guanxi 175
Guo, Z. 66–7
Gutierrez, Nancy 102

Hanban 73–5, 92–3, 95–6, 132, 134, 136, 138, 142–3, 155–7, 159–60; Bridge

258 *Index*

Hanban *continued*
 summer programme 172; conflicting
 relationship between academia and
 115–16; Confucius Institute
 Scholarships 116; funding of CIs 134;
 head teacher scheme 222;
 representatives of 92; sanctioned
 textbooks 220; selection and training of
 teachers for CI 142–3; top management
 92
Han Dynasty 31, 55, 238
Han ethnic identification 31
harmonious world, idea of 25, 90, 113,
 119, 126–7, 219, 237
harmony, concept of 237
Heilmann, Prof 100
Hoover Institute 101
Huawei case 234–5
Hubbert, J. 74, 76, 135, 145, 156, 172,
 176, 180, 185–7, 200
Hu Jintao 22, 25, 31, 35, 53, 61, 92, 113
Huntington's "clash of civilisations" 29, 89
Hu Yongqing 77

ideological other 1, 11, 26–9, 36, 51–2, 56,
 128, 145, 207, 216–17
ideology hegemony 89
implicit propaganda 60
inferior other 1
Institute of Cultural Diplomacy 138
Instituto Cervantes 6, 64, 125–6, 133, 137
intercultural communication 19, 142
International English Language Testing
 System (IELTS) 125
International System Narratives 25
Issue Narratives 25

Japanese devil 36
Jervis, Nancy 128
Jiang Zemin 7, 25
Journey to the East 5, 73, 178–9, 250

Kahn-Ackermann, M. 73, 134, 138, 141,
 145, 151, 203
Kissinger, H. 4, 54–5, 162, 175
Kluckhohn, Clyde 50
knowledge-power nexus 24, 26, 29, 42, 87,
 135

Laozi 22
"The last three feet" 169–90
Leibniz, Gottfried 1
Li Changchun 7, 60, 77, 79, 93, 104
Li Keqiang 93

Liu Yandong 92, 146, 215
Liu Yunshan 60, 105, 131
lobbying 60, 132
Lodén, Torbjörn 141
Ludwig, Jessica 172
Lukes, Steven 23, 61
Lyon Confucius Institute (LCI) 70, 152

McCord, E. 99–100
Manchurian Qing Dynasty 31
manufacturing consent 26
Maoism 51
Mao Zedong 5, 32, 170, 186; definition of
 party 32–3; 'The Great Leap Forward'
 6, 10, 215
Mencius 22
Mercator Institute for China Studies
 (MERICS) 100
Miami University 107
Ministry of Culture and Tourism (MOCT)
 5, 59, 64–6, 69, 221
missionary culture 54
Mohism 22
Montesquieu, Charles de 1
Mosher, Steven W. 99, 106, 117, 132, 138
Mozi 22
multicultural relationship, meaning of 24,
 89–90, 126

National Association of Scholars (NAC)
 100
National Endowment for Democracy
 (NED) 36, 172
National Narratives 25
nation branding 171
Nation Brands Hexagon *62*
NATO's bombing of the Chinese Embassy
 (1999) 39
negative stereotyping 90, 172
network hub 57
New Culture Movement (1912) 129
noble nations 28–9
non-governmental diplomacy (*minjian
 waijiao*) 63; citizen diplomacy 64
non-government-initiated exchange
 programmes 231
non-state-organised programmes 5, 73
Nye, Jr., Joseph S. 9, 20, 22–3, 25, 39, 41,
 51, 54, 59–60, 77–8, 110, 134, 173–4
Nylan, Michael 117

Occidentalism 2–3, 27–8, 34–7, 88–9
'Occupy Central' 36
open societies 60

Index 259

Opium Wars (1839–1842 and 1856–1860) 1, 31
Orientalism 2–3, 24, 26–7, 38, 159; critique of 27–8; *vs* Occidental 88–9
Orientalist perception of world 1
otherness, idea of 1, 5, 28–9, 51, 77, 111, 194, 230
'other' representations 2, 27, 33, 77, 194, 219

Panda Diplomacy 5
Paschalidis, G. 77, 132–3, 145
Patriotic Education Campaign 36
Pavlopoulos, President 233
peaceful evolution 35
people-to-people diplomacy (*renmin waijiao*) 63, 95, 169–70, 190
people-to-people interaction 12, 179, 189, 195, 210–11, 214
ping-pong diplomacy 5, 170
political nationalism 30, 51–2
political subjectivity 101
Pompeo, Michael 28
popular nationalism 30, 32, 38–9, 41–2, 127
power relations 3, 26, 29, 42, 72, 160, 162–3, 218–19
propaganda 58, 59–60, 61, 64, 77, 99, 100, 105, 108, 124, 130, 131–2, 145, 162, 194
public diplomacy 19, 60, 65, 90, 132, 136; of China 62

red threat 1, 28
Ricci, Matteo 1, 238
Rutgers University 107

Sahlins, Prof 99
Said, E. 35, 118; critique of Orientalism 27–8; cultural imperialism 29; Western representations of 'Orient' 27
Saunders, Robert 99
self-censorship 93, 115–16, 144, 148, 173–4
self-identity 7, 30
Shambaugh, D. 22, 35, 37, 39–40, 56, 69, 151, 216, 233
sharp power 4, 12, 71, 172–6, 180, 216
Sino–Japanese War (1894–1895) 1, 31
Sino–US relations 21, 100, 177, 236; as a civilisational clash 234; clash of civilisations argument 233–4; Huawei case 234–5
Skinner, Kiron 233–5

smart power concept 20
Smith, Paul 99
socialist culture 52, 77, 104
soft power 20–4, 39, 56, 59, 174, 215; as an alternative to military and economic might 23; challenge in using 21–2; in China 20–4, 52, 139; media's role 104; ranking 9; sources of 22; *vs* sharp power 173–4
South China Sea issues 33, 161, 235
"Sputnik" analogy 232, 236
State Council Information Office (SCIO) 59, 127
state nationalism 30, 32, 38, 42, 127
state-to-state diplomacy 169
Stockholm University 141, 154
Stop Higher Education Espionage and Theft Act (2018), US 91
strategic narratives 25–6; levels of 25
struggles, types of 87
student exchange programme, case study of 176–89; British students in China, number 177; Chinese students in UK, number 177; Chinese students in US, number 177–8; data analysis and discussions 180–9; data and method 179–80; role of citizen diplomacy 178; students' impressions of China and Chinese people *180–1*, 180–9
Student-to-Student Diplomacy 178
Sun Chunlan, Madame 92
Sun Jiazheng 7, 71
Sunzi 22
Sydney China Yearbook incident 114

Taiwan Institute 76
Taiwan issue 114, 116, 134, 161
Taiwan Relations Act (TRA) 235
Tang Dynasty 55
territorial and national boundaries 206–10
THADD missile defence system 39
three-P incentive structure for China's policy 37, 41
Tiananmen protests (1989) 115, 186
tianxia 13, 31–2, 237–8

Umbrella Movement 36
UNESCO Universal Declaration on Cultural Diversity 50
United Front Work Department (UFWD) 92, 139
universalism 91; Western belief of 89
universalism *vs* relativism 53–6
universality 237

260   Index

University of Aberdeen 107
University of Calgary 107, 174
University of Chicago Centre of CI
(CIUC), closure of 154–61, 171; AAUP
report 158–9; Chicago University
statement 159–61; McMaster case 156;
reasons 155–7
University of Maryland 9, 107
University of Miami 107
University of Minnesota 107, 205
University of Stanford 107
US Centre for Citizen Diplomacy
(USCCD) 169
US–China Civil Dialogue (2018) 231
US–China Economic and Security Review
Commission (USCC) 115

Voltaire 1

Walker, Christopher 172, 174–5, 190
Wang Chen 8
Wang Gengnian 77
Wang Guoqing 175
Washington Consensus 54
Western counterparts *vs* CI, comparison:
constraints in operating model 138;
construction of global legitimacy 126–8;
cultural activities 149–51; government
control 138–9, 144–9; learning from
each other 137; mixture of "pride and
prejudice" 127; national interest 131;
overt and covert differences 130–3;
political values 132–3; pre-job training
222–3; purposes 125–33; purposes,
differences in 126–7; research activities
151–4; similarities 125–6
Western cultural hegemony 28, 42, 131,
159, 162, 220, 229
Western media 12, 103, 106–8, 110, 114,
118, 133, 139, 145, 146, 200, 203
Western other 27–8
Westoxification 35
wounded nationalism 34
Wright, Tim 99

Xi Jinping 7, 22, 31–2, 36, 38, 41, 54, 93,
104, 137, 170, 232; 'golden verse' 18
Xu Lin 92–3, 100, 113–15, 138–9, 155

Yan Shuhan 55
Yan Xuetong 52
Yellow Peril paradigm 1, 28, 88
Yin and Yang concept 55

Zhang, X. 66–7
Zhang Yijun 90
Zhang Zhizhou 52
Zhongnanhai 33
Zhou dynasty 238
Zhou Enlai 94, 170

Printed in the United States
By Bookmasters